THE FINAL DAYS OF
EMI
SELLING THE PIG

Praise for *The Final Days of EMI*

'An addictive blend of tragedy, comedy and insight' – *The Guardian*

'Forde's extensive interviews with key players enliven *The Final Days of EMI*, preventing it from being derailed by endless statistics and legal detail … Impressive' – *The Observer*

'Within Forde's forensic account of the major label's collapse lies a classic tale of human error and hubris' – *Q*

'Meticulously researched' – *Mojo*

'The shocking, yet fascinating, inside account of the decline and fall of one of the former giants of the music industry' – *Choice Magazine*

To Big Annie & Big Eddie. For everything.

THE FINAL DAYS OF

EMI

SELLING THE PIG

EAMONN FORDE

OMNIBUS PRESS

London / New York / Paris / Sydney / Copenhagen / Berlin / Madrid / Tokyo

First edition copyright © 2019 Omnibus Press
This edition copyright © 2021 Omnibus Press
(A division of the Wise Music Group
14–15 Berners Street, London, W1T 3LJ)

Cover designed by FreshLemon

ISBN: 9781913172428

Eamonn Forde hereby asserts his right to be identified as the author of this work in
accordance with Sections 77 to 78 of the Copyright, Designs and Patents Act 1988.

Printed in Croatia

A catalogue record for this book is available from the British Library.

www.omnibuspress.com

Contents

Acknowledgements

Authors are bloviators by any other name and like to regard themselves as lone actors, moving through the world and sniffing out great truths. They are often keen exponents of the auteur theory – that they, and they alone, are responsible for the words you see printed out on the page before you.

But that is so very rarely the case. Books are collaborative efforts and, while the author's name gets put on the cover, many hands and many brains will have helped them get to that stage. Fortunately the acknowledgements section is where they can draw attention to the people who helped them get the book into a shape where it could actually be published and not just languish as a Word document, riddled with typos, on their hard drive.

There are many people I wish to thank for their involvement in this book.

Firstly, David Barraclough at Music Sales/Omnibus who was brave enough to give the green light to the whole project and to hand me that crucial £25 million unrecoupable advance that allowed me to live in the style to which I have now become accustomed. (OK, it wasn't quite £25 million. And it is recoupable.) But he had total faith in me and allowed me to just get on with it, offering support and advice when needed, but mainly trusted me to carry on.

But, rewinding a little, I also have to thank Dave Holley for contacting me on spec to see if I had any ideas for a book in the first place. Without him, he'd not have recommended me to David and I'd probably just be another glorified typist thinking I had a book in me but no one to publish it.

The idea for the book came out of a feature that I wrote in 2011 for the greatly missed *The Word* magazine. While everyone else at *The Word* covered exciting musicians, writers and others, I was given the incredible freedom to write about various parts of the music industry at a time when consumer titles either ignored the business they were linked to or found it desperately dull and not worthy of coverage. Thanks to Andrew Harrison for giving me my first commissions at what was already my favourite music magazine and also to Mark Ellen and David Hepworth for encouraging me to write more about the industry in the pages of the magazine. The original piece I did for the magazine on EMI and Terra Firma ran across nine pages – an incredible luxury for any writer but especially one whose specialism was so niche. That a consumer magazine would regularly allow a writer several thousand words to talk about the business was just one of the many, many reasons why *The Word*, for its short but glorious life, should be cherished. That piece also helped me win Music Business Writer Of The Year at the Record Of The Day Awards, so I have a nice plaque on my kitchen wall as a result.

Also enormous thanks to Imogen Gordon Clark and Catherine Best for their peerless subbing, processing and editing of the initial drafts of the book that saw it all the way to completion (especially Imogen for the essential to and fro of emails with checks and clarifications). Subs are the unsung superheroes of the publishing world – quietly and patiently saving writers' lives. It's not just fixing stray apostrophes; it's making sure writers don't pull the rug from under their own feet (something they are wont to do). Subs save us from the big problems and also steer us out of the way of a million tiny disasters and embarrassments. If you are a writer, cherish these people.

Enormous thanks also to Debs Geddes for promoting the book. It is odd to be on the other side of the PR exchange – as I am more used to going via PRs to speak to people – but it gives me a new understanding of how hard they work and why they fight your corner.

There were many, many people I spoke to for this book. Most are quoted (either on the record or anonymously) and some had informal chats with me that helped shape and refine my understanding of what happened and what it all meant. Without them there would be no book. There were also many PRs who helped arrange interviews and they must also be thanked profusely for helping me persuade key individuals to speak. Endless thanks to all of these people for helping interviews to happen, for giving so generously of their time to answer all my questions and for having their say.

During the research and writing of the book I was also trying to operate as a freelancer, earning a living where I could but also occasionally having to turn down work when the book was the priority. Thanks to everyone at *Music Ally*, *The Big Issue*, *The Guardian*, *IQ*, *The Quietus* and more for understanding when I had to disappear and, what's more, for still commissioning me after I resurfaced.

Of course, friends were crucial during this time, offering support and sanity – but also for giving me the space to not talk about the book. Thanks to Alex Papasimakopoulou for being the best friend I could ever ask for, Greece's greatest tour guide and the person with all the life jackets in the choppy times. An important thing was getting out of the house before cabin fever took hold and my regular saviour here was Louise Haywood-Schiefer and Cultural Friday, our greatest creation and the best day out for those who like half-remembered art documentaries and eating pizza.

Other friends and family members have, in a million ways, been important in the long gestation of this book as people to bounce ideas off or just to let off steam with – even if they might not realise it. So, in no particular order, thanks to Ciara, Declan, Andrew & Lili, Stuart Dredge, Laura Snapes, Mark Wood + John Geddes + Jelly X Duckie, Lars Brandle, Cliff Fluet, Brian David Stevens, Toby Bourne, Ben Cardew, Rob Strachan, Marion Leonard, Jeff Liebenson, Adam Webb and Cathy Brown. And, for arriving with impeccable timing, Sonja van Praag.

Begrudging thanks to the odd and mole-like inhabitants of THIS PLACE, one of the internet's few remaining safe spaces. It's the best (virtual) office I've ever worked in.

Finally, the British Library was an invaluable resource during the research for this book. The fact that such an incredible cathedral of knowledge exists – and what's more is totally free to access – is something to be inordinately proud of. Protect all libraries: they are down payments on the intelligence of future generations.

Prologue

EMI no longer exists. The lights were turned out years ago. But to invert Shakespeare, this book is not here to bury EMI; rather it is here to finally tell the full story of its closing act.

It's a common narrative that EMI, perhaps the pre-eminent British music company, was 'slain' by Guy Hands, the head of private equity company Terra Firma, when he bought it in late 2007 and spectacularly lost control of it at the start of 2011.

Many in the British industry say Hands took three years to kill a 113-year-old icon. Yet this is a reductive narrative, with the initial sealing of EMI's fate taking place back in 1996 when it demerged from Thorn (the company that acquired it in 1979 for £165 million) and became a standalone music company without the safety net of a bigger business with multiple interests. While this move made it attractive to potential acquirers, it also left it exposed in the market where it struggled to compete with the other major record companies, all of whom were stronger in the US – recorded music's biggest market – than EMI.

Its fate was further sealed in 1998 when EMI chairman Sir Colin Southgate rejected a reported £6-a-share offer from Seagram's head Edgar Bronfman Jr; Bronfman would go on to buy PolyGram in May 1998 for $10.6 billion from Dutch electronics company Philips, merging it with his existing Universal Music Group at the start of 1999[1] and creating the music mega-company that would eventually swallow most of EMI at its ignoble end. Next, in 2000, the European Commission blocked EMI's proposed merger with Warner, causing an on-off mating dance between the two companies for the next seven years, with a short break at the end of 2000 when EMI considered buying BMG. And it was condemned for the fourth time when the same European Commission waved through the merger of Sony and BMG in 2004, permitted partly as a result of the impact of digital, which began in 2001 and was to cause the recording industry to nosedive painfully for fourteen more years before it hit a plateau and finally started to see marginal growth thanks to the impact of streaming.

This European Commission acquiescence in 2004 in effect created two super-majors: UMG (Universal Music Group) and Sony BMG (later to be rebranded as Sony Music Entertainment when Sony bought out Bertelsmann's 50 per cent stake in 2008), which precluded the remaining majors – EMI and Warner – from ever combining their recorded music and publishing arms without serious divestment.

That left EMI four options: limp on as the smallest of the majors; have a management buyout and delist it from the stock market, where it took a pounding every six months as it issued its figures in a declining recorded music market; be bought by a major media company (Disney, News Corp and even British Telecom were rumoured to be among those kicking the company's tyres in the 1990s when things were more buoyant, but all walked away); or sell to a private equity firm with audacious plans to cut out the fat, rebuild the company, return it to growth and sell it on for a significant profit several painful years later. How the latter option played out as a reality is the core focus of this book.

The end of EMI is far from a simple tale and it is debatable if anyone could have saved it, either from itself or from a flat-lining recorded music market. But its final few years were unquestionably the most tumultuous of its life. The goal of this book is to explain what happened and why many of the suppositions about the death of EMI are either ludicrously reductive or way off the mark.

CHAPTER 1

Chicken Salad and Chicken Shit

Rather than tell the full story of EMI from its inception (Brian Southall's *The Rise & Fall of EMI Records* provides a meticulous account of that, so I would refer you to it), this chapter focuses on the series of events that stretch over a single decade of its long history, and that eventually led to Terra Firma buying EMI Group for £4.2 billion in May 2007. The deal covered both EMI's recorded music interests and its publishing arm, EMI Music Publishing, with its catalogue of millions of compositions.

Buoyed by phenomenal success in the 1960s and 1970s with enormous international acts like The Beatles, Pink Floyd and Queen, EMI went on a buying spree and acquired a series of smaller publishers (Screen Gems and Colgems in 1976) and labels (United Artists in 1979). Also in 1979, electrical engineering company Thorn bought EMI for £165 million, creating a new entity in Thorn EMI. During their partnership, they bought SBK Entertainment for $295 million and Chrysalis Records for £79 million, but their biggest acquisition was paying £560 million for Richard Branson's Virgin Music in 1992.

In 1996, however, Thorn and EMI demerged, and this is where the domino effect that led to Terra Firma buying it eleven years later really began. The demerging escalated rumours of EMI being put up for sale or of someone making an offer so big they couldn't refuse.

Tim Clark of ie:music, the management company behind Robbie Williams, felt that the demerging from Thorn removed a corporate safety net from EMI and ultimately made it weaker and more exposed than its competitors. EMI could certainly claim it was a pureplay music company now and able to devote all its efforts to its music, but this was to prove a disastrous dismantling of the shield that came with being part of a larger entity.

"The big problem with EMI was it had left that Thorn-EMI umbrella of a big industrial combine and was on its own," says Clark. "It had nothing else. It was just that. When Vivendi bought Universal, they had a company that was prepared to invest. Sony, of course, was part of a huge electronics company."

Remaining a listed company was also seen as a decision that was to haunt the board on a regular basis, seeing a series of profit warnings issued when a major album was delayed and fell into the next fiscal year or rival companies grew their market share.

Chairman Sir Colin Southgate said that taking the company private after it was unshackled from Thorn "was never a consideration",[1] but the managers of two of the label arm's biggest bands were convinced this is where the wheels started to fall off. "EMI should have gone independent and private and not remained a publicly owned company when it demerged," said Chris Morrison of CMO, the management company behind Blur and Gorillaz at the time. "It would have been brilliant if that had happened."[2]

Bryce Edge of Courtyard, Radiohead's management company, concurred, but played up the grimly negative rather than taking the wistful what-could-have-been positive angle. "The day that EMI demerged from Thorn and became a standalone shareholding music company," he intoned, "was the beginning of the end."[3]

EMI was not short of offers at the time, the biggest being from Edgar Bronfman Jr, a recurring character in this story, when he was CEO [chief executive officer] of Canadian distillers Seagram, his family's business. Bronfman's father acquired music company MCA Music Entertainment Group from Matsushita in 1995 for $5.7 billion,[4] renaming it Universal Music Group the following year. "Edgar put in an offer for EMI that Colin Southgate kicked out," says a City source. "It was over £6 a share. That was a few months before they [Universal] acquired PolyGram."

It may be significant that there was a supposed personality clash between Southgate and Bronfman, with the latter accusing the former of calling him a 'bootlegger'[5] (possibly a derogatory reference to Bronfman's Canadian ancestors illegally bringing alcohol over the border during Prohibition). Their talks stretched out for a year while Bronfman vacillated between Southgate and Alain Levy at PolyGram.

EMI and Seagram agreed in January 1998 on a target price of £6.25 a share for EMI but, after conducting due diligence, Bronfman arrived at the gloomy conclusion that EMI was in worse shape than he had originally thought, telling Southgate he was unwilling to recommend the acquisition to the Seagram board at that price. Southgate is reported to have said "there's no deal if it's less than seven [pounds per share]".[6]

Torn between EMI and PolyGram, Bronfman sought advice from a variety of industry and business heads. David Geffen arguably tipped the balance when he asked Bronfman, "Do you know what the difference is between PolyGram and EMI? The first is chicken salad and the other is chicken shit."[7] By May 1998, a deal was done where Seagram would buy Philips's 75 per cent of PolyGram for $10.4 billion and Philips would also receive a $2 billion stake in Seagram. EMI was back on the shelf and it would have to get used to the view from there.

Some feel this was the great missed opportunity for EMI, but it also meant there was an element of unfinished business with Bronfman and EMI that defined the years after Bronfman's departure from Seagram in 2002. (Bronfman was to be fined €5 million in 2011 after being convicted of insider trading[8] while vice chairman of Vivendi, the French utilities company that bought Seagram in June 2000 for $34 billion.[9])

"It should have happened," says a City source of the mooted Seagram deal. "Colin Southgate had so pissed off Edgar that Edgar thought, 'OK,' and went after PolyGram. And he got PolyGram. Colin didn't want to sell out at £6 a share."

In May 1998, just three days after 75 per cent of Polygram was sold to Seagram, EMI publicly stepped off the merger carousel and said it was no longer engaging in takeover discussions.[10] It remained relatively bullish and had plenty of assets beyond its recording and publishing copyrights to see it through. In March 1998, it sold its chain of HMV music shops (a retailer whose origins date back to 1921) to the newly created HMV Media Group. It was not a total sale as EMI retained a 45.2 per cent stake, banking close to £500 million from the sale of the other 54.8 per cent.[11]

The late 1990s was a period of unprecedented boom for the recorded music business, helped enormously by the maturation of the CD market, peaking in 1999 with a global value of $38.6 billion according to IFPI (International Federation of the Phonographic Industry) numbers.[12] That same year, however, peer-to-peer filesharing service Napster appeared and took digital piracy mainstream. For the next decade and a half, the ebullience and arrogance of the global record business was put through the wringer and the market slumped to $14.3 billion in 2014[13] before starting its very slow recovery thereafter.

The turn of the new millennium was a curious time for the record business, when digital and filesharing had only caused papercuts compared to the huge chunks of flesh they would soon tear out of the business. There was still huge optimism due to the vast sums of money sloshing around, and there was also a misguided presumption that litigation would solve the Napster issue. Artists like Metallica and Dr Dre were leading the legal charge by filing suits against the company in the opening months of 2000, and they were soon joined by record labels and industry bodies filing their own actions. There was a feeling of "It'll all be over by Christmas" about it all. Except it was to be Christmas 2015 before any sort of recovery happened.

With all this happening in the background, a process of consolidation was under way. Roger Ames, then Warner Music Group (WMG) chairman, sold his London Records arm to Warner Music International for an estimated $200 million. But this was a mere bagatelle compared to what was being planned at a higher corporate level at parent company Time Warner when it was sold to AOL (America Online) for a traffic-stopping $184 billion[14] in January 2000. The mega-deal was the biggest merger in American corporate history, but it soon soured and was described with hindsight as a "calamity" and "the worst merger of all time".[15]

The dot.com bubble was still a year off from bursting and the markets were puffed up with self-important kingmakers. At the time, Warner and EMI had roughly equivalent market shares – although Warner slightly had the edge due to being much bigger than EMI in the US – yet both were limping behind Sony and Universal. If they could pull it off without regulatory opposition or divestment, the merging of Warner and EMI would create a new centre of power, making them the biggest record company in the world, nosing past even the gigantic Universal to command close to a quarter of the global market for recorded music. Only the thousands of independents in aggregate would have a bigger market share (see charts overleaf).

This was the first major deal on Eric Nicoli's plate within months of taking over as executive chairman at EMI, and he said he met with Dick Parsons of Time Warner, Roger Ames and Ken Berry (then head of EMI's US operations) in mid-September 1999[16] to sketch out a preliminary outline for the deal.

"It occurred to me very early on – in late 1999 and I only took over in July that year – that combining forces with Warner Music Group would have allowed us to create a force at least on a par with Universal, and possibly greater," Nicoli says now, looking back at what could have been.

Such a deal would have fixed EMI's long-running problem: its relative weakness in the US which, at the time, accounted for close to 40 per cent of all record sales globally. EMI's disadvantage there was obvious given its 8.1 per cent US market share in 1999. This was its worst performing market and it held sixth place, some distance behind all the other majors and the combined independents.

4

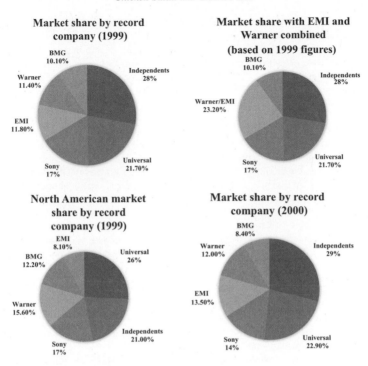

Market share by record company (1999)

BMG 10.10%
Warner 11.40%
Independents 28%
EMI 11.80%
Sony 17%
Universal 21.70%

Market share with EMI and Warner combined (based on 1999 figures)

BMG 10.10%
Independents 28%
Warner/EMI 23.20%
Sony 17%
Universal 21.70%

North American market share by record company (1999)

EMI 8.10%
BMG 12.20%
Universal 26%
Warner 15.60%
Independents 21.00%
Sony 17%

Market share by record company (2000)

BMG 8.40%
Warner 12.00%
Independents 29%
EMI 13.50%
Sony 14%
Universal 22.90%

Source: IFPI

EMI, if it was to compete and grow, had to finally solve the US conundrum – and merging with Warner was the obvious way to do that. Warner was strong in North America but weak in Europe; the opposite was true for EMI (see charts). "The industrial logic was compelling," explains Nicoli. "We had 96 per cent or 98 per cent shareholder approval for the deal. Everybody wanted to do the deal. Except the regulators."

The timing could not have been worse, as the merger of Time Warner and AOL had spooked the antitrust bodies in the US and the European Commission regulators. Getting anything past them in this climate was going to be close to impossible.

"Two weeks before announcing the Warner/EMI combination, Time Warner was taken over by AOL," Nicoli says. "So the owners of Warner Music Group were now in a regulatory review of their own because the regulators were extremely concerned about AOL and Time Warner combining."

Their fear was that this mega-merger would result in the world's biggest internet service provider owning the world's biggest record label as well as becoming "an absolute force to be reckoned with" in an amalgamation of EMI Music Publishing and Warner/Chappell (Warner Music Group's publishing arm). "Ten months after we announced it," says Nicoli, "we were forced to withdraw it because the regulators wouldn't allow it."

EMI had been advised by City law firm Freshfields that a merger with WMG would easily pass the one-month phase 1 for the regulators with few, if any, concessions or divestments having to be made. The looming impact of AOL/Time Warner meant the proposal was shunted into phase 2, a process that could run for four or five months. Phase 2 allowed the independents, spearheaded by trade body Impala in Europe, to put in their objections and they were given, according to one senior source, legal resources from Universal to fight it, less as a means of protecting the indies and more as a way to ringfence UMG's position as market leader.

"They [UMG] didn't want it to happen," says a well-placed source. "But they didn't want it to happen for selfish reasons – not good industrial reasons. The irony was, of course, that Universal in the end was having to talk to regulators [in 2011–12] about how they could accommodate EMI – and they had to give up all the best bits! That's the irony. But that happened much later."

Another issue bubbling under here was how power was going to be shared between two equally matched global companies. EMI had a tiny competitive advantage with an 11.8 per cent share of the global record market in 1999, slightly ahead of Warner's 11.4 per cent, but EMI Music Publishing's 20.2 per cent market share that same year was almost double Warner/Chappell's 10.3 per cent.[17]

"The Warner/EMI deal was going to be fifty/fifty; however, Warner Music was going to have six seats on the board and EMI would have five," says one EMI source who saw the proposals. "Roger Ames was going to be CEO and Ken Berry was going to be COO [chief operating officer]. It was going to be Warner, but only just, as top dog."

Both sides were also gunning for a total merger, and not just of the label arms. "They were trying to merge both recorded music and publishing," says the same source. "Would they have got away with that with the regulators? They were going to give it a try."

Both sides knew there was going to be a lot of work and watertight arguments needed to propel the deal, but they were convinced going into talks that it was really a matter of when rather than if. There were suggestions that Time Warner would jettison its music division if that looked like it could derail the AOL deal but, in the end, it was waved through. That compounded the European Commission's fears about a new type of media giant dominating in content and online but, even so, EMI was being advised that the deal would sail through with only minor concessions.

"We got bad advice," is one source's blunt summation of how it all played out. "All our lawyers at every stage were saying to not worry, that it was simple and that everything would be fine." Even when it was escalated to the more rigorous phase 2, the legal advice was unwavering. "The lawyers kept saying there was nothing to worry about – and these were very, very expensive lawyers," says the source. "Their advice was that, 'Everything is going to be fine.' It wasn't, 'This is going to be really fucking hard. You are going to have to fight and really think about this.'"

As it rumbled on, EMI soon realised it was in an unwinnable situation. "I made that deal on behalf of the business," says Roger Faxon, then CFO (chief financial officer) at EMI Music Publishing and eventually to become group CEO of EMI in 2010. "And then I proceeded to run the antitrust process. As it turned out, the antitrust issues in Europe were insurmountable and the deal was abandoned."

The optimism at the start of 2000 was curdling by the summer. There were rumours that both sides would accept huge concessions as a final push to get the deal over the line – including the possible sale of both Virgin Records and Warner/Chappell.[18]

"The Time Warner deal was a big moment," says a senior executive at EMI based in London. "Everybody thought it was great and that it was going to solve everything ... Roger [Ames] obviously had some thoughts about that [Warner and EMI being a good fit] otherwise he wouldn't have pushed for it to happen. It made sense – but it all fell apart."

The PR spin was that the withdrawal was a means of buying time and allowing them to swing back with a new and improved proposal. "The withdrawal of our application allows additional time to reassess regulators' concerns and to pursue solutions simultaneously in Europe and the US," said Nicoli in a press statement on 5 October. "We have been, and will continue to be, flexible in responding to the European Commission's concerns. However any concessions that are ultimately made must be consistent with shareholder value objectives."

This was seen as clearing away any regulatory reservations over AOL and Time Warner. It was given the green light by the European Commission the following week (11 October) and cleared by the Federal Trade Commission on 14 December, with final approval on 11 January 2001.

AOL and Time Warner had their victory (although it was to prove Pyrrhic), leaving EMI to wake up to the fact it was badly beaten here. "We were totally unprepared," says an executive closely involved in the seesawing of the planned deal. "In the end, it didn't get rejected. We withdrew. If you get rejected, that means legally you can't go back for another merger for two years or something. So we withdrew. Then we were out on our own."

The huge expense of going through this process – estimated to run into tens of millions – did not mean that falling at the first attempt meant all plans were scrapped. A different approach had to be taken and, while a bitter wind was blowing for the industry as a whole, the first signs of a recorded music decline in 2000 – dropping to $36.8 billion by the end of that year, down from $38.6 billion a year earlier – could actually work in the favour of majors seeking to merge their interests to ensure their survival during the most testing of times. The more the recorded music market fell, the stronger their arguments about merging as a survival tactic became.

EMI wasted no time in getting back on the horse. By 10 November 2000, just over a month after accepting defeat at the European Commission, EMI told the London Stock Exchange that it was in early merger talks with BMG, the smallest of the majors. In 2000, EMI actually grew its global market share from the previous year by almost 2 per cent. Only two majors saw their market share slip from 1999 to 2000. No one knew it at the time, but the dual slump of BMG and Sony was to prove their, and not EMI's, saviour.

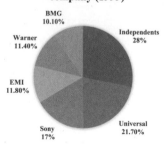

Market share by record company (1999)

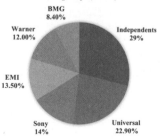

Market share by record company (2000)

Source: IFPI

This proved a very chaste courting that was never going to lead to a full consummation of the relationship and was to turn into more of a fact-finding exercise rather than a solid target for one of the key negotiators.

"We were approached by BMG to have a quick look at whether we could combine with them," says Nicoli. "They thought we could do what we weren't able to do with Warner ... My view, from the beginning of that discussion with Bertelsmann, was that this couldn't work because the regulators were not going to take a different view."

While not having the same concerns over a merging of their publishing arms, it became clear that a meshing of their recorded music divisions would set off the warning sirens at the European Commission.

"Thomas Middelhoff [Bertelsmann's chief executive] and I went to see Mario Monti [EU competition commissioner] and it became very clear that they would resist it," explains Nicoli. "I had already spent a year trying to make this happen [the merger with Warner] and I didn't want to spend any more time on it."

Rather than merge its way out of trouble, EMI decided to take its biggest swing yet to crack America. It was a huge gamble. If they pulled it off, EMI would finally be a big noise in the world's biggest music market; but if they failed, EMI would be even more exposed to a takeover (hostile or otherwise) than at any time since its demerger from Thorn.

In crude terms, the US was always a struggle for EMI. The British company was incredibly strong for its size in the UK and Europe, but could never catch a sustained break in America.

There was some moving of the chess pieces in the second half of 2001. Producer and manager Andy Slater was brought in as president of Capitol Records – the label's fourth head in under a decade, such was the turnover and desperation to triumph in the US market for EMI – and the company's US corporate offices were transferred from Los Angeles to New York.[19]

In a surprise move in October 2001, Ken Berry was fired as chief executive of EMI's recorded music division and head of US operations, with an estimated £5 million payoff. A week later, his estranged wife, Nancy, left her job as vice president of Virgin Music. In their place came Alain Levy (who began his music industry career at CBS in 1972, rising through the ranks and moving to PolyGram in 1988, becoming its worldwide president and CEO in 1991) and David Munns (joining EMI in 1972, before moving to PolyGram in 1987).

Ken and Nancy Berry were a gift for the business pages as the excesses of their lifestyle and rumours of their private lives were picked over with prurient relish. Ken Berry was a long-time Virgin Records executive and was tasked with opening the label's US office in 1978. He met Nancy Myers, then 19, in New York and she became his secretary. The couple married in 1985.[20] She was sneeringly described as "the Hillary Clinton of the global recording business"[21] by *Billboard* in 1993, a sobriquet that was to cling to her throughout her career.

Smarting from having lost out to MCA in March 1990 in the race to buy Geffen Records, EMI chairman Colin Southgate and Jim Fifield, then the president and CEO of EMI, began pushing an accelerated acquisition agenda and alighted on Virgin Records. Their timing was to prove both beneficial and damaging to EMI in the long run; beneficial because of Virgin's catalogue but damaging in terms of the executives that came as part of the package, and who were not necessarily going to bend easily to the ways of working that defined EMI at that point.

The sale of Virgin to EMI in 1992 saw an enormous windfall for Berry, with suggestions that he personally made £25 million out of the transaction. "We're all very, very sad," he is quoted as saying at the time. "But some of us are also very, very rich."[22] He quickly climbed the ladder at EMI and took Nancy with him – and that is where the gossip really started. By September 1997, she was named as vice chair of Virgin Records America, an appointment that Colin Southgate later described as "a huge error".[23]

The Berry reign was arguably the last hurrah of the record industry before the floor started to give way. In their time, they oversaw a number of disastrous and expensive signings, most infamously Mariah Carey in April 2001 for a rumoured £70 million. Carey had a breakdown soon after and was placed in psychiatric care that August. Her *Glitter* album sold just 2 million copies and the tie-in film tanked. Less than a year after signing her to a five-album deal, EMI paid her $28 million to terminate her contract.[24]

It was publicly embarrassing and costly for EMI, but Eric Nicoli backed Levy and Munns' decision to pay her to leave the label. "In 2002, we had an opportunity to cut our losses and I supported Alain and David in doing so,"[25] he said. There was a silver lining in that particular cloud in that, by doing it in January, EMI was able to write off the loss before the fiscal year 2001/2 came to an end. This was, in the words of Levy, "the most prudent course of action for EMI".[26]

Ken Berry himself left EMI but for some, his exit perhaps came too late. One senior UK executive regarded the Berry era as the real beginning of EMI's problems in the US. "I think it started to go wrong when Ken Berry was put in charge of North America," they say glumly.

Another former staff member was not sad to see the end of the Berrys' reign. "I think the Berrys might have been the end of EMI," they say, before adding with a dark flourish, "They were like the Ceauşescus."

With such excess and profligacy leaving an acrid stench in the nostrils of the company, the appointment of Alain Levy as CEO of recorded music and David Munns as vice chair of recorded music was intended to steady the ship and also show that EMI was, with these highly respected and experienced executives at the helm, cleaning up its act and finally ready to take a proper run at the US.

Levy and Munns came as a pair, having previously worked together at PolyGram, growing its market value from $2.5 billion to $10 billion in the five years they were there together. On their appointment, Nicoli called them "a world-class team" and suggested they were employed on a more sensible pay scale than Berry. "His [Levy's] actual salary is a third of his predecessor's and his remuneration is substantially aligned with the interest of shareholders," Nicoli said at the time, hoping to drawn a line under the Berry regime. "They will, frankly, have done very well if he meets his performance targets."[27]

Watching from the UK, Tony Wadsworth, head of EMI's recorded music division in UK and Ireland, felt the Levy/Munns double act provided the shot of adrenaline in the US that EMI so desperately needed at the time. "They are aggressive characters and things had to happen quickly," he said. "What they brought into the company was a new injection of energy, a sense of urgency, and that worked. It came at a time when a couple of signings – Coldplay and Norah Jones – were starting to work."[28]

The company, which had been seen as letting American market opportunities slip through its fingers, throwing good money after bad, was keen to say that things were different now and that it finally had its crack team in place to bring America to heel. "We changed the management of the recorded music business in October 2001," is now Nicoli's summation of that time. "Alain Levy and David Munns came in and Ken Berry departed. We had a decent run in the years that followed."

Former EMI chairman Colin Southgate, watching all this play out from outside the EMI citadel, begged to differ: "I think the move that Eric made from Ken [Berry] to Levy achieved nothing for EMI."[29]

EMI's unrelenting issue with the US was signing and promoting new artists there, even though it did well when exporting UK acts to America. At the time Levy and Munns were appointed, it was estimated that UK repertoire made up 9 per cent of the top 100 sales in the world's biggest music market – and, of that, EMI accounted for around half. This was a staggering achievement that often got overlooked when the company was attacked, though did result in EMI receiving a Queen's Award for Enterprise for promoting and breaking British artists overseas in April 2002.[30] Yet when it came to sourcing global talent in the US, EMI had struggled, and this was the cause of bitter internal fights.

All through this time, while the UK and continental Europe were propping up EMI – both in terms of revenues and also as a talent source, with acts like Coldplay, Robbie Williams and Radiohead helping to keep its batting average up – they had to over-perform to make up for the US situation. The Berrys were the most public manifestation of EMI's problems in America, but the rot went deeper.

"So Munns and Levy were going to turn around America but unfortunately they fell into exactly the same traps as people previously had done – which was to throw their lot in with label presidents who just weren't working," says one senior UK executive at the time. "That cost a lot of money because these guys were paid on a different level from people outside of America." Aside from the pay envy, there was also frustration that under-performing executives in America were being rewarded for what the UK saw as mass incompetence and for which it had to make up the shortfall.

Another senior EMI executive in the London office felt that Andy Slater, as the president of Capitol Records, was strong creatively but was out of his depth commercially and organisationally, and it all unspooled from there. "Andy Slater was a very good creative A&R person – but running Capitol Records is a very different thing," they say. "Andy Slater, for all of his talents, had never actually run a record label the size of Capitol."

Under Levy and Munns' rule, all acts had to be signed on a global basis rather than to 'the world excluding North America', which had often been negotiated by managers and their lawyers. Despite demonstrably having broken Radiohead and Coldplay in the US, the notion of EMI being weak in America was impossible to shake off.

EMI was the front runner to sign Keane, but their manager Adam Tudhope raised concerns about the US. To attempt to placate him, senior UK executives said he should meet Andy Slater when he was in LA the following week and word was sent to Slater to give the meeting his full attention. "He [Tudhope] went to LA and didn't get his calls returned by the head of Capitol Records!" one source says. "He came back and said, 'Look – I really want to go with you guys but I can't go with you ex-North America because you say I can't. And I'm getting nothing back from this guy who you tell me who will deliver us in America. So, I'm sorry.' They were then laid on a plate for Universal and they couldn't believe it." *Hopes & Fears*, Keane's debut album in 2004, was to sell over 6 million copies globally.

"We threw that away because of the dogma thing and also because our American company still had this arrogance of American labels," says the executive. In that climate, and with the decline in CD sales accelerating, Levy and Munns were always trying to push water uphill. The pressure was mounting.

"To me it wasn't that much of a surprise because I think they were showing all sorts of signs of not achieving what they wanted to achieve and what Eric expected them to achieve," says Tony Wadsworth, then CEO of EMI UK & Ireland, of the Sisyphean task Munns and Levy had been lumbered with. "And also America, which was their big focus, was just not happening. Which, for EMI, was a recurring theme in all the years I was there."

Wadsworth's European counterpart at the time was J.-F. Cecillon, who began his career at EMI France in the 1980s, rising to head of EMI UK's recorded arm in the 1990s. He left briefly to work for Sega but retuned to EMI as chairman and chief executive of recorded music for continental Europe in 2004.[31] For him, bureaucracy was an important factor for why Levy and Munns struggled so much in America.

"Alain and David are very good friends of mine," he says. "When they took over the US in 2001, the place was shambolic and they knew it was. They tried everything with the utmost resilience, showing strong charac-ter at all times. They hired A&R guys, signed new artists, restructured distribution and brought financial discipline. But it appeared that the damage was bigger than anticipated. At the same time, Tony was making money in the UK and I was making money in Europe and internationally. We both broke a lot of artists and worked well together. I remember that in Europe, 85 per cent of my non-domestic sales were from UK repertoire and 15 per cent were from US repertoire. The US was a world apart – remote from us and isolated creatively." He feels that EMI should have done one of two things: either forgotten about America and instead found licensing partners to plug the gaps there; or left Levy and Munns to get on with it and stop meddling. It did neither.

Even worse, EMI, out on its own and trying desperately to make headway in America, was to be broadsided by a former suitor finding a new partner and the major label landscape dropping from five to four. Or, more superficially, the birth of a new super-major and the shift into a market duopoly, with both EMI and Warner pushed further to the margins.

The shock creation of a second super-major

In November 2003, Sony and BMG announced they were entering into a 50/50 joint venture. Any speculation from earlier that year that Warner was going to make a move on BMG was blown out of the water.[32] Citing the impact of filesharing and a dwindling physical retail market for recorded music, the companies deftly played a cultural protectionist hand, saying this was the best move for diversity in artist signings, as well as for their continued presence in secondary and tertiary markets around the world.

"If [Sony and BMG] stood alone, we would have to cut artist rosters and even close activities in smaller countries," argued Rolf Schmidt-Holtz, CEO of BMG. "This merger is the best guarantee that we can maintain a broad roster of artists in the current environment."[33]

Despite Warner and EMI being knocked back just four years earlier, and amid fierce oppositional lobbying by the independents via their trade association Impala, the Sony/BMG deal was approved by European regulators without any major concessions or divestments. The feeling within EMI at the time was one of shock, disappointment and rage. Not only had they been stopped from merging with Warner just a few years earlier, but also this pulled the rug from under any immediate plans to woo Warner (and the regulators) again.

"Sony and BMG merging was not good," sighs one senior source, who was close to all the twists and turns here. "That reduced the number of potential partners to one. It was only EMI and Warner. On our side, no one saw Sony/BMG coming. Together they were bigger than we would have been and it just kind of got waved through. After the pain that we had been through, we were like, 'Are you fucking kidding?' That stung. We thought they weren't going to allow another merger through." Others at EMI felt this deal was perhaps a less contentious testing of the regulatory waters than EMI/Warner and could actually play to EMI's advantage.

Sony soon bought out Bertelsmann's stake. "Sony and BMG started as a merger but ended up being a takeover," says Cecillon. "I think the European Commission just played very safely and said, 'OK, let's go from five majors to four majors and see how it works.' Three years later, EMI and Warner attempted to merge again. That was not blocked by the European Commission. The fact it didn't happen was more a reflection of leadership issues on both sides."

With wonderfully symbolic timing, in the same month that Sony and BMG made their first public moves to merge, a suitor from EMI's past seized the deck of cards and threw it up in the air again. In November

2003, Edgar Bronfman Jr led a consortium to buy Warner Music from Time Warner for $2.6 billion.

There was added high-stakes drama, as behind the scenes, EMI was also trying to buy Warner from Time Warner. There had been talks for a number of months between EMI and Time Warner, but the former was keen to cool down any speculation. "Discussions are at a very preliminary stage and there is no assurance that they will result in an agreement acceptable to both parties,"[34] EMI said in a statement, with Eric Nicoli adding that EMI was ploughing its own furrow but "should explore every available opportunity".[35] Few outside of the company knew just how close EMI and Warner came to merging at that time.

"It was hours away," says an EMI executive with close proximity to the negotiations. "We thought we would try again. It was getting existential. If we didn't get this through, the future would be very bleak. We will try our best and we will always have The Beatles and the back catalogue, but this would be fucking difficult."

Roger Faxon, then CFO of EMI, was more sanguine about Warner proving elusive again for EMI. "We had another deal with Warner that was superseded by Edgar's deal," he says. "We had an agreement with AOL Time Warner to acquire Warner Music and that deal fell through at the last minute when Edgar came in with his bid; and he got it for a very good price, actually. That was because he didn't have any antitrust issues. And we, of course, did."

Time Warner said it opted to go with the Bronfman-led consortium as it was, in regulatory terms, a straightforward deal and nothing like the high-wire act that an EMI/Warner merger would be. "It would have taken many months to complete a deal with EMI,"[36] was how Time Warner chief executive, Richard Parsons, summed it up to Reuters. Bronfman may not have wanted to be seen as the path of least resistance, but he almost certainly didn't care. He was back in the music business. The sound recording market might have gone into freefall but green-lighting a Warner/EMI merger was off the table. For now.

In the meantime, EMI had plenty of other problems to fix – notably America, an A&R (artist and repertoire) drain where rival labels were outbidding them for new acts and the growing problem of digital.

A slow and painful digital rebirth

The majors, shaken by the arrival of Napster, set up their own legal download services in 2001. Accusations of collusion were initially sidestepped by breaking into two camps and setting up two competing services. Universal and Sony partnered on PressPlay and EMI managed to have a merger of sorts with both BMG and Warner when they set up MusicNet. Initially they could not cross-license content and both were scuppered by cumbersome DRM (digital rights management, limiting the number of devices music could be put onto or how many times it could be burned to CD), while consumers were put off by the high prices and clunky and confusing interfaces which came with a bewildering set of usage limitations. Paying customers found themselves having to navigate a bureaucratic nightmare straight out of a Kafka novel when all they wanted to do was listen to some music. Even label executives privately admitted these services left them confused.

Apple had already launched iTunes as its music management software in January 2001 (allowing users to rip and organise their CD collections). It flicked the switch and turned iTunes into a paid download store in April 2003 in the US, expanding to Europe the following year. The release of the iPod in October 2001 was arguably the pivotal moment for digital music and helped, via its deft branding, to push digital music into the mainstream.

At the dawning of the millennium, a narrative emerged that has now ossified into fact – namely that the major labels were asleep at the wheel and only woke up to the potential of digital when it was too late, by which time Napster had kicked their legs from under them. Then Apple came along and offered what seemed like a lifeline but was actually a whip, getting labels to bend to its will, not the other way around.

In fact, EMI was, in its way, early to the table and in the early 2000s had invested £75 million to build new systems that would put it at a digital advantage compared to its competitors.[37] While many of the resulting digital deals did not set the world alight, it is erroneous to say it was not experimenting.

"I think that's a really unfair narrative," says Tony Wadsworth, to those who accused EMI of being digitally ignorant. "The first digital download album was actually David Bowie on Virgin/EMI." To be specific, *'hours ...'* was the first major label download album and it was available through both Virgin and Bowie's own websites (as well as a variety of music retailers' sites) in October 1999, a fortnight before its release on CD. Wadsworth feels that labels were more on the back foot here because they were not experts in digital retailing, rather than sticking their head in the sand over digital in general. "The biggest criticism I hear of iTunes is that they got so big and they stole our business from us," he says. "Hold on – they were actually the first mass sellers of digital music for the industry. It wasn't ideal, but it was the beginning of a solution. There were conversations going on about trying to keep the album sacrosanct or maybe only make available two or three singles from an album. There were some exceptions where we were allowed to not break the album up. Radiohead, for instance, were very against their albums being broken up on digital platforms." Radiohead and digital autonomy was soon to become a bigger issue for EMI than anyone at the company could have foreseen.

But before iTunes and even earlier than Bowie's album download, EMI was not exactly in denial about digital. In late 1994, Jeremy Silver built the first Virgin Records websites at a time when few outside of universities and the military had regular access to the internet. He became EMI's first vice president of interactive media the following year. "By the end of 1997, we were talking about things like who owns an act's domain name – is it the label or the artist? – and we started having conversations with people who wanted to do celestial jukeboxes or in-store CD burning,"[38] he said.

Silver also struck a deal in 1999 with a short-lived music service called musicmaker, offering custom CD burning in the US, licensing as much EMI content as they could clear in exchange for 50 per cent equity in the company as it delayed its IPO (Initial Public Offering). When music-maker did eventually do its IPO at the start of 2000, trading galloped far ahead of expectations. EMI traded its stocks on day one netting the company, according to Silver, $30 million in profits.[39]

EMI had plenty of prescient digital cheerleaders on its staff, however their voices were not always heard by those right at the top of labels, who were less concerned about feeding a bubbling revolution than appeasing their existing media partners.

In April 1999, Jay Samit joined as senior vice president of new media at Capitol Records in the US and pushed the company into a catch-up dynamic with regards to digital deals. His policy was to "do as many deals as we can and then see what happens", estimating that the 120 deals he did for EMI netted it $200 million in profit, and adding that at his most prolific he was doing "a deal every nine days".[40]

One US executive – who spent 1999 and 2000 "jumping up and down telling people not to sue Napster" – explains what he and the other digital evangelists were up against at EMI. "I remember distinctly being sat down by a more senior executive at the company than me – and he sat me down with the then-head of video promotion," he reveals. "He said, 'If it comes down to where we have a giant opportunity with AOL Music or Yahoo! Music versus an opportunity with MTV, MTV will win every time.' He looks me right in the eye and said, 'Don't even try to argue your position. You will lose.'" This, it should be stressed, was not a generational divide unique to EMI; it was common across all the majors at the time. Digital unquestionably had its evangelists at EMI and it was not that they were not being listened to. They were just not being listened to all the time.

"In the mid-1990s, EMI was seen as being at the forefront of new media among the record companies – they were often first to a deal, got good terms and moved quickly – but by the early 2000s, EMI had become a bit of a laughing stock," says Barney Wragg, who was senior vice president of digital at rival Universal between 2001 and 2006 before he became global digital chief of EMI. "EMI were getting penalised by analysts for not having a cohesive digital strategy and for not delivering the same kind of ratio for physical-to-digital revenue that the other majors where achieving. That was causing them a real share-price problem."

During this time, exacerbated by the merger of Sony and BMG and a struggle to sign acts before rivals with deeper pockets got to them, EMI was starting to take on water. Something was going to have to give – and soon.

The wheels start to come off

At the start of 2005, EMI was forced to issue a profit warning, with poor sales in the critical fourth quarter of 2004 and album releases from Coldplay and Gorillaz delayed until the next fiscal year. The company said that sales for the twelve months to March would be down 8 to 9 per cent from the previous year and its profits would be £138 million, somewhat short of analysts' forecasts of £168 million.

At the time, Alain Levy called the performance "disappointing" but tried to spin a positive out of the negative, claiming that the physical market "was showing signs of stabilisation" in multiple markets and digital sales were continuing to "develop at a rapid pace". He also tried to explain away the Coldplay and Gorillaz album delays by saying that "creating and marketing music is not an exact science and cannot always coincide with our reporting periods".[41]

Looking back at it now, Nicoli believes they did the right thing by waiting and not forcing acts to rush through albums they were not happy with. But, in doing so, they had to take the inevitable body blows from the City analysts and the stock markets, knowing that the panic from one fiscal year would be parlayed into applause in the next one. "I was supportive of the postponement of the release of the Coldplay album because they weren't ready," he says. "What mattered was the quality of the creative product. We were then obliged, as a public company, to issue a profit warning – to advise the markets that our profits would be less than market expectation and, of course, to explain why. The stock price took a hammering. That was an absurd over-reaction by the market because, six weeks later, we had a magnificent album [Coldplay's *X&Y*] that was the biggest selling album in the world in 2005. And, in the following fiscal year, we had really good numbers – not least because we had the Coldplay album in that year instead of the previous one."

Miles Leonard, then the head of Parlophone (the label both Gorillaz and Coldplay were signed to), feels piling all the blame on delayed albums was a mistake as it would cause friction between artists and labels – something that went counter to Parlophone's belief that it, more than any other label within a major, was the artist's friend. "You may have a date in mind when you think they might deliver, but it is a creative process," he says of the delicate balancing act between A&R and high finance. "That creative process can sometimes happen quicker than expected or, more often than not, it takes longer than expected. Unfairly, EMI used that at the time as an excuse for not hitting their financial targets. That caused a huge relationship issue with both artists that took some time to repair. No one likes being hung out to dry."

This all unfurled as a major PR own goal for EMI and raised the hackles of artists who felt they were being framed for the company's third profit warning in quick succession. "I don't really care about EMI," Chris Martin, Coldplay's lead singer, told a press conference in New York that May. "I'm not really concerned about that. I think shareholders are the greatest evil of this modern world." He added, "It's very strange for us that we spent eighteen months in the studio just trying to make songs that make us feel a certain way and then suddenly become part of this corporate machine."

Bryce Edge, co-manager of Radiohead, claimed that big artists were, in effect, subject to being offered bribes to ensure their albums arrived in a particular financial quarter to appease EMI shareholders and City analysts. "A couple of times we were told, 'If you can get the record out before the end of March, we'll give you blah, blah,'" he said. "Well fuck that – it's not about that, it's about the music and making the right album."[42]

This inadvertent blame-shifting was to cause EMI no end of headaches but this was the reality for a publicly listed company trading in music: the best musicians cannot work to a stopwatch. So there had to be some tongue-biting as albums fell off the release schedule and the City analysts had to be persuaded it was not a cause for panic.

"There was a relentless history of profit warnings and Coldplay was the big one," says one senior executive who had to handle some of the firefighting around this. "They started to say they didn't want to be associated with share price drops and they didn't want to be mentioned in the same sentence as that. They didn't want to be used as the excuse for bad news."

Every six months, EMI had to steel themselves for what the City would make of their performance, and big sellers in one year were not necessarily a cause for total celebration as they knew this could create a vacuum in the next financial year. "A big release like The Beatles *1* album can distort the cycle of profits," says the executive. "When you are exposed the way we had become exposed after the Thorn demerger to scrutiny on the share price and scrutiny in the City, you realise it is really hard to manage the cycle of releases to try and even out those highs and lows. Every time a profile artist has a release scheduled for that year, you know there is going to be so much scrutiny attached to it but it was impossible."

They also argue it became Groundhog Day trying to explain to market analysts why music should not be treated and evaluated in the same way as other consumer goods, because the creative process was at the heart of it and was no respecter of deadlines. "One of the other problems I remember was that the analysts focused on our business were rotated pretty frequently," the same executive comments. "So you just explained how it all worked to an analyst and then they were off and six months later you had to do it all over again with someone else. Managing that City expectation was definitely a nightmarish challenge when it came to marrying that to artists and what artists wanted to do – which was to take the time and to naturally produce the best record that they could."

J.-F. Cecillon says this was the reality of the music business and that the tyranny of the fiscal year for EMI as a publicly listed company was often more about punches than kisses. "When Coldplay and Gorillaz postponed their releases in 2007, the analysts kept a very straight and blind approach to it," he says. "Quarterly reporting obligations in such a volatile industry made the company look dreadful in March at the end of the fiscal year and terrific in May at the start of the new fiscal year. This two-month EBITDA [Earnings Before Interest, Taxes, Depreciation and Amortisation] delay did very negatively impact on the share price, although the album performances were much better than they would have been had the releases been rushed just to please the market analysts."

* * *

Unwittingly, EMI's board had planted a bomb under its future at a point where they thought the CD-powered good times would never end; this was to play a decisive role in making EMI increasingly vulnerable to a takeover during the digital famine years. A company cresting a commercial wave had badly misjudged a re-mortgaging of its future.

"There was that moment where we gave a lot of money back to the shareholders at the end of the 1990s," says a senior international executive. "It was something like half a billion pounds. After that, then we had the issues with the debt. That was another key moment because it made us very weak and susceptible to takeovers."

Another executive concurs that this is where EMI's many problems over the next decade could be traced back to. "It all started to go wrong really in 1996 or 1997 where Sir Colin Southgate did a massive share buyback that was funded by debt," they say. "Up to that point, EMI was not heavily indebted. That is where the debt came in and, in hindsight, just at the point where the market was peaking. EMI was basically fucked from that time on."

Saddling EMI with such debt put it at a huge strategic disadvantage, according to one executive who was party to all the failed merger talks that happened in the 2000s. "EMI's debt was a massive problem for us as we didn't have any money," they say. "So we couldn't acquire anything sizeable. A merger or a sale was the only strategic option for the company. As the market stopped growing, it was only a matter of time before we were fucked."

The company was forecasting operating profits of £150 million for the year ending March 2001 but had to make a move to soothe jittery investors about its debt. To this end, it agreed a refinancing with the banks that gave it an £800 million facility that was spread across three years and an additional £500 million as a bridging loan.[43]

With this new financial wind in its sails, EMI steered a strategic course to bulk up its size in the market, just as the downturn was starting to bite. Expand and survive or stand still and atrophy was the logic. In 2000, EMI signed a joint venture with indie label Heavenly which had a knack for spotting talent before most others, putting out early records by Manic Street Preachers and Saint Etienne. The deal was serendipitous, bringing in Doves, whose first two albums went platinum (sales of 300,000+) and gift-wrapping The Magic Numbers, whose debut album sold over a million copies, for the company.[44]

Tapping into the indie sector was a deft play as it gave the company a new – arguably sharper – A&R resource and also credibility by proxy. In May 2002, EMI made its biggest acquisition in years by acquiring Mute for £23 million.[45] Mute had long been hailed as an indie pioneer, initially putting out singles in 1978 for The Normal, the recording name of founder Daniel Miller. It quickly spotted Depeche Mode and steered them to enormous global success. Mute was envied for its ability to find genuinely pioneering artists and help them recalibrate the mainstream, a reputation founded on the incredible success of Moby's *Play* album.

Mute had a long-standing licensing deal with Virgin Records and the acquisition was termed a "natural progression of our relationship with Mute"[46] by EMI Recorded Music chairman Emmanuel de Buretel.

Daniel Miller, looking back on that time, was keen to stress that this was different from a major buying up a well-performing indie and squeezing it into its business and corporate culture. "We were more than an imprint," he says. "We were a standalone label and apart from distribution and manufacturing we did everything ourselves. We weren't connected to EMI UK as the deal was with EMI Continental Europe." He did, however, quickly become aware of a very different culture and operational strategy that stood in sharp contrast to the way lean indies have to bootstrap themselves. "I remember going to Brook Green [home of EMI UK] and seeing the offices of the MDs," he recalls. "I thought this was something from the past – massive offices, a grand piano, huge sofas, big desks. It was from another world."

The company may have been expanding its roster at this time, but it was drastically cutting its staff numbers, laying off 1,800 employees in March that year and pushing through a major restructuring in the wake of a £59 million profit in 2000 inverting into a £2 million loss in 2001.[47]

A further cost-cutting programme swung into effect in March 2004, with 1,500 jobs going (equal to 20 per cent of the workforce) as the recorded music market continued to tumble. The company said the job losses were part of a "continuing drive to maximise efficiency and effectiveness in the changing global music marketplace".[48]

A welcoming home for the mavericks

Even with the recorded music market going into a nosedive, EMI was still seen as a great place to work and more artist-friendly than the other majors. Murray Chalmers, head of press for Parlophone at the time, says the label was all about making the mainstream bend to the outsiders, rather than vice versa, and this is what powered it through the 1980s and 1990s, breaking acts like Pet Shop Boys, Radiohead and Blur. "It was the home of the mavericks," he says. "The mavericks gatecrashing the mainstream, which is the best thing ever."

Speaking to the BBC in 2005, Tony Wadsworth, the chairman and chief executive of EMI Music UK & Ireland, outlined how the company took the long view with its artists and stuck with them even if success was not immediate. "For the first two albums Blur were on a downward sales curve," he says. He explains how they stuck with them and led them to huge commercial success with *Parklife* in 1994. "*Modern Life Is Rubbish* sold twenty-odd thousand. It was quite desperate […] An accountant looking at the books would probably say it is the time to get out. We decided to stick our neck out as we believed in what they were doing [...] We want creative self-starters, who have a point of difference and are going to be around for a long, long time."[49]

Wadsworth was something of an anomaly in the corporate world of the majors – an executive who was widely loved, not just admired, by staff and artists, and seen by all as fiercely loyal and unwaveringly honest. In March 2005, for example, Wadsworth came tenth in the 'most highly rated boss' category in a *Sunday Times* poll of the best places and bosses to work for in the UK. EMI was named the fourth-best media company in the country (and thirty-ninth overall across all company types).[50]

Sadly, Parlophone's culture – and how it spread across the company when Wadsworth took over the running of EMI recorded music in the UK – was identified by several staffers as part of the problem for EMI in the long term as it calcified into a certain musical aesthetic in the company and a wariness of signing shamelessly commercial acts. "Tony's biggest mistake was putting Terry Felgate in charge of EMI Chrysalis and Miles Leonard in charge of Parlophone," one EMI staffer said. "That meant you had people who had a very specific type of music that they loved [and signed]. Miles not so much because they had Kylie, Supergrass and Radiohead, whereas Terry [had one taste in music]. That's where it all went wrong as it wasn't ambitious or forward thinking at all. They weren't very broad. EMI had this fascination with being way too cool for school."

Another staff member felt that Parlophone, in many ways the engine room of the UK company, was guilty of coasting on past glories after Wadsworth took over the running of the whole UK company. "What Miles was great at doing was creating a fun and family atmosphere," they said. "He was great with artists and great with staff. It was a great atmosphere and I adored it. But what he wasn't doing was signing anything himself – or bringing anything new or original into the company in a time when things were massively changing." With acts like Blur, Radiohead and Supergrass, Parlophone had ruled in the UK in the 1990s, but it struggled, or refused, to adapt to a very different set of market conditions in the mid-2000s. Parlophone was revealed to be out of step with the UK market and started to cede power and influence to labels like Polydor, part of Universal Music Group.

"Parlophone was a cool label – but that was the problem," argues one EMI executive. "They only wanted to sign cool things. They didn't want to sign stuff just because it would make lots of money [...] Parlophone kept passing. EMI Publishing had signed James Blunt and offered him to Parlophone UK but they said they didn't want him. They did lots of that because they just wanted to be cool. They got lucky with Coldplay as they were a band who were cool enough for Parlophone but would still sell a shitload of records. That enabled them to be safe for a couple of years. Lucian Grainge at Polydor was signing everything – Girls Aloud, Ms Dynamite. He didn't fucking care and Polydor just became the biggest label. They totally eclipsed Parlophone. Universal UK was on fire at that time."

Meanwhile, EMI was suffering from something of a log jam and being outbid for hot acts or just struggling to break the ones they had signed. "They had some successes with Corinne Bailey Rae and LCD Soundsystem but they also had quite a lot of misses," says one department manager tasked with helping to break some of these new acts. "They were signing lots of bands that weren't really doing anything [...] Robbie Williams and Coldplay at that point were effectively keeping the company going."

DFA Records had brokered a distribution deal with EMI in the UK which gave it the rights to big-selling records by LCD Soundsystem, which was clearly great for the company. What was less great for EMI was that it also had to take anything else signed to the label in the US – and none of these could sell records like LCD Soundsystem. "DFA was able to sign whatever they wanted," says one department head of the negative knock-on effect of this deal. "Prinzhorn Dance School. It was just shocking." Prinzhorn Dance School's debut album in 2007 became a running joke among music journalists at the time as they – and this writer included – were sent multiple copies of the album because EMI simply couldn't sell them and had to clear the shelves. Ever-more apocryphal tales would circulate among music critics that the album had sold fewer than 200 copies. Eventually the total was lowered to twenty copies as the schadenfreude got ramped up.

While this was not profligacy on the scale of the Berrys a decade earlier, there was still a spending issue throttling EMI internally. There was, of course, a series of layoffs and belt-tightening measures happening on a regular basis, but deep and sombre austerity was not exactly implemented across the board. This would be pounced on and amplified dramatically out of proportion by Terra Firma when it took over in 2007, which was keen to discredit the former management structure and point the finger of blame at them for not cauterising budgets. But there were genuine issues and occasionally, as one staff member put it, a "last days of Rome" mindset at the company in the UK. This person, who was still in a relatively junior position, recalls going to a staff party in Brighton where everyone had a sea-view room at the Grand Hotel and arrived to find a gold disc laid out on their bed. Company away-days could cost upwards of £500,000, but this was seen as a way of keeping the staff happy and loyal, with long-serving team members being presented with plaques on key anniversaries and treated to dinner at the Ivy in London. "They prided themselves on that," says the employee. "The other major labels had a much higher staff turnover. Nobody left EMI because it was great [...] They would come around and do what they called a desk assessment and if you said you weren't happy with your chair they would come back two weeks later with this throne!"

A happy workforce, runs the corporate logic, is a productive workforce, but EMI's largesse was occasionally taken advantage of by staff out of the line of vision of the senior management. "They had an in-house bike desk there because people were couriering so much stuff," recalls one EMI department head. "There was a guy sitting in the basement whose sole job was to handle that – Ian from Wings. I would courier a banana across London to my boyfriend – just taking the piss. Or you would have them picking up your dry cleaning."

This was seen by staff as at best benign and at worst high jinks, but there was also said to be a culture of late-night excess among some staff members.

This sporadic hedonism by the staff could, if we are being generous, be read as a deflection technique to take their minds off the wider problems of the company as budgets were being slashed and colleagues were routinely being laid off. The low hum of merger or sale rumours after the failed Warner deal in 2000 soon rose to become a form of corporate tinnitus and staff talked about the miasma of uncertainty that was enveloping the company in those years. No one knew what was going to happen to the company and the music trade press and financial pages of the broadsheets were often the first place EMI staffers would learn about what was happening, or what could happen, to the company.

There was also a cultural divide between Wrights Lane in High Street Kensington, where EMI's corporate and international offices were, and Brook Green in Hammersmith, where the UK label operation had its headquarters. "It felt like crossing the Rubicon to go to Wrights Lane," says one EMI UK staffer. "It felt like this mystery place that no one ever got to go to. We never got to go there. That was like Harrods compared to what we were in. We felt at Brook Green that we were doing the proper jobs and they were corporate over there."

There was unquestionably an us/them divide between the two offices and those in Brook Green felt, as the creative drivers of the business, they should not have the perks of their jobs taken away. "There were stories that A&Rs would get a cab to Wrights Lane and leave it running outside when they did the meeting and then take it back to Brook Green," reports a Brook Green employee of a journey that would take fifteen minutes each way to walk. "There are a few moments where they said they had to cut the taxi bills. There were inklings of, 'Fuck! Maybe this isn't going quite so well.'"

A department head suggests that Brook Green was shielded from a lot of the fiscal handwringing in Wrights Lane and that, as far as they were concerned, it was business as usual – until they were told otherwise. "There was always a sense from when I joined onwards that we were in an unstable business – that things could fuck up and the sales weren't there," they say. "But at the label, things continued as normal. We still had expense accounts and cab accounts […] We were still overspending. There was still all of this stuff happening." They add, "Was it like the glory days of the 1990s had never ended? To a certain extent, yes. We were still able to spunk a load of money on a photoshoot that then got junked because it wasn't good enough. You could have a marketing spend that was just ludicrous. That was because even if you had a flop album you still might have sold 40,000 copies. If you sell 40,000 copies these days you're a fucking genius! We were all just getting on with things."

Tony Wadsworth was the buffer zone between Wrights Lane and Brook Green – sheltering his staff as much as he could from the corporate issues gripping the global head office. To achieve that, he took the Parlophone mindset and applied it to the UK arm. And this worked in his favour when they were demonstrably breaking artists as this afforded them a layer of insulation from any squeeze that Wrights Lane might want to impose.

"My way of running Parlophone and subsequently all of EMI UK, which I started running in early 1998, was to protect, as much as possible, the company from what was going on with all the corporate stuff on the outside," he says. "When it came in and I couldn't stop it, then I saw the company suffer as a result of that. Prior to that, I tried to run it on our own terms. I was able to do that because we were producing the goods. We had an incredible 1990s and that continued into the first few years of the millennium. We signed Kylie and Coldplay in the same month in late 1999. That was a good month's work! Financially we were delivering well above our budgeted and targeted profits every year. For that reason, I was able to be relatively bolshie on behalf of my UK team."

One outsider who had a close working relationship with EMI felt that the Brook Green/Wrights Lane dichotomy was both a blessing and a curse for the company, explaining it in terms of the different personalities and styles of the two men at the head of the different offices. There was a geographical divide but, more crucially, there was an ideological divide between them and this was a major factor in creating the problems EMI found itself in during the opening years of the millennium because they could not always move in lockstep on everything.

"Everybody loved Tony and actually lots of people liked Eric Nicoli – but there was a real gap between Tony and Eric," they say. "Tony was off being the creative genius and allowing – some would say indulging – all these artists to go off and make these incredible records. But somewhere in the gap between him and Eric, the business stuff was falling down. It just wasn't working. It was all going terribly wrong."

For those on the UK side of the business who were party to what was being discussed at the corporate head office, they were keenly aware of the pressures the company was under, the turnaround it had to try and achieve and just how painful it was all going to be.

"I think there was a sense of fatalism in EMI," says one very senior source based in Brook Green at this time. "The thing with EMI was that we had gone through so many restructures, so many rumours, so many profit warnings – that, actually at the UK record company, were above and beyond our control – and so many changes of staff at the senior executive level. Tony had been in charge of the UK company for a long time and there was a strong sense of stability; but around us we were working in an environment that was relentlessly changing and striving to become something else new or different. What was it we were trying to get used to? And here we were trying to get used to something again."

They add, however, that what was happening at this stage in EMI's history was not that out of the ordinary and that a corporate squeeze was common even when the company was breaking UK acts globally and the CD market was at its absolute peak. "We were a little like punch bags and that chaos was totally normalised," they say. "I had been there for many years and every single year that I had been there, there had been a company restructure of some significant type. And that was even in the good times. Even the so-called glory years there would be a sales force restructure or there would be some kind of uncertainty."

Those on the digital side had a better understanding of what EMI could be and were perhaps less caught up in the romance of what it used to be. As such, they believed that there were ways to transition the company and make it ready for future challenges – but believed there was possibly a sense of nostalgia causing a corporate inertia.

"There was a lot of exhaustion in the company and we just wanted some certainty," says one digital executive. "I always felt that the music industry had lacked a traditional business acumen that was able to structure and organise the company with an eye on profitability and not purely on artistry. The industry was always more heart than it was head. I thought if you managed to keep some of the senior A&R leaders and

27

creatives, but bring in somebody who was able to turn their hand to any business and make it a success based on the principles of business, then you would be in a good position."

Another digital executive agrees with this synopsis to a point, but says that at this stage, because all the major decisions were being made in London, EMI had a competitive and structural advantage over the UK arms of the other majors that were headquartered in Japan and the US. "The whole music business at that time was still managed at the top by some people who had been around for a long time and weren't necessarily ready for that [digital] change," they propose. "I would say EMI was a little bit like that. However, we had a team in the UK – and the UK for EMI was the global HQ, unlike at Universal, Sony or Warner – so a lot of what we decided was driven out of the UK for the rest of the world. You wouldn't necessarily have had that in some of those other companies."

While its London-centric set-up was a boon in some regards, it remained a problem, and a growing one as global record sales shrivelled up, with regard to EMI's eternal white whale – America.

"I had to deal with that," says Tony Wadsworth of the need for the UK arm of the company to compensate for the money pit and talent tundra that the US was proving to be for the company. "But the pressure was to produce the profits because America wasn't – *and* to deliver the acts because America wasn't. And sometimes those two aims clashed. In order to deliver the acts, it takes investment. And investment isn't necessarily something that pays back tomorrow. So managing that dynamic was a challenge. But that's what I was paid to do and that's what the people working for me were paid to do. And I think we did it pretty well. But it did become very onerous from around 2006 where I was squeezing out the profits required but also losing out on one or two signings, purely because of money."

The contrast between EMI and Universal in terms of market share in 2006 was pronounced (EMI had 12.8 per cent, slipping behind Warner with 13.8 per cent while Universal had 25.7 per cent[51]) and the competitive imbalance meant that Universal was more able to spend its way to success, widening the gulf between the biggest and smallest majors. Plus, Universal was incredibly strong in the US where EMI was left floundering.

"Universal had worked out that they had the deep pockets," says Wadsworth. "They used the deep pockets which come from having a well-balanced organisation – i.e. one where as much money was coming from their American artists as from their own domestic artists. It really should be something like 50/50 [domestic/American] at a UK major. We were 80/20. They were 50/50. Therefore, their whole was bigger. Much bigger. They were making big profits from American artists and were able to use those profits in the UK to create, through signing artists like Amy Winehouse, Keane and Snow Patrol, real competition to our own domestic success."

*   *   *

A series of haymakers had landed on EMI since the late 1990s, and like Wile E. Coyote the company was running across thin air above a ravine, its eyes yet to bulge out in shock at the vertiginous drop below it. The Thorn demerger had left it exposed while the other majors were ring-fenced; digital had given the entire record business a punishment beating; Universal ballooned into a behemoth that showed no signs of slowing down; EMI had been blocked from merging with Warner and had to look on in shock, awe and envy as Sony and BMG became the second super-major label; Edgar Bronfman Jr, the man whose overtures a supercilious Colin Southgate spurned in 1998, reappeared and bought Warner Music from under EMI's nose; it was taking a pounding on a regular basis when it published its accounts to the City; it was losing acts to labels with deeper pockets; the global recorded music market was cratering; and EMI still hadn't broken America.

Something had to give. EMI was approaching the end of 2006 and had a plan. But, as was becoming a motif in its recent history, what EMI wanted was not always what EMI got.

CHAPTER 2

Be Careful What You Wish For

While not quite a 'death of the majors' scenario, February 2006 opened with Arctic Monkeys' debut album (*Whatever People Say I Am, That's What I'm Not*) selling 363,735 copies in the UK in its first week, making it the fastest-selling debut album in British chart history. This was on Domino, an independent label that was set up in 1993, at a time when industry trade bodies like the BPI (British Phonographic Industry) in the UK and RIAA (Recording Industry Association of America) in the US were strenuously arguing that piracy was killing the record business. This same piracy argument was key to Sony and BMG's justification for a merger almost two years earlier – they asserted that they needed to consolidate to survive and invest in the artists of tomorrow.

What the success of Domino proved was that indie labels could steal acts from right under the majors' noses – there had been a furious A&R scramble to sign the Sheffield band the year before – and break them bigger than the majors ever could; and all in a period of sharp decline for record sales. It was a triumph for the indies, but also showed that the majors were asleep on their watch.

Midem 2006, the music industry's enormous annual trade fair and conference in Cannes, came around the same time. Here was a tarnished symbol of where the industry now found itself. Six years earlier the harbour was packed with yachts and parties with endless free food and drinks, champagne corks popping through the night. But now it was turning into a wake, the conference panels full of handwringing and low-level panic over the future of the record business. Expense accounts were visibly tightened, the overpriced hotel bars on the Croisette noticeably quieter than a few years before and the yacht parties were a mere memory. The self-indulgence was turning into self-flagellation.

At Midem, Eric Nicoli was asked if EMI would merge with Warner or if they would remain separate, albeit somewhat diminished, forces by the time Midem 2007 came round. "Yes or no," he said, swerving the question and then quoting Al Capone. "You get a long way with a smile, but you get a lot further with a gun and a smile [...] What [Capone] meant, of course, was that the multi-media approach increases your chances of success."[1]

In April, two key EMI acts hinted at where their digital futures lay and both were to have seismic repercussions for the music company in the coming years.

"Radiohead are indicating a move away from issuing new recordings simply via album releases to releasing tracks digitally as and when they are ready," reported *Music Week*.[2] "The band, who are currently out of a recording contract after coming to the end of a deal with EMI, spoke of a possible new way forward as plans for a European tour and UK summer festival [...] were unveiled."

Later that month, Neil Aspinall of Apple Corps, during a legal dispute with Apple Inc. over its name given recent moves into music with the iPod and iTunes, was quoted in the High Court in London on the digital plans for The Beatles, saying their music would be made available digitally after it had been remastered. "I think it would be wrong to offer downloads of the old masters when I am making new masters," he said. There were also suggestions that CD remasters and digital remasters would come out at the same time for maximum impact. "It would be better to wait and try to do them both simultaneously so that you then get the publicity of the new masters and the downloading. [That way] you can just try to market the product properly really, rather than just doing it ad hoc."[3]

In May, there was the reappearance of the Warner rumours, with reports of EMI's approach of a $4.23 billion cash-and-sales offer being knocked back by Edgar Bronfman Jr, who was apparently holding out for a higher offer. Bronfman, speaking during a company earnings call, confirmed an approach had been made but claimed it was turned down as it was not deemed to be in the best interests of the shareholders. Speaking to an audience in New York the following day, he poured yet more water on the EMI rumours. "Consolidation for consolidation's sake doesn't make a lot of sense," he said. "Ours is not a business that requires scale economics."[4]

EMI was down but not out, quickly issuing a statement on the matter and hoping to keep the merger plates spinning. "The board of EMI continues to believe that an acquisition of Warner Music by EMI would be very attractive to both sets of shareholders," it said in a statement.

"But [EMI] will only pursue a transaction that delivers enhanced value and earnings accretion to EMI shareholders."[5]

Things started to reach boiling point in June and July as both sides scrambled to buy the other. EMI tabled a bid of $28.50 a share for Warner but had it kicked into the long grass as Warner laid down a counter-bid of 315p a share for EMI. In an escalating game of tit-for-tat, EMI snubbed that bid and raised its original bid by $2.50 a share. Bronfman turned his nose up at that offer of $31 a share and swung back with a raised counter-bid of 320p a share. EMI said no.[6]

"It was a move which set the two companies on a route which is likely to result in an aggressive takeover during the second half of 2006," proposed *Music Week* in a feature headlined 'EMI and Warner declare war'.[7] Bronfman was reported to have grown the worth of Warner from $2.6 billion in 2003 to $4 billion in just three years and was bullish that Warner should be the acquirer and not the acquiree. EMI, meanwhile, was considering issuing new shares, rather than taking on more debt, to raise $4.5 billion to buy Warner.

"There was some thinking internally that we would buy Warner and that would solve all our problems," says a senior EMI source party to these plans. "There were task forces of people who met in shadowy rooms to talk about strategy in terms of how we would approach that. Warner were doing the same thing to buy us."

A matter of weeks later, however, a bomb dropped. The Court Of First Instance ruled to annul the European Commission's green-lighting of the Sony/BMG merger, a move that put more power in the hands of indie label trade body Impala to stem further consolidation. Sony and Bertelsmann looked like they would have to re-submit their applications to merge and any EMI/Warner marriage was never going to happen with this rumbling on in the background. In August, both EMI and Warner publicly mothballed any plans to merge, accepting the regulatory climate was against them while Sony BMG's future hung in the balance.

Even though the health of the recorded music industry was heading rapidly downhill at that time, a Warner merger might have been deemed possible in theory; however, it was regarded as simply too big a risk to take. "We thought it would have been very difficult to achieve a full merger with Warner – for recorded music and publishing," says a senior source. "You probably could have done elements of both but with some divestment."

Nicoli says that EMI "had the means and the strategic rationale to acquire Warner Music Group" and it made more sense for EMI to buy Warner, rather than the other way round. "Edgar wanted to buy EMI," he suggests. "But he would have been buying a public company and would have had to persuade that public company's shareholders to sell. I did have a meeting with Edgar where he proposed acquiring us. But then the Sony BMG deal went back into review – and at that point both Warner and we decided we should forget it. Whoever owns it, it's not going to happen. The regulators are just not going to approve it in this climate."

Another senior source claims that "there was no Plan B" after the Warner talks were derailed, and that internal thinking was that Bronfman agreeing to sell would be both panacea and the catalyst for new growth – plus helping to finally make EMI a force to be reckoned with in the world's largest music market.

"The plan was to become part of a bigger thing; we had to be bigger," they say. "If we had bought Warner there would have been lots of synergies and cost savings. That helps. It would have made us bigger and it would have fixed fucking America. The biggest global repertoire comes from American and we didn't have any apart from Norah Jones."

While nerves were frayed at the corporate head office of EMI in London, down the road in Brook Green the UK recorded music arm was jubilant. Speaking at the company's autumn conference, where it outlined its key releases for the final, and busiest, quarter of the year, Tony Wadsworth was defiant, saying EMI made up 33 per cent of sales by UK acts in the year to date while Universal limped behind with 20 per cent. EMI UK was firing on all cylinders. "In the past two years, there has been a significant swingback to UK music in the UK," said Wadsworth, alluding to the market that EMI historically over-performed in. "Two years ago, UK music made up 50 per cent of the UK market – now it's up to 60 per cent. We [EMI] pride ourselves on being number one for UK music."[8] Acts like Corinne Bailey Rae, The Kooks, KT Tunstall and Lily Allen were all held up as examples of EMI's domestic success.

EMI UK might have been roaring into a strong Christmas, but in Wrights Lane hearts were in mouths as a whole new chapter in the company's future was on the brink of being written. A potential new owner was waiting in the wings – and it wasn't a music company. Spooked by the potential unravelling of Sony BMG, which put the kibosh on any Warner deal, EMI's senior executives were courting someone who had plenty of money and who came with zero regulatory risk, potentially allowing the company to move from publicly listed to private, the move many said should have happened after the Thorn demerger.

This was a leading European private equity firm, founded as Schroder Ventures in 1985 and rebranded as Permira in 2001, expanding in the early 2000s into the US, Hong Kong and Japan. Its acquisitions in the early 2000s included telecommunications company Debitel, Jet Aviation,

Spanish pizza chain Telepizza, UK TV, film and digital production/distribution company All3Media, Principal Hotels[9] and 85 per cent of German luxury fashion brand Hugo Boss in August 2007.[10]

John Gildersleeve, described as a 'big beast' of the City,[11] had been on the board of supermarket chain Tesco from 1984 to 2004. On leaving Tesco, he became a non-executive chairman at EMI and had rich experience in high-finance deals, helping to sell Gallaher to Japan Tobacco for close to £10 billion in 2006. He was to become a driving force in the sale of EMI. "John Gildersleeve turns out to be a very key person in all of this," says a source who worked closely with him at this time. "EMI did have a really good board when you look at some of the people on there. Gildersleeve came from Tesco. Good bloke. He had risen right from the bottom of Tesco and was a very impressive person. No nonsense. Doesn't suffer fools gladly. But not a twat."

On the horns of a dilemma over EMI's survival, Gildersleeve and Nicoli had to land something big – and land it decisively. "John and Eric had concluded that there was no other option but to look for a buyer for EMI – rather than a merger," recalls one well-placed source. "Warner could end up being a buyer, but the problem there was the uncertainty around antitrust issues. Really what they wanted was a deal that could deliver certainty."

Certainty was far from a given, with the Sony BMG merger at serious risk of unspooling at the hands of the European regulators. EMI needed a sale – and not just to help shore it up during the endless and bitter digital winter that was causing the record business to slip, slide and pratfall. It also needed to jump before its debts killed it.

"The main reason why we had to sell the company was because of the debt covenants that were in place with the banks," says one senior EMI source. "There were four or five banks who had essentially lent EMI all of its money. Although the company was trading profitably, it was not making sufficient profits to meet its debt covenants. We had to report to the City every six months. The issue was, the ratio between its profits and its debt had to be within a certain band, otherwise at that point the banks could step in and seize control."

Few outside of the EMI board knew how loudly the time bomb was ticking – but it was getting deafening and Permira seemed the fastest and cleanest way of defusing it. Except when the numbers started to be combed through, a huge problem in the world's second-largest music market emerged that put the whole deal at risk. "Talks had begun towards the end of 2006 with Permira," says a senior executive. "That was for the sale of EMI. The whole thing. Permira came in and they did quite a lot of due diligence. A major problem that arose when they were doing their due diligence was that they had looked at an agreement between EMI and Toshiba in relation to the Japanese business."

EMI's Japanese business was called Toshiba-EMI, where EMI owned 55 per cent and Toshiba owned the remaining 45 per cent. A clause in the agreement stipulated that in the event of any change of control of EMI Group, Toshiba had a put option, where it could sell its stake for an agreed multiple of profits before a certain date, in respect of its 45 per cent.

The music industry had been made keenly aware of the uncertain ground around put options in 2002 when Clive Calder sold Zomba to BMG. It all dated back to 1991 when BMG bought 25 per cent of Zomba's music publishing division and followed this up in 1996 by buying 20 per cent of its recorded music arm. A put option was granted to Calder in 1996 where a total BMG buyout would be based on a multiple of earnings made between 1999 and 2001.

In that period and just before digital piracy kicked the chair from under the business, its Jive division had a phenomenal run. Backstreet Boys' *Millennium* album in 1999 sold an estimated 30 million copies globally and 2001's *The Hits: Chapter One* did around half that. Also in that time, the first three Britney Spears albums sold over 50 million copies, making Zomba/Jive the pre-eminent pop label at the turn of the millennium. The net result was that the label's key signings were arguably at their commercial peak, operating in a genre where careers are often brief, and Zomba's earnings were dramatically inflated. Calder's deft playing of the put option saw him walk away with $2.74 billion having, in the eyes of the *New York Post*, "fleeced" BMG.[12]

Permira would have been sharply attuned to what a put option could mean for its takeover of EMI. "Toshiba could put its share in Toshiba-EMI at a certain multiple of profits," explains one source. "That would have been fine except for at some point in 2006 Toshiba-EMI had done a sale and lease back on one of its offices in Tokyo and had sold the freehold for a large amount of money. That resulted in a one-off huge spike in profits for Japan that year. That had nothing to do with trading and nothing to do with selling lots of records; it was simply the fact that we had sold the building and leased it back and caused a huge profit in Japan. Unfortunately, the joint venture between Toshiba and EMI, in the calculation of the put option, did not eliminate one-off spikes in the P&L [profit and loss statement]."

It is understood that EMI came within a whisker of closing the deal, but Permira was said to be concerned about clauses in the joint venture with Toshiba. It turned out that this was to stall discussions. Those wrinkles in the clauses were swiftly ironed out when EMI bought out

Toshiba's 45 per cent stake for an estimated £93 million to take full control of the Japanese arm; but this solution arrived just too late. As the buyout was happening, Permira announced its acquisition of German media operator ProSieben, a company it had at the top of its watch list. "Permira had been let back into the ProSieben deal that they had been kicked out of some weeks earlier," says a City source of this last-minute switch in focus. "[F]or two weeks they had been riding both the ProSieben and EMI horses." The deal was a combined effort between Kohlberg Kravis Roberts in the US and Permira in Europe, acquiring a 50.5 per cent stake in the broadcaster that valued it at €5.6 billion.[13] ProSieben's gain was very much EMI's loss.

EMI tried to put a brave face on it all, issuing a statement confirming the talks had collapsed but not saying who those talks were with. "The EMI board has not received an offer that fully reflects the prospects for and value of the company and which it could recommend to share-holders," it said, pushing a 'business as normal' line. Shares in the company immediately dropped 8 per cent to 276p.[14]

EMI might have ended 2006 frustrated and dejected, but 2007 was to put it through the mangle in a way no one could have imagined.

New year, new panics

EMI was losing ground to its other major label rivals and this was going to damage its share price. For 2006, EMI's global market share had slipped to 12.8 per cent according to IFPI figures, its worst performance since 1999. To rub salt in the wounds, Warner was now ahead of it with 13.8 per cent. EMI was now the smallest major in a declining market.[15]

Desperate times would call for desperate measures. The new year opened with a shock double firing. Alain Levy and David Munns were called back from America, the market that EMI continued to struggle in, and were sacked. Part of the blame was put on a poor performance by EMI in Q4, triggering two profit warnings at the start of January. The early departure of two high-profile executives came at a heavy cost: Levy was reported to have been given "an extraordinary pay package worth at least £4.6 million".[16]

Eric Nicoli immediately took over as chief executive, with John Gildersleeve moving up to become chairman, and quickly announced a restructuring plan to shave 20 per cent off its cost base as well as adding an extra £110 million in savings.

The sacking of such high-level executives as Levy and Munns never happens on a whim and it was clear that the US had been underperform-ing for years. Perhaps some outside of EMI were shocked by the departure of such senior names, but those within the company knew that it was a sad, but inevitable, conclusion to that particular chapter.

Despite the blood still soaking into the boardroom carpets and the Permira failure still smarting, EMI went straight back out to court or respond to potential private equity buyers, among them One Equity, Fortress and Cerberus, the firm named after the multi-headed 'hound of Hades' in Greek mythology that would play a bigger, and accidentally more damaging, role in the coming months. Even Warner was not retreating fully into the shadows at this stage. "Edgar was always looking," says Nicoli. "Not disrupting, but always looking."

By February, Nicoli had merged Capitol and Virgin in the US, appointing Jason Flom as chairman of the newly amalgamated division. EMI barely had time to lick its wounds after another profit warning on a loveless 14 February, when it found itself back in merger machinations as Warner Music made a shock move in March. Warner's aim was to nullify independent label opposition to its plan to buy EMI.

It struck a deal with Impala, the body representing Europe's independent labels, to lend its support to Warner's proposed takeover of EMI. As part of the agreement, Warner would agree to provide funding for Merlin, the digital rights agency for the indies, as well as committing to divestment of certain recorded music assets. There was also the promise of a more nebulous commitment to "pursue various other 'behavioural' commitments to benefit the market as a whole". Alison Wenham, CEO of UK-based indie body AIM, said, "The purpose of our organisation is to improve the market for indies, which means improving the behaviour of the majors."[17] This was not good enough for some of her member labels, with both Ministry Of Sound and Gut Records immediately quitting AIM in protest. Other AIM labels were also said to have serious reservations about Impala's backing of a merger but did not resign.

EMI confirmed later in March that it had received a non-binding proposal from Warner to buy it (pegged at 260p a share) but batted it back as it was deemed inadequate.

In Brook Green, staff were aware that the future ownership of the company was being jostled over, but were instructed to put it out of their minds and carry on as normal. "There were rumblings [of a takeover or merger] but that was all happening at Wrights Lane," says an EMI UK executive. "We felt insulated at Brook Green and we were told that whatever happened it wouldn't affect us. It was just a change of the business structure and would not affect our day-to-day activities. Don't worry about it. We're fine."

Tony Wadsworth confirms that he was shielding the UK part of the company from what was happening at the group board level, but adds he was often as much in the dark as his staff were, with the team at Wrights Lane only keeping him abreast of events as and when they saw fit.

"This whole environment of uncertainty and will-they-won't-they? and so on made me even more keen to insulate the UK company from what was going on outside – it's just a distraction from artists and music," he says. "I was [party to those corporate discussions about a sale or merger], but only up to a point. For example, no one ever discussed Permira with me. I only heard the deal had collapsed through rumours. The old-fashioned structure that was the EMI board – which was a legacy of Thorn-EMI, in a way – at the time, which was chaired by Eric, didn't have any of the heads of the major territories on it. So it was still a case of, 'These are the people who run the company at the top and you are the music people.' So I wasn't in that upper cadre of people who were party to these discussions, really until Terra Firma was a fait accompli."

In March came a symbolic defection that foreshadowed an artist exodus when EMI was to eventually find its new owner later that same year. Paul McCartney, one of the four architects of EMI's phenomenal global run from 1963 onwards with The Beatles, signed to Hear Music, a joint venture between Concord Music Group and coffee shop chain Starbucks, for the release of his *Memory Almost Full* album that June.

"I have left the family home, but it doesn't feel bad," he said at the time. "I hate to tell you – the people at EMI sort of understood. The major record labels are having major problems. They're a little puzzled as to what's happening. And I sympathise with them."[18]

Across the Atlantic at Warner, however, things were accelerating at a rate of knots.

"When Edgar came in and acquired Warner, he always had his sights set on EMI," says one highly placed source at the company's New York office. "That was always part of it. The private equity guys were definitely up for it." They reveal that large-scale divestment scenarios were already being mapped out to appease the regulators should EMI agree to a sale. "One was that we could sell Warner/Chappell and keep EMI Music Publishing," they say. "Or we could [...] create a pool of assets to satisfy the regulators and then sell those [...] There were various options that we were looking at in terms of how we could either immediately sell one of the assets or pool together some assets and then sell them. You can park the acquired assets until it clears regulatory approval."

They also suggest that corporate ego – or, more specifically, corporate protectionism – was a constant threat that could blow merger or acquisition talks out of the water. "There was no question that EMI management absolutely hated the thought of a Warner acquisition," the

Warner source claims. "They were clinging on for their lives. The competition between the companies was incredibly striking. Warner at the time, and I might be biased, was performing much better. Warner was also strong in the US which EMI was not [...] In terms of the top of the senior management team, I think it was clear that Eric Nicoli wouldn't survive. Or he would take some kind of interim secondary role. There were even discussions at the time between the two companies where it was pretty much agreed that in the event that Warner was the acquirer, I think they knew that the senior management team wasn't long for the world. I don't think anyone would have objectively looked at the top tier of EMI management at that stage in the revolution and said, 'Oh, these are the best of the best!'"

They also claim that EMI was trying to queer the pitch to spin it that the British company was gunning to buy the American one, feeding stories to analysts and business writers to try and get them to repeat this narrative as fact. "It was a presumption that we [Warner] were going to be acquired!" they say with disbelief. "It was just assumed! And there was a level of arrogance to it that we found incredible. The day that we made a bid for EMI and it became public, I think everybody was shocked. There was a Reuters story that basically said that the conventional wisdom had turned out to be wrong as no one thought that the acquirer was going to be Warner at that time. That's when it really heated up. I remember that EMI had leaked the story to CNBC – and we were a public company the time – that they were going to acquire us. You can imagine how disruptive that was internally. Once that happened, then it was on! It became a big battle in the financial press between the two companies."

Nicoli, for his part, denies that this was ever the fight to the death between him and Bronfman that played out across the business pages by writers keen to make this corporate story as scurrilous as possible. "I know it was characterised as Edgar against me," he says. "Corporately, it was a bit. But it was never personal. Could I have worked with him? Certainly! Edgar's all right."

While these corporate lurches were happening at the board level, EMI still had to get on with its normal business. If the sacking of Levy and Munns was a tacit admission that America was to remain its existential nightmare, the company was very keen to prove that it was adapting fully to the digital future.

Barney Wragg joined EMI in late 2006 to spearhead its digital operations, having joined from Universal Music Group where he was senior vice president of digital in its eLabs division. He had a remit to shake things up and put EMI back at the forefront of digital developments.

"After five good years at UMG, I had gone to EMI to do some fairly radical stuff and I wanted to move the game on faster and drive change across the industry," he says. "When I joined, Levy and Munns gave me carte blanche to be able to do stuff within digital that they hadn't previously been able to do."

The first, and most significant, change he pushed through was to be allowed to unify and globalise all digital decisions and deals. "Companies trying to get licensing deals done in 2005 and 2006 would say that EMI was impossible to deal with," he says of the system he inherited. "Inside EMI you needed something like twenty-seven signatures on one physical piece of paper to get a deal approved in North America. It had to get FedExed from coast to coast because it had to be signed in a particular order. I spent a lot of time rejigging a lot of that kind of stuff. Taking out bureaucracy and trying to empower innovation."

EMI was, Wragg felt, being held back as deals were being done in territorial tranches and therefore its digital plans were unable to move in unison. "Munns and Levy gave me the ability to be able to determine things on a global basis for the first time," he says. "Previously, there hadn't really been any corporate strategy. You had policies set and decisions made in the US that were different from the UK, that were different from Europe and that were different from Asia. It was very, very fragmented. My job was to pull it together and give it some direction. Because it was so fragmented, it was very slow, which meant EMI was always the last into a deal, especial new deals that were with emerging global players. EMI was always seen as a laggard, really."

One of his first big coups was with YouTube, a deal he felt should have been signed off a year earlier. He was also keen to drop the industry's obsession with putting digital restrictions on CDs and legal downloads as he felt this was not in the consumer's best interests. He saw this as a way for EMI finally to be painted as a digital pioneer.

"One of the first things that I wanted to do when I got board approval to go DRM-free was to be out in the market ahead of everyone else – and to do it as a big corporate strike," he proposes. "It was to send a message to the market that, under this new regime, EMI was open for business and that it could and would do things."

The statement deal that EMI desperately needed was to arrive in April with the biggest digital retailer of music in the world: iTunes. It was also a deal, as was becoming all too common in their negotiations, that very much played in Apple's favour too.

EMI made its digital catalogue on iTunes available stripped of DRM (digital rights management), albeit at a higher price (£0.99 for DRM-free tracks at an improved audio quality versus £0.79 for 'standard' DRM-encased tracks), announcing the deal in the company's Wrights Lane offices with Apple head Steve Jobs in attendance.

"Without Eric, we wouldn't have got the DRM-free deal done," says Wragg. "Eric's background is in physics and he had a broader understanding of technology than a lot of other executives inside the industry at that time. I could sit down with him and explain that, despite our best efforts, we had lost the battle on DRM. We were trying to sell a download with protection limitations on it that we didn't add when we sold a CD. We knew by that time that we would never stop selling CDs, so why wouldn't we offer the consumer the same product when they bought it as a download as when they bought it on a disc? Eric completely got that – and very quickly."

Breaking from the pack, Apple was hoping EMI would force the hand of the other majors and get them to follow suit. "EMI is pioneering something that is going to become very popular," said Jobs at the event. "There are always leaders and there are always followers." Finally, EMI was being acknowledged as 'pioneering' and a 'leader' by a technology head whose cultural impact was so profound that he was worshipped in almost messianic terms. EMI, after a tough six months, could be allowed to puff its chest out with pride.

The jaws of debt open wider

While a celebrating Nicoli was sharing a stage with Jobs in the atrium of Wrights Lane, gnawing at the back of his mind was the need for an EMI sale to happen before the end of the summer. EMI had saddled itself with serious debt covenants and, like stones in its pockets, these were pulling it under water. "There were four or five banks who had essentially lent EMI all of its money," reveals a senior source. "Although the company was trading profitably, it was not making sufficient profits to meet its debt covenants. We had to report to the City every six months. The issue was, the ratio between its profits and its debt had to be within a certain band otherwise at that point the banks could step in and seize control."

EMI had its debt covenants measured twice a year, the test dates landing at the end of March and September. It had hit the buffers in the March test but managed to get a workaround. It was understood that EMI refinanced its debt on 29 March 2007 via an unsecured £700 million facility made up of a £400 million loan and a £300 million revolving facility (where a loan can be withdrawn, repaid and redrawn multiple times within an agreed timeframe).

"On those measuring dates, the amount of debt that it was carrying had to be within a certain ratio of the amount of profit that the business was making," explains the same senior source. "As it was getting closer to March it became clear that we were not going to get through that covenant test in March. What the banks agreed to do, rather than let EMI breach that covenant, was that just before the test date they readjusted the covenants so that no matter what its profits were, it would still be within the covenant tests."

EMI had, despite the odds, secured itself some wriggle room in March, but this reprieve would not be bounced down the line to September. "The banks said they would agree to move the covenants in March but they would not agree to move the covenants in September. They said we must make the March covenants or suffer the consequences."

From this vulnerable position, September – if the covenants were breached – was looking as if it could torpedo the company. EMI's board was, it seemed, having to pull off a miracle if it was to survive beyond the company's 100th birthday. "Eric and the board did not believe that we would make the September covenants so they realised at that point that the company would have to be sold," claims a source. "Otherwise it was going to hit the rocks."

The problem was that this all left a smoking gun for anyone looking to buy EMI. But only if, according to the same source, they did their due diligence properly. "If a buyer had done due diligence they would have had access to all of our debt documentations," they explained. "They would have seen the profits that we would have had to have reached in the September test in order for the banks not to call in the debt. The banks could have said if we did not make the covenant test that we would have to pay back the loan. If EMI had not been able to pay back the loan at that point, the bank would have forced the sale of the business."

EMI had interest from several private equity firms, but all the tyre-kicking (Warner's boomerang-ing acquisition aspirations aside) had resulted in not a single bid from the private equity world. "There were lots of companies sniffing around," says an EMI executive close enough to follow the daily twists and turns here. "Everyone was leaking to the press left, right and centre. But nothing actually happened. Nobody made a formal deal. It was John Gildersleeve who set the deadline. That was it. EMI could not function like that."

A time and date were set of 9 a.m. on 21 May to weed out the time-wasters and also force the hand of any external company that might have been vacillating. "Gildersleeve was the one who accelerated it," says a senior source about this decisive rolling of the dice. "Because that hadn't happened before. Eric wasn't in charge at this point. He was the CEO. But Gildersleeve was the chairman. It was his auction. He was running it."

It is understood that One Equity submitted an indicative bid – rumoured to have been between 250p and 260p a share – in the final week of April. That was good but, as far as EMI was concerned, not good enough.

Thought to be the front runner, Cerberus was seen internally at EMI as a solid buyer. But another suitor suddenly appeared, led by "a dishevelled six-footer with an unkempt bouffant and tombstone teeth"[19] who had struggled at The Judd School in Kent due to his dyslexia and dyspraxia but still managed to make it to Oxford University. From there, he went to Goldman Sachs in London where he became head of bond trading within four years. He then left to join Japanese bank Nomura where he was hailed as a rising star and fiscal whizzkid. On his ascent he made a vast fortune, estimated at £100 million,[20] leaving the Japanese banking giant in 1994 to set up his own private equity company, Terra Firma.

Guy Hands had just come knocking at EMI.

* * *

Terra Firma was, as far as EMI was concerned, the outside bet in the steeplechase to acquire it. They were both, however, on the rebound: EMI from Warner (multiple times) and Permira; and Terra Firma from Boots after it lost out to Kohlberg Kravis Roberts' £11.1 billion bid for the high-street pharmacy chain in April 2007. Each spurned party needed to get a big deal done – EMI to ensure its future and Terra Firma to finally be taken seriously by the City as a dealmaker without equal.

EMI was, however, not a new target for Terra Firma. It had considered making a move for the company as far back as 1994, and also in passing at the end of 2006, according to Guy Hands. "I felt very strongly that the music industry was losing touch with its customer and it didn't really understand what was going on," he says. But 1994 was a period when the record business was entering an accelerated boom and Hands backed off.

Some thirteen years later, however, things were very different. The good times appeared to be over and the record business was in sharp decline. The pain seemed endless, but Hands claims he had spotted how to salve, ease and end that pain and, secondly, how to nurture the business into recovery.

"We saw two things happening," he says of the bitter landscape of 2007 that had replaced the glittering one of 1994. "One was that the customer base was going to change and how they would experience music would change. Two, the technology was slowly changing, and that technology changed your ability to control your customer in the same way that you had been able to ... What was attractive, however, was the catalogue. The catalogue was attractive in 1994 and it continued to be attractive all the way through. Both recorded music and publishing; both catalogues were attractive. What we felt was that that was not being focused on as much as it should have been. What people were really focusing on was very much new music."

Hands was adamant a change had to happen and he saw parallels with the pharmaceutical industry, where the creation was separate from the distribution. "If you are a small technology company making a bio-technology drug, you make that by yourself and then you get a major drug company to distribute," he explains. "Very few of the major drugs today are developed all the way through by the drugs companies. They will tend to buy them later. To some extent with music, what was happening was that EMI and the other labels – but for some reason EMI was particularly bad at this – were spending an absolute fortune on trying to find the hits, rather than using their strengths to basically distribute and market the hits. They were literally just throwing stuff at the wall."

This model, he felt, is where the music business needed to move itself. Terra Firma was ready to pounce, but this was perhaps its first mistake – it pounced too fast. Or, more specifically, it came back with a proper acquisition plan mere weeks before the bidding deadline closed. Hands says there were very clear reasons for this, to do with confidentiality clauses relating to mergers and acquisitions. "We had looked at the business briefly at the end of 2006 and we asked for the information that has been given to Permira and they [EMI] wouldn't give it to us," he claims. "If they weren't in the sales process, they weren't obliged to give it to us."

This information would have afforded Terra Firma a longer run-up to buy EMI, but it kept a watching brief on the music company anyway. As it turned out, it was then approached in April by David Wormsley at Citigroup – a bank Terra Firma had worked with on seventeen trans-actions in the previous five years totalling £27 billion, elevating the private equity firm to 'Platinum' client status – to see if they would consider a formal bid. But time was against them and this was going to cost them dearly.

"Terra Firma came in very quickly," says one high-up source at EMI. "As senior management we didn't know very much about it. We would have weekly board meetings and senior management meetings and I remember Eric, then acting as CEO after Levy, telling us that they had accepted a bid from Terra Firma. It had all happened very, very quickly."

Hands says that Terra Firma knew that EMI Music Publishing was a robust business that ran efficiently and this could be the part of the company used to regenerate the struggling recorded music side. "Our view was that the publishing business could be securitised and we could add onto it by buying further catalogues," he says. "We were always going to hold onto publishing. That was what we were going to rely on to repay the debt and to give us our money back. We saw that as a safe business that we would be able to make two times our money on. As it was a little bit more than half the cost, two times your money meant that you would have a profitable deal."

It is understood that Hands and Nicoli met to discuss the bid in the first week of May and Hands stressed that he would require help in accessing the assorted due diligence documentation to expedite the bid. Within a matter of days, EMI had given Terra Firma access to the electronic data room so it could start to comb through the information at hand.

Both sides, for their own reasons, were keen to get a deal done, with some claiming that Terra Firma – obsessed with getting a deal done to cancel out its chagrin over the Boots failure and also dazzled by the showbiz-by-proxy of owning a music company – went through its due diligence at breakneck speed. This was to prove an extremely costly mistake for all concerned.

"They only did a few weeks of due diligence and that really showed," claims one senior executive at EMI about Terra Firma's sprint to get its bid in. "Their lack of understanding of, well, everything quite honestly was quite phenomenal. You would almost think they had done zero due diligence from some of the conversation you had with people [when they took over]."

Hands admits that they did rush due diligence on EMI – and this was in large part born out of necessity. They were last-minute entrants and had to go through the process speedily to trump the competition. Or, what they thought was the competition.

"It [the due diligence] was something like four weeks from start to finish," reveals Hands. "The due diligence that was done was done in an incredibly short period of time and it was done in what we thought was a competitive situation. We believed that Cerberus was bidding against us."

City sources say that both Terra Firma and Cerberus were in the running until the latter pulled out a few days before the bidding deadline set by the EMI board. It is understood Cerberus was struggling to get its banks aligned just as the financial crash was starting to bite.

As the pack started to thin out, through all this Warner was sitting on the side-lines, crossing its fingers these deals would fall apart and it could swoop in and get EMI for a knock-down price. "But at the same time, we knew that we weren't really being given a fair chance because EMI management was so against us acquiring the company," claims one Warner executive involved in the bidding. "Talk about be careful what you wish for! In the hands of Warner, it would have been a much healthier company. Their knight in shining armour was Guy Hands and we saw how well that worked out!"

Things started to turn toxic between Warner and EMI at this stage as it increasingly became clear that private equity was where EMI was seeing its future. In doing so, claims a Warner source, EMI treated their company's bid with contempt. "There was a meeting on video conference where the senior teams from each company were to meet to go through certain aspects of the bid," they claim. "A lot of people from the EMI side didn't even show up. In the middle of the meeting, an announcement went out about them agreeing to sell to Terra Firma. That's the way they were playing it. The announcement went out and I recall the Warner executives just walking out of the room thinking this was just theatre. They felt they were just pretending to entertain other potential bids but it was so obvious that they were rigging it so that they could hold onto their jobs."

It would take several years, and a new owner, before Warner would get its hands on at least some of EMI.

The deadline looms

Any bids, given EMI's status as a public company, required 90 per cent shareholder approval so even if the bids were accepted by the board, there was a purgatory period where the senior team and the prospective buyer would have to convince shareholders that this deal was in their best interests.

In these final, rushed days, Citigroup approved its financing for Terra Firma, but the terms had still to be agreed between the two sides. Time was of the essence and so Terra Firma ploughed on with a loan in name but not in final shape – something that was to prove a costly oversight.

At the deadline loomed, Cerberus was bidding at 262p a share and Terra Firma, claiming it had been advised by Citigroup what Cerberus was offering, went hard with an offer of 265p a share. This was to prove a combustible claim that was to threaten the survival of both the bank and the private equity firm in the next few years.

"We were told the number [of Cerberus's bid]," asserts Hands. "There is no question that we were told the number. Citigroup disputes who told us the number. I don't think they have ever told us who told us the number but they have said they never told us the number. But we were definitely told the number. No one disputes that we were told the number because it is everywhere. It is in every single document we had – just about. We believed it was 262. Because of the competitive situation it became a very fast deal. Deals are all based on competition. It is like buying a house. People don't like to think of it like that. People like to think when you were buying a big business it is different from a house. It is actually like buying a house. If you believe someone else is bidding, you do things quickly. If you don't believe someone else is bidding, you do things very slowly."

A senior source, over a decade's remove from the rapid speed of developments at the time, argues the deal was never as do-or-die as others around them now claim. But, with a duty to EMI's shareholders, they say Eric Nicoli could only green-light a bid that came in above any minimum figure the board had agreed on.

By lunchtime on 21 May, EMI's board had accepted the Terra Firma bid. Soon after, EMI issued a statement on its future that, given the previous seven years of near misses, only the quixotic thought possible.

"The EMI board received a number of proposals from several different parties," said chairman John Gildersleeve in a statement. "Terra Firma's offer is the most attractive proposal received and delivers cash now, without regulatory uncertainty and with the minimum of operational risk to the company."

Terra Firma had won the bidding, paying £4.2 billion for the music company. The term 'won' is a misleading one here: you cannot really win if you are the only runner in the race. Cerberus had dropped out mere days before, but Terra Firma did not know this. It would soon find out, however, and this revelation would spark one of the biggest, and most disastrous, court cases in corporate history.

The bitter accusations and recriminations that played out in New York and London courtrooms were still in the future. For now, this was a time for celebration. Eric Nicoli had helped EMI scramble clear of the maw of debt and Guy Hands had landed the biggest deal of his life. That afternoon, Nicoli and Hands arranged to meet at the Chelsea Flower Show to raise triumphant glasses to the deal that had, despite the odds, been pulled off.

Earlier that same morning across London in Greenwich a fire tore through the *Cutty Sark*, the iconic 138-year-old tea clipper, which had been awaiting a £25 million refit.[21] Over at EMI, the first spark was unwittingly ignited that, over the next three years, was to rip through another British icon in desperate need of modernisation.

As Nicoli and Hands clinked champagne glasses in the Chelsea afternoon, the last thing on both men's minds was that over a century of British cultural history was about to go up in flames.

CHAPTER 3

The Horror ...

The EMI board may have accepted Terra Firma's offer, but there was still some distance to the finishing line. There was plenty of speculation that Warner would swoop in with a last-minute offer, although that would come with huge regulatory risks. The day after the EMI board accepted Guy Hands's bid, the European Commission finally approved Universal Music Group's £1.1 billion purchase of BMG Music Publishing. But this had taken eight months to clear the regulators and was contingent on the divestment of Rondor UK and Zomba UK.[1] EMI could ill afford a delay in the deal, so Terra Firma was the regulatory path of least resistance; yet that did not stop the music trade press and others in the business exchanging rumours that Terra Firma was only there for asset stripping and was planning a quick flip of the business, possibly spinning EMI's recorded music arm off from its publishing division. Terra Firma's previous deals should have been an indicator that it, compared to more ruthless private equity firms, had a slightly longer view on its investments and the necessary restructuring plans.

David Kassler was an operating partner at Terra Firma and had previously worked on the turnaround of Tank & Rast, the German autobahn service operator, calling it the private equity firm's "most successful deal ever". Terra Firma had been keeping an eye on the business and finally bought it in November 2004. Its 338 filling stations and 382 service areas around Germany gave it an annual footfall of around 500 million customers a year,[2] but it was tarnished as a brand.

"German customers weren't stopping there because the retail offering wasn't great and the products were quite expensive," says Kassler. "The local German food suited some people, but not everyone. The toilets were dirty and very often you would have someone at the door trying to get you to pay €1 or €2 for the privilege of stopping there. We reinvented that situation and installed very high-quality turnstile toilets. You paid

€0.50 to go in but then they gave you a voucher to use in the restaurants or the shops – so effectively it was costing you nothing. We could use the money that was generated in the retail [side] to make sure that all the loos were incredibly high quality, clean and staffed 24/7."

This was arguably the deal Terra Firma was proudest of and Hands would regularly refer to it when talking to EMI staff and executives as proof that he knew what he was doing and where he could take ailing businesses – identifying the core problems, fixing them and returning the companies to their former glory.

Kassler says it was also evidence that Terra Firma did not operate at the same pell-mell speed of other private equity companies, playing the tortoise rather than the hare. "Terra Firma tends to hold companies for much longer than a typical private equity company," he says. "The typical hold time is seven or eight years; whereas for other private companies it might be three or four years."

Three months prior to the Tank & Rast deal, Terra Firma had bought the Odeon chain of cinemas in the UK[3] for an estimated €650 million, then paid €350 million for the UCI (United Cinemas International) chain that year, merging the two into the UK's largest cinema operator.[4] Terra Firma had plenty of experience of big deals and recovery plans, but it was oblivious to the fact that its latest – and certainly most glamorous – deal was to be the one that almost sank it.

There was still a lot of red tape to scythe through before Guy Hands and his team could start hammering EMI into a new and, they hoped, improved shape. As a public company, EMI's board needed to get its many shareholders to approve the deal before Terra Firma would take possession of the keys. They needed to convince 90 per cent of them that this was the best deal for them and the best deal for the company. In terms of due process, Terra Firma had twenty-eight days to produce a formal offer document and shareholders would have sixty days to consider it, with *Music Week* suggesting an ultimate cut-off point of 17 August.[5]

Getting to that 90 per cent shareholder approval was to prove more arduous than either EMI or Terra Firma had anticipated. "There were a couple of extensions on that," says one senior source as they struggled to get the final few shareholders to back the sale. "At one point we had to rely on the fact that there was a postal strike [in early August][6] to get an extension from the takeover committee to allow us a few extra days. We argued that some votes may have got lost in the post – but obviously not many votes came in the post as they would come by email. We successfully argued that, because of the postal strike, we should get an extension. In the meantime, there was a massive scramble to get the institutions over the line to approve the deal. Which they subsequently did. It went right down to the wire."

If they failed to get to 90 per cent approval, the bid would have to be scrapped and there was some talk at the board level that Warner could be allowed back in. That, however, would not only present multiple regulatory hoops to jump through but also, because of the delay this would cause, would mean the banks having to accept another adjustment to the covenants due that September.

"If that had not happened, the banks could have taken control of the assets and put the company into liquidation," says a very senior source at EMI. "They could have seized the shares and ultimately the shareholders would have lost their money […] Eric did not want to be the chairman of a company that went bust and left shareholders high and dry."

Meanwhile Terra Firma needed to convince the naysayers in the financial world that it was a serious contender and that it was now moving to the upper echelons of deal-making. "Guy had to weigh up the reputational risk for him of having 88 per cent of shareholders wanting the deal to happen but he walked," says a well-placed source. "It's all very well with hindsight – ten years and two court cases later – for him to say what he thought at the time, but it was very clear that he wanted to own the business. Very clear."

Hands reveals something that was not made public at the time. He claims that both Terra Firma and Citigroup were hoping against hope that EMI's board would fail to convince shareholders that this was the right deal. If they could not get 90 per cent of shareholders to back the sale, both Terra Firma and Citigroup could walk away with impunity, their reputations intact, breathing enormous sighs of relief.

In effect, getting to the 90 per cent approval rate was the worst possible outcome for everyone involved in the deal – except EMI. Terra Firma would be saddled with a debt just as the markets collapsed and Citigroup would not be able to syndicate its loan and so would be exposed in a massively turbulent market to the tune of £2.6 billion.

"Both Citigroup and us were hoping that we would not get to 90 per cent," suggests Hands. "Neither of us wanted to blame the other, though. By the last week, I was just hoping it wouldn't get to 90 per cent […] There were three groups involved. There was Eric Nicoli and his advisors, who were [investment bank] Greenhill & Co., and who were desperately trying to get every vote out there. You then have Citigroup and Terra Firma. Neither Citigroup nor Terra Firma under any circumstances want to be seen as trying to stop the deal. Citigroup and Terra Firma have to be seen, from a reputational point of view, to be doing the best to get the deal done."

Everything went into slow motion in the closing days as Nicoli and his board did everything in their power to get every single vote they could. Some within Terra Firma were petrified that it would happen while others were trying to put a brave face on it and focus only on the positives.

"So you had this group of people who were watching the clock tick and watching the votes come in with completely different motivations," says Hands. "You had EMI who wanted it to happen because, if it didn't, it was going to be horrendous. You had us split with some people believing in the deal and other people scared shitless. I think the difference there was the difference between whether it was your own money or it wasn't. So the people who had done the deal passionately believed in the deal and still felt positive. I, on the other hand, had pretty much all of my net worth invested in Terra Firma. I was just thinking that if this happens it was going to be difficult to get it done."

Along with using the Royal Mail strike as a reason for an extension, there was also the issue of the dead register (essentially shareholders that, for various reasons, could not be found). But following the granting of extensions and a final desperate push, they got over the 90 per cent threshold on 1 August. Just. When the figure reached 90.3 per cent, this allowed them to force the sale of the remaining shares. It was announced on that day that EMI would stop trading on the stock market on 6 August.[7] EMI was now technically a private company, but its every twist and turn for the next three years was to play out in the most blatantly public way imaginable.

The race to secure the loan

Its fate now sealed by just over 90 per cent of the EMI shareholders, Terra Firma had a concurrent race against the clock to deal with – and it was also going to go right to the wire. It was all tied to the first tremor that would ultimately see the demise of Guy Hands's mega-deal ambitions. A City analyst was quoted in *Music Week* saying there was a chance the financing of the whole deal could fall apart because of changes to the credit market since Terra Firma had its bid accepted in May. There was talk of the "appalling state of the debt markets", with a crisis in the market having already impacted on the private equity acquisitions of Alliance Boots and automotive company Chrysler.

"There is a much different credit market and EMI's performance has continued to lag," the nameless analyst said. "EMI and Terra [Firma] have ticked all the boxes, but Citigroup have still to make the deal."[8]

EMI was quick to send out a message to quell any panic this might cause, with Eric Nicoli claiming all the material conditions of the offer had been satisfied. Citigroup added that, given over 90 per cent of EMI shareholders were backing the deal, they were steadfast in their commitment to raise the capital Terra Firma needed to buy the company. "We've signed up so we are obliged to do it,"[9] a Citigroup spokesman told *Music Week*.

Behind the scenes and away from the media, a monumental struggle over the debt structure was happening – one that would have enormous ramifications for Terra Firma's ownership of EMI. Effectively, Citigroup had agreed to lend Terra Firma the main chunk of the sale price (£2.6 billion of the £4.2 billion total) and Terra Firma had agreed to borrow it; but the actual terms of the loan had not been agreed on. In a strong debt market, such a cavalier attitude was normal. But between originally discussing the loan and coming to the stage where both sides had to work out the precise terms, the first tremors of the global financial collapse were being felt. The rules had very quickly – and shockingly – changed.

"The belief was that you would sort out the documentation on the financing during that period," says Hands of the original plan that would lead into the final structuring of the loan. "Citigroup had agreed to lend us the money. We had agreed to borrow the money. But the actual terms were still to be negotiated. Is that common? At the time it was very common. It became less common [after that], but it is becoming common again now [in 2018]. In a buoyant debt market, it is very common because if the lender who says they are going to lend you the money doesn't, you can just go off and borrow from somebody else. In a very bad debt market, it virtually never happens. Let's say you really want to buy a house and you need a mortgage. You might go to your bank and say you need to borrow the money as you need to get the bid in by tomorrow. In a buoyant market, if you don't like their terms, you just go down the road. In a bad market you might say that you need to understand the terms fully."

At the start of the process, Terra Firma had a term sheet and "everything was sweetness and light" according to Hands. Citigroup was, he claims, focusing on what percentage of the loan it could sell on and working out its fees while Terra Firma was charging forward with utmost confidence. Then the pungent reality hit them both squarely in the face.

"Then the debt market started to collapse," says Hands. "By the beginning of July, the debt market was in a terrible state." He argues this was all a process of terrible timing, and if they had done the deal six months earlier, they would have got better terms; if they had done it six months later, they could have bought EMI for much less than £4.2 billion. "If it had been done at £1 billion less, it wouldn't have been an issue," hypothesises Hands. "At £1 billion less we would have reduced the debt by almost half. If we could have cut the debt by 40 per cent, the deal would have been absolutely fine. To cut the debt by 40 per cent, you need it to cut the price by 20 per cent."

Another bone of contention between lender and borrower was how the £2.6 billion loan was packaged up. Citigroup was offering it as a single loan and Terra Firma wanted it as two separate loans – one for the recorded music assets of EMI and the other for the publishing part of the business. Terra Firma's logic was that it was buying a business where one half (publishing) came with virtually no risk while the other (recorded music), because of the reconstructive surgery it was planning, was almost all risk. Hands and his team wanted a 'safe' loan for publishing to mitigate against the high risks of the loan for recorded music.

"We saw there being a publishing deal which would get us our money back and make a small profit; and a recorded music deal which would be a difficult deal," explains Hands. "We always saw recorded music as being a difficult deal but we thought that we were always going to get our money back through publishing. The big argument between us and Citigroup was over whether it was two deals or one deal. We saw it as being two debt packages."

Citigroup was not budging so Terra Firma went for what it thought was a stopgap solution. "What we did was that we put in an interim loan with the intention of putting in permanent financing at a later stage and that we would do a securitisation," Hands continues. "Between agreeing to do the deal at the end of May and when we finally closed the deal at the beginning of August, the market started to go to Hell in a handcart on the debt side […] Citigroup and Terra Firma could not agree on what the final debt package would look like. In the end, Citigroup gave Terra Firma an ultimatum, which was if we were going to move from the interim package to a permanent package, the permanent package would need to be done on the basis that the loans are joint and several. So if something goes wrong with recorded, we can use publishing to pay off recorded. In other words, if recorded goes wrong, you lose publishing [too]. Terra Firma wanted a situation where if recorded went wrong, we still kept publishing. We agreed on joint and several loans. So they were basically merged. There were two loans, but if one went under [Citigroup] could call on the other."

He adds, "The problem was that the debt package that we had finally agreed with Citigroup, once the markets had changed, was a very different debt package from the debt package that we had envisaged when we did the deal. The team who did the deal always presented it on the basis that we would always get our money back on publishing, and recorded music – we could make a fortune on or it could go wrong. We had a way of making a fortune on it, but the question was whether or not we could do it."

This reluctant acceptance of Citigroup's single loan structure might have provided the necessary capital to get the EMI purchase through but it was to come back and plague Hands and his team. For now, however, the sighs of relief were deafening.

After all the internal uncertainty, the numerous false starts over sales or mergers, the job losses, the budget cuts, the dwindling market share and regular pastings in the financial press, the feeling internally at EMI was that – finally – the ground beneath their feet had stopped shaking and they could see the company they loved return to glory.

"I don't remember Googling Guy Hands, but I do remember being excited at the possibility," says a senior executive based in Brook Green when the deal was finally confirmed. "We had already looked at some fairly radical restructuring of how we were doing business because we knew that the record industry was changing. All bets were off. We had to look at what we were doing, how we were doing it and why we were doing it. We had already considered various options to try and get a little bit more efficient."

Another senior executive at EMI UK said that EMI delisting on the stock market meant that restructuring plans that had been put on ice for eighteen months during accelerated merger and acquisition talks could now be implemented.

"This covered cost savings and the new ways of doing business," they said. "There were lots of radical structural changes that really needed to be made under the radar. Because we were a PLC, every fucking thing we did would be in the financial pages along with a picture of Kylie Minogue or Robbie Williams. That was not good. I thought this [deal] was good because there would be a period of certainty and we could do things under the radar." With that last sentence, they dramatically rolled their eyes.

EMI needed to change and everyone working there knew it. A lot was being pinned on Terra Firma to alchemise a leaden company into gold.

But before any of that was to happen, it was announced on 29 August that Eric Nicoli was leaving. This was possibly intended as a statement of intent. His payoff was said to be £3.3 million,[10] and Terra Firma named one of its own, Chris Rolling, as COO of EMI Group as well as CFO of both EMI Group and EMI Music. Additionally, Ashley Unwin was appointed as director of business transformation for EMI Group and EMI Music. Both he and Rolling were MDs at Terra Firma and would now take seats on the EMI board.

As if this changing of the guard at the very top of EMI was not enough, the EMI board would now have to report to a new supervisory board chaired by Guy Hands and one of his closest lieutenants, Julie Williamson.

"The new management structure will allow EMI to benefit from Terra Firma's experience in strategically transforming businesses and driving operational change," said Hands in a statement. "The initial focus will be to maximise the value of the significant assets in EMI's publishing business and to realise the digital opportunity in recorded music."[11]

Nicoli says that his departure was far from the shock that the media reported, the sub-narrative in press reports being that Hands wanted all the power to himself and that, to achieve this, Nicoli would have to be thrown under the bus. "It never occurred to me that there was a role for me under Terra Firma's ownership," he says. "It was nothing to do with style or my assessment of their capabilities. They had been very successful with other deals. For me, it wasn't about Terra Firma; it just seemed clear there was no role for a group CEO under the new owners."

Other senior executives claim that, just ahead of a private dinner in a City club in London where the senior EMI team was about to meet the Terra Firma team (including Ashley Unwin and Chris Rolling), Nicoli took key confidants aside and told them he had just been ejected from the company. The impression they were left with at the time was that Nicoli was not leaving by his own volition. "Shortly before that dinner, Guy Hands told Eric Nicoli that he was fired," claims one source. "Up to that point, Eric seemed to believe – and I think he had been told – that he was going to remain in place [...] Terra Firma up until that point was implying that all the management was safe."

Also going out of the door at the same time as Nicoli was Martin Stewart, the company's CFO, who left without an official statement as to why. This author was unable to officially confirm why his departure was so abrupt.

Guy Hands, however, offers some insight into what may have transpired here. "When we closed the deal, I was expecting Eric to be CEO for some time," he says of Terra Firma's immediate plans on taking over the company. "It was a huge shock to me that roughly two weeks later we were considering him going. The reason was very, very simple. He [Eric] and the CFO [Martin Stewart] fell out. Martin went and we had a discussion within Terra Firma about the fact that we had bought the company on the basis of having Martin and Eric. Eric had said Martin was great and now, literally within a week of us taking over the company, Eric had fired Martin."

This put Terra Firma in a very difficult position, according to its senior management team. "We get a report that the CFO has been fired," recalls Hands. "We sat down and said, 'What the fuck?' We had just bought a business that the debt looked a nightmare on. The CFO was going to be the person we were going to rely on to help us with regard to the debt. The CEO told us two weeks earlier that the CFO was great – so either he is the most appalling judge of character or he knew that the guy was bad when he told us the guy was good. Our belief was that he had already made the decision to fire him before we closed the deal and that he didn't want to tell us in case it made us find some way out of the deal."

He continues, "I would regard it as a pretty material thing when you run a business and the CFO was fired. It's not great. There was a debate about whether or not Eric Nicoli continued or whether the fact that we had just bought a business relying on the CFO being there and the CFO had suddenly gone – and the CEO has been the reason for him going – meant that we should get rid of the CEO as well."

There was no other option that Terra Firma could see. Because Stewart had gone, Nicoli had to go too. That meant that Terra Firma was now in the unenviable position of being left holding a company where the two most senior executives were immediately jettisoned.

"We have a belief in Terra Firma which has served us very well for a long time – but I'm not sure whether it served us well or badly here," says Hands on why his company took an intentionally hard line. "The belief is that culture is absolutely key in a business and culture starts at the top. If the CEO tells you that the CFO is good and then wants to fire him, they both should go. It's just a rule we have. The question is: did we break our own rule or didn't we break our own rule? It is clearly a horrendously difficult decision. Some people would say that you were almost mad to have such a rule. Some people would say it's a mad thing to do. You are putting a morality above a business sense. We would say that if you are trying to run a business where you can't trust your CEO then you are mad as well ... you are damned if you do and you are damned if you don't. We just had a horrible choice. But we never meant to get rid of Eric Nicoli and we never meant for the CFO to go."

A vote within Terra Firma was held with regard to succession plans. Everyone, with one exception, had already voted for Nicoli to be cast out but no one had put themselves forward to be the CEO of EMI. Two names were eventually suggested by others – and Guy Hands was one of the two. "There was another vote," says Hands. "There was one vote for the other person and the rest all voted for me. So suddenly I found myself nominated and in there as CEO."

The original plan had been, had Eric Nicoli and Martin Stewart not been removed, for Stephen Alexander to take over as chairman and work with the existing executive team. There was no contingency plan for the shock eviction of the old guard of the company, so there followed a necessary process of improvisation.

"We often change management teams, but it is normally over a three-to-six-month phase," says Hands. "It is not within a month ... It would have been very unfair if I had said I was not willing to do it [become CEO] because lots of people here have done it. It is an organisation where people lead from the front. If we have a problem in Australia, people go down to Australia. It is what we do. We are an operating private equity firm where, if a problem exists, we go. Sometimes people go in at quite low levels and sometimes they go in at very high levels."

This executive game of Jenga was just the latest in a long line of things going in the diametrically opposite way to how Terra Firma had intended. It was, unfortunately, going to have to get used to this, as things going to plan were, from this point on, going to be the exception rather than the rule.

"It was not a job I wanted to do," says Hands of his new role of CEO under duress. "I had a day job and we had just raised a fund. I like looking at businesses in terms of what, strategically, they should do and then have management teams do it. Going in and doing it myself isn't my natural skill. I am not a natural operator. It is a very different role from what I do day to day ... It would have been crazy for me to say no [to the CEO role], but I would far rather have had three to six months to work it out in advance. Instead what happens is that you go in and from day one you are firefighting. And while you are firefighting you are also trying to do the strategic stuff. I think it is fair to say that having to do both at the same time was very tough – emotionally and physically tough besides just being tough intellectually."

* * *

When Terra Firma first moved in during August, they set up base camp in Wrights Lane, Guy Hands establishing his nerve centre in the recently vacated chief executive's office. "Guy stepped in as a group CEO and in fact moved into Eric's old office almost as soon as Eric had vacated it – the corner office on the fifth floor," says a senior Wrights Lane staffer. "Guy was then spending two or three days a week in Wrights Lane. He liked being in the building [and he] was starting to get a bit of a taste for the music business."

A cultural divide was immediately apparent. Historically those at Brook Green had dismissed the staff at the corporate head office as the 'squares' of EMI, deriding them as bean-counters who didn't get – or simply didn't care about – the creativity that powered the UK division. Wrights Lane was where the money happened but Brook Green was where the art happened. When Terra Firma's team moved in, the staff at EMI immediately began to regard the interlopers as the real 'squares'.

"The Terra Firma guys were pretty easy to spot as they were wearing suits and ties," says a senior source at Wrights Lane who watched this all play out. "And they didn't have BlackBerry phones. This was the year of the BlackBerry. We all had them but no one at Terra Firma did as Guy Hands did not believe in them … When they came to EMI they would all sneak off to the IT department and get a BlackBerry without Guy knowing."

Very quickly, however, some Terra Firma people – according to several EMI employees this author spoke to and who all used the exact same phrase – "went native". "The suits and ties were replaced with jeans and trainers," says an EMI employee who watched it happening in growing disbelief. "You could see them starting to think, 'Hey! We're in the music business now!' They started to behave a bit like music people. Guy started to get annoyed that some of the Terra Firma people had started to go native. They started to go to 'meet and greets' with the artists and their pictures started to appear in *Music Week* with Katy Perry or The Rolling Stones. He felt they should be different from the old [EMI] world."

Several people identified Ashley Unwin as the most visible manifestation of this. He had taken to wearing jeans and leather jackets in the office, except they were designer and, as such, seen as a desperate simulacrum of rock'n'roll rebellion. "Some of the Terra Firma people, not all of them, were really drinking the Kool-Aid," says the source. "They could wear jeans, they could go to gigs, they could order CDs – for free!"

This was not just confined to head office, as Terra Firma staff started to infiltrate Brook Green. An EMI UK executive says, "They would start coming to marketing meetings in Brook Green. People would come out of these planning meetings and they would be squeaking with excitement and amazement at some of the things that were being suggested."

Guy Hands confirms this ideological crossing of the floor by Unwin but he refutes claims that it caused a schism between them. "There were undoubtedly people in Terra Firma who thought he had basically gone native – that is definitely true," he says. "One of the problems of running an organisation is that often people put words into your mouth, particularly when you're quite a colourful character in the first place ... I didn't fall out with Ashley at all. [But there] was a lot of focus, as one can imagine, on EMI from our investors. What I did say to people was, 'Look, I don't really care what you wear at EMI. I'm going to continue to dress the way I dress because I have to meet investors on a regular basis, but I do think, if an investor is coming in, it probably makes more sense that you are dressed in a suit than you are dressed in tight black trousers and a leather jacket.'"

One of the first outings for the new owners was to see The Rolling Stones at the O2 in East London. The band played three nights at the arena as part of their UK tour, but a delegate of EMI and Terra Firma executives went on the middle night – Thursday 23 August. This was the first real time the two sides had socialised together at a gig – a regular occurrence for EMI staff but something of a rare treat for those from Terra Firma – and it was starting to become clear that they came from very different worlds.

This cultural mismatch was only going to become exacerbated as Terra Firma took tighter control of the company, but one executive was more initially surprised by the rapid turnover of Terra Firma executives. They appeared to be parachuted into the company and then yanked back out with seemingly little notice, meaning the management team repeatedly found themselves back at square one with their new owners.

"Mike Clasper was given a big brief but he was only there for a while,"[12] says one source watching this revolving door spin faster and faster. "Chris Rolling was an exceptionally nice guy who tried his best and just got destroyed, I think. Julie Williamson was there all the time. Guy trusted her. But you just saw her crumbling by the month. She just seemed to never go home ... He was throwing every piece of crap at her ... I felt really sorry for her because she was put under a massive amount of pressure."

Terra Firma's first senior appointment of someone from outside its business was Mark Hodgkinson, joining EMI from Virgin Money, where he was CEO. He was named consumer development director at EMI Music on 12 October and would work with Barney Wragg, EMI's existing head of digital, to define its future online strategy.

He had met Guy Hands at an awards dinner in April 2007 and was sounded out about a job in EMI in August. "My experience of the music industry was pretty minimal before that," he admits. "I was in a band at university and that was pretty much it." Initially he was to be in charge of marketing, and then digital was added to his remit. "What became quite clear was that marketing in the music industry at that time was done in a very, very traditional way," he says. "There are a lot of conversations about 'the ear' – where a lot of the A&R guys would use their ears to say if something was going to be a hit [believing they had an innate understanding of what made good and successful music]. I have a consumer background, so what I came in to do was to make the marketing much more consumer-focused and to align digital with the marketing function. Increasingly our view was that the way to market music was through digital channels and digital means."

In what was to become a recurring pattern for outsiders coming into EMI, he says he faced "a lot of resistance" from the staff there. He was tasked with looking at unifying marketing within EMI globally, but found it to be "scattered across all the different labels". "The way I try and do this generally in business is not to try and eat the elephant in one go," he says. "Guy was very clear about what he wanted to do. He wanted to look at the opportunity to have more global functions rather than just the label fiefdoms."

One name was to prove critical in bridging the two seemingly incompatible cultures. And he was to outlast even Guy Hands at EMI.

"David Kassler was a nice guy and was probably, of all of them, the most human," says a senior source who had very close dealings with him. "He didn't have that arrogance that some of the others had where they thought they knew what needed to be done. He was asking us to tell him what was going on so he could make a more informed decision on things. He was a nice guy and he actually stayed on long after Terra Firma. He chose to put in his lot with EMI."

Looking back at this opening period of Terra Firma's ownership of EMI, Kassler recalls feeling he had to move carefully and sensitively. "People were nervous for their jobs as private equity is often a byword for cost-cutting," he says. "I had a job to do of rebuilding the management team and rebuilding morale … I would say there was a bit of a malaise about the company. Brook Green was a pretty sad place. It was a bit of a rabbit warren with shut doors – people not really communicating – and there was not much team spirit at that point. Maybe understandably there was a recognition that the previous ownership and management structure hadn't really worked."

His peripatetic upbringing and career meant he had lived in thirteen different countries by that point and he says this all shaped his approach in the office – keenly aware he was the outsider and that had to earn the incumbents' trust. "I always spent the first three to six months sitting at the back quietly listening and trying to understand the way that things tick," he says of his first months in a new business. "I think it is only if you really understand the way that things are working today that you can hope to improve them. Actually, a lot of your preconceptions when you first go into a new industry are wrong."

Kassler was, in the world of Terra Firma, very much an outlier. Roundly praised by just about every EMI employee spoken to for this book, Kassler's operating style was the complete inverse of that of his colleagues.

"There was a feeling of uncertainty as we didn't know what the credentials of Guy Hands and Terra Firma were," says a senior UK executive. "When they first came in there was a sense of the people from Terra Firma not having an understanding of the music business. They were very bold in their remarks, suggesting that no one in the music business knew what they were doing. There were some big bold statements like that – and how they were going to revolutionise both EMI and the music business … The tone, the language and the body language they used in those initial meetings and discussions with us just felt out of touch. The way they talked about the employees in the company and the way they talked about the artists and talent we had was somewhat alarming. Alarm bells rang very early on. A number of our artists could sense this change and felt uncomfortable."

This sense of Terra Firma imposing its superiority on the company was also being felt by those people one tier down in the EMI hierarchy. "They [Terra Firma] very quickly became dismissive and arrogant to the point of making sweeping judgements and statements, putting in changes that would affect the business negatively without any real understanding of or care about the repercussions," says a digital executive at EMI. "There was a belief that these guys [at EMI] were too soft, too sensitive and the artists were commodities who should feel lucky to be signed to us."

This particular staffer was one of the few at EMI calling for radical change to the business, but they felt Terra Firma's people were going to do more damage than good because they were trying to push through seismic changes without thinking them through – in effect, doing the opposite of what EMI had done in the past simply because that was seen by Terra Firma as the root problem in the company.

"I think reappraising the structure of new [recording] deals was a really healthy thing," the EMI employee says. "But applying that thinking to existing deals for acts like Radiohead was just arrogant and irresponsible … Certainly for me and for the people in the record industry that I identified with as being part of the future, we believed there was definitely an opportunity with somebody like Terra Firma to put some rigour and some traditional business principles behind what we were doing."

It became immediately obvious it was not going to work out this way. "What that translated into, unfortunately, was a whole host of people coming in and finding out very quickly that it was far too much driven by the heart and getting very confused very quickly about how they would address that balance," says the same source. "They were not really seeing a clear path as to how they would do that ... that just turned into arrogance. From not really understanding why there was more heart than head and not really being willing to go into the details as to why, they very quickly became arrogant and dismissive to the point of not understanding it and just saying everyone else was doing the wrong thing."

One label head took a wait-and-see approach and having grown up in the post-punk independent sector until being acquired by EMI just five years earlier, he was actually keen to see a staid major label shaken into life again.

"My reaction was, 'Whatever – let's see what happens,'" says Daniel Miller, the head of Mute. "I thought there were positive things about it, somebody from outside of the music industry [buying them]. I thought EMI was overly entrenched in the past. I thought it was good because it was somebody from outside the industry; and I thought it was bad because it was somebody from outside the industry."

Having spent the past half-decade getting to know how the old bosses worked, Miller recalls meeting Terra Firma's head and leaving the meeting reasonably impressed – but mostly bemused. "Guy Hands went on an information-gathering mission," he says of when he first met the new owner of EMI. "He always had henchmen around him. I went in to see him and he asked me about Mute and what we did. He was very friendly. He was quite interested in the fact that Mute was a bit different to the way that EMI worked. That interested him a bit – on a very surface level. That was the only time I met him, right at the very beginning. It was a one-on-one meeting. There was a queue. Like going in to meet the headmaster."

EMI staff at Wrights Lane talked of being "swarmed" not just by Terra Firma employees but also by teams of consultants brought in to forensically comb through every part of EMI's business, although their focus was heavily on the recorded music side. EMI Music Publishing was the market leader and publishing had not been affected by digital disruption to anything approaching the level of recorded music. EMI Music Publishing had long been a profit centre for the company and Terra Firma's time at EMI left it pretty much unscathed – in part because it was carrying on and making money as usual, and also because the enormity of the job facing Terra Firma with recorded music seemed to

63

double in size every time they dug into it and thought they had got a handle on it.

One executive at EMI's head office said that Terra Firma had gone on a hiring spree in the years before and had too many staff and a growing need to find them something to do.

"It created this really farcical situation where you have people running around looking for roles inside EMI and a very competitive mindset within Terra Firma," they said, as they saw the corridors at Wrights Lane get busier. "It was like having a weird balloon debate in terms of who was going to be the last one without a job. They were fighting among themselves for what the jobs were and then fighting within EMI for what the jobs were. I watched all of that happen from August through to December 2007."

* * *

Hands had bold ambitions for EMI and was adamant it was in desperate need of radical overhaul. The company was, he feared, about to sleep-walk off a cliff. EMI needed saving, he felt, and mostly from itself.

In July, even before it was sure it was even going to take control of EMI, Terra Firma worked up a framework business plan for the company. Using a code, EMI was referred to as Dice Music, reportedly after The Rolling Stones song 'Tumbling Dice', and the document was circulated internally on 30 July 2007. A copy of the report was subsequently leaked to this author.

It worked through the numbers of the recorded music and publishing side of EMI, forecasting the severity of the decline the former was going to face in terms of falling CD sales up to 2012 and how that contrasted with anticipated growth in digital income. It predicted a decline in physical sales of 11 per cent CAGR (Compound Annual Growth Rate) through to the financial year 2012 but expected digital to see a 32 per cent CAGR over the same period. It also outlined that it was planning cost savings to net £90 million by 2011.

Its economic modelling aimed to "[r]eturn Dice Music to historic market share by 2012 through organic growth", picking up on the potential of the long tail theory with regard to EMI's catalogue (forecast-ing earnings of £50 million by 2012) as well as a move into 360-degree deals (taking a cut of acts' total income, not just that from recorded music sales) that could see the company earn £36 million in 2012 from its share of touring and merchandise income alone. There was also a curious reference to plans to run advertising on acts' official websites and split the resulting revenue with them, stating this could net £6 million a year by 2012. This, had it been implemented, would have made acts like Coldplay recoil in disgust. It was not going to be an easy sell so, fortunately for Terra Firma, it remained hypothetical.

One of the first things that Terra Firma had to change was the part of the business that was costing EMI the most money: A&R. Standing for "artist and repertoire", this is the creative and commercial engine of a record company. It involves finding new talent and breaking them, as well as retaining existing talent while enabling their artistic and financial evolution. The returns can be enormous but the investment risks are terrifyingly high. Signing a new act and getting their first music into the market can cost a major label anywhere between £500,000 and £1 million – and that is before anyone has had the chance to recoup a penny.

All of this, plus an accepted industry figure that said 90 per cent of signed acts fail to deliver a return on their investment, set off warning bells within Terra Firma. This business – in fact, no business – could survive with this level of risk.

"I felt they had to change the way they did A&R," says Hands. "It had to be done in a new way. It was just ludicrously expensive. We kept seeing this model changing and the model, particularly at EMI, seemed to get under more and more stress. The secondary CD sales [consumers rebuying their existing collection on a new format] disappeared – and it was inevitable that was going to happen at some time. The customers changed – and changed radically. That was very difficult for the music industry to accept. EMI was the one I think that found it the most difficult. EMI's ability to do urban and hip-hop ... they just weren't any good at it." On top of this, EMI had always struggled in America – the biggest market for music sales and the biggest source of new global talent. It was doubly disadvantaged there.

One source with considerable industry experience, brought in to advise on both artist development and the American conundrum, made it clear to Hands and the Terra Firma team that everything hinged on A&R – especially in the US.

"My view was that it needed an awful lot of help," they said of where Terra Firma's efforts within EMI had to be focused from day one. "It had to be significantly re-engineered. It needed a significant infusion of artistic and creative juices and input. It needed great artists. A record company always starts from the creative process on out. That needed to be done. If it wasn't done, whatever money spent [would have been wasted]. Lousy music in, lousy music out."

Citing acts like Robbie Williams and Coldplay, Hands agreed that EMI could break acts at the highest commercial level, but the deeper problem was that it was becoming too reliant on a handful of acts. When they drilled into the numbers, Terra Firma felt that there was simply too much waste, especially with regard to new music.

As any City firm would do, Terra Firma started auditing EMI's P&L sheets for the years 2004 to 2006 and came back with numbers that sent a chill up its spine. "You had a situation where you had high-level numbers when we bought the company that looked quite good but once we started to actually use what I would describe as more transparent accounting standards, those numbers looked terrible," says Hands. His team concluded that sales and marketing at EMI were good but "our ability to choose the right artists and our ability to control what we spent on artists was just not good". He claims that a mere six acts – Coldplay, Norah Jones, Celtic Woman, Beastie Boys, Lenny Kravitz and Ben Harper – were responsible for 100 per cent of the profits for EMI in the US in the three years they audited.

In the UK, traditionally EMI's best market, things were not much better. "In the UK, Robbie Williams, Coldplay and Kylie Minogue were 55 per cent [of the profit]," he says. "So in both the US and the UK, you have got over 50 per cent of the profit coming from two or three artists over a four-year period. You couldn't say that we couldn't promote. What we did was to ask what was going wrong here. Some of that was a question with regard to the economics of it; we were just spending a huge amount of money on the tail and getting nothing back for it. So if you were an artist, your A&R had an allowance that they could spend on you each year. Surprisingly, everyone spent what they could spend! We were just spending money that there was no chance of ever seeing a return on. It was just a complete waste of time."

There was, thought Hands, a very simple and immediate solution. "Once we discovered the issue, it was a very easy issue for us to deal with," he says. "We just stopped spending the money. We basically cut off about £100 million of expenditure post-April 2008."

The long-term goal, it seems, was to unapologetically slash perceived waste and focus on a handful of mega-acts so, in theory, the company was going to be delivering pure profit. It was suggested that Hands wanted to ultimately reduce the EMI global workforce to under 1,000 people (a fifth of what it had been when he took over) and take the frontline A&R numbers to 10 per cent of what they had been.

"If you had just concentrated on where all the money was, you could probably have run EMI with sixty people," he says. "In terms of where we made the money, it was so concentrated that you don't need the rest of the people. You just need your insights team, a marketing team and sales people. You don't even need an A&R person with the vast majority of artists. Therefore, you spend your time on the artists where you can really add value."

There is an element of retrospective logic here, of course. Looking at hugely successful acts like Coldplay and Norah Jones after they had achieved global success, it is easy to say a company needed to sign more acts like them and not the other 90 per cent of acts that were losing money. But this is how the culture industry, for better or worse, works. It is based on enormous bets at the earliest stages of an act's career and then tries to build a runway to take them to global success. There are no guarantees here – which is the great beauty and disaster of the music business.

This author asked Hands if what he was trying to do here was to reverse-engineer logic onto an inherently illogical business, but he disputed that this was the case. "I disagree," he says. "I didn't find the music industry illogical at all. It seemed to me to be totally the same as if I had looked at the newspaper industry or the book industry ... In venture capital, 98 per cent of your investments don't make money ... Or the movie industry. Most movies lose money."

He took it a step further and claimed that it was inherently unfair that hugely successful acts were being penalised, via the terms of their contracts with regard to royalty rates and signing away ownership of their masters, for the other 90 per cent of acts they shared a label with but which lost money.

"The catalogue of The Beatles was subsidising every mistake that EMI made," he claims. "As was Coldplay. So why should Coldplay and The Beatles subsidise artists who don't succeed? Finding those artists is clearly going to be an A&R role but then going and testing them and seeing if they work is a totally logical role for the insights team to do. It is about putting the discipline in around it. We all think we are geniuses and we all think we find things that work, but we don't."

Much of the problem in the company boiled down to, as far as Hands could make out, an endemic and isolationist structural problem within EMI that went all the way to the top. A diversity problem was preventing EMI from covering every base in every market.

"When we looked at EMI when we bought it, it was basically a white, male, over-50s establishment," proposes Hands. "It was self-fulfilling. It was the same type of people supporting the same type of music with the same type of views. You had positive bias to basically say the same things. I remember going into the first board meeting I had there and told them that, if this was a bank, they would be in trouble – that they wouldn't be allowed to have an executive team with no women and no one of any colour. It was just a bunch of white men over the age of 50."

* * *

Four major consultancy firms were brought in to look at different parts of the business, identify waste or weakness and then work up actionable solutions that would feed into Terra Firma's overall strategic review of the company. They were: KPMG (doing a profitability analysis of the artists on EMI's books); McKinsey (looking at its vast catalogue); Capgemini (audience analysis and segmentation); and OC&C (forecasting where and how EMI could fit into the wider music business value chain outside recorded music and publishing copyrights).

"We were brought in with the remit to look at the wider music industry for other opportunities that would support them in the recorded music business and publishing," says one of those consultants. "We went through a whole bunch of models, helping them understand how the music industry worked and what the opportunities were ... There was nothing particularly controversial there. But what was fascinating was the total lack of awareness of how these things worked. I know that is why you hire consultants and I know they hadn't bought into a live business, but we were still surprised."

According to Charles Allen, the former chief executive of ITV who was to join EMI at the start of 2009, the first year of Terra Firma's ownership of EMI was "consultant heavy", and he says consultancy costs in that time ran up to £40 million. One of his first jobs was to pull the plug on this ongoing expenditure and to actually start to implement their recommendations.

"There was some good stuff in there but what I did was stopped all the consultants," he says. "They had done a lot of the work but they were still doing follow-up. I said we didn't need it and we literally stopped at that point in time. We stopped all the consultants in the business. It was distracting everyone. Because they had brought in four different consultants, there wasn't a joined-up plan because they had effectively all recommended different things."

When told by this author what the final consultancy bill came to, one of the many consultants paid by Terra Firma turned white. "Jesus Christ!" they gasped. "We clearly didn't charge enough!"

Guy Hands, however, disputes that figure. "I think Charles is being slightly disingenuous to say the least there," he says. "A lot of the initial due diligence was done through the consultants. So some of that £40 million is the initial due diligence budget. Some of the £40 million is the consultants involved in the redundancies and the firings. You have to use a consultancy firm on that. We got rid of something like 1,700 people. You have just got to [use consultants]."

Daniel Miller questioned why the company was spending so much money to try and find out information that any record industry person worth their salt would know. The money being handed over to them also felt like a slap in the face to staff within EMI, especially at a time of mass layoffs. "There were people from consultancies being paid a fortune while we were having to fire people," he says. "That pissed off a lot of people. There were consultants costing tens of thousands of pounds a week just telling us what any junior product manager would know. That was very frustrating for people."

Another source who saw the consultancy work close up felt that the overall approach was too scattergun and this only heaped confusion on top of more confusion for the man who, given the scale of his investment and the size of the bets he was making, desperately needed precision and prescience.

"It was very unwieldy and there were too many people involved," he says of the packs of consultants let loose on the company. "One of the criticisms of Guy was that he would listen to people but he would literally only listen to the last person who talked sense to him. He was so willing to change his mind based on another conversation. With all the consultancy projects, he just wanted someone to give him answers. He was spending a lot of money on people who couldn't give him any answers. He could have done a much easier job by just getting a brain trust together – maybe just twenty people with some selective consultancy and just get on with it."

Another well-placed source working in an advisory capacity believes an inability to listen was Terra Firma's key failing here, putting it at a serious disadvantage right from the off.

"It wasn't about getting rid of everybody and having change for change's sake," they said of their advice to Hands and his team in those critical opening months. "There were some really good people there and what needed to be done was to first walk in with my eyes wide open and ears wide open. As I said to them, 'You have two eyes, two ears and one mouth. So you watch and listen twice as much as you talk in the beginning.' But that obviously wasn't Guy's style."

Lord John Birt had been director general of the BBC between 1992 and 2000 and left a hugely controversial legacy at the corporation. Variously seen as "the Antichrist, the devil himself, the man of mission statements but no mission, the architect of the mighty Beeb's ruin, its fall from Reithian grace",[13] he began working with Terra Firma in 2005. His first job was to chair WRG, a waste disposal company the private equity firm had acquired. Students of semiotics within EMI did not have far to look for their punchlines.

While he was at Terra Firma at the time of the EMI bid, Birt was not involved in that part of the process. "Because they were trying to take over a public company, it was only done on a need-to-know basis," he says. "I knew nothing whatsoever about it until the purchase went through."

But later, when the deal was happening, Birt was asked to become chair of Maltby, the holding company for the EMI purchase. "That was effectively the board of EMI," he explains. "It is quite common in private equity for the real holding board which holds the assets to not necessarily have the name of the company. It was specifically for EMI. It didn't do anything else."

His initial remit was handling governance. "There has to be formal governance in the environment where you have a single shareholder but a lot of debt," he says. "There is a proper formality in the running of the company – like monthly board meetings, reporting of accounts, so on and so forth."

For someone with a huge amount of experience in restructuring and cost-cutting in a long-standing British institution made up of a three-letter acronym, it was an obvious move to bring Birt's BBC experience to bear on EMI. "I was also asked by Guy to oversee the strategy process and that was, in many ways, my main role at the beginning," he says. His immediate reaction walking in the doors of EMI was that this was a business mired in crisis. "It was a troubled company," he says bluntly. "In a troubled sector." But he claims he also saw a lot of parallels with his former employer and, as such, felt he knew exactly where the scalpel should be applied.

"EMI was very like the BBC, in many ways, culturally," he says. "It was characterised by, at its best, [being] full of very dedicated and very skilled people who passionately loved their music, just as the BBC was absolutely chock-a-block [with] people who just care about one thing. That is its great strength – but it can be a weakness."

He elaborates. "When those qualities dominate an institution, the institution finds it extremely hard to adjust to fundamental change; they don't really understand what is happening to them. But there is a second characteristic of institutions like that. When they have enjoyed strong market positions over a very long period of time, they tend not to develop very sophisticated business systems. Again, EMI was not the exception; but EMI was a case in point."

He calls the KPMG analysis of artist profitability (or, more specifically, lack of profitability) the first and "the most important" of the four different consultancy-led research projects.

"This was an organisation which made investments without having any data which would tell it what the payback on that investment would be," he claimed. "KPMG was the first study and it proved to be exceptionally difficult for KPMG to do because, as you would expect in an organisation like EMI, every part of the world had kept its information in different ways, so it was extremely hard to aggregate that information and pull together all the costs and the revenues associated with a single artist … But we set out to do it because, without that information, you were flying blind in the business."

He says this research came back to say that only 10 per cent of artists were profitable. This was, for anyone working in the record business, hardly news and had been a commonly quoted figure at major labels for years where the business, by its very nature, is high risk; namely that 90 per cent of recording artists will lose money but the 10 per cent that are profitable should ideally pay for everything else.

Birt says the biggest drain on EMI profits was in new music, with the recording and marketing costs so high to break a new act that tens of millions of pounds were, he believed, being wasted here. There was a feeling that EMI had normalised this 90 per cent failure rate as part and parcel of working in new music, but Terra Firma was on a mission to apply the rigours of City finance to what it was increasingly seeing as a flaky business that was in desperate need of being brought to heel.

"Not every artist is going to be a huge success," Birt says. "Nonetheless, if you're going to run it as a business, you have to be disciplined in your decision making. You have got to make investments based on good quality information about what has happened in similar circumstances before and when you distributed different artists in different countries. None of that information was available. By gathering this database, we had for the first time good-quality information about actually what happened – and indeed what some of the pitfalls of the industry were, one of the pitfalls being paying huge sums of money for an artist that turns out to be not profitable at all, or which proves to be a huge drain on your resources."

This was eventually to feed into a series of ideas that were considered but dropped (scrapping artist advances and working towards a model that shared risk and profit with the acts, plus slashing frontline A&R to 10 per cent of what it had been) and some that were implemented (applying the logic of the fast-moving consumer goods world to music and driving audience insights through every part of the business, from talent spotting to digital marketing).

He says that EMI had, split between active artists and those in its sprawling catalogue, around 30,000 recording artists, a number they deemed too unwieldy for the new EMI they were starting to formulate in their PowerPoint presentations.

Birt argues that his role was not to expunge the creative roles in the business – notably A&R and marketing – but to amplify them by building up expertise in other parts of the company so as to make it all more cost-effective. It was not, he claims, a war on art.

"This was an organisation that desperately needed an injection – not of musical skills but of other kinds of skills," he says. "In a healthy organisation, those people work in a team. This is in any environment. This is an absolute commonplace where you have a company that is challenged – it is challenged not because it doesn't have a feel for its sector but because it doesn't have the right additional skills to help it navigate change."

Well used to the brickbats at the BBC, Birt says he knew this would meet resistance from those at EMI who were perhaps too long in the tooth and, therefore, most resistant to the upheaval caused by the implementation of new ideas. He says there was "certainly a lot of rolling of eyes" when ideas and plans started to be shared within the company. He was there, he feels, to do a job that was always going to be painful; he was not there to make friends.

"I'm sure that was a terrible shock to the system and not everybody liked it," he says of the changes they were starting to formulate. "For a lot of people who had been used to having a lot of authority to make their own judgements, I'm sure it was completely unwelcome. But I disagree with those people."

One head office executive reports that the appointment of Birt was not a popular one among EMI employees but the mood lightened somewhat when an introductory video was created to introduce him to staff. What started out as fear and paranoia started to edge a little closer to ridicule for those who saw the video, fostering a view of Birt they found hard to shake afterwards. "We spent a fortune on this video when John Birt came in," they say. "It was this massively expensive production. There was him going through the revolving doors at Wrights Lane with his coffee, walking through the building and saying hello to people. Which he never did because people would have probably spat in his face! He was talking about all the exciting things they were planning. And this cost tens of thousands of pounds at a time when they were laying people off!"

With different rafts of consultants sniffing through every corner and contract at EMI, Birt went on his own fact-finding mission, meeting with senior executives and key artist managers to get a better understanding of what, exactly, they did. He reported back his findings to Guy Hands. "He came into my office with some young lad who sat on the sofa," reveals one of the executives Birt met on his navigation around the upper tiers of the company. "His first question to me was asking where I was educated. 'Where did you go to school?' I thought it was very archaic that he just wanted to hear about some private school that he could relate to – that old boys' network. He asked me a lot of questions, one of which was if I had thought about halving all of my advances [for signing acts]. I think it was the most bizarre hour that I've ever had in the music industry. And I have had some quite odd and bizarre moments in this business! Sitting there with him and this young lad with a clipboard going through a list of questions about me, the label and the artists."

There was a similar story coming from other executives who were put through the same process, with many wondering what his questioning was going to elicit. "I did an interview with him [Birt]," says Daniel Miller. "I felt sorry for him. Well, I didn't feel sorry for him because he was probably being paid an absolute fortune. But he was half asleep. He had been interviewing almost every member of staff. But this was way into the process."

Another senior EMI executive immediately took against Birt and felt that he was a poor ambassador if Terra Firma was hoping to get the old guard of EMI to fall into line with its plans. "Lord John Birt came in to see us – and I really didn't fucking like him," they say. "He asked me a lot of questions and they were very leading … He put my back up. He was asking a lot of questions about people for me to pinpoint the weak links. I also felt he didn't have an understanding of what we did. That set the tone for me. I didn't like him at all. No one liked him at the BBC, either."

Another source who dealt with Birt during this time claims they found it impossible to fathom why he had been appointed with such a major remit. "No disrespect, but what the fuck does Lord Birt know about the music industry?" they asked. "He was one of the most unpopular BBC director generals of all time."

As managers of Robbie Williams, Tim Clark and his business partner David Enthoven (who passed away in August 2016) had something of a love/hate relationship with EMI, having formed The Black Hand Gang a few years earlier for managers of acts signed to the company to meet, share information and work on common goals. They were high on Birt's list.

"He came to our offices and David and I sat with him here – looking out at what was his fiefdom [their office in West London faces the back of the old BBC Television Centre building]," says Clark. "He sat here for half an hour or forty minutes, asking us about EMI and the business ... I know for sure that we talked about recorded and publishing [to work more closely together] because that was one of our pet things ... We spoke about the problems that would face EMI, like declining sales, and what they would have to do about it."

There was also a bulking-up of PR (Public Relations) teams to go alongside the existing corporate communications executives at both EMI Group (in Wrights Lane) and EMI UK (in Brook Green). Terra Firma had its own PR staff and Guy Hands had a personal PR manager in Andrew Dowler, but it also brought in City PR specialists Maitland and Outside Organisation to deal with the mainstream media.

"You had all of these different comms teams briefing and, for the most part, counter-briefing against each other," said one well-placed source. "And then you had Amanda [Conroy, head of corporate communications at EMI Group] stuck in the middle of this maelstrom of PR activity and not knowing who said what next."

Another, equally well-placed source, backs this up and explains that winning over the media was a key objective even before Terra Firma had properly rolled up its sleeves. "Guy said, 'The EMI story is going to be won or lost on perception. It's going to be all about PR. Everyone is going to hate me going into this as I am taking over a national treasure and people are going to see me as an interloper.'"

Mere weeks into his ownership of EMI, Hands made his first PR gaffe – but it was going to be far from his last. Attending the Royal Television Society's annual gathering in Cambridge on Friday 14 September, he was quizzed by reporters about his move into the music business. "We look for the worst business we can find in the most challenged sector – and we get really happy if it's really, really bad," he said. "EMI, our most recent investment, is a classic example. We're just hoping EMI is as bad as we think it is."[14]

When this was relayed back to the staff at EMI at the start of the next working week, the air at both Brook Green and Wrights Lane turned blue. Those at the top level of EMI already knew how badly Terra Firma viewed them. Now the whole company knew.

Staff were, according to one senior executive, "offended and hurt" by the comments. Hands was forced to issue a statement to the company but, says the source, "stopped short of denial and apology".

Hands is, with the distance of a decade, not fully repentant about the quote that ended up framing the opening months of Terra Firma's ownership of EMI.

"The quote is correct if everything else is correct," he proposes. "If your financing is all in place and you're getting on well with the bank, then the worse the business is the better because you have got time to turn it around and change it. The issue is that you do need time."

He does, however, accept that it would have landed very badly with the staff at EMI, anxious to find out what the new owners were planning. "It wasn't meant to be done that way," Hands says of the highly negative way it was received by his new staff. "That is why I never wanted to be a CEO and it is why my wife has said I could never be a politician. I am very dyslexic and use of language is not necessarily my greatest skill when it comes to tactfulness."

He argues context is all here and suggests that if EMI staff "had heard the whole speech, they would have been fine", but they didn't. So he feels that, albeit retrospectively, he should provide the full context in which the comments were made. "It was [from] a debate about newspapers and publishing, music and the internet," he says. "Somebody said, quite fairly, 'For God's sake, you've bought EMI and it's the fourth of four music companies. How the hell are you going to make any money out of that and get that to work? We'd be delighted to hear.' I gave a long answer and in the middle of that there is no question that I said, 'When we do buy businesses, we often buy the worst business in the worst sector. And with EMI we have definitely done that.' To some extent I was agreeing with what other people were saying at the time – but it did sound terrible, I agree. I wish I hadn't said it, obviously. But it wasn't meant [the way it came across]. Was EMI the worst of the four music companies? Yes! It absolutely was."

But surely he must understand that this was not the best opening message to deliver to EMI staff worried about the future? "I know," he sighs. "It probably wasn't a nice thing. But that's why I'm not a CEO. Or a politician."

Guy Hands was correct that everything was going to be won or lost on perception and, setting up a PR pattern that was to repeat with increasingly calamitous results, he'd just driven the needle screaming into the red.

"Having been on the 1st September a bright-eyed, bushy tailed, Tiggerish optimist, by the end of September, I'm starting to have these dark clouds over my head," said one high-level EMI executive as the whole situation started to unspool. "A colleague said it was like one of the final scenes of *Apocalypse Now* with Marlon Brando talking about 'the horror'."

CHAPTER 4

Punks, Petrol and Popcorn

Up to this point, meetings with the Terra Firma team were mainly confined to senior management and most activity was happening in Wrights Lane. Staff further down the hierarchy were having developments filtered to them by their superiors or were hungrily gleaning crumbs of information about their new owners from the music trade press and the business pages of the broadsheets.

Internal emails were already being leaked to the media. This was not uncommon in music companies, with business writers often receiving major company-wide emails that they would quickly turn into stories. But things were going to be different this time.

"Even with notes to Terra Firma's investors, what are called the limited partners, I think the record was nine minutes from pressing the button to send something out to the limited partners to it appearing in the media," says one PR executive. "Nine minutes! To call it a sieve would be a disservice to the structural integrity of a sieve. It was hugely difficult."

This was to become an escalating problem for Terra Firma and very quickly it was normalised to the point where anyone senior on the team writing a company-wide email did so knowing it would be regurgitated on multiple websites soon after it landed in the staff's inboxes. "Never have I known a private equity portfolio company under as much scrutiny," the same source says. "It was enormous ... I don't think Guy had realised how much public scrutiny EMI would be under."

For the many hundreds of employees in the UK, much of their knowledge of Terra Firma came second-hand, while encounters with the new owners were by proxy. This was inevitably going to lead to all manner of unregulated misinformation and misunderstandings becoming baked into fact. As the maxim runs: a lie can travel halfway around the world while the truth is still putting on its shoes.

To cauterise the rumours and head off many of the leaks (and to quell the panic caused by the Royal Television Society quotes), Guy Hands decided that he should meet the staff and outline his vision for the company. Unmediated. This would, he hoped, be a defining moment for his ownership of EMI. He was right. It was defining – but not for the reasons he intended.

Due to the huge numbers of employees at both London offices, if Guy was to address everyone en masse, they needed to find a venue large enough to accommodate them all. A decision was made to use the Odeon cinema on Kensington High Street. It was not quite equidistant between EMI's two main offices,[1] but walkable from both. There was the added symbolism that this was a recent Terra Firma investment and so EMI staff could see with their own eyes the meticulous surgery the company was currently performing on a cinema chain that had a long history – dating back to 1928 – but that had been allowed to fall into disrepair due to management apathy. The symbolism was ripe.

Before the day itself, there was a huge amount of preparation and refinement of topics. This was the first time the vast majority of people on EMI's London payroll would hear Hands speak and he knew he had to win them over. Like whipped dogs, after the long years of mistreatment caused by failed mergers, the staff had to be treated carefully and respectfully, with Hands assuring them that he was going to do his very best for the company and, by implication, for them. This was to draw a line under all the uncertainty of the past and point the company, collectively, towards its sparkling future. Guy Hands knew he had one chance to win them over. Everything that was to follow rested on how these two town hall meetings played out.

The idea was first floated at the senior board level to gauge reaction and take in feedback. "I hadn't met the majority of people in the organisation at that point," says Hands of why the town hall idea was taken up. "I had met about 100 people and worldwide there were about 6,000. It was actually a worldwide tour. It wasn't just London. There was a general view that I should do this meeting – which I agreed with totally."

Then came the issue of what the theme and tone for the meetings should be. "Guy said at one of these early meetings he was going to do a town hall meeting at the Odeon and asked us what he should focus on," says a source with rich knowledge of what was discussed. "We talked about the heritage of the company and its great artists – and [told him] to focus less on the financial aspects." They hoped he would take their points on board but were soon to discover that Guy was convinced he knew the best way to handle this and was determined to plough his own furrow. "He just completely ignored us," they sigh.

In the planning meetings leading up to 18 September, with certain details of what was said being leaked to Music Week the following week[2] the rooms were filled with the existing EMI corporate communications teams as well as the external PR person that Hands had brought in.

"I remember there were a lot of people there, protecting various interests," says a source at several of those meetings. "At this early stage the goodwill was essentially still there from my point of view. I was still optimistic and thinking this could be great. It did definitely turn on the day of the Odeon for me."

One person closely involved in the planning of the Odeon event says they knew it was a gamble as they believed Guy was at his best around a boardroom table, but anything smaller or anything bigger would risk leaving him floundering. "He is incredibly awkward one-on-one and wasn't great in a big arena – but put him in a room of twenty people and he will shine," they say, before making a curious and somewhat gob-smacking analogy. "He is a throwback to someone like Michael Milken, the junk bond king. Milken would bamboozle people with science and make things sound incredibly convincing. He was a very charismatic and smart guy. He had made millions and people believed him because he was rich."

Lights, camera, action!

On Tuesday 18 September, two presentations were given to EMI staff. Owing to crowd numbers, they were split into two sessions; Music Week reported that the first was for the staff at Wrights Lane as well as those at EMI Music Publishing while the second was for the staff at Brook Green and EMI's studio operations. The air in Kensington was crackling with anticipation.

Staff attending the September event were divided before they got to the Odeon and even more divided afterwards, with some, as reported in Music Week feeling a lot better but others feeling even more negative than they did before. As they arrived, some were prepared to hear Hands out and reserve judgement until he had outlined his plans for EMI. Others were already fearing it would be the opening salvo in a massacre that would see many of them laid off and left with few options of work at record companies, given that all the other majors were still suffering a sharp decline in their own revenues.

"It was horrific," says one Brook Green staff member. "We weren't even allowed to get cabs. We had to walk in a line there like we were going to be fucking crucified!"

For Murray Chalmers, head of press at Parlophone, it was the moment that convinced him that the time had come where he should leave EMI, as he knew it would never be the same again. "It was like lambs to the slaughter," he says of the ten-minute walk to the Odeon. "I have a memory that I had already decided to leave by then. I remember feeling angry, but not for myself. People were literally walking along en masse along Kensington High Street. Incredible times."

The media were barred from going into the cinema, but this author has spoken to multiple employees who were inside at those two meetings about what happened and what was said. What becomes clear from those accounts is that by the end of the afternoon the already pessimistic had all their fears confirmed tenfold and all the optimists had their sanguinity punctured.

"There was a sense of anticipation that we were either going to get a sermon from the mount where we would gasp in amazement that we were saved, or we were all going to think we were fucked," says one EMI employee at the second session. "We all knew we were going to see Guy Hands for the first time," they continue. "We knew our shit. Every single person in that room knew the music industry. We weren't convinced he [Hands] did."

Hands spoke about his company's success with Tank & Rast and also, gesturing around him with the silver screen behind him, how Terra Firma was resuscitating the Odeon.

"They [Terra Firma] were obsessed with the success they had had in Germany after they bought Tank & Rast … so they were on a bit of a high," says a senior source from Wrights Lane who sat through the day's first meeting. "Guy began his opening remarks by telling everyone in the audience that Terra Firma also owned the Odeon cinema chain. He tried to make a joke about how, when we had come in, we would have smelt money and popcorn."

Hands continued to talk about the ownership of the Odeon chain and how they had managed to turn it around. "He said the owners before they bought it had stupidly thought they were in the film business rather than the popcorn business and they had to put them right," says the same source. "They found that the managers were all flying all around the world to go to screenings and premieres when really what they should have been focusing on was selling more Coca-Cola and popcorn. That was the simple change that they had made at the Odeon."

Hands points out that Odeon relied only on one form of income from blockbusters from California with little control over its distribution, but that through staff initiatives they made several changes, including through the sale of food and drink as well as extending revenue of the venue beyond cinema tickets.

Another senior executive at EMI, who had met Hands several times by this point, started to feel that his anecdotes and case studies were running on autopilot and becoming dangerously dull. "The German toilet stories were wearing thin and becoming overdone," they say.

Hands did have a third example up his sleeve which he pulled out for these special meetings, talking about his turnaround of the Unique and Voyager pub chains in the 1990s when he was at Nomura. They sold the 4,189 licensed houses to a consortium led by Cinven and Enterprise Inns for £2.01 billion in March 2002, netting the Japanese investment bank a profit of £300 million and Hands a £50 million bonus.[3]

"When he had bought them, they had been spit and sawdust," says a source who heard him expound on this story for the EMI staff. "They realised that what it took was to have nice wine and nice food so that women would come in. That was it. Everyone who worked at pubs probably knew this but there just hadn't been a chance to do it. Simple changes that had a big impact. That was their job."

While some were tiring of hearing the same stories trotted out again, some who were hearing them for the first time felt they were utterly irrelevant to the job ahead of him at EMI. "How could you compare that to what you're going to have to do here?" says one who regarded Hands's talk of the economics of petrol and popcorn as having no relevance to music. "He had no idea what he'd actually got himself involved in. It was all about how he could keep the investors happy."

With both Tank & Rast and the Odeon, Hands talked about how they had identified the fundamental problem of each business and applied a turnkey solution. As outsiders, the logic ran, they had the requisite distance to see what was really pulling the businesses under – something those right in the thick of it were blind to.

Some at EMI, while knowing it was in dire straits, were dumbfounded that Terra Firma was walking into the music company believing it just had to locate the one problem at the heart of the business in order to flip it back into rude health.

In the speech, Hands pointed out that the recorded music business was struggling because it was based on a model that had not been changed or reviewed for a long time. Quoting directly from a transcript made of his speech that day, Hands said, "We need to work out how we serve our artists, how we maximise their income, how we serve our consumer customers, how we maximise their choice and their convenience and we need to be part of an industry which is about serving the consumer and the artist and not serving the interests of a few highly paid executives who move from label to label". Hands argues that the transcript shows that what some EMI sources claim they recall from this part of his speech that day was not what he actually said.

"Guy said they had revolutionised the German service stations and it was all down to the toilets," they recall of that day in the cinema. "He said, 'I want to find what the toilets are at EMI.' He thought there was one thing he could change that would revolutionise the way we did business. He was never able to find that one thing because there wasn't one thing that had to be addressed."

A senior executive at EMI UK who had not met Hands or any of the really senior Terra Firma people by this stage quickly found their cynicism levels going off the chart. "It was a dictatorship dressed as a revolution," they say of how the meeting unfolded. "I had never seen private equity at play. It was fascinating. It's like watching termites on an apple. Or piranhas. It's all gone. They're all over you."

Hands to this day believes he made the point that relatively small things were capable of making a significant difference and that initiatives came as much from staff of the companies that they worked with as from Terra Firma.

Hands knew that showing the private equity successes under Terra Firma's belt was only part of his charm offensive. When the meeting was opened to questions from the floor, Hands was asked by someone they suspected to be a plant what sort of music he liked. "He said he loved The Enid," says an EMI employee who was there. "The Enid were a little-known progressive rock band." One source claims Hands also said he liked punk.

Born in 1959, Hands would have just turned 17 in November 1976 when the Sex Pistols released 'Anarchy In The UK' on EMI. The label soon after dropped them as their notoriety exploded. Hands was the perfect age to become a punk. He says this came from a place of genuine fandom. He had been a punk and was advised that he would be asked about music on the day so to prepare an answer. "I was told I had to say an EMI band, so I said the Sex Pistols," he says. His first choice – the tediously scatological and wilfully politically incorrect sub-punks The Macc Ladds – was vetoed.

"I think that would probably throw people!" he laughs. "'No Sheep 'til Buxton'![4] I sometimes put The Macc Lads on in the background at dinner parties. It's quite funny because you see people sitting around the table and I really like doing it. You do it with a bunch of smart people from London and you put it on. The words are quite difficult to understand because of the accent. But then slowly people start to ask if they really said what they said. And they suddenly realise it's about sheep! It is quite funny. I thought about [picking] Joy Division, but it's just too depressing."

Hands said that he would regularly see The Stranglers and other bands play in London in the late 1970s. Then he tells the most extraordinary tale of how he narrowly avoided arrest as a punk while at university.

"It depends what you mean by 'arrested', but I was with my wife in Oxford when I was a student and I didn't have the guts to do real piercings so I never put safety pins through my nipples," he says. "But I had a classic black ripped T-shirt and so I put safety pins through that. Instead of having the right type of black trousers, I had some trousers that were quite shiny and looked quite authentic. So I was going through Oxford with [the woman who became] my wife, who was very different in her musical tastes to say the least, and this police van draws up literally beside us. People say the police will not arrest a man who is with women. I say go out dressed as a punk with a woman who's dressed normally and I promise you they will arrest you! This van draws up and these two coppers jump out, grab me and are about to throw me in the back of the van! Julia had to tell them that I was with her. They stopped manhandling me and left me alone."

The image of Hands as a 1970s punk fan was not convincing to many of the EMI staff. One claims, "There was unconstrained sniggering because here was this 50-year-old man in his suit claiming to have been a punk. It just didn't sound true. It just made it so stark that he was not one of us. People thought he was an idiot and that we were fucked. We felt he didn't understand musicians and that he didn't understand artists. We felt he didn't understand the creative endeavour. He understood business. Purely business."

Hands, over a decade on, feels that this ire was somewhat misdirected, arguing that the EMI board when he took over the company was made up of "the most conservative people" he had ever encountered.

"I went to the boardroom and they were all in tight black jeans and tight black T-shirts and thought they were all anti-establishment," he says. "I just looked at them and thought, 'You are a bunch of 50-year-old men trying to pretend to be different.' … I probably hated the establishment far more than any of them did. I went through a very difficult childhood. My parents were lovely. They couldn't have been nicer. What happened to me at school [being bullied] and trying to get through that didn't leave me in a particularly happy place. To some extent, when I find myself talking with some of the artists or talking with some of the managers, their relationships with things like drug abuse, suicide, problems with the establishment, et cetera, were things that actually, on a human level, I could talk to them about and relate with them quite well. It probably shocked them. And it wasn't fake. I didn't try and turn up at EMI dressed in a leather jacket and tight black trousers. I had my job to do but I could chat with them and it was fine. I didn't really have a problem."

He was asked only a handful of other questions in the two sessions. Key among them were one about the EMI pension scheme, and another about possible redundancies.

"The first session threw up a question on the pension scheme and their commitment to it," says one eyewitness. "Guy fudged by saying they were reviewing the previous management's plan."

One senior EMI executive, who already had close knowledge of Hands's operational style, walked into the Odeon fearing and preparing for the worst but walked out feeling that, while not perfect, it all went better than they could have hoped for. "Guy was starting to listen and take on board feedback," they claim, "and that day's speeches very much addressed staff concerns well."

Another Wrights Lane executive with a lot of direct dealings with Hands at this point read the day very differently. "What was supposed to be a rallying of the troops turned into everybody leaving with their hearts in their boots," they say. "There was a feeling that they were just interested in the money and were not interested in the artists."

Those more junior and mid-level employees who were seeing Hands for the first time in the flesh, were sceptical. "He talked vaguely about how he was a fan of music," says one. "Yeah, whatever! You're a guy from the City who's going to talk to us about how great you are at business, why we are not very good at it and why that was the end of it. There were a lot of disappointed people who came out of that room afterwards."

The staff all returned to their desks and received a follow-up email from Hands inviting them, in a spirit of transparency and collaboration, to send in suggestions about things they felt could be fixed, added to or improved within the company. "He said he didn't want us to hold back in any way," recalls one recipient of this email.

"The idea of these ideas boxes is that you get hundreds of suggestions and two or three work," says Hands of the point of this exercise. "There were two conflicts going on. One was that we needed to do stuff as quickly as possible so let's just fucking get on with it and who cares about what the people think. The other was that we needed to get hearts and minds with us so let's listen to what people say and see if there is some overlap between what they say and what we say. If we say it is their idea, it is going to be much better than if it is our idea. The ideas box was to tie into hearts and minds and the 'let's just get on with it' thinking was just to tie in with let's get on with it. And meanwhile the clock was ticking."

Some staff members dutifully sent in their suggestions but many others who didn't want to were beginning to feel railroaded into emailing a response. There was already growing paranoia that anyone who didn't reply would be seen as part of the problem, not part of the solution; as such, they were fearful that anyone who failed to engage in this exercise would be placed on a watch list. Hands categorically denies this, saying all suggestions that were sent in were completely anonymised.

Hands says that ideas submitted by staff that were ultimately implemented
by the company included: a customer insights programme (garnering feedback on customers' musical and consumption preferences); firm-wide music sourcing (where A&R input was encouraged across the company to help locate new talent); and "rationalising and refreshing EMI's back catalogue of acts and music".

If Hands was hoping the Odeon appearance would win the majority of staff over and get them to trust him as the man who would save EMI from both itself and the ravages of the market, it didn't seem to have worked. One Brook Green staffer said, "In my opinion he really made a fucking dog's dinner out of it."

Hands disagrees. "But I can't say it was what I had expected to be my introduction to the majority of people at the company. By the time I got to LA and Memphis, things were getting a lot better."

He suggests his speeches that day ran to thirty minutes each – they would later swell to an hour as his tour of the international EMI offices rolled on and he became more assured in his delivery – and covered a number of things. It was primarily to publicly flesh out his vision for the company over the next twelve months but, at this stage in his tour, they were still refining what that structural vision was going to be so what he said, he feels, lacked the necessary focus and tone.

"It was supposed to be much more of a rah-rah speech – but I am not good at rah-rah speeches as it is not my strength," he says. "Plus, I was far happier when I could actually start talking about specifics of what we were going to do than the generalities. Part of the problem was that the generalities weren't going to be very good. We knew we were going to let a lot of people go as we were over-staffed."

A plan for the future

In the September Odeon meetings, Hands had asserted that Terra Firma was in this for the long haul, suggesting they planned to stay in charge of the company for at least the next eight years as they nurtured it into growth again. As this was the case, he also categorically ruled out a merger with Warner.

"All the majors are swimming in the same direction," he is reported as saying to staff in their cinema seats. "We need to be different, and that means not selling EMI's recorded music division to Warner."[5]

As part of his recovery plan for the music company, he outlined three key objectives: "to complete a fundamental analysis of the business; to agree the vision and its execution; and then to involve all staff in the planning and execution of that vision".[6]

The London town hall meeting would be followed by similar ones at EMI's offices in Nashville, New York and Los Angeles in the week starting 8 October. Meetings in other key international markets would come next as Terra Firma took their message and plans global.

A subsequent meeting at the same Odeon cinema, where Hands outlined his plans to cut the global EMI workforce by 2,000 people[7], took place in mid-January 2008 and became a public event. Hands arrived at the Odeon to a media scrum.

The advice he got about which entrance to use was mixed with EMI's PR department advising him to use the front entrance while Terra Firma's PR team advising him to use the side entrance as they knew there would be media there but he felt this was "cowardly" and so he walked the five minutes from Wrights Lane and headed for the cinema's front door.

"Going around the back would have been really stupid," he says now. "And also quite dangerous because it was a much narrower entrance. I didn't think it was going to be an issue."

It very much became an issue. Chaos ensued.

Hands, in a pinstripe suit, light purple shirt and purple patterned tie, was photographed walking into the Odeon, linking arms with Andrew Dowler, Terra Firma's PR man. It had been drizzling and spots of rain were detectable on both men's suits. Closing in around them were TV cameramen, photographers and journalists wielding boom mics. In some shots, Hands looks panicked by the scrum; in others he looks passive, almost resigned; and in yet more photos he looks defiant.

Visibly agitated when asked to replay the walk into the Odeon, Hands claims it all got terribly out of control, by which point it was too late to do anything but try and get through the hubbub of reporters and into the sanctuary of the cinema lobby.

"I have never had cameras being thrust into my face, microphones being thrust into my face, people pushing and shoving," he says, wincing with embarrassment at the memory before revealing a darker side. "It was quite dangerous. For me, beside the fact that they were trying to push cameras in my face, it wasn't actually that dangerous; it was dangerous for some of the reporters and some of the photographers. One guy got pushed over and I was worried that he was going to get trampled on. I stopped so they could back off just to let the poor guy stand up again. The whole thing was just a hullabaloo. It wasn't something I had ever experienced before. And it shocked me. In some ways it was a good thing to experience. It gave me a good understanding of how people say silly things when they have got cameras shoved in their face."

He now accepts it was "a complete mistake".

Regardless of whose advice Hands had taken, some at a senior level at EMI remain cynical that this was not planned by Hands to get as much media attention as possible and to give him a sheen of showbiz, in which his previous investments had been seriously lacking.

"The fact that he didn't avoid the cameras and he knew that they were there, it does make you wonder if that was part of a strategy to make this a little bit more public than we would have chosen it to be," they claim.

The semiology of the photographs that catalogued the day in January was ripe – the City millionaire going into one of his businesses to talk of his latest purchase, their PR man by his side struggling to shield him from the hordes of reporters, a security man on his other side trying to prevent him from being crushed against the wall. Behind the hubbub, on the wall in the background, was a film poster for Charlie Wilson's War. Guy Hands's own war was just about to start.

Hands says that the scrum outside the cinema knocked him for six and he believes his subsequent speech suffered as a result.

"When I got into the actual cinema, I was shaken," he claims. "I had a script. I do my speeches in very big print and I do them in different colours. Like most dyslexics, I find focusing on a page quite difficult. The middle of the page is red, the left of the page is blue and the right of the page is blue. You don't read left to right. You read the centre, then you read the left and then you switch over to the right. That enables me to focus on the words. It is the only way I can read publicly otherwise the words just get [scrambled]."

His coping strategy for reading out a speech in public collapsed badly. "I was shaken up and I should have just sat there and read it very slowly," he says. "Instead I tried to give a natural speech. It was OK but it wasn't as good as I would have liked. I think the Q&A went better than the speech went."

Looking back at those meetings with over a decade's remove, Hands feels the context of what was happening around him needs to be taken into account to really understand what was happening here. "I don't rate myself as the greatest CEO in history by any means – but I did a damn sight better than the previous few CEOs at EMI!" claims Hands of how he was trying to bring new focus to the company, before adding he was doing so under exceptional circumstances.

"I have never been the CEO of a company before in my life. If you're thinking about it rationally, to take a guy who had never run the company and, as their first job, get them to turn around EMI in circumstances where you have got a bank and the sword of Damocles hanging over you was probably not an easy job to do! I don't think I did the perfect job of it. I really don't. But I would say that I got enough done for us to basically transform the economics and put in place the building blocks of what could be a great business."

Foreshadowing what was to happen through the coming years, Hands also said that Terra Firma's strategy coming into companies was normally to strip out a layer of senior management as they were often too entrenched in the old ways. In their place Terra Firma would put in new management who were more critically objective and therefore better placed to push the company through the pain barrier.

The conclusion from all of this was clear. EMI would be sailing into clearer waters alone, and Guy Hands would be the captain.

Just over the horizon, however, an iceberg was looming.

CHAPTER 5

Artists up in Arms

"It fucking ruined my Christmas ... "

The Odeon meetings had failed to get all the staff behind Terra Firma's plans for EMI. Meanwhile, there was another equally important community Guy Hands desperately needed to buy into his vision for the music company: the artists.

The timing of what happened next, however, could not have been worse, from either EMI's or Terra Firma's perspective. One of the biggest bands on EMI's books had just decided it would not renew its contract with Parlophone – the label that had signed them back in 1991 when they were still called On A Friday. EMI had taken them to a level of commercial success and afforded them almost total artistic freedom, which made them the envy of every artist who wanted to become a megastar on their own terms. Not only that, they were going to release their new album online themselves, letting fans pay whatever they wanted for it, thereby setting a bomb under a business that was still struggling to turn digital into a net positive.

On Sunday 30 September, just hours before the calendar flipped into Q4 and marked the start of the major labels' busiest and most profitable retail period, Radiohead guitarist Jonny Greenwood posted a message on the band's *Dead Air Space* blog. "Hello everyone," he wrote. "Well, the new album is finished, and it's coming out in 10 days. We've called it *In Rainbows*. Love from us all."[1]

This seemingly blasé post to announce their seventh studio album was followed up by the details of the release. When it became clear what precisely they were doing, all hell broke loose – not just within EMI but across the entire record business.

In Rainbows would be available, with no record company involvement, on 10 October directly from their official website and fans could choose how much, or how little, they wanted to pay for the download version.

The band had seen out their six-album contract with Parlophone with the June 2003 release of *Hail To The Thief*, but the long-serving executives at EMI who had backed them since the early 1990s had regular communication channels running with the band and their two managers – Bryce Edge and Chris Hufford of Courtyard Management – and were working out ways for Radiohead to renew their contract and stay with EMI.

The company knew that a deal similar to that signed by the band in 1991 would not work, but they had already tested the water with new deal structures to retain their biggest solo artist a few years earlier. In October 2002, following a complex negotiation led by Tony Wadsworth on behalf of EMI and both Tim Clark and David Enthoven of ie:music, EMI renewed its contract with Robbie Williams, not just to cover his next six albums but also for the company to take a cut of all the other ways he made money – from touring and merchandise to his earnings from music publishing and brand endorsements.

This 360-degree (or multi-rights) deal was erroneously pegged at £80 million,[2] a figure that has since ossified into fact. There was talk of him receiving an advance of £25–30 million for the *Escapology* album and a compilation of his hits,[3] but this was never confirmed. The reality of the deal was that it was more complex than the frothy media speculation and was dependent on certain commercial targets being hit before escalating to the next stage. All his earnings would be fed into a holding company, called In Good Company, from which he and EMI would take their agreed shares. Neither side would make public how the money was split, but this author has been told by highly reliable sources that the deal was very quickly extremely profitable for both music company and artist.

Not helping the tabloid speculation about how much money was handed over to secure his signature, Williams, dressed in a sleeveless Mötley Crüe T-shirt, a more reticent Tony Wadsworth by his side, greeted the press assembled outside his managers' office by cartoonishly bunching both his fists and bellowing, "I'm rich beyond my wildest dreams!"

EMI could do new types of deals – deals that were much more in the artists' favour than their standard ones – in order to retain its biggest stars, and so hoped it could pull off something similar with Radiohead. A new contract would necessarily have a different shape to the Robbie Williams one, but EMI was open to experiment and so conversations were ongoing between the label and the band's managers.

Tony Wadsworth and Keith Wozencroft – the EMI executive who had originally signed the band sixteen years earlier – were the key contacts and would travel regularly to the band's studio in Sutton Courtenay in the Oxfordshire countryside, as they had done for years, to hear songs and recordings as they progressed. They were not naive enough to think that the band were not going to be talking to other majors or even large independent labels (singer Thom Yorke's solo album, *The Eraser*, had come out in July 2006 on XL Recordings and Yorke had a close relationship with Richard Russell, the indie label's head), but they felt they had a bond of trust with the band. They also held their catalogue, which was to prove a hugely important negotiating chip.

Reliable sources say that Wadsworth had travelled to the band's studio at the end of August to hear what everyone understood to be an album nearing completion and, as such, could have a release date some time in 2008. As with many acts, Radiohead would work on tracks and either scrap them or mothball them for release years down the line, so label heads and A&Rs always worked on the understanding that they were never hearing the final recordings until they were told by the act that these were the finished product. Plus, after the share-price issue tied to the late arrival of the Coldplay and Gorillaz albums in 2005 and the delicacy of the Radiohead negotiations, no one wanted to rush them into putting the album out.

Wadsworth reportedly met again with Hufford and Edge around three weeks later to discuss Supergrass – another Oxford band they managed and who were also signed to Parlophone – as well as to catch up on Radiohead developments. So even as little as ten days before the *Dead Air Space* blog announcing *In Rainbows*, EMI UK's most senior executive was still working on an understanding that a deal could be done with Radiohead.

A source close to the developments and negotiations says that Wadsworth was phoned by Radiohead's team the day before the blog posting and informed what the band were going to do. They were going to do this without EMI.

This was no 'surprise' release; behind the scenes it had been carefully plotted for months, yet few were allowed into the tight circle of trust that consisted mainly of the band, Edge, Hufford and Brian Message, the band's business manager at Courtyard. The team, however, were forced to bring in Jane Dyball from Warner/Chappell, the publisher the writers in the band were signed to, in order to slice through a Gordian knot related to the performing rights for the album. Letting fans set their own price for the download version (there was also a deluxe physical version that could be pre-ordered for £40) caused huge complications, as Dyball had to take the album out of the Performing Rights Society (PRS), which traditionally owned and administered those rights on behalf of artists. That took protracted negotiations and a lot of brinkmanship, but she was able to do it[4] and the October release date was quickly set in stone.

As Radiohead's circle of trust were working furiously to clear the way for this ground-breaking and controversial release, Wadsworth and Wozencroft were most assuredly not consulted at any stage. As far as they were concerned, the contract negotiations were still ongoing. Radiohead, in their minds, could remain one of EMI's marquee signings.

The news of *In Rainbows*, when it came, ripped through Brook Green like a dirty bomb. "Tony was devastated," says one senior source who had to help pick up the pieces in the immediate aftermath of the announcement. "Oh my God, he was devastated when he found out they were doing it a different way. They had been in negotiations and Tony was convinced they were going to sign a new deal with EMI. It was a massive kick in the teeth for him. He was so close to them – the band and the managers – and I think he genuinely felt that everyone was negotiating in good faith and that the deal was going to be done ... It was a shocking betrayal really – to be going through the motions but at the same time planning something else."

Radiohead's management team declined all approaches to be interviewed for this book.

Many at EMI were floored by the move, with suggestions that the band took everything the label had done for them for granted. One source said that the band were teetering on the brink of becoming a one-hit wonder in the US with the success of 'Creep' in 1993 (a track that was re-released in the UK before it became a hit), but Parlophone stuck with them through *The Bends*, their second album, which was a slow burner. When it came to picking the lead single from *OK Computer* in 1997, EMI suggested the six-and-a-half-minute 'Paranoid Android' as a statement of intent which surprised even the band, with more immediately radio-friendly tracks like 'Karma Police' or 'No Surprises' perhaps being the more obvious choices to set up a new album. EMI also backed the band when they took an increasingly experimental turn in 2000 from *Kid A* onwards.

That said, the band and their managers had an occasionally strained relationship with the US arm of the company around this time. Bryce Edge talked of banning Roy Lott, who had been made head of Capitol Records in 1998, from an EMI conference to launch the *Kid A* album. "We did not want him involved in the marketing of the record," Edge said. "He was the head of the US label and we had just sold millions of records there but we did not want him involved."[5] EMI UK had always felt that it was close to the band and was seen as their protector against the US. That, ultimately, counted for little by 2007.

EMI may have been badly bruised and extremely embarrassed by the online release of *In Rainbows*, but they were not totally out of the running just yet as there was still the standard album release edition to come at some unspecified date in the future. And there were also the albums that would follow that.

A story this big, however, did not go unnoticed by Guy Hands and the team at Terra Firma. This arguably seriously damaged Tony Wadsworth's standing in their eyes. They had been led to believe that he was not just an exemplary executive and boss but also a confidant for artists – someone they loved, respected and trusted. If, Terra Firma wondered, Tony was as close to the acts on EMI as everyone said, how on earth could he have let *In Rainbows* slip through his fingers?

While Tony Wadsworth and Keith Wozencroft felt they had been frozen out of developments leading up to *In Rainbows*, another senior name at EMI had been ushered in even closer and had to eventually develop a split working personality, on the payroll of EMI but also deep inside the Radiohead camp.

"It impacted on me because I did their PR," says Murray Chalmers, Parlophone's head of press at the time. "Then all of a sudden they were out of contract [in 2003]. They wanted me to carry on doing the PR. Obviously I still wanted to ... Tony very graciously let me, but it also worked for them [EMI] with me carrying on doing Radiohead's PR."

Chalmers claims that he was let in on the *In Rainbows* release strategy reasonably late in the process, but suggests before this happened he was already aware that the band were probably not going to re-sign to Parlophone. "The day that it was announced that they wouldn't re-sign [to Parlophone], I knew that everything would change for me," he says. "I wasn't aware of hiding things – although maybe I did – from Parlophone. To be honest, I would have done because my allegiance has pretty much always been with the bands. I don't remember that I did, but then I wouldn't have had any qualms about doing so. But I wouldn't have lied to Tony, for sure."

In this interim period, when EMI was trying to get itself back in the race to sign the band again, Chalmers had to meticulously split his time between his wider obligations for the other EMI acts on his PR roster (including Kylie Minogue, Lily Allen, Pet Shop Boys and Coldplay) and his Radiohead work.

"I had two laptops – my Parlophone one and then I set up a different email address on another one, initially just for Radiohead," he says. "I was very thrilled about it at the time because I got the IT department at EMI to set up my other laptop. I was wearing two hats, really. But I had an eye on the future."

Tony Wadsworth's immediate future involved biting his tongue and re-opening negotiations with Radiohead to see if something could be salvaged here. What was really at stake as far as the band was concerned was ownership of their master recordings. Traditionally in a record deal, certainly at a major label, an act will sign but the label will own the masters in perpetuity, even if the act eventually repays all the expenditure (such as the advance and marketing costs) out of their royalties. If the act leaves the label after seeing out their deal, the masters will normally stay with the label. If, however, they want to renegotiate at the end of the deal – and they are still commercially successful enough – they will often ask for three things: more creative control; a higher royalty rate; and ownership of their masters.

For the very biggest of acts, however, they can use their leverage to start renegotiations earlier and put in place a deal that will see them extend their original deal in exchange for certain concessions such as return of their masters and higher royalties. This is, according to well-placed sources at EMI, something Coldplay did quite early on in their deal with Parlophone, turning what was originally a five-album deal into a seven-album deal in the wake of the success of 2002's *A Rush Of Blood To The Head* album.

The Radiohead renegotiations were always going to play out a little differently. "When we were four albums down, after *Kid A* in 2000, we were trying to have conversations with them about what they called 'realigning their deal'," says a highly placed source at EMI. "Which is basically making their deal better. It was less about higher royalty rates as, like all artists, they wanted to ultimately own their masters. It's almost a standard thing that when an act becomes a worldwide name, they have the negotiating power with the record label to start to claw back ownership of something which they had signed away at the very beginning of their deal. They signed that away because, at the time, the record company was risking millions of pounds in bringing them to the market."

EMI had already bent to Radiohead at the time iTunes was growing in the market. The band had not wanted their digital albums to be 'unbundled' as the iTunes model was primarily about consumers being allowed to buy any track off an album that they wanted. Radiohead were solid in their belief about the sacrosanct nature of the album as a body of work and so EMI initially would not let iTunes offer cherry-picking of tracks by consumers. This issue was also to trigger a legal dispute between Pink Floyd and EMI. The courts ruled in Pink Floyd's favour in March 2010,[6] but by January 2011 they had reached a new agreement with the label to allow unbundling.[7]

EMI had also given Radiohead higher royalties midway through their contract. The feeling internally was that Radiohead and their team were taking but not making concessions in EMI's favour, repeatedly stalling over the contract extension issue. "A negotiation can't be, 'I want all of these things,'" says someone within EMI who had a strong working knowledge of the oscillations between label and band. "They never got anywhere – these conversations. After the fifth album came out [2001's *Amnesiac*], this became quite urgent to EMI. It was pretty clear that they [the band's managers] weren't engaging. And they weren't being very straight about why they weren't engaging."

Reliable sources at EMI claim that the label was tabling the reversion of the masters of one catalogue album for every new studio album the band added to their contract. Their management vacillated coming into 2007 and it is understood that EMI could have gone as far as giving back two catalogue albums for every new album added to their contract. And then *In Rainbows* arrived and those talks crashed into the ditch.

With Terra Firma now in charge of EMI, the negotiations would have to work on a different level from how they had done in the past. This was the private equity firm's first serious test and how this played out would define the shape, speed and scale of how it dealt with EMI's acts in the future. This would be a statement negotiation for all.

A tougher kind of love

EMI had long claimed it was the artist's friend, but some at other major labels felt it had over-indulged its biggest names and become an easy touch. Terra Firma was going to come in with a clean slate and artists and managers were soon to discover that cuddly old EMI had grown fangs. Everything was not going to go their way.

One senior executive at Wrights Lane believed that EMI tying itself in knots to sign Radiohead again was always doomed to failure. The market had changed and, crucially, the band had changed. "We would probably have lost Radiohead anyway without Terra Firma coming in because they didn't want to be signed to a major any more and they wanted their catalogue back," they say.

As mentioned earlier, Terra Firma's research into EMI's business had revealed that 90 per cent of signed acts were losing money and naturally they wanted to turn the odds better in their favour. Any record label's biggest upfront cost when signing an act was the advance – a figure that could go through the roof if other labels were after the same act. It could run into hundreds of thousands of pounds for a hot new act and millions for a mega-act. The memory of the catastrophic and incredibly wasteful Mariah Carey deal in 2001 still haunted EMI, and Terra Firma increasingly believed that this needed to change.

"Guy didn't understand why we had to pay artist advances," says a senior EMI source. "He thought it was ludicrous and he thought that the whole model was completely broken. He wanted to change it going forward so that artists would only be paid according to the success of the record. He was asking why we would pay all of this money up front when you didn't even know if the album was going to be a success."

Hands had been hugely impressed by what Laurence Bell at Domino had done with Arctic Monkeys at the start of 2006, looking at how indie labels did not get into the same chequebook A&R game as the majors and so could sign acts for lower advances and therefore make their sales much more profitable.

"He constantly wanted to reinvent the business model, so they were looking at ways to reinvent the relationship with the artist," says the same source. "But he did that without realising we were in an incredibly competitive business and we had a market share of only around 10 per cent at that point. So it was going to be incredibly difficult to attract talent if we weren't going to be doing the same deals as our competitors – in other words paying advances. He didn't quite realise that artists still have to live in the meantime between recording something and earning their first royalty cheque. It could be up to eighteen months or even two years. They wanted to change the whole system; but from a position of a 10 per cent market share they were not going to be able to do that."

There were also suggestions that Hands was considering taking EMI out of frontline A&R entirely – seeing the signing of new acts as too much of a gamble, especially when they could be mining the company's vast catalogue instead. It turns out that this was seriously being considered at the time. One major idea being worked up by the team at Terra Firma and its assorted consultants was effectively to mix church and state by rolling the recorded music catalogue into the publishing side of the business.

"We were going to put it into a rights business that focused purely on B2B [business-to-business]," reveals Hands. "Catalogue we saw as a B2B business in that your consumer didn't come along and say, 'I want to buy that.' We got some sales that way. It normally came because you did a promotion. You packaged it up and put together the greatest hits of The Beatles or whatever. Or you re-recorded The Beatles. You enhanced it somehow. If we were doing it today, we would do it with holograms."

The Terra Firma team was divided, however, on getting out of frontline A&R entirely. "Some of the team wanted us to just sell new music ... Some of the firm wanted to do that. Some of the firm actually felt that we could make it very profitable if we cut the costs down to the core and we switched the way that we evaluated new music ... And some believed that we could make a very profitable business using insights and technology ... So you had three groups. I was in the insight group. I wanted to stay doing frontline but do it differently. My view was that we cut out all the overheads, switched it to a marketing and sales business with insights telling us which records we should release and why."

The fear, of course, was that cutting frontline A&R entirely was a short-term solution and the long-term negative impact would be that by not having hits today, you were vaporising the catalogue of tomorrow.

"Some believed that the hits of today were becoming shorter and shorter ... and they were largely the financial side of the firm," says Hands of how this was splitting the company. "The very operational side of the firm was largely of the belief that we could run this better. And the ones in the middle were like me and were more strategic; they were less financial and less operational, but more strategic. So we had these three different groups."

What followed was deadlock.

"In the end we could never do it," says Hands. "We did put together a plan ... to license all the new music for a period of time which would have got us the catalogue after a period of time. It is a little bit like leasing a house as you get it back eventually. The reason we looked at that was because we were not selling enough new music to justify our distribution costs ... The idea was to either get somebody else to buy it and take it or close it down. It never happened. But I was definitely of the view that we could do new music but I felt that we had to change the model hugely to do it."

These ideas were all percolating through the Terra Firma team as they looked to reinvent EMI, and this provided the backdrop to Hands's meeting with Radiohead's managers as they tried to strike some sort of deal. Hands was the new head of the company and this was one of their biggest and more celebrated acts threatening to defect. He had to be involved.

The issue for those inside EMI was that Terra Firma was going to apply hard City thinking to something that defied spreadsheet logic: dealing with creative people who often swing between bellowing megalomania and crashing self-doubt.

"The issues for me with Terra Firma were to do with the lack of understanding of artistry, artists and the culture of the company," explains one observer with a long history of artist liaisons and having to tiptoe through the emotional minefield here. "It is a touchy-feely thing in a way. But why do people want to sign to a label? Why do they want to go to XL or Domino or Parlophone? It's because of that culture that has been developed over many years. And the people who understood that, Terra Firma didn't respect or listen to."

Another senior A&R source explains the delicate steps that often have to be taken in situations like this. "Artists are people who have inflated egos but are also very sensitive and paranoid," they say. "The art of actually working with your artists is to create trust and discussion. Immediately this new person had come in and had not worked in music before, did not speak the language and was just telling them what they were going to do."

One highly experienced advisor says they had explicitly warned Hands not to take a tough line with artists, but rather to learn the delicate language of diplomacy that the most successful label heads were fluent in. That did not mean automatically acquiescing to their every demand; it meant finding ways to let them down gently, or getting them to understand the other viewpoint. This advice, they felt, fell on deaf ears.

"There is an art to managing art," they say, paraphrasing what they told Hands and his senior team. "You are not going to be totally successful by capitulating on everything every time there is an artist or manager who stands up and jumps on the desk. There is a point when the word 'no' is a fair and right answer. But that 'no' has to be based on objectivity and directness. They might not like it, but in the end they will respect it."

There were also suggestions that Terra Firma initially did not fully understand what managers did. Hands reportedly would refer to them as "agents" and not managers, mistakenly applying Hollywood industry terminology to the wrong industry. Agents in music work on the live and touring side of the business, not in management.

"They massively underestimated the importance of managers," says a UK employee whose day-to-day work involved nurturing these very relationships. "We weren't dealing with the artists every day – it was normally the manager. That is a constant and very fragile negotiation. They never understood any of that. They never understood those weird intricacies and nuances of the industry. Because there is no reason why they should have done. You can't [understand those political complexities] unless you're in the middle of it."

Not only did Guy and his team not understand how to deal with artists or their managers, some claim they actively disliked artists and felt they had been cosseted and given too much freedom. They behaved like spoilt children and, Terra Firma believed, EMI had given in far too easily to their incessant demands and foot-stamping.

"With Radiohead – that whole mini storm – one of the issues behind it was that Guy really didn't like the artists or the managers," claims a well-placed source. "He thought they were arrogant. He didn't like the feeling of being held to ransom. He didn't like the way the organisation bent over backwards for them. Or the extraordinary amounts of money [spent on them]. One thing he was right about was that the wastage was breath-taking. Money was just sprayed around in all directions at EMI without much care."

Talks between EMI's new owners and Radiohead's managers, with Hands having visibility on the key negotiation points, ran into complications. "That didn't go well at all," claims one EMI executive. "I believe it was related to the deal and what they were asking for. Guy's attitude was that they should take what they were being offered."

On the other side, the same executive claims that Radiohead's team had little understanding of, or sympathy for, the enormous pressure Wadsworth was under in these talks. This was Guy Hands observing Wadsworth up close in his natural environment – the space where he excelled. He was under intense scrutiny and how it all played out would define how Terra Firma viewed him and the role he played for the company.

"I think Tony was let down," they say. "I don't think Chris, Bryce or the band took into account what was happening and what a difficult situation Tony was in where he was managing Guy and he was also managing the whole thing. One of the things here is about relationships and about the culture of the company."

The meeting is understood to have hinged on two issues: the band's digital rights and ownership of their catalogue. There was talk of EMI being in the running to have the full CD release of *In Rainbows*, but the band would retain all digital rights. This would, in effect, be a pressing and distribution deal, possibly also having EMI involved in the marketing and promotion. This was something that could have been worked with, but Hands dug his heels in over the catalogue. The band wanted everything back and Hands was not prepared to consider any reversion of masters.

"We worked out roughly what the economics were," said Hands of how Terra Firma arrived at its first offer. "They said no to that. We came back with an offer that we thought was ludicrous and they suggested an offer that was even more ludicrous."

No consensus had been reached yet, but Courtyard Management had, by this stage, made up their minds. Someone else was going to get to release the CD version of *In Rainbows*. They reportedly said they had lost all faith in EMI and that Terra Firma's ownership of the company was going to be "a bloodbath". They wanted no part of it.

The make-or-break meeting with Radiohead's management danger-ously undermined Wadsworth in the eyes of his new boss and this was to have serious repercussions over the coming months for the man who had always fought Radiohead's corner. "It definitely weakened Tony's pos-ition," says an EMI executive who had a long working relationship with the avuncular head of EMI in the UK. "I kind of felt that Tony went after that. My feeling was that they [Terra Firma] thought he didn't have a [close] relationship with the band. I didn't understand why Radiohead did that [to him]."

Perhaps partly to appease staff worrying about what this would mean for EMI and partly to save face, given that negotiations with the band had collapsed, Hands sent a memo to all EMI employees about *In Rainbows*. This was subsequently passed to this writer. He argued that while some in the record industry had "expressed shock and dismay at this develop-ment" he believed "it should have come as no surprise" to those working in the business. "In a digital world, it was inevitable that a band with the necessary financial resources and consumer recognition to be able to distribute their music directly to their fans would do so," he wrote.

He went on to explain how "there are some important lessons to be learnt which support our analysis of what needs to change in the recorded music business model". He claimed that EMI still had a powerful role to play for "the vast majority of artists" that are brand new or breaking, but they would continue to be the ones that typically lose money. For the small number of profitable acts – the ones that subsidise all the losses – Hands felt they would increasingly question why they should make up for the shortfall of the loss-making acts "or for that matter their record company's excessive expenditures and advances".

As such, the company needed to look at new contracts that were "fair to both sides", suggesting a move away from deals defined by large advances and towards ones that provide "a true alignment of interests and transparency". He said the recorded music arm of EMI needed to think and behave much more like the publishing arm of EMI in terms of taking a wider and longer view on copyright exploitation.

The memo ended by saying that EMI needed to lead the way for a record business that has "stuck its head in the sand" by properly embracing the digital opportunities, and to stop relying on CD sales. "Radiohead's actions are a wake-up call which we should all welcome and respond to with creativity and energy," he wrote.

The subtext here was that *In Rainbows*, rather than being thought of as a defeat, should instead be thought of as a new type of opportunity. The optimistic took this as a sign of a company being fast to learn from its mistakes; the cynical saw it as little more than Orwellian doublethink.

The CD edition of *In Rainbows* eventually went out on XL Recordings in December 2007, going to number one in the UK. It came out in the US in January the next year on TBD Records and also went to number one.

Ed O'Brien, Radiohead's guitarist, said they were "really sad" to be leaving the label that discovered them and turned them into one of the biggest bands in the world. He pinned pretty much all of the blame on the new owners in an interview with the *Observer Music Monthly* at the start of December 2007. "EMI is in a state of flux," he said. "It's been taken over by somebody who's never owned a record company before, Guy Hands and Terra Firma, and they don't realise what they're dealing with. It was really sad to leave all the people [we've worked with]. But he wouldn't give us what we wanted. He didn't know what to offer us. Terra Firma doesn't understand the music industry."[8]

Terra Firma told *The Times*, "Radiohead were demanding an extraordinary amount of money and we did not believe that our other artists should have to subsidise their gains." Some suggestions pegged the amount demanded at £10 million, including an advance and marketing spend commitments, as well as reversion of catalogue ownership.

This was denied by their manager. "We were not seeking a big advance payment, or a guaranteed marketing spend as discussions never got that far,"[9] claimed Bryce Edge.

Hands, however, maintains that this was about wringing as much money as possible out of their erstwhile record company. "They did it – they absolutely did it," he says of their excessive financial demands. "They wanted a lot of money and we couldn't make money on what they wanted. And they wanted their masters back, which we valued even more. At our valuation, it was millions and millions that they wanted. And we just weren't going to do it. I think their view was that they wanted to do the experiment. I don't think they saw it as an experiment. I think they thought it would work. I think they felt that if they were not going to do this then they needed a really big offer."

The fact these famous musicians were taking to the media to air their grievances against Terra Firma also caused consternation at the private equity company. "Guy took these comments from artists personally – like they were attacks against *him*," says a well-placed source. "He did not take them well."

Exacerbating the already bad and very public situation, singer Thom Yorke waded in by posting a blog on the band's website. In it he denied that the band wanted "a load of cash" from EMI. "What we wanted was some control over our work and how it was used in the future by them," he wrote. "That seemed reasonable to us, as we cared about it a great deal." He claimed Guy Hands was not interested in striking a deal. "So, neither were we. We made the sign of the cross and walked away. Sadly."

He added with a flourish, "To be digging up such bullshit, or more politely airing yer dirty laundry in public, seems a very strange way for the head of an international record label to be proceeding."[10]

Tensions between the band and the new owners of their former label were about to get worse. Much worse. On 10 December 2007, EMI issued a box-set edition of the six studio albums it owned (along with an album of live recordings). They also issued a USB edition – a short-lived format that was briefly in vogue at the time – containing all their EMI releases. The USB came in the shape of a demonic bear face that had become a default logo for the band in recent years. The members of Radiohead were reportedly incensed at this as they had no creative input in the release.

"Contractually we were allowed to release [the box set]," explains an EMI executive. "Radiohead didn't want to do that and it didn't feel right creatively from them at that point in their career. It can suggest that your best years are now behind you. Guy Hands pretty much said he had the rights to put a [box set] out and it was going to be in time for Christmas and a big release. He still expected them to re-sign to the company when he had pretty much gone against every wish."

More salt was to be rubbed in wounds the following June when EMI put out the two-disc *Radiohead: The Best Of* compilation. This, once again, enraged the band, partly because they had no input and also because a *Best Of* is traditionally a last-gasp cash-in when a band's career is in commercial and artistic freefall. The band felt this could not be further from the truth.

One senior EMI source says this compilation was "done out of spite" by Terra Firma, who were still smarting from the band walking out on them. "Guy said, 'We'll work this catalogue in the way we want to work it.' Talk about lighting the blue touchpaper with Radiohead!"

Another source close to Radiohead on the EMI side added, "Any conversation with them fell apart at the point Guy Hands said he was going to put a *Best Of* out. Was it intended as a 'fuck you' to Radiohead? I think so. But when you get into a 'fuck you' with your artists, that's all that ends up as. And they fuck off!"

Hands flatly denies it was a 'fuck you' to the band. "They weren't happy," he says. "I wasn't happy either. Apart from the fact that they had basically refused to do the next record with us, they said something like they had walked away from the devil [Hands]. My view on it was very simple. The economic cost of doing a deal with them was just outrageous. I know they deny they demanded it, but I know they demanded it. They can deny it all they like. It's just not correct."

Interviewed in *The Word* magazine just ahead of the compilation's release, Yorke made his frustrations and disappointment clear, before having another angry swing at Terra Firma. "It's a wasted opportunity in that if we'd been behind it, and we wanted to do it, then it might have been good," he said. He responded again to claims that the band had simply demanded too much money to sign to EMI again.

"It fucking pissed me off," he raged to *The Word*'s Andrew Harrison. "We could have taken them [Terra Firma] to court. The idea that we were after so much money was stretching the truth to breaking point. That was his PR company briefing against us and I'll tell you what, it fucking ruined my Christmas."[11]

Rather than going out of his way to upset the band, Hands claims they had a simple economic choice to make: they needed to boost EMI's revenues and, as they had the rights to Radiohead's catalogue, it was inevitable it was going to be commercialised as much as it could be.

"They wanted money and they wanted control over their music," is how he sees it. "Then they publicly go out and humiliate us. My view was, 'Fine!' The financial department came to me and said they could make X amount of money by just doing this. We put it on hold when we were having the negotiations with them. They asked me if I wanted to push the button on it or not. At the end of the day, it was my decision as to whether we pushed the button or not. I said, 'We have a bank that is staring us down and now they have basically told us to f— off, I don't think we have a huge amount of reasons to be nice to them. We need the money for the bank, so let's do it [the reissues].' So I took full responsibility and I did it. And if it spoiled his Christmas, I'm sorry! At the end of the day, I take responsibility for that."

Hands claims the band were fully aware a box set and a compilation album were being planned, adding that it was raised during the failed contract renegotiations. They knew, he says, that if they walked from EMI then EMI could and would release these products into the market.

"Was the artwork that was finally used the artwork Radiohead had approved or not?" he says. "I have no idea. Was the track listing in the order that Radiohead wanted? I have no idea. But this had been worked on for months before. It wasn't like Radiohead said no to us and then two weeks later we released this as we had suddenly come up with it. It had been worked on all the way through. It was part of the negotiation. What happened in the negotiation was that we said no to what they wanted financially and they wouldn't accept our offer financially. That meant everything else fell away."

He adds, "I would be astonished if they were stupid enough not to think that if they chucked that they were going to lose this. But maybe they did. Maybe they thought they were so important that, even though we had 5,000 employees and 4,000 other artists, we were not going to take the opportunity to release this. And it was a very profitable transaction for EMI. It wasn't something we were going to say no to."

Anyone serving in the trenches at a record label for any length of time will warn you never to go to war with an artist in the press – even if they are demonstrably in the wrong. They will almost always have the public's sympathy and the 'suits' and 'fat cats' of the music business will always come off worse. You let the artist have their say, you bite your lip and you hope the brouhaha subsides quickly. If anyone told Guy Hands this, he didn't listen at this stage. He had become a storm chaser and EMI was driving right into a tornado.

CHAPTER 6

Out with the Old

"It felt like it was open season and anything could happen ..."

Losing Radiohead was an early PR disaster for the new EMI; but if the company had bent over backwards for the band, it would have set a dangerous precedent for future negotiations with other major acts coming to the end of their contracts who would demand parity at least, if not a much better deal. It was catch-22. EMI hadn't necessarily stopped being 'the artist's friend' but it was sending out a clear message that it was no longer the artist's toady.

Terra Firma went into November in stealth preparation mode. Keen not to disrupt long-term planning that was leading into the critical Christmas period, the company said it would outline its restructuring plans for EMI early in the new year – traditionally one of the record industry's quietest periods and, ergo, the best time to implement a major overhaul. To show just how heavily the record industry relied on the closing weeks of the year, BPI figures for the UK in 2007 show that 21.1 per cent of all album sales that year happened in December compared to just 7.1 per cent in January.

The private equity company was looking to sell down (essentially syndicating) between £200 million and £300 million of the £1.5 billion equity it had locked up in the company, doing this by coming back to the financial partners who had invested in the music company, of which there were 220, with a new proposition. "Partners with co-investment rights can now take a direct stake in EMI, but it will necessitate them paying the private equity company for that right,"[1] wrote *Music Week*, suggesting this could mean Terra Firma effectively halving its own exposure to £1.1 billion.

Hands, hoping to quell any staff panic over this, sent a company-wide memo at the end of October explaining what the thinking was here. "In all major private equity deals, equity is sold by private equity managers to their investors and other private equity firms," he wrote. "Indeed, Terra Firma has done this on all previous deals and it is something we proactively market to our investors."[2] The company suggested that "anything and everything" would be considered as part of the strategic review, but Hands was ruling out the then-fashionable '360-degree deals', similar to the Robbie Williams deal in 2002 that gave EMI a cut of all his revenue sources, from providing the building blocks for the company's new future. EMI would move in a different direction from the other majors, who effectively all copied each other's leads. EMI was going to be an outlier.

Hands, in the same memo, talked of "a fundamental change in how we approach the music business" and the "interconnected triangle" that is the consumer, EMI itself and its artists. This was also part of a plan to put clear blue water between the way things used to be done at EMI and how they would now be done, blaming many of the company's current woes on the old management bequeathing "a universal culture of [not] working together". The company would also be much pickier in terms of the acts it signed, with a precise and selective A&R strategy compared to the more scattergun approach that was apparent in the company in the past. This was a Year Zero rationale.

A story appearing in the *Independent* on Saturday 3 November[3] based on the same leaked memo from Hands was to have explosive consequences. "The memo has fuelled intense speculation about potential casualties of the new owners, though the memo did not include specific names," wrote the newspaper, before then listing a series of acts that "industry executives" had told Amol Rajan, the writer of the piece, were about to be axed. These include The Magic Numbers, Athlete, Captain, Badly Drawn Boy and Air Traffic.

It seemed that Hands was sending a shot across the bows of the artist community. "There has been a lot of talk about what labels offer to artists and to the consumer," Hands wrote. "However, there is not much talk about how artists should work with their label. While many spend huge amounts of time working with their label to promote, perfect and endorse their music, some unfortunately simply focus on negotiating for the maximum advance ... advances which are often never paid."

This was spun by the *Independent* that Hands was effectively waging war on artists that he saw as greedy and lazy.

On reading the piece, the normally placid Tony Wadsworth was reportedly apoplectic. He had to swing immediately into firefighting mode, trying to appease managers and artists that they were not about to be junked by the label. He is understood to have told Hands that this was not only undermining the UK arm of the record company but was also freewheeling into a PR disaster as it risked turning the artists signed to EMI violently against the company.

Hands claims that, yet again, he had been misquoted, possibly alluding to a smear campaign against him that was being orchestrated internally. "I never said artists didn't work hard," he states firmly. "It was just somebody in the room who decided to be mischievous and take it out of context and basically say that what I was saying is that artists aren't working hard enough. We didn't even discuss the artists. It was just a misquote. But misquotes in the music industry just happened all the time."

Hands, according to sources, stuck to his guns – arguing that advances were most assuredly out of control and that most acts on EMI's books were, collectively, losing the company vast sums of money, possibly damaging the company to the tune of billions of pounds according to his calculations. He is understood to have said that his PR strategy was right and that they needed to send out a tough message to artists and managers that the days of enormous cheques were coming to an end.

He admits that he and his team looked in great detail into scrapping artist advances altogether and instead offering something closer to a profit-share arrangement – but only for artists renewing contracts. "We didn't think it would make it competitive at all with starting artists," he says. "When you looked at your big catalogue artists and long-term artists, a lot of them didn't need advances. They were more interested in having control of their content and they were more interested in getting a bigger percentage of the profits. We felt there was a way to do a more commercial negotiation with those artists."

He claims that it never went beyond the hypothetical stage as they got immediate pushback from the management community when they got wind of it. "Philosophically the artists were quite keen on it," he says, "but the managers were quite negative on it. The maths was very simple. The managers liked the fact they got their percentage upfront, as did the lawyers … When we put it to the managers there was a universal no because it was cutting them out. So we didn't push it. We didn't have time. If we were going to push it, we needed the time to really focus on it."

He adds, "It would have been a difficult thing to do. And you would have had to do it with one artist at a time. Our money was so concentrated, if we did it with thirty artists, that was going to basically release an enormous amount of money that could be split between the artists and us."

One senior executive warned Hands that slashing A&R in this way was only going to inflict so many internal wounds that EMI would drown in its own blood. "The whole A&R side just dropped away," they say of what happened as a result of this hard line on artists and signing budgets. "Yes, he put out records, but the whole pipeline of music and the marketing of the catalogue just got stuck. It's not surprising that sales went down faster than our competitors. The record business is heavily driven by new music. People will look at it and say that the catalogue is wonderful … The Beatles, they do their thing, but the margin on The Beatles isn't very high. It is a big part of your business and you have to keep renewing it. You have to keep moving along. I finally went to Guy and showed him a model that explained to him why he had to continue to invest in new music. Because they weren't sure that they ought to."

Statements like these from Hands also upset labels who had come into EMI on one set of terms and found them changed almost overnight. Speaking to *The Guardian* in 2015, Jeff Barrett, founder of Heavenly Records, who had brought acts like Doves and The Magic Numbers into EMI as part of their joint venture, claims he saw the writing on the wall very early on and wanted to extricate himself from the situation as quickly as possible. What's more, he instantly took a dislike to Guy Hands from merely seeing his photo in the press. "I looked at a picture of this big Etonian fuck and said to Martin [Kelly, Barrett's business partner until 2010], 'He's going to unplug the jukebox, it's over.' And it was. Everything froze. I got my lawyer on the phone and said, 'Get us out as fast as we can.'"[4]

While there was a feeling that Hands and his team did not know how to talk to music executives, this was multiplied tenfold for their dealings with artists. The lessons of the Radiohead negotiation had not managed to stick yet.

"This was the only bit of advice I gave him [Guy Hands] – which he completely ignored," claims one senior executive. "I said, 'If you accept nothing else that I say to you, do understand that this business is a people business.' He did not grasp that. I said, 'This is a people business. Your product is alive. Your product has an opinion. Most of the people who matter in the success of your product do not report to you and are not beholden to the company. I am talking about lawyers, agents, producers – all these independent people who surround your artists; they are not employees of the company. You have to motivate them to help you succeed.'"

The executive claims that this advice went in one ear and out the other with Hands. "He said something like, 'Bollocks! When we are the best music company in the world, people will be kicking down our door to work with us.' I said, '*If* you are the best music company in the world, they may. But if you want to become the best music company in the world, please believe that this is a people business.'"

Another EMI employee working in digital at the time adds, "Music is a relationships game and I think this is where Terra Firma came undone. No artist manager is going to want to sit and be cool with Guy Hands or any of the people who worked with him."

This was all going to be a very steep learning curve for Terra Firma. It was also going to be a very painful rebirth for EMI.

Birt steps in

One of the architects of EMI's suggested divorce from its troubled past was Lord Birt. He was tasked with working out a new budget strategy for A&R to make it leaner and more precise. He was also sent around the recorded music division and its satellites, notably artist management companies, on a fact-finding mission.

He says that, as with his time at the BBC, he found internal resistance to change and disruption at the senior executive level and this hardened thinking had to be chipped out.

"I am not going to talk about any individual but I am happy to characterise them," he says. "As I found in other sectors, as I found in the BBC, these were proven industry professionals. They had got to their position for good reason. They had shown good judgement of music, they had the confidence of the industry and often the confidence of the artists – so that was three ticks for all of that. But as a group, they were missing some important skills."

An email dated 4 November 2007 from Birt to Guy Hands, and subsequently passed on to this author, was punitive in its findings about the old guard and the old structures. In it, Birt said he had found that "pretty much everyone realises that the existing A&R model, invented in a different era, is bust, and has to change" but that "almost no-one has done any serious systemic thinking about a viable alternative".

While everyone at EMI would agree that A&R needed to be reconfigured in an age of online, customer fragmentation and big data, Birt did not hold back in the email when pointing out where the real problems for the company lay. "Though not everyone is willing to say it bluntly, it is clear that the creative leadership of A&R in the UK is generally seen to be weak," he wrote. "Two of the major UK label heads were embarrassingly exposed under our gentle but persistent cross-examination. They appeared listless and almost despairing, and had no knowledge at all of their most basic numbers. The creative leadership in the UK will need massively strengthening."

He ended with a damning flourish. "Our over-arching insight is that EMI is a hopelessly run organisation, and that by introducing rigorous business processes, we will greatly improve its profitability. I remain very optimistic about the outcome – although I have no illusion that the transformation process will be very challenging, and I am sceptical that we will find anyone from the current music industry capable of leading the charge."

Weak. Listless. Almost despairing. Hopelessly run. When a leaked copy of this email quickly made its way round the senior team at EMI UK, the reaction was one of fury, followed by a terrifying sinking feeling.

"By November, the people that he is talking to are just thinking, 'For fuck's sake! What is going on here?'" says a senior source who saw this email at the time. "He [Birt] is asking me questions that I don't really understand. All he asked me for were names, emails and some financials. That was it. From that he decided that the creative leadership of the UK was weak! Did he ask me about my job or my history with the company? He wasn't the slightest bit interested. By November, my morale was underground – as was that of the other people he was talking to."

When interviewing Birt, this author showed him the email to gauge his thinking on it all a decade later. "I did talk to some of the people on the labels," he says. "I can remember that exact meeting, but I won't say who it was with and I didn't put it in the email. But I can remember the complete sense of – and this was at a more junior label level – what I described there as 'listlessness'. I can remember the meeting because I was shocked by it at the time."

Asked about the "hopelessly run organisation" line in the email, he says, "I don't have anything to add to the exposition I have given you. It [EMI] didn't have data, it didn't understand its customers, it didn't have proper processes, it was not a well-run company … That's why private equity operates. It comes to tech companies which were challenged in some way or other and tries to sort them out and make them better … Plainly the kind of picture that comes out of something like that tells you that, in many parts of the world, EMI was destroying value. It had non-profitable activities. It had non-profitable artists. That is how you become more efficient, by trying to reduce barriers that are value destructive and increase those that are value accretive. That's what you do in any organisation."

On his role here in meeting the senior EMI team, he says he was merely collating evidence and insight to pass upstairs to Guy Hands and his close team. "I was information gathering," he says. "I wasn't the chief executive. I was trying to understand not only the formal business challenge, but I was [also] trying to understand the cultural challenge as well. That wasn't my job; that was the CEO's job in the end to populate the new structure in the right kind of way. But it was true that there were people in there that seem to have lost the will to live."

Two days after the Birt email, Guy sent an email to senior Terra Firma and EMI executives outlining key challenges for the company. This email was subsequently leaked to this author. In it, Guy said that "there is a level of dissention, distrust and unwillingness to work together between the US and the UK labels within EMI" that was in urgent need of repair. He also said he was appointing David Kassler as chairman of a new committee focused on artist projects to coordinate all efforts globally and budgets as well as resources assigned. This lack of centralised activity was, he felt, a cause of immense frustration for artist managers.

In the same email, his exasperation with the inherited working practices of the company he had just bought was becoming evident. "There currently is not a forum within EMI that ensures, from a management team perspective, that major projects and their resulting implications are presented in a coherent and timely fashion," he wrote before mentioning an example that he felt exposed this problem.

Following the previous day's meeting of the newly created Music Management Board, chaired by Hands, he said he had returned to his office to see an article in *The Times* about a deal between Kylie Minogue, EMI and Facebook. (It was a marketing initiative involving the creation of a Kylie app that allowed users to send a 'Kyliebot' avatar to their friends on the social network.[5])

He said this was "for me the absolute last straw" given they had talked about "these very topics in the MMB" but no one had thought to mention it. He added that his own 17-year-old son had texted him about it that afternoon when he got out of school. "Clearly," Hands wrote, his vexation palpable, "he is more on top of EMI business than we are!"

At the most senior level at EMI, vast quantities of petrol was now being poured on the flames.

For the rest of the staff, they were now going to be subjected to psychometric testing – a means of assessing their skills and knowledge as well as understanding their personality types. This was a common process that prospective employees in the financial sector, for example, were put through when applying for jobs, but it was an utterly alien concept in the music industry. As such, it was met with a mixture of scepticism, paranoia and gallows humour within the offices of EMI.

"I had to go off to some place in the City to do this psychometric test," says one source who went through the process. "Fuck – I wasn't expecting that! I had three hours of testing. It was the Terra Firma test and included things like business comprehension where you had to read a paragraph and say what it meant. Then you had to do a statistical interpretation of a load of data."

Not everyone, however, did the tests and it was telling that the one group of employees who dodged it were the people in the company that Terra Firma arguably understood least. "Everyone in the company went through psychometric testing except the people in A&R," says a senior source. "They were frightened that if they didn't come out well then they were gone – these A&R people who they [Terra Firma] saw as wildcatters who were out at night getting off their heads. They didn't understand that."

Several employees claim that a very different type of testing was talked about, but ultimately not implemented. "I have clear memories of them saying that they were going to drug test every single member of staff," says one UK label executive. "'What? Are you kidding me?' There were psychometric tests for staff, but I think that was only if your job was under threat."

Hands denies that this was drug testing for artists or staff but rather a tacit acceptance that drugs were part and parcel of the job for some employees and that Terra Firma needed to provide a safety net for them. "We were never going to do drug tests on the artists; we were going to introduce a ... drug safer-use strategy," he claims. "My view is that drugs are taken recreationally. I am not convinced that drugs are necessarily more harmful in society than alcohol or, indeed, obesity. But they are undoubtedly very harmful to some individuals. My view was that we needed to identify the problem and help. I was thinking of introducing both some help with regard to drugs and some actual monitoring of drugs. The information I had was that drugs were very prevalent in EMI. Not just at concerts and with regard to entertainment, but also with regard to people at work. In the end, I backed off on that. What I did do though was make it absolutely clear that we were not paying for anything that was inappropriate. There were rumours about how much money it saved. Some people claimed it was saving £10–20 million a year. I have no idea [if this is true]."

Then he makes an astounding assertion. "I was warned about threats from drug gangs in EMI because I made it essential that people give receipts and explain where the money was going," he says. "The rumours were that this had annoyed the drug gangs who were supplying drugs. That was quite a thing. We had one guy – and the police had to be called – who wanted to attack me on the premises. A dealer – just a small-time dealer. My driver had to go and have police training because they were very worried I was going to get attacked. I did have one manager warn me that I needed to understand there were people out there who felt that some of the stuff I had done with regard to expense controls was not appropriate."

Around this time, the business press were running stories about the alleged excesses of the old guard at EMI and how the music company was allegedly propelled by profligacy. Among the stories were a bill that topped £700,000 a year for just one London taxi firm,[6] a £5.6 million Mayfair mews house, an executive indulgence that was barely used[7] and a monthly bill for candles that ran to £20,000.[8] There was also much euphemistic talk in the media of huge sums being spent on "fruit and flowers".

As with stories of this nature, the truth was a distant relative of what was printed. Several senior sources at EMI say these stories were a cartoon exaggeration of what really happened. The executives flatly deny that there was a drugs and prostitute budget, but other junior staff say each office was genuinely supplied with fresh fruit and this was seen as an office perk for the long hours and late nights that came with the job. The taxi budget had been consistently slashed in the late 1990s and early 2000s and was nowhere near as high as the stories suggested. "That may well have been the sum total of taxis for the whole bloody company for a period of time," says one well-placed source before having to accept it appeared excessive. "It may be that there were some savings to be made on that taxi account."

The mews house in Mayfair was regarded by the company as both a cost-saving measure and a deft investment. It was used by the upper tier of management in the UK if working late in London and was also used by international executives in London for meetings. It was deemed preferable to paying for hotel suites. Colin Southgate had, according to one well-placed source, bought it for the company in the 1990s for £700,000 and, when it was eventually sold, it made eight times the original purchase price.

The candles story had a long and curious history and was said to have been a one-off in America in the 1990s that triggered a serious internal review at EMI and the swift introduction of stringent budgetary control. It was not a quotidian indulgence. It turned out to have been for an artist album launch at the Bel-Air home of US executive Nancy Berry. When the bill was sent to London to be paid, all hell broke loose and any marketing or entertainment expenditure even approaching that level subsequently required sign-off at the most senior level.

As for the 'fruit and flowers' bills? "The idea that the board would approve a budget for drugs is preposterous," splutters one senior source. "Preposterous!"

Senior executives within EMI were at a loss to explain how and why these stories were appearing in press, but were quick to question their veracity. By this stage, however, the fires they were required to fight were multiplying on a daily basis. They could deny the stories all day long and point writers to evidence that exonerated them but, as more and more outlets regurgitated these tales as fact, the management knew this would be a Sisyphean task.

Externally, senior executives at EMI believed the company was being unnecessarily dragged through the pages of the business press; but a more pernicious destabilisation was happening in the corridors of Wrights Lane and Brook Green.

Two tribes going to war

The world of music and the world of the City were never going to rub along comfortably with each other. There was always going to be a culture clash, but in the opening months of Terra Firma's ownership of EMI, that disconnect escalated quickly. And it just kept escalating.

The incoming team from Terra Firma were met initially with suspicion but that was quickly replaced by hostility as the feeling was they had a binary approach to it all. If Terra Firma staff and new hires were the anointed saviours of EMI, then everyone at EMI was part of the problem.

"The view from Terra Firma was that everybody at EMI was an idiot because the business was crashing and burning around their ears and so if they were any good they would have been able to save it," says one senior executive. "So everybody at Terra Firma were geniuses. They thought that everything that the entire industry was doing in digital was wrong. Not just EMI. They thought that about everybody … The hubris they had! There was the idea that, 'We are Terra Firma and we are the greatest private equity firm in London at the moment. We are just masters of the universe.' That was just unbelievable. Terra Firma's approach was that everybody at EMI was clearly just a moron."

Another independent observer backs this up, saying that they were taken to one side early on in the process by senior management at EMI to try and broker some sort of peace by getting the new owners to at least listen to the old bosses. That fell on deaf ears. "The Terra Firma guys were arrogant and thought they knew better," they say.

"It was so overriding – their sense that everything we had done was wrong and stupid," adds another EMI executive at that time. "In any meeting about marketing music, emotion played no role in it whatsoever. You can put as many statistics on a board as you like, but emotion is a hugely important factor in music and it is what sparks people to buy things and listen to things. They just went, 'No, it's not!' To me that was, 'You've got it wrong, guys. You're in the wrong business. You have bought something that you simply don't understand.'"

Hands suggests this was simply an unfortunate by-product of this takeover – but admits that some Terra Firma appointees went into the company more altruistically and tactfully than others. "It is inevitable when you take over a company and things aren't going well, whoever you bring in [will not be popular]," he says. "David Kassler and some others made a very big effort to find out what was going on. Julia Williamson did. Pat [O'Driscoll] did. There were a number who did. The group was split between: those who felt they had a plan and the consultants have done it so they should implement it; and those who felt we have a plan, we needed to check it was right and then we needed to decide how to implement it. I was sort of in the middle of this trying to referee it."

In trying to rationalise why it unfolded in this way, Hands suggests that the strategy of putting so many Terra Firma executives into the company so quickly was perhaps heavy handed.

"There were thirty-three people from Terra Firma in the business," he explains. "I met with them as a group twice a week for about two hours on average. That was probably, of all my weekly meetings, my worst weekly meeting. The [artist] managers, by comparison, were a doddle. I had these two sides and they totally disagreed with each other. The one side just wanted us to get on and do it. And the other side wanted us, if we did it, to do it much more slowly ... What happened was that we moved on certain areas quite quickly and we were slower in other areas. I think what people find slightly frustrating was, and this is from a Terra Firma perspective, that the areas we moved on quickly tended to be the areas where the individuals made the better relationships with their people because it was easier to move on with them."

Arguably, EMI staff were frightened of having to change and change quickly so they could have come across as equally belligerent to the team at Terra Firma. This created a situation where the two sides were only going to butt heads until one of them fell down unconscious.

"The whole 'resistance to change' thing is crap," argues an EMI UK executive, saying that the idea of change was not the issue: it was the way Terra Firma was looking to impose it from the outside in. "They came in, they didn't understand and they tried to change things without that understanding. When you do that, you are going to get resistance. They will just explain why that won't work but how we could make it work is like this. But they would say, 'We didn't like that and that's not what we got into this business for.' Well I don't know what you got into this business for!"

Looking back at it now, Hands concedes that there was far too much demanding and not enough persuading in terms of how his team went into EMI. But, he argues, Terra Firma, with the terms of its loan from Citigroup snapping at its heels, could not afford the luxury of the slow-but-steady approach. It had to make changes and it had to make them immediately.

"I probably would say there was too much stick and not enough carrot," he recalls of the opening months. "But I think the thing we probably couldn't share with them [EMI's staff] was that we also had a huge amount of stick over us as well. It was a case that we were getting absolutely beaten by Citigroup. We were having regular meetings with Citigroup where they were basically saying the performance wasn't good enough. 'Hang on a second! You guys lent the money to this company for twelve years. You knew everything about this company you could know and now you're basically beating us up and we've only been there a few months? Let's get real.' If Citigroup had allowed us to work over seven years and we hadn't had the pressure of the debt, we would have done these things differently."

He denies, however, that this harsh strategy was a result of Terra Firma being dangerously flustered by its debt and taking it out on the staff at EMI. "It wasn't panic – it was a controlled, almost military, approach," he suggests. "I brought in thirty-three people. I would never have brought thirty-three people in [normally]. It was all we could do to get it done really quickly. At the end of the day, we had to be in a position to cut the costs really quickly. We just didn't have the luxury of time."

This was not a clash that was confined to the UK; it was also happening, albeit at some remove, in the US. "When they came in there were things about their mindset that I think really hurt them," says a US-based executive at EMI. "They had the perspective that anyone who had any music industry background was not listened to. That meant that people like Barney Wragg [were dismissed]. You were talking about some of the best digital executives who were out there. But that didn't matter [to Terra Firma]. As far as they were concerned, if you came from the music industry, you were an idiot. You were the ones who allowed this mess to occur in the first place so you were not to be listened to."

Even those at EMI who had been calling for radical upheaval within the company for years felt that Terra Firma came in with the completely wrong approach and attitude so this was always going to amplify any resistance they would have naturally faced.

"We had seen this a lot in the music industry since 2000 where people thought they had the silver bullet and they could change the music industry, how it was perceived and the money that it could make," says a digital executive who had been trying to push their own changes internally long before Terra Firma arrived. "They had the belief that anybody who came before them had the trappings of the old music industry that wouldn't allow them to see the future through a Terra Firma lens. And that just wasn't true. I wanted somebody with traditional business acumen to come in and apply that. But they had to work with people … It was always like they felt they just needed to make sweeping statements and representations about what they were doing so that the press would think these guys were really turning around the music industry."

They add, however, that there was something of an institutionalised problem within EMI that meant any changes had to be negotiated and implemented slowly, thoughtfully and carefully so as not to upset the management. Set that against people explicitly tasked with tearing up the old manual and problems were always going to appear. "There is little collaboration in the music industry because it is hierarchical and people fear for their jobs because there is so much change," they suggest. "So people at a senior level present this belief that they know more than you do and if you don't agree with their decision that's probably because you don't understand them. Terra Firma was as guilty of that then as were the people before them and [they] still are today. They all think they've got this silver bullet."

If this meeting of contrary worlds started badly, it was going to get worse before it would get better.

"Both sides were totally incompatible," says one EMI UK executive who quickly started planning their exit strategy as the new regime flexed its muscles. "There was also that feeling pretty early on that they thought we were a bunch of Muppets. And that is quite offensive. When you go into a company that has been around for over a hundred years, not everyone is a fool. And if you think the company's worth buying in the first place then presumably you have to respect some of the people who have been running it, some of them for quite a long time, and treating them with a bit of respect. I'm not sure any of that respect was really demonstrated. That probably wasn't a great start. It just became clear, from the more exposure that I had to them, that we were going to be fighting a bit of a losing battle with a bunch of people who didn't get it at all. And didn't necessarily realise that they weren't getting it and therefore didn't have much instinct to try." They add, glumly, "They didn't know from one minute to the next what they were trying to do. I think they weren't listening to anyone else."

A senior UK executive says this all set off a domino effect that the company was only going to become acutely aware of months later. "One of the central reasons why this was such a shit-show was that I think there were fundamental misunderstandings by Guy Hands and all his people about what EMI was and about how the music industry worked – to the point of almost banality," they say.

This ideological divide between Terra Firma people and EMI people soon found a physical manifestation, exacerbating a situation that was already gripped by wariness and paranoia.

"They had a room by the mezzanine and they put blinds on the windows and we were told that was the Terra Firma room and we couldn't go in there," says a Brook Green employee. "That's where they housed all the drones. Some of them weren't all bad, but some of them couldn't believe their luck. One minute they were management consultants and then the next they were in the building where you might have Thom Yorke in reception. They started to dress down and wear chinos. But you could always spot them. It was like *Invasion of the Body Snatchers*. You always knew who they were."

Some at EMI felt there was a very clear and very intentional 'divide and rule' strategy being rolled out here. "Largely it was felt that the bosses were being ignored and they were picking other people to head up special weird squads," says one senior UK executive. "It was intentionally divisive. That's what private equity does. It sees who wants to spill the beans. I was fascinated by the fact that people can come in and think they can do this better than you. I imagine that is the basic premise of private equity."

In telling stories from this time, most EMI staff are quick to point out that David Kassler was the exception to the rule here. He was the one Terra Firma appointment they felt was at least trying to understand things from their perspective rather than just trying to bend everyone to their will. "I remember speaking to him a couple of times," says one UK executive. "He wanted to understand. He took the time. And he was personable."

Kassler himself was well aware of the enormity of the job in front of them all, not just him, but also everyone Terra Firma brought in and the staff at EMI who remained. He felt that carrot was preferable to stick and that the staff should feel involved in the changes happening to them rather than regarding themselves as victims of those changes. At the heart of this, he believed, was introducing more rigorous business ideas to something the EMI culture had perhaps romanticised into a state that was deemed sacrosanct, believing that art should always trump cash. That was workable in the 1990s when the CD market was buoyant, but it was utterly impractical now.

"The music industry has always been built on gut feeling and the guys who built the catalogue at EMI were extraordinary executives," he says. "But as the world became more complicated and it became a multi-channel business with lots of digital channels and lots of physical channels and radio stopped being the only route to the consumer, it becomes too difficult to do that by gut feel."

Ever the diplomat, he says his approach was one of gentle encouragement, but his ultimate boss always had a different strategy that he was used to but that the people at EMI found difficult to accept and work with. "Guy is a larger-than-life personality," he says. "Typically, he would make quite controversial statements intended for a City audience who are very used to hearing about transformation and reinvention of a company's business model. Inside the music industry, people are much more sensitive about it." Kassler found himself – by default – having to act as Terra Firma's peace-keeping envoy.

The team in the UK felt they were being punished most as they were immediately in Terra Firma's line of vision, and that the biggest problem at EMI was still being ignored. This could only feed into the victim mentality that was starting to grip elements of the old guard.

"The UK seemed to be the only place that was getting any heat from Terra Firma," says one executive on being put through the wringer. "We were the biggest profit provider and the biggest artist provider in the world of EMI. And we were only a small percentage of what is a global company. He bought a global company and only seemed to see it from outside of his office door ... I can't believe how fundamental a misunderstanding that is. The UK company got all the heat. Particularly in those first few months. The US company was haemorrhaging money. That was their thing. If I had bought a company, I would get my arms around it a bit more than simply squeezing the most successful bit of it. Weird. I thought it was remarkably short-sighted."

They claim there was "no focus on America" at all in the run-up to Christmas 2007. That felt to them less like a company with its priorities in the wrong order, and more like a company that had no idea what any of its priorities were in the first place.

"All of the criticisms, questioning and undermining – and the revolving door of people that he brought in – was all done in the UK," says the same executive. "You just thought, 'If you had looked at your numbers, which you're supposed to be so good at doing, you'd see that the biggest expenditure that you make every month on rent and salaries isn't in the UK. And if you also look at your numbers, you'll see that the people who are earning you the money and the artists who are making the money are signed here and not over there. So are you shining your spotlight in the right areas so soon after you have done the deal?' It honestly felt to me that they had an incredibly short vision of what they thought this EMI company was."

The first Christmas under new ownership was not as Scrooge-like as some had feared. Hands appeared at a staff party in December to gee up the troops, but as a sign of the coming austerity, costs were cut. Even so, EMI staff were determined to have a good time and park any worries about the challenges ahead of the company – if only for one night.

"They didn't spend any money on it so all the DJs were just people who worked at EMI," says one source at the party. "Guy Hands put in a song request – which was 'Two Tribes' by Frankie Goes To Hollywood. He came on the mic and said, 'You're all brilliant! We have had a shit time but now we can all look to the future. You have been distracted by Warner [and the merger rumours] and it was like two tribes. But now you can carry on without the distractions.'"

One eyewitness at the party claims that, at one stage in the evening, Guy Hands energetically took to the floor when ABBA's 'Dancing Queen' was played, manically flailing around. EMI staffers looked on aghast as their new boss – the only person dancing at this stage – careered around. Very quickly, according to the eyewitness, several Terra Firma staffers took to the floor, creating a protective wall around Hands so he would be spared the discomfiture of dancing alone in full view of banks of face-clasping EMI staffers. "It was," says the eyewitness, "toe-curlingly embarrassing."

By January, any optimism or laughter-against-the-odds feelings engendered at that bash had withered like the balloons taped to the party room wall. As UK staff returned to their desks in January, they were unaware that the one person they had hoped could protect them was being negotiated out of the company.

On Tuesday 8 January 2008, it was announced that Tony Wadsworth, having risen through the ranks to run EMI's recorded music arm in the UK and Ireland since 2002, was leaving the company after twenty-six years. Terra Firma revealed that Roger Ames, head of EMI in the US, would take charge of UK A&R while Terra Firma board member Mike Clasper would take over the rest of Wadsworth's responsibilities.

This was genuinely shocking news as many in the UK music industry felt Wadsworth was like the ravens in the Tower of London – if he left EMI then it was all over. The media all ran with similar stories, praising Wadsworth for being a music industry executive like no other, calling him the "artists' ally"⁹ and talking about his unwavering honesty in an industry that many saw as the enemy of rectitude.

"We loved Tony and I thought Tony was one of the nicest people I've met in pretty much every industry I have seen," claims Hands who says he offered Wadsworth a more creative role within EMI while simultaneously cutting off his financial say in the company.

"We tried to offer him a job that took him away from having economic responsibility," he says. "It would have been something like a relationship chairman. He would basically have been the guy who talked to the artists. The main thing I wanted to take away from him was his control over budget … You have got two things here. You have got running the commerciality of the business and you have got running the operations of the business. Tony, I felt, could have done an absolutely wonderful job as a senior relationships person."

Hands was adamant, however, that Wadsworth was never considered for the CEO role. But then he reveals who was top of Terra Firma's wish list to run EMI: the chairman and CEO of Universal Music Group, the biggest music company in the world. "Lucian Grainge I thought would have been superb," says Hands. "If we had been able to get Lucian Grainge, I would have hired him tomorrow."

He did not make it clear how he was going to lure away the global head of the biggest major and make them the head of the smallest major. "The music industry had, bluntly, taken out all of the good talent and put it somewhere where it was making money," he says in a way that could only be read as him believing that EMI, in executive terms, had been left with the runt of the litter.

Inside EMI UK, the news of Wadsworth's exit meant that the mood was funereal. And the employees took it incredibly personally. "Staff knew him and, because he had a very relaxed personality and was very good at staff presentations and meetings, people felt like he was like their dad," says a source who worked closely with him for several years. "And then when someone says they don't want your dad here any more you go, [mock horror] 'Why not?'"

Another senior EMI executive from the corporate office felt this was a symbolic scalp and that Terra Firma was sending out a clear message that they alone were in charge and no one was irreplaceable. "There were no sacred cows," they said of the symbolism of this change at the top. "Absolutely nobody was safe. They were very clear on that."

Even speaking a decade on, several people who worked under Wadsworth became visibly emotional when talking about hearing the news he was leaving. "Tony was a very patriarchal figure," says one. "He felt strongly for the people who worked for him and the people who worked for him feel strongly about him. Him leaving ripped the heart out of it. When Tony went we knew it was all over at that point. It felt like it was open season and anything could happen."

Another adds, "That's when it started to dawn on people at EMI that, oh fuck, we're not in Kansas any more. Tony felt like the spirit of the company in the UK."

A non-EMI source who had a close working relationship with EMI had mixed feelings about Wadsworth as a business executive but was effusive about his A&R skills, saying both Terra Firma and EMI would be all the poorer after his departure as he was the best person they had in the company to deal with artists. "Tony wasn't the best executive there has ever been but he was absolutely the right executive," they say. "He could speak to Kate Bush, Robbie Williams and Damon Albarn. Speaking to those three alone is, I can imagine, an absolute minefield."

Some EMI Music Publishing staff, however, felt that someone had to be held accountable for EMI's recorded arm being a shadow of its former self so when the axe at the top started swinging, they were not surprised. "I have sympathy with people on a personal level," says the senior publishing source. "It was difficult for them and people lost their jobs, but the business was long overdue someone getting their hands on it and taking the waste out of it. There were too many sacred cows in that business. 'You can't get rid of Tony! What will Kylie say if we get rid of Tony?' Subsequent reviews showed that these people cared about their careers and if you could show them their career was in a better place with Person X, they are going to be fine with that. They are still focused on the big picture in their career … This would not be a popular opinion with my recorded music colleagues, but for a long time that hadn't been a proper business. They had not operated well. They were huge amounts of fat in the business and there was spending that there shouldn't have been."

The door had barely shut tight after Wadsworth walked out through it when another senior executive was pushed out. On 16 January, it was announced that Barney Wragg, worldwide head of digital at EMI, was leaving and he would be replaced by Mark Hodgkinson, executive vice president of global marketing.[10]

To the outside industry, this looked like Terra Firma's scorched-earth policy at the boardroom level. Hands, however, says that the removal of a top tier of executives was just continuing the restructuring that had been put on hold from 2006 when the company was aggressively trying to sell itself.

According to Guy Hands, Eric Nicoli and Roger Ames had provided him with separate lists of executives that they felt were expendable when the Terra Firma sale went through – high-level redundancies that would have been difficult to make when the company was still listed on the stock exchange.

"They were expensive to get rid of – the biggest payment we did to get rid of someone on this hit list was $20 million," says Hands of why the mass sacking of the old guard did not begin on the day they got the keys. "They had huge contracts. It was very, very expensive to get rid of people … As a public company, EMI just hadn't spent the money. So they decided that, rather than getting rid of someone … they would keep them."

The Terra Firma team believed that some EMI executives no longer had their finger on the pulse of the company and so needed to go. "What had happened at EMI, which happens at a lot of businesses, is that if you are at the top, you spend your time not doing any more than seeing people; so you end up seeing more and more senior people and getting further and further away from the coalface," explains Hands. "When you actually looked at it, you had these people who worked for them who knew the artist managers just as well; they didn't necessarily know the artists, but most of the artists you didn't see that much – you just saw their managers."

He alleges that, despite the fact that EMI liked to present itself as an artist-friendly label, Terra Firma was hearing quite a different story when it consulted with the acts on EMI's books. "I spoke to a lot of artists and they had a few people that they liked but for the most part they were pretty negative on EMI," he claims. "You saw them and they did nothing but complain. Some of the complaints were with vitriol. If I was going to criticise us, I would say it took us a very long time, because of the way the redundancy laws in the UK work, to actually get rid of that top list."

Roaring ahead in 2008, Terra Firma clearly meant business. This was very much the old brigade being cast onto the bonfire. Executives going was one thing, but now the staff were becoming aware of just how deep the cuts were going to be. Hands revealed that up to 2,000 jobs – from a global staff of around 6,000 – would vanish as part of a £200-million cost-saving programme. They were also going to seriously cut down on the 14,000 (including frontline and catalogue) acts on EMI's books. Terra Firma had recently drawn down £250 million in new investment and it was rumoured that £40 million of that was earmarked for redundancy packages. EMI was going to be squeezed like never before.

Hands was keen to outline some of his company's visions to the management community and perhaps right some wrongs of the recent past in regard to his misguided statements about artists, their workloads and their financial demands. He was already meeting with groups of managers when Wadsworth was still at the company and these interactions continued.

An observer at some of these meetings felt they were a massive missed opportunity as they went in with the right intentions but had sent the wrong envoys. "They would hold these open forums for artist managers in the atrium of the EMI building [in Wrights Lane]," they say. "It was a great idea and EMI hadn't done that before. But they'd get the wrong people there from Terra Firma as they didn't know anything about music. So the whole thing backfired. Guy would bring along his key executives who needed to be there but they just couldn't speak the right language to the managers. There were lots of things like that where they had the right idea but the wrong execution. That is ultimately the story of their time there."

Hands claims none of these meetings were "particularly difficult" or "particularly extreme" but adds that years of bullying at school had given him a thick skin. "You build up a certain amount of resilience, so getting screamed at by an artist manager in a meeting is not a big deal – it really isn't," he shrugs. "I think this is one of the things that artist managers were a little bit shocked by. I think they thought I would be very typical of the City and very similar to most people in the City."

He recounts one meeting with a major artist – one he personally refuses to name but who some inside EMI suggest was Joss Stone – that went as badly as any meeting could, primarily as he had to break a promise made by his predecessors at the company. "Eric [Nicoli] had told them they were going to get a £12 million advance," he claims. "They hadn't legally signed it, but clearly the artist had been told this. The manager came in and talked to me about it. We had run the numbers for that artist and there was just no way that you could ever pay back the £12 million. It was just the most absurd concept. I said no and there was lots of screaming and shouting. They left. Somebody came in from EMI and said that conversation sounded terrible. I said, 'They're upset! It's not surprising. They thought they were going to get £12 million and we are offering £3 million. Of course they're going to be upset!' They said it was horrendous but I said it wasn't. We didn't have £12 million to give them. I said I couldn't magic it [up]. It doesn't make sense."

That, however, was not the end of the story. "Eventually the artist came to see me," he continues. "The artist was really nice and polite and they explained that they had basically set their heart on a house and they wanted to buy this house but they now couldn't afford it. They were really upset. We sat down and they had obviously decided they wouldn't try the screaming approach; they were going to try the charm offensive.

Of course the charm offensive didn't go anywhere either. There was nothing I could do."

Relations with the management community, however, threatened to curdle beyond repair when Tim Clark, co-manager of Robbie Williams, gave an interview in which he made a reference to Guy Hands and plantation owners.

Hands was born in South Africa, while Clark was born in Kenya before moving to London in the early 1970s to work for Island Records, where he became managing director. Both were children of the colonies so any mention of the word 'plantation' was going to be an emotionally loaded one, coming as it does with associations with slavery and racism. Hands reacted to this by threatening Clark with legal action.

"That was an extraordinary quote," says Hands looking back at it and the diplomatic incident it caused. "It slightly upset me because my parents are South African."

Clark has always denied he said it the way it was interpreted by Hands, stressing that he had warned that Hands was at risk of behaving like a plantation owner if he carried on the way he did in his dealings with artists. "I said that it seemed to me to hark back to the days of plantation owners," says Clark looking back on this incident that could have exploded into a court case. "He took umbrage at that. He threatened to sue. [That quote] was based on everything that was happening at the time. It was the people who were being let go and it was the people who were being brought in who were not record company people and that we felt didn't understand what this industry was all about."

Despite some senior executives at EMI advising against this route, a legal letter was issued to the co-manager of one of the biggest acts on EMI's books. "I was well aware that plantations weren't necessarily all staffed by slaves, but I absolutely understood how that could be misconstrued," says Clark. "Fortunately, we had a very clever lawyer who wrote a letter, we sent it off and didn't hear anything back."

Perhaps filed in anger, the response from Clark's lawyer managed to calm things down and soon after an olive branch was extended when Clark, along with his business partner David Enthoven, was invited to dine with Hands in order to reach an armistice.

"We went and had dinner," says Clark. "This was our first direct meeting with him [Guy Hands]. It was David, myself, Guy and another Terra Firma person. It [the legal threat] was the great unspoken, I think. It might have been alluded to but it wasn't really spoken about. It was a dinner about what we could do with this industry. That's what we were all focused on, really. It was trying to find answers to the disruption that was occurring. We were all trying to find answers and tackling it in different ways."

The enmity dissolved even before they had moved on from their starters. "We got on really quite well!" recalls Clark. "We had a pretty good chat. And he was engaging and engaged. I think he gave us a good listen. He might not have agreed with everything that we said, but I think he gave us a good listen. He was fairly open. He didn't actually touch on anything to do with Citigroup or any of that. But really it was talking about the company, its good bits, its faults and so on. And what we thought about the industry generally. From what I recall, we had a pretty open and friendly conversation."

Hands concurs that, after such a bumpy start, things were eventually back on an even keel. "We all calmed it down and moved on," he says, admitting a valuable lesson came out of it – namely not to conduct wars with artists or managers in public. "It was a very fast learning experience," he concedes. "I hadn't expected to do it and I suddenly found myself in the middle of it! It was an horrendous experience. I learnt more from it than anything else I've ever done. But it was the most gruelling, challenging and difficult thing I have ever done."

Defection of the megastars

Hands had only met Radiohead's managers rather than the band itself. But in January 2008, he met with Mick Jagger to discuss the future of The Rolling Stones on the label. Hands had a major quandary he was having to get his head around quickly: EMI had lots of big names on its books putting out new albums, but very few of them were making any profit. "We had a whole list of artists where they were just ludicrously overpaid and lost money," he says. "We had a cultural decision to make, which was to send a message to the firm that we were going to start focusing on making money."

Radiohead going was a watershed moment for the company, but Hands says the dealings with The Rolling Stones were equally important as a statement for Terra Firma sticking to its guns and being prepared to see major names walk away.

"A lot of the money that we were losing was based on very small sums – but hundreds and thousands of them," says Hands of the macro-economics of EMI's A&R strategy. "Twenty-four thousand pounds was our average loss – but it was lots of £24,000s. We were losing about £100 million on A&R-ing new music each year and it was made up of an average of around £24,000 for each artist. That's around 4,000 artists. This is something that Roger Ames said to me. He said, 'Don't think it's all the big numbers.' It was actually about fifty-fifty ... So we had about 2,000 acts that we lost on average £24,000 on and we had a few artists that we lost £50 million on. The problem was that if we were going to tell the A&R guys to be disciplined on the small side, which was the fruit and flowers comments that got into all the papers, we had to be serious on all the other stuff as well."

The Rolling Stones liked to release new albums, but primarily as a hook for their record-breaking tours where they made the lion's share of their money. There was a feeling within EMI, one that had been around long before Terra Firma, that contracts like the one the Stones were on were effectively vanity deals – super-fans might buy a new album but they were never going to be the crossover success they needed to be to get the investment back. Having a band of that calibre on the label was good for EMI's image but less good for its bottom line.

For Hands, if the Stones were to re-sign to EMI, the deal could not just be a repeat of the past, where the company was effectively compelled to put out loss-making albums just to keep the band (and their post-1971 catalogue[11]) on the label. It had to be more than just the records.

There have been a lot of rumours about what happened in that meeting, suggesting that Jagger walked out in a mixture of anger, disbelief and exasperation. There were suggestions that Hands had put together a presentation of what EMI could do for the Stones and this included Stones Idol, a TV talent-search format looking for members of a Stones tribute act where Jagger and guitarist Keith Richards would be the judges, going all the way to a mooted Stones-themed hotel that included a pre-trashed room for the authentic rock'n'roll experience.

"The press mischaracterised it," sighs Hands. "I didn't tell them that they had to go and do the TV series or anything. I brought along a presentation of all the things they could do to increase the exposure of the band to a younger generation and earn money. It was a brainstorm. It had everything out there. It included *Guitar Hero*, it included touring, it included TV shows, it included just about everything."

He elaborates on some of the options discussed and the ideas pitched. "This was a smorgasbord of everything you could do," he says. "For example, with Coldplay we talked about having electric toothbrushes that played 'Yellow'. It was about how we could commercially do things. We [he and Jagger] sat down and we had a very nice lunch and a half-bottle of white burgundy. And we chatted about business. He's a bright guy. He is a grammar-school boy from Kent. He is a bit older than me, obviously, but I am also a grammar-school boy from Kent. He went to LSE. I didn't get into LSE! ... We had a lovely lunch and we talked about business. What was very clear was that they had absolutely no need, and no interest, in trying to scrape every dollar. They made more than enough money from touring. Everything else was really incidental. We could continue to sell their catalogue, but that was all the income we were going to get."

Soon after that meeting with Hands – some claim the very same day – Jagger went to meet Universal Music and took the Stones' post-1971 catalogue (previously on Virgin) with him, effectively reuniting it with their pre-1971 catalogue (on Decca, owned by Universal) for the first time. In May 2010, a remastered reissue of their 1972 album *Exile On Main Street*, put out by Polydor within Universal, went to the top of the UK charts, giving the band their first UK number one album in sixteen years.[12]

Hands denies it was as simple as Jagger walking out of EMI and into Universal's willing arms. The band's deal, including their post-1971 catalogue, was subject to an auction among interested parties. "We had a final look and we could have won it if we wanted to," claims Hands. "We knew what we had to bid to win – and we couldn't afford it. It was just too much money. And I don't think you were going to get the money back ever. They weren't going to give us any share of their [other] rights. The Stones are an extraordinary band but you only earn so much from catalogue … So when we bid, we bid to lose. I decided that we could not afford to keep the Stones. They were just too expensive. So Universal bought them. If you had a successful music company, the Stones would be a great addition. But we weren't a successful music company; we were trying to recover and start to make money. They were just a luxury that we couldn't afford."

The start of Terra Firma's first calendar year ownership of EMI did not open well. Another major act was defecting; staff layoffs were going to cut the company by a third; the head of the company's digital operations was shown the door; and the most beloved executive working in the British music business was now gone.

It couldn't get any worse than that. Could it?

CHAPTER 7

EMI.com

When the complete numbers for recorded music sales globally for 2007 came in from the IFPI, they spelt out the full extent of the challenge now bearing down on record companies. The decline that began at the start of the millennium continued and the overall market was 8 per cent down from 2006, slipping to a value of $19.4 billion. Physical sales (primarily CDs) remained the bulk of the market ($15.8 billion), but they had dropped an unlucky 13 per cent over a twelve-month period. Digital revenue was growing, surging forward by 34 per cent, but with a value of $2.8 billion for the year, it only made up around 15 per cent of labels' revenues. A dual dynamic was defining the record business: first, the biggest part of its income was falling off a cliff; second, the only growth sector was utterly incapable of offsetting the losses from the sharp CD sales decline.

Digital really only started to appear on IFPI's sales numbers from 2004 onwards but it was a tiny sliver of the bar charts IFPI was producing that year. This was primarily down to the arrival of Apple's iTunes Music Store in the US in April 2003. But as iTunes gave with one hand (showing there was a market for paid downloads), it took with the other (allowing consumers to cherry-pick tracks from albums rather than having to pay for the whole album). Not only was the CD album market falling through the floor, the idea of even buying a full album was starting to look anachronistic.

This presented the record industry with a financial crisis. The album, since the late 1960s, had been its economic backbone and the CD reissue boom of the 1980s and 1990s had propelled it to new heights; but this proved a monetary *trompe-l'œil* as it was effectively an artificially inflated market that was always going to run out of steam. It also presented the record industry with an existential crisis. Albums were how artist contracts were measured out, so acts signed, for example, a six-album deal at the start of their career. If the album as a creative entity as well as a commercial product was looking endangered, where did that leave the record business and the rules and traditions it had clung to for the past half-century?

Going into its acquisition, Terra Firma knew that digital was the weakest part of the record business but also knew that digital was the only way to haul itself out of the hole it now found itself in.

As such, the first major digital initiative for EMI under new ownership was going to make a statement. It was going to be about the company regaining control of the means of distribution and retail that had been seized from it first by the arrival of online filesharing and then by the likes of iTunes. This was very much Guy Hands's pet project where he was going to show the other labels that EMI could rip up the rule book. He was also going to show the nascent legal digital services that he could play them at their own game and win.

In 2008, 'digital music' at scale really amounted to iTunes, which industry estimates at the time controlled 70 to 80 per cent of the legal download market, and MySpace, where anyone could upload their music and whip up industry and consumer interest. MySpace was in a period of accelerated growth when Terra Firma was starting to rebuild EMI, with Rupert Murdoch's News Corp having paid $580 million to buy it in July 2005 when it had 22 million users,[1] and by August 2006 it had already rocketed to 100 million[2] users. Its growth was going to continue for a while but by June 2009 it was losing ground and was being overtaken by Facebook at the biggest social network in the US.[3]

There was a lot of quixotic thinking at the time that these two services marked the death of the record label – Apple had seized the whip hand and was dictating terms to labels, while MySpace was the hottest A&R resource on the planet and could theoretically do away with the need for record labels entirely. Hands, having told staff that Radiohead's release strategy for *In Rainbows* in October 2007 was a wake-up call for the industry, was keen to be ahead of the next wave of disruption to come crashing down on the music industry and for EMI to be the one that wrote its own digital future.

In the background were the first rumblings of Spotify, which was in stealth mode, and YouTube, which launched in 2005 and was bought by Google in October 2006 for $1.65 billion.[4] Both, however, were for the music and tech aficionados and had not become the new centre of gravity for the music industry that they are today. The digital music business was still putting on its shoes and Hands felt EMI should try and hit a home run here when, just a few years earlier, PressPlay and MusicNet, which were backed by majors, had barely left the dugout before they tripped over their laces.

"It would have been the first real streaming [platform]," he says of what his vision was, wilfully overlooking other services already in the market. "It would have been early. It got huge resistance from the business. I wanted to go out and get agreements with the other labels to do a streaming service, effectively unlimited and pure subscription, in 2007. So you would have paid a subscription fee and you would have got music unlimited. I wanted to get other catalogues in there or to do it as a joint venture."

He says he was not concerned about the monopoly and collusion issues that shackled PressPlay and MusicNet, arguing that the arrival of Apple into the market had changed the centre of power so much that it permitted a label coming in with its own offering. Well, to an extent.

"The legal advice that we got was that because you had iTunes, and because we were effectively improving the consumer's position, we would be able to get through it," he says. "We certainly could have done it for catalogue. The issue was with regard to new music. The argument around new music was more around having to give access to the independents. So long as all labels could be on there and as long as we could redistribute the money, there was no reason why we couldn't have done it. All it would have done was give the music industry the ability to not have to deal with an intermediary. That's all it was. We had pretty good legal advice that it could work under those circumstances."

As this project was coming right from the top, it had to become a company priority. "Guy decided that was going to be the first easy win – a new website," says a source at Wrights Lane on Terra Firma's first big digital play. The project was going to be a consumer-facing one, branded as EMI.com – offering a music experience for users. Beyond this, however, sources disagree on what, exactly, it was going to be. Therein lay its first big problem: what it was going to be and what it was going to do were never fully defined from the off.

Incredibly, EMI did not own the EMI.com domain name which, in 2007, was taken as a sign of just how far behind the company was. It operated with the emimusic.com address and @emimusic.com format for emails, but another company had beaten it to the ownership of EMI.com and so a deal had to be struck for the music company to purchase the domain name and then start populating it.

Those working in digital at EMI during this period prior to the takeover had been playing catch-up, but were quick to do a series of deals when Barney Wragg joined at the end of 2006 to run digital operations globally for the company, notably the DRM-free deal with iTunes in April 2007. There was a feeling within Terra Firma that EMI was not moving fast enough here and was also doing a series of deals that were desperately lacking or simply never going to amount to anything. In contrast, the feeling within EMI was that Terra Firma was charging into digital with no vision and no strategy – so this could only end in disaster.

"What became clear to me by the end of 2007 was that Terra Firma were obsessed that digital was going to completely transform the business – but they really didn't have a clue what they were talking about," says a digital expert at the music company. "Suddenly they were wanting to second-guess all the decisions that we wanted to make. They wanted to reconsider things in a way that was very fragmented and slow again ... They were hiring people who they thought were digital experts but were coming out of online banking [meaning Mark Hodgkinson from Virgin Money] and not really related areas who had no media experience – people who knew nothing about digital media. For me it felt like I was hitting the buffers and concrete was being poured around us. I just didn't want to be in that environment."

One digital source, when the initial plans for EMI.com were outlined to them, thought it was dangerously flawed but also felt it was being railroaded through the company without the involvement of anyone senior on EMI's existing digital team. "That was the kind of thing that Terra Firma was talking about in late 2007, but I just looked at it and [sighs with exasperation]," they say. "They had these people coming in who had no experience in the media business or the record industry to see where the problems were within EMI and they were talking about applying a lot of research and development to that. What I found so frustrating was that nobody at Terra Firma wanted to have a conversation about it. They would lock themselves in rooms and decide these things on their own. That might have been fine if they had got it right and my opinion might have been wrong. But I looked at what they would be doing and I saw no merit in it."

They also felt making EMI.com a consumer destination was a waste of effort, resources and budget that really should have been used internally at EMI to ensure it was futureproofing itself for how digital would change it on a business-to-business and workflow level.

"One of the things that they did do that I thought was wrong was hiring a whole development team on the West Coast," they suggest. "They were fixated with building things – be it EMI.com or different apps. My view is that that isn't the role of a content business. The role of a record company is to service its artists as best as it can. That was a big distraction and I wouldn't have advised them to do that. There are things that you need to build – things like good asset-management systems and good data-recording systems. But consumer-facing platforms that are all built by one record company? We all tried that in the 1990s in the first dot.com boom and quickly realised that this is not what record companies do."

The same source claims that any attempts to persuade the new team being put in by Terra Firma to reconsider investing in this project or focus their energies on other things that needed to be fixed first were ignored or rebuffed. "Did I try and persuade them otherwise?" they say. "Yeah, but they were completely fixated on it. They wanted to invest more, develop more and do more stuff. We had got a business that was falling apart and we had problems with artist liaison. We had real problems with A&R. We had real problems with the actual business of being a record company. And they had armies of people wanting to build EMI.com? I just felt that they were fiddling while Rome burnt. It's just a lack of experience."

Consultant Shamsa Rana was brought into the company in summer 2007 to take charge of what eventually became EMI.com and also to advise on other digital opportunities that she spotted in a music market and a digital landscape that were both dramatically in flux. Her background was in digital consultancy, having previously worked at KPMG and online bank Egg before setting up her own company to work with private equity and venture capitalist companies on their digital strategies.

"When Terra Firma was looking to buy EMI, Guy reached out to me to do some initial due diligence," she says. "That was around the digital side of things in terms of where the future of music was headed. My due diligence was not on the company itself but around the future of music."

She says she was "obsessed" at the time with futurist Gerd Leonhard's 2005 theory of 'music like water'[5], which essentially argued that music would become a utility, much like water, gas and electricity in the home, and would be available everywhere for a monthly fee. Her first job for Terra Firma was doing an audit of emerging models in the digital world that Terra Firma should be aware of and possibly even look to acquire. She claims she put forward both music-recognition company Shazam and the nascent Twitter as possible acquisition targets for Terra Firma/EMI.

"The other part was around how EMI could position itself for the future," she says. "I advised Guy to focus around digital distribution. It was not to move everything from physical to digital but to focus around digital partners. To focus on online players who were distributing content – so focus on third-party partnerships. And to focus around potentially having a direct-to-consumer offering as well."

This is where the seeds of EMI.com were sown – just before Terra Firma took ownership of EMI – and Guy Hands wanted to put wheels in motion as soon as they got the keys for the company.

The company also did an audit of all the deals EMI had done with third-party services to try and figure out the shape of its digital footprint in both quantitative and qualitative terms. The results were not encouraging. "What we found was that they had been pretty much been deer in the headlights when the digital world exploded and they had basically entered into partnerships with everyone," says Rana. "There were quite a lot of unprofitable relationships. There was a lot of hand-holding going on with a lot of partners that wasn't really leading to any benefits … The vast number of deals that they had entered into were very unprofitable ones. The top ten relationships were responsible for driving about 80 per cent or 90 per cent of the revenue. Then there was a long tail of relationships that really made no sense."

Mark Hodgkinson was drafted in at this stage to shut down the huge number of unprofitable or unviable deals that had been signed by the company before Terra Firma came into the picture. In his stocktaking of these legacy deals, he concluded that over half of them were dead losses. "We looked at how many were ever going to survive beyond a year," he explains. "The industry had got hooked into [the thinking that] if they signed a deal and got an advance fee, as a PLC that was how you hit your quarterly targets. It was a constant cycle of, 'Let's sign up more of these people, get more advances, that all goes to the bottom line' … We analysed 5,000 [deals], worked out that only 2,000 of them stood any chance of making any money and, of that 2,000, only ten would be likely to make a significant impact on the business – and iTunes was one of them. Then we started to talk to the guys who were setting up Spotify and that was another emerging model."

He describes the Spotify negotiations as "fascinating" especially as the music business at the time was waking up to a new type of deal structure where a substantial advance and a high royalty rate (which, invariably, drove the nascent service to bankruptcy) could be swapped for an escalating royalty rate contingent on the growth of the service and, crucially, an equity stake in that service.

The thinking across the industry at the time was that, by having equity, they had a vested interest in the new service succeeding and reaching its exit strategy of selling to a bigger company or going through an IPO, at which point the equity could be cashed in. There was also the wider move to ensure that companies that built their name and their market size on music could not sell without their licensing partners receiving a substantial windfall. The sale of Last.fm to CBS for $280 million in May

2007[6] was held up at the time as a warning to music companies in their dealing with start-ups to get equity and get it early.

"A lot of what I was doing at that time was negotiating longer-term deals with some of the digital partners," explains Hodgkinson on how EMI was now going to work out deal terms with new entrants looking to use its music. "Some of them went through several days and nights. MySpace proved to not be the best use of my time! But we spent three solid days and nights negotiating that deal with them [Spotify]. We got that over the line with some equity. What we were trying to do was to shift from this very short-term attitude of services giving us cash and us ticking that box and if they fail in a year then so be it, to looking at how we could get to a point where, if they are more successful, then we are more successful [too]."

EMI.com, however, was going to be different as here the licensing partner was also going to be the 100 per cent owner. EMI would continue to license to what it deemed viable partners but it would also be taking its own start-up to market.

"Guy was a key driver behind EMI.com – and that's really important for you to know," says Rana. "He believed in it before anyone else did. The purpose of EMI.com was threefold. One was to really begin to build a relationship with consumers that focused around our artists and actually present to the world who our artists are. What you had was a fragmented world where artists had their own music websites or they were working with Apple or someone else. The quality of the offerings varied and there was a lack of consistency in what consumers were able to do, we wanted to provide more functionality to artists and consumers. The second element was to learn. It was to learn what was going on with regards to how people consume music, which artists they were interested in, the type of content they are interested in. The third element was around streaming of music. There was never any interest in providing people with another direct-to-consumer downloading world."

Avoiding downloading and going for streaming in 2007 was either a reckless move or an incredibly prescient one. Downloading was the only growth engine for recorded music at the time, and streaming, while it existed with services like Rhapsody and the fully legal incarnation of Napster, was an incredibly niche activity. It would take several more years – driven by Spotify's sharp growth as well as Apple's move into subscription with Apple Music in June 2015 – to go mainstream. EMI.com was intended as a very early effort to get the company a first-mover advantage when the consumption of digital music moved from an ownership-based model to an access-based one.

Except Spotify was able to explode as it had, barring the occasional superstar hold-out, by licensing 30 million-plus tracks from all the major labels and pretty much every independent that existed. EMI.com, in contrast, would initially only have music from EMI artists. And as the smallest major with a market share that barely made it into double-digit market share, it was already on the back foot.

Added to this, it was not going to be squeezed into any revenue model. There would be no subscriptions and the music would not be paid for by ads either. Unlike Spotify's 'freemium' strategy (a choice of the free tier with limited functionality and regular ads or the paid tier that had no ads and much richer functionality, including offline play on mobile), this would be completely unmonetised.

"It was not ad-supported; it was absolutely a free offering," says Rana. "It was very much to build relationships between artists and consumers. We only developed it for a desktop experience but it could have gravitated towards a mobile experience."

She adds that it was about EMI having a cohesive identity online and the end goal was less about earning money off every stream and more about gathering data on people's consumption patterns and using that to build a tighter and richer relationship with them that could be monetised elsewhere.

"It was a direct-to-consumer offering and we wanted the data in terms of how people engaged with the music [as well as] what they were most interested in in terms of different styles and different artists," she explains. "It was also an effort to really professionalise the websites that were available for different artists. Some of them were very good in terms of being able to stream music; but on the whole they weren't very coherent in terms of the information that you could get, the ability to stream music, the ability to look at pictures and all this other stuff."

Data, for Hands, was where it could really come into its own, envisaging it as a central hub for acts to plug all the other social sites and web properties into. "It would have been like Good Reads for music," he says. "You could discover new music, you should go and connect with the artists, it would be open source so you could put your own content on there. My view was that it could really transform music in terms of saving costs and getting A&R on it."

This was, some crowed, basically a 'me-too' version of MySpace – but four years after MySpace. It was, they felt, a digital gewgaw that exposed how woefully out of its depth Terra Firma was digitally.

"The great white elephant", is how one source who saw the different iterations of EMI.com described it. "They were going to turn it from a website into a D2C (direct-to-consumer) site and allow all of the music on the catalogue to be streamed there. It was not a bad idea – but just a bit too early and impossible to execute." In brief, they felt the underlying idea was solid, but that was all lost as the idea developed and more limbs were stitched onto it.

"I thought it was a good idea – if it was designed right," says the same source. "The fact that you could let the EMI catalogue be effectively sampled [by consumers], that was pretty forward thinking. But there were some wacky things around it. They wanted to build the celestial jukebox for the record industry. I asked what they were going to do about the other content. They said if someone searched for Beyoncé – as she was on Sony – they would have the tracks there but the user would have to be sent off somewhere else to hear them. I said, 'We've got a problem.' Did they not understand cross-licensing? No, they didn't understand pretty much anything."

Hands was confident that, when it was up and running, the other labels would be willing to strike a deal. Many, however, saw the name as a barrier here as Universal, Sony and Warner were not going to be happy to license music to a service branded in the name of a rival label.

"The name [EMI.com] was an irrelevance; the name was just what we were using," counters Hands. "It was like a working title. We needed to see if we could technologically do it. I didn't give a damn what the name was … You could have called it any name you wanted. We had one person who did try and think of all sorts of different names for it. You wanted something like music.com but that was already taken. I don't think we ever got to the point where the technology was good enough that we could have actually given the streaming service a name."

Sources claim that Hands was massively inspired by a pre-release BitTorrent tracker called OiNK, which emerged in 2004. It was an ever-evolving database of, in this case, unlicensed and shareable media files that sat on a variety of peer computers and facilitated the accessing of them by other users. It was eventually shut down in October 2007 as a major source of pre-release album leaks,[7] so it would have dominated industry headlines in Hands's opening weeks at EMI. "OiNK was the thing inspiring Guy at the time," says a well-positioned source. "He wanted to build an OiNK."

They argue that Hands's legal version of OiNK was symbolic of what was to follow – a good idea in essence, but one that was implemented poorly. "He wasn't that much of an idiot in terms of the strategy," they say. "He was spot on. He just couldn't execute it. That started with EMI.com which was a dog's breakfast of a project."

Many within EMI felt that, beyond any flaws they might have seen in the proposed functionality, the branding was the biggest problem.

No one outside of the company itself, they said, cared about the EMI name; so trying to get consumers to suddenly care about it was a fool's errand.

"If the brand has no resonance for the consumer and if the brand does not deliver a coherent proposition to music fans in general – and we are not featuring the biggest acts of the day if they are not signed to us – it will just not connect," says one source on the EMI digital team during this period.

One of their digital colleagues added, "EMI.com was very misguided as the label is not a brand [as far as the consumer is concerned]. It is the artists who are the brand."

Other executives at EMI felt that record labels in the twenty-first century could absolutely drive changes in society through art and the artists they signed, but the only companies that would drive changes in society through technology were Silicon Valley behemoths like Apple, Google and Amazon or emerging Scandinavian firms like Spotify.

"I think they thought they could force the pace," says one EMI executive of where they believe Terra Firma came unstuck with the EMI.com project. "When they came in they thought the record companies were missing a trick and they thought they could force the consumers into behaviours that the consumers themselves hadn't even understood. I think they had a belief that they could force all areas of the market in the same way. Despite the very granular dissection of various audience groups, they still didn't understand there was a whole host of people who would move only when they were ready."

Even Mark Hodgkinson, an executive brought in by Terra Firma, so not as knee-jerkingly critical as EMI employees could be, was unsure it would ever fly. "To be very straight with you, I was a bit sceptical about whether or not it would work," he says. "The problem with EMI.com was that you would only have a quarter of the music."

Despite all the negative feedback percolating through the EMI team, Rana forged on, with Guy's complete backing, with the project. This was partly because Hands saw it as an asset to be nurtured and, ultimately, sold for a considerable profit.

"I am convinced that if we had done it and we had done it cheap enough, we would have got ourselves enough members," he says of his quixotic ambitions for the platform. "And if we got enough members, we would have been able to sell it to someone like Google. I am absolutely convinced that it would have worked."

Silicon Valley comes to the record business

In April 2008, a major hire was to bring a whole new digital strategy to the company and EMI.com was to get trampled by the company's subsequent stampede in a different direction.

Douglas Merrill had come up through Google, joining in 2003 and becoming vice president of engineering before being appointed chief information officer there. He joined EMI on 28 April 2008 to lead all of its digital efforts globally, splitting his time between Los Angeles and London.

He came into the company to find the EMI.com project well under way but he was firmly of the belief that this was something that should be put out of its misery as quickly as possible. "I was very not-hands-on with it because I thought it was a terrible idea," he says of inheriting the EMI.com project. "We were taking time and money to solve a problem that wasn't a problem. Apple's iTunes was a perfectly good sales vector. What we didn't have was a way for people to discover new music; and we didn't have a way for people to engage with our artists and engage with our art. Building another store front was not going to change any of that. It was a project that was very important to Guy – so it was one to get done."

Hands says he was fully aware of his new digital head's objections to his pet project and understood how it was becoming a symbol of a philosophical divide within the company. "Douglas certainly wasn't a fan of EMI.com," he says. "I think the major reason he wasn't a fan of it was because he thought that we were trying to do something that other people could do better. But then you had within the organisation – and the music industry as a whole – a view that we owned the content and so we should be able to do this. There was a debate about if this should be done by the technologist, which is where you would say Douglas was, or if it should be done by the content owners."

Rather than suffocate it there and then, Merrill says he felt obliged to guide it to completion. But he was not planning on make it a core part of the initiatives he was going to implement thereafter within the company. "I am a good soldier and my boss told me to get it done," he says of why he, begrudgingly, worked on it. "So we got it done. I put two of my best guys on the project to finally shepherd it across the finish line to the response that we expected, which was 'Meh'. But we got it done. What I want to be clear on is that I thought it was a bad idea from the start. And I said so."

Rana quickly became aware that the project was going to splutter to a close as EMI had a new digital team and they would, naturally, want to define their own projects and not necessarily look kindly on the ones they were bequeathed.

It also became clear to her that, while Guy was effusive about it, many in the company were taking the opposite view and that the time for her to leave was imminent. "There was a lack of enthusiasm for the offering [EMI.com] within the business," she says. "The view was: why are we doing this? We found it a very hard sell."

She negotiated with Guy to fulfil her contract by taking EMI.com to launch and then exit the company. "I was very loyal to Guy," she says. "Guy had brought me in and he had wanted to deliver EMI.com. He had the vision for EMI.com before anyone else."

Looking back on it now, she feels it was never given the chance she believes it deserved. "It [EMI.com] was an under-utilised resource," she argues. "I thought it was an interesting platform that could have really repositioned EMI's relationship with consumers. I am not saying that it would have been ground-breaking. It was no Spotify, but it would have helped us to understand the consumer ... But I thought it was a real missed opportunity for the company ... I raise my hat to Guy as he was a real believer in EMI.com. He supported it and he was probably the key person who wanted to drive it forward. What the company did with it afterwards was up to the team that he put into place."

While Rana describes the project as being "bootstrapped" and says that it possibly cost under £500,000 to develop and build, others in the company regarded it as an unnecessary money pit, where good money was being thrown after bad. They made their opinions clear to the company's new head of digital. "I had so many fights with Douglas about EMI.com," says a senior source at EMI's head office who had sight of project costings. "He was pedantic and ridiculous about it. It was a spiralling budget – getting out of control. It was outrageous."

Merrill was undoubtedly happy to starve EMI.com of oxygen and that is what happened as soon as he came into the company in April. He had his sights on bigger projects, notably unplugging DRM across the board and finding a way for the company to both learn from and work with the filesharing and torrent sites the rest of the industry was trying to sue out of existence. EMI.com would be an ignoble footnote.

Changing the guard

In April 2008, while EMI.com was rumbling on, Stephen Alexander, MD at Terra Firma, was named executive vice president of EMI Music Catalogue, Compilations, Studios & Archives. The biggest changes, however, were to happen in America that month – the market that Terra Firma was yet to tackle head on.

Roger Ames had been put in charge of EMI's US operations in April 2007, soon after Eric Nicoli's sacking of Alain Levy and David Munns at the start of that year. Following the exit of Tony Wadsworth in January 2008, Ames had his role extended to become North American and UK labels president. It was a short-lived role, as by the end of April, it was announced he was leaving, but would continue to be an advisor to Guy Hands and Terra Firma.

There were lots of rumours that Ames and Hands clashed several times during their brief association and the belief was that Hands wanted to appoint, rather than inherit, his own head of the US. As Ames's departure was announced, it was also revealed that Nick Gatfield would be running the US for EMI. Gatfield, a former member of Dexys Midnight Runners in the 1980s, began his label-side career on leaving the band before rising through the industry to become president of Island Records in the UK, part of Universal Music Group, in 2001.

Poaching an executive from the biggest record company in the world was a significant coup for Guy Hands. "As well as developing some of today's most popular artists and music around the world, Nick Gatfield has also demonstrated his talents for embracing and delivering change," said the Terra Firma founder in a statement. "At Universal, he has led a complete turnaround in both creative and financial terms and built it into the most successful domestic repertoire label in the UK. The combination of Nick Gatfield and Douglas Merrill working together will enable EMI to reposition itself in new music."

A fervent Gatfield added, "My goal is to nurture the culture of creativity and change [at EMI], working in true partnership with the talented artists and A&R people. I am extremely excited about EMI's determination to embrace a new way of working with artists that recognises both the importance of the history of the labels but also the importance of new technologies."[8]

At the same time, EMI announced that the existing EMI Music management board would be replaced with two new boards: a chairman's board, which Hands would lead and which would be focused on long-term strategy; and an operating board, chaired by president and COO Chris Rolling, which would handle day-to-day issues. Buried right at the bottom of a *Music Week* story on the executive changes was the fact that the consultation period, which could see up to 2,000 people leave EMI, was still under way.[9]

At the annual Music Week Awards that same month, Tony Wadsworth was the recipient of The Strat – the night's concluding honour, given to someone who has made a long and lasting impact on the music business. Presenting him with the award, KT Tunstall revealed she called him the Thames Barrier when she first moved to London and ended up signed to EMI. "I didn't know how it works," she joked, "but I was glad that it was there."[10]

Wadsworth, on being handed the award, expressed what many of his former employees were increasingly thinking.

"It has been," he mused, "a funny old year."

CHAPTER 8

The Matrix is Everywhere

Something that soon became apparent to Terra Firma when it took over EMI and started to assess its working structure was that it was made up, in their eyes, of a series fiefdoms and power centres. These were defined by a sense of protectionism and, as such, Terra Firma felt the organisational dissonance prevented the company from moving in lockstep.

This was not just a dichotomy between recorded music and publishing – even within the label side, there were a series of subdivisions that sometimes pulled in the same direction but often pushed up against each other. It was nowhere near being on the same combative level that Lucian Grainge had introduced to Universal UK – where internal labels were encouraged to view each other as the competition as much as they viewed any of the labels at Warner, Sony BMG and EMI as the competition – but Terra Firma felt it was an unworkable system that was holding EMI back when it should be propelling it forward. A new command structure was needed, Guy Hands believed, and a matrix system was the solution.

"It always slightly amuses me: on the one hand, people say we didn't do enough; and on the other hand, it sounds like we did quite a lot!" says Hands, reflecting on the matrix system he and his team implemented. "Some of what we did with the matrix system was very standard to the industry. It was just that EMI hadn't done it."

The recorded music side of the company was already being divided up into three distinct business units, all focusing on different areas: there was frontline (signing and breaking new acts as well as building and maintaining existing signings); catalogue (covering inactive artists and anything that was now out of promotional cycle, which could mean anything older than eighteen to twenty-four months); and label services (the business-to-business side of the company, offering marketing and distribution as well as retail through a direct-to-consumer arm).

On top of this was to be layered the matrix system that created new lines of command in each market and also across regions. This was being sketched out at the end of 2007 and was seen by some EMI staff internally as the way Tony Wadsworth was to be manoeuvred out of his job as head of UK and Ireland for EMI's recorded music operations.

"The unfolding strategy they were coming up with was to do away with territorial and regional breakdowns so it was going to be a matrix," says one senior source privy to the restructuring plans as they were being plotted out and refined. "That is how he was able to fire Tony as they'd no longer have a head of the UK. They said, 'Our strategy, which is unfolding, is to not have territorial heads. Therefore, there won't be a head of the UK. So we will no longer need Tony.'"

Another senior source at Wrights Lane outlines, in theory, how this new model was going to work. "One of the things that Terra Firma did early on was to restructure the way that the company was run along three lines – frontline new signings, catalogue and what they called 'artist services' which included merchandise and all the other rights [associated with an artist]," they explain. "So you had these vertical reporting lines and horizontal reporting lines at the same time. So you still had the European structure, the UK structure and the global structure going one way and then cutting across that you had new music, catalogue and artist services. So you had heads of those three streams but also the heads of regions."

Hands says the economic imperatives of pursuing this strategy were obvious here and this was something EMI had to go through if it was going to not just survive in a dwindling recorded music market but to actually grow. "What we found was that we were losing money in most of the local markets," he says. "We were losing money for two reasons. One was that the local area was not getting support centrally. So if we had a really good band in Holland that could be an international band, because it was in Holland it didn't get support. Two, the local offices would sign bands when they have absolutely no chance of ever doing anything and they were signing too many. You had a double whammy."

The problem, as he saw it, was that, as EMI was headquartered in the UK, many of the international markets were not getting the focus, attention, investment, resources and support they needed.

"The central area didn't care about them and they were losing money because they were just trying to do too much," he argues. "We had to solve two problems. One problem was that we had to make the centre have some responsibility for them so they cared. The second was that we had to make them actually have some discipline around it. So bringing it in meant that if we signed an artist it would not just be the local office's responsibility; it would also be the central office's responsibility. We would also have sign-off on the artists being signed. It also, frankly, meant that we didn't need to have quite a lot of senior people in the regions just doing administration and management."

On paper, this made a lot of sense, but when it came to implementation, that is where the flaws and obstacles became apparent. "It created this enormous confusion because it became unclear who was actually really responsible for decision making," says the same Wrights Lane source. "Was it the regional head or was it the head of new music? Who was driving catalogue? Was it the local MD or was it the head of catalogue? You had everybody suddenly treading on each other's toes because you had this new matrix which cut through the way the company had traditionally been organised and reported into."

While intending to break apart the fiefdoms in the company and thereby end the squabbling and power plays between them, it soon became apparent that Terra Firma had created a whole new series of headaches and hurdles for itself.

Beyond the internecine politics, there were clear economic reasons for trying to rebuild the structure of EMI from the ground up. Joining EMI as a non-executive chairman at the start of 2009 while this rebuilding of EMI – or the switching-out of engines mid-flight, depending on what side of the divide one speaks to – was going on, former ITV chief executive Charles Allen explains the rationale of the system that predates his arrival but that he was to eventually inherit.

"There was a lot of duplication in overheads so there was no need to invest more," he says. "But to do that, you had to take away every label having its own infrastructure. We created a back office infrastructure which serviced all of that ... This is when they put in the matrix structure. You had people like Ernesto [Schmitt, president of catalogue] driving the digital plan; you had the operational teams looking at things differently. Caryn [Tomlinson, senior vice president of artist relations] and I were doing a lot of work with the talent. We were in the papers a lot because of the legal situation with Citi[group], so we spent a lot of time with the talent personally to calm that down."

He denies that it was as Byzantine and counterproductive as its critics claim, believing it brought a more transparent reporting system to a company that was previously only united in its discord. "People were wondering how [the matrix structure] could work," he says. "Practically, we had to get the senior team – so David [Kassler], Ernesto and all the regional people – working much more closely together. It was a two-key system that asked what we were going to do and how we were going to do it."

David Kassler was clear on where he saw the problems with the old system – in terms of both budgets and power centres – and why a matrix system would make EMI much more efficient and effective. "I think it was run as a cottage industry," he says of the fundamental flaw dragging down the pre-Terra Firma EMI. "Every label was resourced as if it was a full-scale national enterprise. It would have its own sales team, its own marketing team, its own digital team, its own back-up admin, its own lawyers, its own finance people, its own A&Rs. I, and Terra Firma, didn't think that model was scalable. It was about sharing best practice and sharing resources across labels. The label ultimately became an A&R hub with some marketing support within the label. But if you have the best digital marketing people in the UK, you want to share them across labels."

He says some would see this as centralisation but he would prefer to regard it as resource sharing. "It's a hub-and-spoke model where the labels are all spokes and they effectively feed into a central hub where you have the best people that you can recruit in the industry," he explains. "Across all the markets there was a general cleaning-up needed … People had got out of practice of having sensible budgets that covered sensible reporting, normal accounting practices and financial controls."

At the heart of it all were some hard existential questions that the record business was having to ask itself in a period of digital turmoil sparking off against digital opportunity. Consumers' preferences were changing dramatically while the economics of the old business were collapsing like a house in a Buster Keaton routine. Kassler outlines the big questions everyone in the company was having to ask themselves in 2007 and 2008: "What is the role of a label? What is the role of a country? And what is the role of a region?"

For the music business, change was no longer a luxury. Change was a necessity.

An EMI executive felt that this new matrix system was being dreamed up by people who had never worked in any division of the arts, let alone music, and so it was always going to be a case of applying paint rollers to something that required precision brushwork. They felt they had to intervene before too much damage was done.

"You saw these people coming from industries that couldn't be more remote from the creative world, tuning up and imposing their presence in meetings, imposing their words in meetings, imposing their views in meetings," they say. "I was thinking, 'This is interesting. I am going to have to talk to them one by one and just realign them to the position that I believe they should be in in terms of their behaviour.' Which I did. After a few weeks, it was completely squared. But I had some very serious one-to-one conversations. I mean serious. No joke. No prisoners. One to one. I warned them all. After a few weeks, I was left alone. With some of them, it was very confrontational."

They argue they were not obstinate for the sake of it but felt that ripping out experienced music executives from the company at the same time as pushing it through a massive structural reconfiguration was a case of going in too hard and too heavy from the off. "Some of their ideas and thinking were not bad, to be honest with you," they accept. "Let's recognise that. They had some good people who came with good ideas, but Guy managed to fire executives and hire executors ... When you take the meat off the bone, the muscle and everything, what's left in the end? It's just a bone. There is nothing to eat and there is no strength to it. It's finished!"

Long-time executive Bob Mercer, who rose to prominence in EMI during the 1970s, said he regarded the matrix model as utterly "unworkable" and even when Terra Firma executives explained it to him by breaking it down to its component parts he was left nonplussed. "That has my bullshit buzzer going overtime,"[1] the exasperated executive told them.

The matrix system that was eventually implemented was not as extreme as it could have been, with one senior source at EMI's head office claiming that it could have seen the entire top structure in every regional office removed. "There was an idea to fire all of the MDs around the world and put this matrix system in place – so there were going to be no MDs," they say. "It was J.-F. [Cecillon]'s idea to keep the MDs but give them one of the matrix positions – which was usually head of new music. They had a head of new music, a head of catalogue and a head of music services. Guy wanted that matrix system and to fire all of the MDs."

Hands felt there was incredible financial waste happening here and that reducing the headcount in smaller offices and changing the reporting structure was going to make less actually go a longer way. "You'd have a manager for the office who is also responsible for the country as the country head and they are probably paid £200,000," he says. "But what are they doing? They are managing one A&R person, one secretary and two people who go to concerts."

In his mind, the matrix system was going to have a tripartite transformative impact. "One was that it saved costs; two, it imposed discipline; and three, it meant that if we did have opportunities in these countries with really good artists, they would get proper focus," he says. "I think we did a very good job on the first two, but it is very difficult on the third. How many bands from Denmark become international bands? Sweden is an exception. My view was that we should be able to spot that."

This was, at the planning stage, going to be a complete inversion of how EMI – and, indeed, other international record companies – were run. "Historically, the regional heads had run the business, but what Guy wanted to do was to flip it on its head and have the heads of the matrices run it," says a key source before adding there was strenuous internal resistance to a structural change as pronounced as this. "We said that someone had to be in charge. The MD is usually the person who is closest to the artists – so you can't fire them. The compromise was that the MDs mostly became the heads of new music – so each territory had a head of new music, a head of catalogue and a head of music services. And the MD, depending on their background, who is usually the head of new music. That is what J.-F. managed to negotiate with Guy before he left [in July 2008]."

The same source thought this radical change was utterly unworkable and feels EMI would have suffered badly if it were implemented as originally intended. "You don't fire the MD because they are generally the best guy we have in each market. It was a ridiculous idea. And it got worse later on."

May 2008 saw a dramatic reshuffling of the UK team as part of the matrix structure. Miles Leonard was made president A&R at Parlophone (he was previously MD) while Ferdy Unger-Hamilton became president A&R at Virgin. For the latter, it was short-lived as he left the company almost immediately afterwards. It was announced around the same time that Mark Collen (EMI Music UK's senior vice president) and Terry Felgate (MD of EMI Records) would be moved to unspecified new positions, but they both, like Unger-Hamilton, left the building soon after.

Mike McMahon (EMI senior vice president, commercial) also exited at this time, being replaced by Matthew Crosswaite. Mark Terry was shifted from being GM of Virgin Records to the newly created role of marketing senior vice president for EMI Music UK & Ireland. Meanwhile, Mike Allen (EMI Music's international marketing senior vice president) was also leaving. This was a rapid-fire change at the executive level in the UK and left no one in any doubt that Terra Firma's plans for the company were extreme and they were going to be pushed through.

A common criticism at this time was that Terra Firma was parachuting in people from outside of the music industry and putting its own staff to work in the company, defenestrating the old guard of music executives. But it did also bring in people with music industry experience, in part to replace some of the long-serving executives who left or were pushed out during this first year of upheaval.

Nick Gatfield had joined from Island Records in April 2008 but the year before, Terra Firma had brought in Billy Mann as a creative advisor.

The American songwriter and producer had written for acts such as Celine Dion, P!nk, Backstreet Boys, Robyn, Joss Stone and Kelly Rowland. By the end of 2007, he had been promoted to chief creative officer at EMI.

He suggests that Terra Firma was prescient in its restructuring of EMI, implementing ideas and systems that are now common practice in the record business. "I feel that the basic fundamentals that Terra Firma put into place are in many respects now what the major companies are doing," he says. "They have all done the separation of catalogue and new music. They have all not just looked to centralise but also to isolate physical distribution ... Key was the separation of catalogue from new music – which is a very difficult pill for anybody to swallow. You can make a lot more mistakes if you know the catalogue sales of those legacy Queen albums will gloss over the projects that you signed but that didn't work. Now all the companies have done this."

He primarily dealt with the regional offices of EMI and the MDs there, helping them to work on their signing and developing of new artists, but he felt they were at the mercy of purse-tightening that ultimately pushed EMI into a fallow A&R period in 2008 and 2009.

"The bulk of resources that was spent on A&R were really focused towards the US and the UK repertoire and Nick [Gatfield] really got the lion's share of those resources," he says. "That made sense because you're talking about two of the biggest markets in the world. Unfortunately, they didn't really hit anything through in repertoire that pre-existed Terra Firma – like Katy Perry and Coldplay. That left not as much investment money available for new music in the international territories, who really had to fend for themselves."

This all caused issues in the regional offices of EMI as they felt they were being starved of both budget and power. "They felt disheartened and disenfranchised by the changes because it was very centralised," he says. "All of a sudden everything was UK focused and US focused under Nick Gatfield's leadership at the time."

Mann, however, was able to fight the corner of some of the European offices and get sign-off on particular projects. He says that when Simone Bosé, head of EMI Music in Spain, was looking to sign and develop Pablo Alborán in 2009 there were issues related to the deal and budget, which had to be approved in London first. Mann's advice was that everything should be thrown at the singer to break him. This was all the more pronounced given Spain was one of the most ravaged recorded music markets in Europe due to piracy and the impact of digital (slumping from a trade value of $429.6 million in 2005 to $245.9 million in 2009, according to IFPI). "Take all the marketing money and just triple down on this guy!" Mann told Bosé, advising him to pour 80 per cent of the company's marketing budget that year into Alborán.

EMI Spain were also moving into promoting concerts, so if they broke a recording act they could also benefit from their touring. This is something, Mann argues, that all the other majors are doing today.

Mann also says he managed to get EMI to treat French DJ and producer David Guetta as a global priority during this time. Guetta was signed to Virgin and his first three albums between 2002 and 2007 were building his profile in Europe, but doing little outside of the region. A single released in April 2009 was, however, to help break him internationally.

"I met David in a taxi going to a Coldplay concert and he played me 'When Love Takes Over'," he recalls. "I said, 'This song is a smash and we're going to go for it.'" There was, due to the matrix system governing A&R and marketing spend, initial resistance. "The line I got back from the finance department was, 'Why should we invest in an artist who is over 40 and who neither sings nor dances?'" he says. "David of course went on to be one of the biggest new artists on EMI during that entire time." The album the track came from, *One Love*, gave Guetta his first number one in his home country and made it into the top 100 in the UK. The album after that, *Nothing But The Beat* in 2011, was an international number one and got to number five in the US, turning Guetta into a superstar act in the exploding EDM (Electronic Dance Music) market there.

Mann may have been seen as someone fighting the corner of the European divisions of EMI, but those back in London were far from impressed. "I remember Billy Mann coming in," sniffs one UK executive. "Billy Mann is a B-list songwriter. I always used to joke that he's the man you hire when you've got too many hits on a record and you want some album tracks."

The matrix system was going to struggle to end the long-standing snobbery and superiority endemic among some in London who were convinced they were the real drivers of creativity in the company and that Europe was, in terms of international acts, a busted flush.

Uli Mücke was in charge of frontline for EMI GSA (Germany, Switzerland and Austria) during this period and explains how all the changes being imposed from London impacted on the regional offices.

"When Terra Firma came in, the whole structure and organisation of the company worldwide was affected by this takeover so dramatically and everything changed," he says. "At the time, I had three bosses. Billy Mann was one of them in terms of the A&R business; Bart Cools was my boss for marketing; and the German CEO Wolfgang Hanebrink was in charge of the local company. I had three bosses and, of course, that was a kind of terror; but this is something you can observe in a lot of matrix organisations today."

Domestic signings were struggling to break in GSA at the time, with Mücke saying that to classify as breaking in Germany, acts had to sell at least 100,000 albums. Schlager (a Teutonic twist on easy listening) singer Helene Fischer was EMI Germany's biggest act during this time and the company also managed to have success with Sunrise Avenue, a rock band from Finland that were signed locally in Germany, in 2006 and 2007. Against this uphill struggle with domestic A&R, EMI was using Germany as a test market for new types of deals that went far beyond acts' recorded rights.

"Billy was trying to move away from the typical industry thinking and the typical industrial philosophy," explains Mücke. "He wanted to bring more input into artists' careers — trying to give them the support everywhere they needed it. It was not just asking for 360 deals or rights participation. It was about starting to think more like an artist manager so that you really supported the artists in all the different parts of their activities and, in the end, their revenues and, therefore, [you] could ask for a share of the different revenue streams. Some countries followed that very closely – such as Spain."

A restructuring was already happening in the German-speaking markets before Terra Firma took over, seen most obviously in the centralisation of EMI GSA but also in the closing of local pressing plants and the subsequent outsourcing of CD production. As such, when Terra Firma introduced its redundancy programme, GSA saw its staff headcount only shrunk by about 15 per cent, bringing employee numbers from around 200 to 170. These were significantly less swingeing cuts compared to the UK and other European markets.

Mücke argues, however, that A&R budgets were dramatically scaled back at this time at EMI GSA so the company had to really punch above its weight.

"What I had as a yearly A&R budget at hand to sign artists and to invest into production was really tiny," he says. "Why? Because Germany had those very profitable artists where, for the GSA company, they were pure cash cows. Probably after the UK, Germany was the most profitable company [in Europe]. We had profit rates at that time that nobody could have imagined. I remember a very famous executive at that time asking me, 'Wow – what is that margin like in your domestic P&L? Are you not investing into artists?' After looking at those numbers, he immediately understood that the spending on new talent was tiny – otherwise we would never deliver such an enormous margin on the frontline label business."

There were severe roster cuts happening in mainland Europe during the first two years of Terra Firma's ownership of EMI, aggressively weeding out unprofitable acts and cutting their losses rather than doubling down on them to spur them into the black. They also had to operate with one or two A&R managers per territory while the UK had over twenty in London alone. The added complication of the matrix system bearing down on talent-spotting and artist development was that anything signed in any of the European offices had to be approved by London first. That, of course, included signings in the UK.

Hands describes a hypothetical situation to illustrate how it was all intended to work. "Let's take a silly one," he proposes. "Let's say an A&R wanted to give an artist £12 million or whatever it was they wanted. What we had discovered was that A&R would do that with Eric Nicoli's sign-off. I said that I was not signing off on anything unless finance had signed off on it. So they would have to go to finance to get finance to do an economic modelling of whether or not we were going to make money. The finance and A&R [executives] would come to the management committee … Obviously I have to take responsibility because I am CEO, but I'm not going to make the decision unless I have had advice on it."

Hands says this was simply taking the risk-assessment logic of the venture capital world and overlaying it onto the music industry that had, until that point, romanticised the 'golden ears' of A&Rs over and above the building of a robust business case for signing – or not signing – an act.

"Every time that I consider a deal, I have twenty or thirty people who then go and look at the deal and see if they think it is actually going to work," he says of how Terra Firma itself is run. "Lots of people test it."

He also offers an example of how it could have warded off costly mistakes in EMI's recent past. "Robbie Williams got paid an enormous amount of money, released *Rudebox* [in 2006] and it was a disaster," he claims. "And they spent a fortune advertising it. What they should have done under my system is that the A&R said, 'This is *Rudebox*. We want to spend X million.' Finance says it wants to know what marketing thinks, what sales thinks, what distribution thinks and what A&R thinks. Once they got all of that, they will produce a report which then goes to me and the management team – and the management team then votes and says yes or no … People say this is a matrix system, but to me it is just common sense. And then you don't have problems like *Rudebox*."

These are, of course, hypotheticals where it is relatively easy to say that X would lead to Y which would lead to Z long after the fact, but the actuality can be markedly different. As such, those under the cosh of the matrix system felt it did not go as smoothly as in Hands's idealised conjecturing.

"For me personally, that was a very bad side of the entire experience," says one head of a continental Europe office. "Whenever I had the situation of signing new artists, it always went through a special committee in the UK ... [the decision] whether you sign an artist or not was not being made in my market. It was being made in the UK. That was a pretty strong centralisation strategy from Terra Firma who created those communities because they saw everywhere they looked in the different territories what kind of crappy business A&R people were doing at that time. They sometimes signed crazy deals and they lost so much money."

This was also where Terra Firma was treating market research and audience analysis as gates through which A&R had to pass before giving the green light to a signing. "You always had this controversy where they said, 'Why don't you research it first before you sign it?'" explains the same regional head. "This was always going to be like *The Clash of the Titans*. That was years of an ongoing argument between the global people at Terra Firma in the UK and the territories. It was always the same."

They knew that the old days of signing ten acts and hoping the one successful act would pay for the losses of the other nine were long gone. In their place came analytics and spreadsheets.

"Terra Firma created those committees and they engaged themselves in these decision-making processes in those territories," they explain. "I understood that – but as the guy in charge of signing or dropping artists, it was a pain in the ass because I couldn't do my job. I couldn't do this without always following the UK. As you can imagine, this was not the best situation. When you are talking to artists or managers, you could never tell them your decision because you had to double check everything with the UK."

Begrudgingly, however, they say this worked in making EMI more efficient than it had been in living memory. "What came out of that strategy and that strong regulation was probably the most efficient record company of all time," they claim. "Worldwide, the numbers that EMI made at that time and the profit rates [that were] generated were enormous. It was a huge change compared to the time before."

The problem, however, was that this was suffocating domestic A&R and merely turning the European offices into the sales and marketing arms of the UK and the US. Tasked with lowering spend and exceeding targets, pushing international repertoire at the expense of local repertoire became the path of least resistance.

"I had more successes on my roster with the international stuff," says a European executive. "We were very strong with that. With international repertoire, I didn't have origination costs and I didn't have to take care of the production or the videos or anything. I always had a very good profit on those international projects."

Marco Alboni was head of pop/frontline division at Capitol Music Group/EMI in Italy when Terra Firma took charge of EMI and says that piracy in the country was out of control – not just online but also in a major black market in counterfeit CDs and cassettes. The numbers around the decline are stark. According to IFPI figures, the trade value of recorded music sales in Italy collapsed from $504.9 million in 2005 to $252 million in 2009.

Against the odds, Alboni claims the company in Italy managed to hang on. "It was a challenging time and sometimes it was very difficult, but the experience I went through was very motivational for me and for the team," he says. "We really managed to re-motivate the team. We managed to retain the artists. We also managed to extend some of our contracts with the local artists to include additional rights. That, at the time, was very pioneering."

Terra Firma's restructuring plan for Italy was decided at the start of 2008 but could not be implemented immediately due to having to agree terms with the unions representing the staff. This was a delicate issue as it was EMI Italy's second major restructuring in two years.

There was also a knock-on effect on A&R and EMI found itself seriously compromised in trying to sign local acts and hold onto those nearing the end of their contracts, with rival labels able to move faster and also outbid them.

"It was challenging for us to sign new artists because the competition was really tough," says Alboni. "The terms that they were offering were much more attractive for artists than the ones that we were offering. The overall view from top to bottom was that we were not really after market share growth but we were being a consumer-led company offering a lot of different services to the consumer to connect with artists ... To sign new artists was achievable, but in terms of competing with the other labels to sign established artists who were coming to the end of their contracts with us, that was extremely difficult. None of them were considering us as a company with the necessarily stability that they were looking for to commit to a contract for three, four of five albums. That was a real struggle."

The focus was about trying to hold onto existing acts and do so under new deal terms where the label got a share of other revenue streams and used that to push any losses on record sales into net profitability when all income sources were accounted for. "What I was really focusing on was renewing the contracts with the big artists who were already on EMI and to retain them. It was also about expanding the rights basis of the contracts – so that we could make more with them rather than less with them," he says.

"We got the merchandise [rights] from one of the biggest local stars, Vasco Rossi," says Alboni by way of example. "[Previously] it was a very traditional contract and then we stepped in and I managed to close a deal to sell his merchandise rights on tour and via traditional retailers. That was a big step for the company."

A quirk in Italian tax laws, however, was able to work in the label's favour and was also used to convince two of EMI's biggest catalogue artists to make certain concessions in terms of retail expectations in the country. A large percentage of catalogue sales in Italy went through kiosks but some major acts had insisted their records could not be sold this way. In a rapidly declining legal market, however, this was about to gradually change – although for the biggest acts it was to prove just too late for Terra Firma.

"This is peculiar to Italy and Spain and is down to VAT reasons," explains Alboni. "If you sell CDs with recordings at the news stand together with a publication – like a magazine or a daily newspaper – the VAT was 4 per cent at the time. If you sell a CD now, the VAT is 22 per cent, but at the time it was 20 per cent. That is one of the reasons why the kiosk business is big here … At the time, I managed to have all the local artists sold at the kiosks which was something that before this wasn't happening. That constituted a huge and solid revenue line with a very important margin. With our colleagues at EMI we also managed for the first time to sell The Beatles and Pink Floyd at the kiosks from 2011."

With planned redundancies across EMI globally running upwards of 2,000 people in 2008, the matrix system was not just about making the company operate more efficiently – it was about doing so with considerably fewer staff.

"When they started to put structures in, it became clear they didn't know what they were doing," says a head-office executive who watched the roll-out happening with mounting incredulity. "They put it in the matrix structure and they were getting rid of swarms of people. At Wrights Lane, there were two or three floors that were completely empty – and they were doing that to start to move the Brook Green people in [in early 2009]."

One of the quickest ways to get the global headcount down was to close entire regions, which Terra Firma did with impunity. While Europe and the UK were being pared down to the bone, EMI was retreating from entire markets.

"When Guy Hands bought EMI, he made a speech where he said he was going to cut staffing by X, costs by Y and overheads by Z," says a senior source who witnessed this happening at close quarters. "When he came in, the only way to do that would have been to close down whole regions."

* * *

First to be amputated was a large part of EMI's Asian operations. "We had issues in Asia," is how Hands justified the dramatic reduction to EMI's global footprint. "Europe was quite simple; we owned it and we had control. There were all sorts of very strange deals that had been done in Asia. We worked out that if it worked then we didn't make any money and if it failed then we picked up all the costs. So it was a question of closing everything down, selling what we could and then going back in clean."

In August 2008, EMI sold its interests in China, Taiwan and Hong Kong to Typhoon, its joint venture partner in China. The joint venture was due to laws in China that only allowed international companies as part of an arrangement with a Chinese company in which the foreign company could hold no more than 49 per cent.

"The relationship that we had with China and our joint venture partner there, as well as our joint venture partner in Taiwan, was a mess," proposes Hands. "We had to clean it up. We didn't have any choice. We felt that the relationship that we had meant that we were better off focusing on other markets. It didn't mean that we wouldn't come back into that relationship or that market later. The structure economically and in terms of control [was an issue]."

Typhoon was run by Norman Cheng, former head of EMI Music Asia, and he bought out EMI's stake in Typhoon in China, the Gold Label in Hong Kong and EMI Music Taiwan for 100 million Hong Kong dollars.[2]

"They had closed the regional office in Hong Kong pretty much as there were about three people left there," says a well-placed source. "They were dismantling the companies. In the case of markets where we had some local repertoire, like Indonesia, they tried to sell them. The Philippines also."

EMI Japan – fully owned by EMI after they bought out Toshiba's 45 per cent stake in 2006, when the board scrambled to try and save the doomed Permira deal – was granted a stay of execution, albeit with an executive reshuffle. However, EMI Japan was looked at again just two years later and came close to being sold off.

"There was a period of about a year where EMI was working with JP Morgan to try and sell the Japanese company to Universal," reveals a senior source. "This was around 2010. Eventually, for whatever reason, it didn't come to anything. They made an offer, Guy didn't accept it so it stayed as it was."

Latin America had been in a perilous state since 2006 after a major accounting fraud was discovered at EMI Brazil,[3] but Terra Firma ultimately felt that overall the region was a more immediately worthwhile investment than much of Asia.

The US, which had long been the leak in EMI's hull, was also briefly considered to be put up for auction rather than a protracted and painful rebuilding. "At some stage, the Terra Firma guys would have thrown about ideas about closing America completely and just licensing it out to another major," says a source.

Hands confirms this. "If we had had more money, and we had not been fighting for survival, and if Citigroup and us had been united, we would have tried to do something in America," he says. "We had a number of different alternatives. The one that, in some ways, made the most sense was to do some form of merger so that we could try and save a lot of the costs that we had and concentrate more on the A&R side. The value-add would have been in having the right A&R people. We were very good in country and crossover and very, very good in gospel. In urban music we were just a joke."

One mooted idea here was to find a way to work with Warner Music Group. It was not going to be a merger, more a conditional collaboration that would have improved EMI's standing in the US and Warner's standing in Europe – but done in a way that would not have had the regulators in the European Commission and antitrust authorities in the US swiftly erecting roadblocks.

"In a situation where we had the strength, not the weakness, we had a debt package that worked and the timing had been different, the deal clearly to do would have been for us to have taken over distribution, sales and marketing for them in Europe on a licensed basis and for them to take over distribution, sales and marketing for us in the US," explains Hands.

It went beyond the conceptual, with Hands revealing that he discussed initial ideas with Warner head, Edgar Bronfman Jr. "But we were never in a position where we could do something," he says. "We were just too weak economically. We had a debt package with Citigroup that was huge and we couldn't agree a way to deal with that. Without getting an agreement on that, we couldn't ever really consummate any deal with anyone."

While EMI's recorded music division was being melted down and poured into whole new – and smaller – moulds, EMI Music Publishing was left untouched. Right from the initial bidding, Guy Hands knew that publishing was the safest part of the purchase. It was the world's leading music publisher and immensely profitable. It would have been reckless to try and tinker with that winning formula. Those in recorded music looked on enviously as publishing was allowed to carry on as normal.

Roger Faxon, as head of EMI Music Publishing, was highly protective of the division and had taken steps to ensure that it was left out of the dramatic restructuring programme tearing through its sister organisation. This was, in a very large part, because Faxon was already implementing his own overhaul of the business and was able to convince Hands to leave him to it.

"We presented a business plan that showed how we were going to restructure the business – what we had done and what we were in the process of doing," he says. "We had the evidence that it was actually driving additional revenue, reducing the costs and increasing the margins. Everything that they could have said we should be doing, we were already doing. And that was not true on the record side. Not true at all. There was a requirement in the loan agreement that a certain amount of the debt be allocated between the record company and the publishing company. Because the record company's EBITDA [Earnings Before Interest, Taxes, Depreciation and Amortisation] was so low that it could not meet its covenants from day one, they shifted as much of the debt onto the publishing business. It was an astounding number – 11.8 times EBITDA."

This walling-off of EMI Publishing dates back to Faxon's replacement of Marty Bandier as the head of the publishing arm in 2006 where he was able to negotiate with Eric Nicoli to be granted substantial sovereignty. "Frankly, I had seen the messiness of the record business and the way in which that worked and I wanted to have a lot of autonomy," he says. "I had that in my contract. When Guy came in, the first thing he wanted to do was to give me a new contract – which would take all of that away. Basically, I told him no. Guy is not good with people telling him no. But I was down his list in terms of things that he had to get done."

Just as Terra Firma were moving into EMI's offices in London in September 2007, EMI Music Publishing was moving its headquarters in New York, relocating from Midtown to the Meatpacking District.[4] This came with considerable cost savings, something that landed well with Guy Hands when he saw the details of it all. It was far from a given that Faxon and his team would be totally immune from change and the budgetary scalpel, but the costs-to-profit ratio it was delivering on was the best armour it had.

"I was concerned about the possibility of not being left alone," Faxon admits. "I never was worried that they would come into the publishing business and try and do something – like fire me. Other than when I told him I wasn't changing my contract, there was a possibility [then] that he might fire me. Even though I had lots of autonomy, there was a lot of effort to intervene in the business but we absolutely resisted it and we didn't feel we were going to lose that game. We were going to win. We were delivering. And the other part of the business [recorded music] was not delivering. Therefore, they did not need to spend the time on us."

Coldplay deliver the blockbuster everyone needed

The biggest album under Terra Firma's watch to date came during the middle of this massive structural cataclysm and it was, thankfully for Hands and his team, a success straight out of the gates. Released on 17 June 2008, there was a lot riding on *Viva La Vida*, Coldplay's fourth album. Lead single 'Violet Hill' was offered as a free download from the band's official site from 29 April for a week.[5] At a time when there was much industry bellyaching about free music online, this was a clear statement that the new owners of EMI were prepared to make big and bold statements by swimming against the tide.

They also ceded some control to the band's manager, David Holmes, as part of an effort to get one of the biggest acts on their books to embrace the changes they were pushing through. "David Holmes," wrote Brian Southall in his history of EMI, "realizing the importance to EMI of his act's new release, had shrewdly done a deal with Hands that gave him control over the campaign and – more importantly – the marketing spend."[6]

Towards the end of May, the band also appeared in a major iPod and iTunes ad in the US performing the album's title track, a huge coup for EMI and a powerful marketing set-up for the album's release a matter of weeks later. It was a massive international hit, going straight to number one in the US, the UK, Japan, Australia, Canada, France and Germany. It was precisely the kind of blockbuster Terra Firma needed and, unlike the release of *X&Y* in 2005, whose late delivery from the band to Parlophone was partly blamed for an EMI profit warning, this album was intentionally delayed by the label.

Incredibly, Hands had insisted on that delay as he felt the album was not quite ready. "One of the stories that probably no one will tell you was that when I got the first version from Coldplay of *Viva La Vida*, we delayed it by six months," he says. "I listened to it and it didn't make one's feet tap. That's the best way of saying it. I know nothing about music but I phoned the A&R guy up – I think it was Miles [Leonard]. I spoke to whoever I spoke to and they said, 'You need a record now, don't you?' I said, 'Is this the best that we can get?' They said, 'It's the best we can do now.' I said, 'If you were given six more months, could you do a better album?' They said, 'Yes.' So I said, 'Fine. If I tell you that you don't need to do it for six months, what would you choose?' They said, 'I wouldn't do it. I'd spend some more time on it.' I said, 'Fine. You've got more time.'"

This may sound like extreme bloviating, but other sources close to the band at the time confirm this played out exactly as Hands says it did.

Hands claims the extension drastically improved the album and, he feels, helped propel its global sales. "What they had with me for a year was somebody who was willing to make decisions which were in the best interests of the company and the best interests of the business," he says of his time as CEO. "And someone who was happy to be different in doing that and wasn't going to run it on the basis of what we had to do to hit profits. We were going to do what's best. That is the situation where I basically chose to do something completely different. I am convinced the guy on the end of the phone was completely shocked."

He was unconcerned about pushing back the company's biggest new album that year – even if it did mean it was effectively postponing critical revenue coming into EMI to help meet Terra Firma's debt commitments. "I was fighting with Citigroup about a lot of things," states Hands. "Delaying the Coldplay album until Coldplay were ready to release it was going to be the least of my problems, frankly."

* * *

The moving around of executives on the corporate chessboard in May had barely time to make an impression when things were switched around again. In July, J.-F. Cecillon stood down as EMI Music president, and it was announced that his role would be split between Billy Mann and David Kassler.

But the biggest change of all was the appointment of Elio Leoni Sceti as chief executive of EMI Music to be in charge of its recorded music arm, a move that allowed Hands to step down from the role he never wanted in the first place but felt obliged to take on as an interim measure. Leoni Sceti was previously executive vice president at Reckitt Benckiser, specialising in FMCGs (fast-moving consumer goods). It did not take long for the sobriquets to be wheeled out – among them 'Mr Muscle' and 'Mr Cillit Bang'.

"I'm delighted Elio is joining as chief executive of EMI Music to lead the most exciting business transformation in the music industry," said Hands in a press statement. "His career achievements and outstanding leadership qualities are ideally suited to ensuring that EMI is a successful business."

Speaking to *Fortune* about his appointment, Leoni Sceti accepted it was a big job but also signalled that Terra Firma was looking to inject outside expertise into EMI to radically modernise it. "I don't have the silver bullet [for the music industry's woes]," he said. "I think the industry as a whole has not been able to anticipate where the market is going. There is a gap between consumer need and the industry's capacity to leverage it. What I'm going to do is not only catch up but to try and take a step forward and get to where they want us to be."[7]

Slipstreaming the appointment of the company's new global chief executive, Guy Hands issued an internal memo claiming a "dramatic improvement" in EMI's performance in the first fiscal quarter of 2008. EMI's recorded music arm had positive earnings (before interest, tax, depreciation and amortisation) of £59.2 million compared to a loss of £45.1 million in the first quarter of 2007. Total revenue was up 61 per cent to £288.1 million.

Hands said it was still "early days" for the turnaround of EMI, cautioning that "the recorded music business is extremely volatile and we cannot count on future quarters always being this good".[8] But this news and the arrival of Leoni Sceti sent out a clear message to the entire music industry. EMI would roar back to its former glory, Hands was tearing up the rulebook to achieve it and no one should ever have doubted Terra Firma when it said it meant business.

CHAPTER 9

Brands Over Bands

"There were a lot of inefficiencies in the system.
The question was where to find them."

The arrival in July 2008 of Elio Leoni Sceti as chief executive of EMI's recorded music division was significant in a number of ways. First, it would allow Guy Hands to stop being CEO (a job he had only accepted under duress), and to step back into a non-executive role. Second, it was a symbolic appointment, bringing in an experienced executive from outside who was not tainted by association with the old way of doing things in the music business, something that Terra Firma adamantly wanted to distance itself from. And third, it sent a message to the company and the industry as a whole that the logic of FMCG (fast-moving consumer goods) was now going to shake the record business into new life and teach this very old dog some important new tricks.

Leoni Sceti had worked his way up from Procter & Gamble in Italy and France, joining Reckitt Benckiser in 1992 and eventually becoming executive vice president of Europe at the company, which traded in cleaning products like Cillit Bang and Dettol, to a guffawing media's delight.

"His career achievements and outstanding leadership qualities are ideally suited to ensuring EMI is a successful business," said Guy Hands on welcoming him to EMI.

"This is a hugely exciting time for the music business and for EMI," said Leoni Sceti of his appointment. "The potential that can be realised in this industry is massive, music consumption is growing more than ever across the world and I cannot wait to get started and to work with EMI's artists and employees."[1]

Rather than running pell-mell through the company and bending it into whole new shapes, Leoni Sceti waited four months, until November that year, to unveil his new plans for the company. He did so at a company-wide meeting at Shepherd's Bush Empire in West London. Adding a new layer to the already divisive matrix system, the new chief executive would separate the company into three operational divisions: North America and Mexico; Europe; and the rest of the world. This was a rallying cry for the record business to take control of its own destiny.

He outlined his plans in an interview with *Music Week* where he also revealed he would add 'president of new music' to his existing CEO title. "If you think about the last big innovation in music ... the iPod, who did it?" he asked. "Not us. The innovation of how music is experienced has not been done by the music industry. I think we have the ambition, the capabilities and the vision to regain that leadership in innovation of how music is experienced."[2]

Maltby, Terra Firma's holding company for EMI, had looked into the profitability of acts on EMI's books and found that 88 per cent of them were making a loss and so, along with ongoing staff redundancies, Leoni Sceti would also have to dramatically pare back the estimated 14,000 acts pulling EMI into the red. An awful lot of blood was going to have to be spilled.

He, was, however, keen to say that he was not going to impose cold FMCG logic on EMI; rather he would take a more sympathetic strategy. "It is ridiculous to think [of] marketing music like a brand; it is not a brand," he said in his first major interview in *Music Week*. "A brand is a set of physical values, an expression of physical values. Music talks to your soul, to your heart, to your inner senses. It doesn't talk to your physical senses."[3]

There was another executive expansion announced at this time, with head of EMI's digital business Douglas Merrill also becoming COO of new music. Leoni Sceti also revealed to EMI staff that Ernesto Schmitt would be joining from consumer electronics retailer DSG International to become president of catalogue.

The Triple E Era was about to arrive: Elio and Ernesto's EMI.

Who is Elio Leoni Sceti and will he save us?

No media profile of Elio Leoni Sceti at the time was complete without a headscratcher about why this executive from the brands world was given such a high-profile job in the music business when he had zero music-business experience. He still feels the need to justify his appointment at EMI, a decade on, and to explain that he was not the musical arriviste that some thought.

"My personal background is a mix of creative and disciplined financial," he says. "My mother was a composer and my father was in property development. I grew up with those two sides to myself ... I have always been somebody who grew companies rather than cost efficiency."

On being approached about the job by Terra Firma, he says that Guy Hands wanted him to help bring two distinct disciplines to the company. "One was about financial discipline and the other was about consumer discipline," he says. "The second one is a very highly debated objective because a lot of people without an understanding of what that means or its context might perceive it to be that he wanted to craft a music world where certain types of music would be developed to fit consumer tastes. Which, of course, had never been the object or the case. The objective was to ensure that, while music is being developed, you insert into this industry the same data-rich information that allows for that music to find its fans faster and more efficiently and therefore to bloom and grow in a more informed way."

Leoni Sceti already knew Eric Nicoli as their children went to the same school. He said they spoke about the music industry regularly so he was not coming into EMI blind. Quite the reverse, in fact, as he felt he was eagle-eyed enough to pinpoint exactly where the long-serving executives who had only ever worked in music were coming unstuck.

"The industry had been run by individuals who had been grown in that industry of certain behaviours and assumed consumer understanding which was not optimised," he argues. "It was very much relying on the few A&Rs with 'magic ears' based on their own [taste] and personal experience. From a cost perspective, it was running quite wild in the industry, with lots of things which were perceived to be the right thing to do but which were really not monitored or measured to be the right things to do – i.e. costs that could have been optimised simply by measuring results and choosing which one to do. There were a lot of inefficiencies in the system. The question was where to find them."

There were often very public criticisms from Terra Firma of the old guard of executives at EMI who they felt had not so much painted the company into a corner as kicked it towards a cliff edge. Leoni Sceti believed that while this was causing inertia in thinking on the top floor, the staff several executive levels below were the ones that could take the company forward.

He found them "truly dedicated, committed, hard-working and passionate about what they were doing" and called them "impressive people for the reason that they were motivated by passion as opposed to being motivated by a function". It was this dichotomy between the executives and the rest of the staff that he felt could be harnessed by him and his plans for the company.

"The opportunity was even larger than I thought," he says of what surprised him most coming into EMI and meeting the staff. "That was because the lack of industry sharing was enormous. At the top, the industry in my mind was, and still is, basically led by people who think they have been anointed by the Virgin Mary. That therefore brings a consequential arrogance that does not want to know what others do or how to do it better because you know it all. That is a huge opportunity if you're entering into an industry. Basically what it means is that you can learn from everybody, but everybody will not learn from you. So you can retain your competitive advantage while learning from others."

He knew his appointment was going to be met with huge suspicion, but says that his nomadic life and career, having been born in Italy and having lived in seven different countries at this stage, as well as being a polyglot, made him very adaptable to new environments and situations. He accepted it was going to be an uphill struggle coming into a company less than a year into its new, and extremely tempestuous, ownership. "I had my antennae up," he says, "but I didn't need very long antennae. It was quite obvious I was somebody brought in by the new owner of the business and the new owner of the business was vastly rejected and disliked and, therefore, I was equally rejected and disliked before I even spoke!"

He had to win over not just the staff, but also the artists and their managers, many of whom were getting extremely anxious about the very public discussions about far-reaching cuts to the existing roster. "I met with pretty much all the meaningful managers – for Coldplay, Robbie Williams, Katy Perry and new acts like Tinie Tempah who was signed and launched in my time there," he says. "Queen, Pink Floyd and The Beatles, of course. I met them. I met them sometimes one-on-one for lunch, sometimes I met them at industry forums and sometimes I met them at gigs."

He knew time was against him and he had to work fast to both outline his vision for EMI and, more importantly, get company-wide buy-in to that vision. "The first few months were really trying to gain my place in people's agendas and minds. It is a journey so you cannot start on day one. You might start on day 200! Time was a factor. But I did meet with all the meaningful ones, for sure. I made a point of doing that. I made a point of being as active a member of the industry associations as possible. I shared my vision openly. I don't think that doing things alone in an industry that is in need of change is as effective as doing it with the rest of the industry players. I shared my consumer views."

In many ways, Leoni Sceti represented an extension of the thinking that was parachuted into EMI right at the start of Terra Firma's ownership of the company with the appointment of Mark Hodgkinson. Coming from Virgin Money, Hodgkinson had very different skills from those who had worked for years in record companies and the thinking was that this would fast-track EMI's transition by bringing in new knowledge and working practices right at the top.

"When I came on board, we had lots of data but we weren't really using that data for much insight," says Hodgkinson of what faced him when he came into EMI at the end of summer 2007. "Part of the initial challenge was to work out what we had got in and how we were going to make more of it. That was very much within my remit. We were therefore challenging the way you would traditionally go about promoting artists."

He argues the global promotional junkets for mega-acts worked well in keeping them in the public eye but were commercially rash when applied to mid-tier acts who had not yet ascended to global ubiquity and the vast record sales that came with it.

"The bit in the middle was the most interesting part because it enabled us to do what I would call consumer marketing," he says of how Terra Firma was starting to tackle this. "Doing what I used to do at Virgin in the music industry therefore enabled some of those artists to be much more successful by using the data and the insights as well as using more digital content – all of those things that everybody now probably does without thinking about it … A lot of what we were doing in the first two years was really understanding what was there, working out how to do it better, starting to make some of those things happen and then starting to show the success of doing it that way so there was more belief in doing it that way."

This strategic disruption was clearly going to be pushed through by the new wave of executives who felt they were not hidebound by the old ways of doing things at record companies. They did not have to rip up the rulebook, simply because they had not been indoctrinated by it. What they were doing, however, was met initially with bemused resignation from the old team at EMI – but this quickly escalated to vehement opposition.

"Elio came in very arrogantly from Reckitt Benckiser, thinking we were a bunch of idiots," says a senior Wrights Lane executive watching the global roll-out of this new strategy. "When Guy started, he had some EMI heavyweights around him like J.-F. Cecillon, Roger Ames and Tony Wadsworth. They were still in place running their bits. But by the time Elio came in they had all gone and he surrounded himself 99 per cent with non-industry people."

One executive with music-business experience was less damning of Leoni Sceti and felt that, under the circumstances, he handled himself well despite some of the incumbents willing him to fail. "I think Elio did an amazing job, frankly," says Billy Mann. "He was someone who walked in with zero music-business experience, had to look at the state of things and had to make some order out of it. I feel that that is often overlooked. He's the guy who came in and didn't get the secret handshake. And he never cared. He went in and he did a job that he had to do according to the way he saw it. As you can imagine, there was a lot of tension and stress internally."

Lord Birt was also effusive, saying that he was the breath of fresh air that EMI – and Terra Firma – desperately required at this stage in its restructuring and recovery. "[Elio] brought a muscularity and a different kind of experience to the business," he says. "This was a business that needed other kinds of muscles."

An external source, albeit one working closely with EMI during this time, felt the new senior management were right to call time on the way EMI had worked. They felt it was running on autopilot, oblivious to the fact that the market in 2008 was very different to the one it was used to. "Elio was used to market research and product testing before launching them," they say. "Market research as far as the record industry does it is, 'Let's put out a single, make a video and see how it goes.' You can't do that today. It's not the 1970s any more."

The wider fear was that EMI under Terra Firma was sacrificing too many experienced music executives as part of its scorched-earth policy, believing the only way to build the company's future was to eviscerate its past.

"It's very difficult to come in and run a company like that with no background in the industry anyway – especially when you're also surrounding yourself, or Guy has surrounded you, with a bunch of other people who know nothing about the industry," says one senior executive. "Apart from a few people, like David Kassler, everyone else assumed that everybody who had ever worked in the record industry were a bunch of idiots. Universal was upset by this as well, watching from afar. They were told by Guy that they were also a bunch of idiots who didn't know what they were doing. Guy tarred the whole industry with the same brush."

Another senior UK executive says that the company's new chief executive was doomed from the off as he had inherited a global structure from Terra Firma's first year and was forced to work within its flaws and restrictions. "Elio could have been an incredibly successful global CEO," they say. "However, he had a structure that Guy and one of the big consultancy firms they worked with had put in place that was never going to work. The problem was they had a global team and then domestic teams. The domestic teams had all the relationships with the artists and the managers. But they were seen as second-class citizens compared to the global team. But the global team had no experience in music. Elio wasn't part of a global team; he was the boss. But underneath Elio, he had lots of global roles. And that wasn't working."

Another Wrights Lane executive also feels Leoni Sceti was catapulted into an unwinnable situation where Terra Firma was trying to do too much, too quickly. "It felt to me like they were trying to reinvent everything at the same time," they say. "They were throwing everything at it. With the exception of publishing as that was a bit that wasn't broken and that actually made money."

Given this, the same source has a lot of sympathy for the new head of the company and what he was trying to do while facing what were inconceivable odds. "Elio came in in July but was dropped into this mixture of confusion and lack of direction, but was expected to run everything despite not knowing anything about the music business, not really knowing anything about EMI and not really knowing anything about Terra Firma," they say. "It was a pretty hard gig for him to get to grips with quickly."

One senior EMI source who worked closely with the newly arrived chief executive felt he was horrifically out of his depth. They say they understand why an outside executive could be transformative but feels Terra Firma picked the wrong executive to pilot that transformation. "I agree, up to a point, with that idea that you need an outsider in the situation that EMI faced," they say. "But you also need somebody who really understands transformation as your CEO. And Elio did not understand transformation. He was a marketing-driven person. Frankly, in the record business, marketing is a micro thing. You have got hundreds of little brands and trying to reform that part of the business, which Elio never really did, [is the trick]. He did a couple of really fantastic things, by the way. Don't get me wrong. But he just wasn't capable of running the whole business. And that was obvious from day one. It wasn't like it seemed he could run it. He could not. He didn't understand the dynamics and he didn't have people around him who were able to give him that insight he needed. And he had Guy yelling in his ear all the time. Plus he was faced with covenants that were impossible to make without getting fresh cash in. He was in a really difficult position."

The same executive was equally damning of the structural changes being pushed through at this time. "Then they tried to organise the business in a way that is completely nonsensical," they sigh. "It so misunderstands things. They tried to implement worldwide functions – worldwide marketing, worldwide A&R, worldwide everything. But the implementation of these things has to take place in the localities as these are local markets. What happens is that every decision about how you are going to take a record and get it into the marketplace has to go up through three silos, right up to the top to get agreed. Then it goes back down. And when it comes back down, as you can imagine, it is very different to what went up, even though the people at the top think they are saying yes."

Despite Leoni Sceti saying he went out to meet all the key managers and artists as soon as he started, some felt that he did not learn from the mistakes Guy Hands had made in the preceding months and ended up causing animosity internally when he was supposed to be creating affability.

"Elio, and this was possibly a cultural thing as he had come from a big European corporation, really didn't like it when there was any danger of any besmirching of his image," says a senior EMI UK executive. "If an artist was being really difficult with him, he would agree with him and then deflect the pain down the line. They were now dealing with properties that could talk back rather than brands … He really couldn't handle that. There were a couple of times we were put in situations where the deflecting of an artist's ire came and smacked us around the chops. Stephen Alexander [Terra Firma's operational managing director who had taken on various senior executive roles at EMI] wouldn't do that. He would try and have a reasonable discussion."

Rather than take criticism on the chin, the executive feels a blame-shifting culture started to take over. "If Guy Hands had upset Thom Yorke, he'd try and blame the people at the label," they say. "If Elio got it in the ear from an artist whose career was struggling, he'd try and blame it on his underlings instead of trying to have a reasonable discussion with the artists. That was really painful a lot of the time."

As there were generally two oppositional schools of thought here – Terra Firma's 'change at all costs' ideology versus the old guard's sandbagging its existing working practices – they were always going to clash. Some at EMI felt this had to be fought against but others felt the new team would, given enough rope, soon hang themselves.

"Compared to Guy Hands running around causing chaos, I guess there was a level of stability [with Elio]," says one long-serving EMI execu-tive. "But I would definitely say that none of us thought these guys would be around for very long. That's just because of the way they went about things. It just felt like they were making the wrong decisions and things kept cropping up all the time."

Not only that, but a company accused of not being analytical enough in its thinking and operations in the recent past had now swung to the opposite extreme. The veneration of the innate was eliminated by PowerPoint inanity.

"It was endless meetings," says an executive who had been with the company for several years before Terra Firma arrived. "EMI became Every Meeting Imaginable. There were meetings about meetings about meetings. It was just endless presentations about why we should be doing this. And then we would have to go off and give presentations about why we couldn't do it or why this or that might be able to work. We were constantly having to go through this process of proof. It was all done in endless meetings."

While the executive was more sanguine about Leoni Sceti, he was utterly scathing about the executive brought in to run catalogue. "Ernesto Schmitt was a very humourless man," they say. "He simply would not listen to any other opinion."

This was not an isolated opinion. Schmitt was seen by many within EMI as being, by some considerable distance, the most divisive appointment made by Terra Firma during its entire ownership of the music company.

Schmitt arrives and the gloves come off

Unlike many Terra Firma recruits, Schmitt not only had music business experience; he actually had EMI experience. During the 1990s, he worked at the Boston Consulting Group as a consultant on the post-merger integration of Universal and PolyGram and became fascinated by the coming digital disruption for the music business – what he calls "this mass explosion and fragmentation of content". Fired up by this, he set up online music community site Peoplesound in 1998 – effectively a proto-MySpace – but it was too early into the market to have a pronounced impact.

"The mistake I made at the time, being an optimistic 27-year-old man, was to think that if you build a better mousetrap the world would beat a path to your door," he says. "What I hadn't really understood was that the music industry didn't want to be changed or disrupted. The vested interests of the incumbents in the industry were such that the idea that you could use technology to somehow deskill the A&R process and change the marketing process was deeply threatening rather than enlightening."

Peoplesound was sold to music website Vitaminic in June 2001 for £20 million[4] and Schmitt was invited into EMI by senior executives in the US, but he was unaware their time at the company was coming to an abrupt end. "I was brought in by Ken Berry and Tony Bates to do some of the transformative digital work but they both got fired two weeks after I started and Alain Levy came in," he says. "He [Levy] didn't have that agenda at all; he just wanted to cut costs. That was not going to work." Schmitt left soon after.

It might have been a brief time, but it was partly why he was headhunted for the job by Terra Firma. It was a job, initially, he did not want.

"They told me they had created this global division for the first time for catalogue and they asked me if I would be interested in running it," he says. "I said, 'I have absolutely no interest whatsoever. The music industry is in deep trouble. EMI is a deeply troubled organisation. Good luck!' They said I should go in and meet Guy and meet Elio. I did and I was hugely impressed. Guy had gone in and had effectively replaced the majority of the management team and had put in some very, very impressive people. Guy had stepped away from trying to run it himself, which didn't work. He had brought in Elio, who had just joined. Elio is a class act. He is a world-class consumer marketer. He's a very, very sharp commercial operator. He knows his stuff and I really felt that I could learn from him. I took on the mandate of running the global catalogue division."

He says that looking at the numbers underlying the catalogue division made it clear why Terra Firma wanted to protect these 'crown jewels' and also why the company had toyed with cutting frontline A&R completely and focusing instead on maximising the catalogue. According to revenue numbers that Schmitt saw, catalogue made up 70 per cent of the revenues and the vast majority of the profits for recorded music at EMI because new music was losing money and the music services arm was just about washing its own face.

"I inherited a fairly sceptical organisation," he says of what he faced when he first came into the company in 2008. "They were really all united only on two things: 1) their scepticism of the new private equity owners. 'Here we go – yet more bankers trying to do music. What do they know?'; and 2) their scepticism of me. 'Who the hell is this guy? What is he going to tell us?'"

Building up rich consumer analytics and segmentation within EMI was to be his first major task. "What I did was put in place structures that allowed a quarter of a million consumers across all the main territories to provide real-time data – that was updated once a week – on musical preferences, habits, listening awareness, the whole thing," he says. "This was the consumer insights division and was all part of my team."

He identified eleven distinct consumer groups in the market and found that EMI was super-serving just a fraction of them, meaning A&R within the company operated as a form of confirmation bias. "I got everybody at EMI to do a test to see which segment they fell into," he recalls. "It turned out that 95 per cent of them fell into just two segments – and 100 per cent of the products and services they were building were for just those two segments. The first 'Aha!' moment was seeing that there was a much bigger world out there."

This aesthetic echo chamber was one of Guy Hands's initial suspicions about EMI when he bought the company and met the top executives; now Schmitt had the data to bear it out. Those consumers who focused on artistic credibility and those desiring luxury box sets were well catered for within EMI, but the other categories were being ignored – and it was costing the company heavily.

"What we actually found was that the impediment to consumption was not whether or not the music was any good but it was the problem of what I call 'de-averaging'," he says, adding that they looked to the airline industry for inspiration in terms of how pricing and experience worked there.

"[If] you can de-average what is effectively just a plane ticket, you could do exactly the same [with music]," was his premise. "That had a fundamental impact on everything. It impacted on what products you would develop, how you would price them, how you would market and distribute them, what the commercial skill set would be that you could bring to the table. It was transformative. It energised and galvanised the entire catalogue team. It brought in a whole bunch of new skills where we completely repriced the entire catalogue for digital and completely countered the logic of the music industry in terms of how to price."

He adds, "We were doing the opposite of what Steve Jobs wanted us to do digitally – which was maximising single prices and lowering album prices to get better conversion. We adopted a completely different approach to product development where, instead of launching single catalogue reissues, you would have a basic version, a discovery experience and an immersion product and that would range from £5.99 to £200 for different attributes. The whole thing revolutionised the catalogue business."

This modelling was not just to change the division he was in charge of, it was also to have a domino effect through the rest of the company. "It was in fact so infectious that Elio looked at me and said, 'What you are doing here is not just fundamental to catalogue, it is fundamental to the whole of EMI.' Hence he gave me the responsibility of being global

CMO as well as running catalogue and running the transformation agenda for EMI overall."

EMI had, of course, done its own market research and audience analysis before Terra Firma arrived, but the feeling with the new executives coming in from disciplines and with experience across other product categories was that it was dangerously lacking.

"There were two problems," says Leoni Sceti of the work EMI had done before he arrived. "The first was that it was generic. In the belief that you have to appeal to everybody, you test with everybody. That never works because you need to segment. Nothing appeals to everybody. The second problem was that it was fundamentally not believed by the leadership. The president of Label X said, 'Bullshit. I really don't think so.' And then that piece of research was scrapped. So if you have universal and generic learnings that are not endorsed by the leadership, you might as well save the money! It serves no purpose."

This segmentation eventually found its way onto every desk in EMI as a means of getting the whole company to think in the same way and, ultimately, pull in the same direction. Branded internally as EMI Music Key and presented in a CD jewel case, it was designed to explain to staff how consumer insight worked alongside product development, marketing and financials.

The eleven consumer segments were plotted across "most engaged with music" on the X axis and "spending more" on the Y axis. The categories worked as follows:

1. Post-Music (10 per cent of consumers where "music is of no interest")
2. Disenchanted (7 per cent of consumers who "actively want to buy music, but are frustrated by not knowing what to buy, or where to buy what they want")
3. Pre-Cash (10 per cent of consumers who are without credit cards or bank cards)
4. Casual (25 per cent of consumers who are passive in their music consumption, who "enjoy music, but it does not form an active part of their lives")
5. Orphan (16 per cent of consumers with limited disposable income and "the most willing to compromise on quality in order to pay less")
6. Pop Idol (12 per cent of consumers who are fascinated by celebrity and reality TV)
7. First In Line (3 per cent of consumers who will pay a premium to have music first and "get close" to favourite acts)

8. Collector (12 per cent of consumers for whom "music is collected and displayed for all to admire")
9. Nighthawks (8 per cent of consumers who exist where "fashion, brands, image, lifestyle and music are all interlinked")
10. Gadgeteers (4 per cent of consumers who are "visual, digital, mobile and into gaming")
11. Cutting Edge (12 per cent of consumers where "music is a social experience and part of their social glue")

(To note, the numbers add up to more than 100 per cent, as some consumers can exist across two or more categories at the same time, e.g. a young teen could easily fit in the Pre-Cash and Pop Idol segments simultaneously.)

There was also a six-tier product overview:

1. Music To Go Edition (essentially a cut down or budget release)
2. Standard Edition (self-explanatory)
3. Live Edition (instant live recordings of shows available at the venue)
4. Experience Edition (deluxe and limited-edition packaging)
5. Immersion Edition (adding in extra online content)
6. Collectors' Edition (featuring collectables and rarities in numbered editions)

This was all presented in a CD-sized cardboard wheel (dismissively and sarcastically known among certain EMI staffers as The Wheel Of Destiny) with the eleven consumer types on the outer rim and the six types of product in the inner section that would be revealed via punched-out sections in the cardboard. The outer rim could be turned and would quickly show each type of consumer's music spend, level of music passion and segment size. Regardless of what department they worked in, staff were encouraged to consult this to help inform what they did and how they planned their projects. Outside of the insights department, this appeared, based on anecdotal evidence, to be quickly secreted at the back of desk drawers and was only referred to in the most mocking of terms.

Schmitt felt this was, nonetheless, an incredibly powerful tool for the staff at EMI – but one that had to be used correctly. "The point is that any segmentation will only answer the questions that you ask of it," he says. "Unless the questions are deeply rooted in 'What am I supposed to do differently tomorrow? How am I supposed to price differently, how am I supposed to promote differently, how am I supposed to reach one segment as opposed to another differently with my marketing?' Unless you are really in the roots of how you operate, market segmentation is an intellectual exercise that has no practical worth."

Hands himself claims that artists, perhaps used to being indulged by EMI, were sceptical of how this insights division was being built up within the company and used to help direct their careers. But, he says, when the benefits were explained properly to them, their enthusiasm for it snowballed.

"We got some big pushback initially from the artists when we did this," says Hands of the early stages of the process. "But then you showed them the data and the information ... But this was not about the information, this was about the process. I don't think we were teaching them to suck eggs. We were teaching them how to use the eggs they had [already] sucked. It was a different thing."

It was part of a bigger concerted effort to push the company – willingly or otherwise – into the future. To add extra credence to what they were doing, Schmitt and his team brought in experts in psephology (the study of voting trends and statistics), including one who had worked on President Obama's first electoral campaign, to teach the company how to use micro-segmentation.

"Then I brought in skills around commercial modelling and pricing to do the pricing optimisation," says Schmitt. "So I enhanced the team of music operators with new skills. That combination made for an incredibly effective, highly motivated and dedicated operating team. They turned from being the most sceptical team to being the most loyal, committed and highest-performing team ... At the time the Terra Firma people spoke of the work that we were doing as being a transformational agent for the business."

If Terra Firma did one thing in its time at EMI that even some of the refuseniks within the company had to praise (no matter how begrudgingly) it was the work on audience insights and segmentation. Some may have hooted in derision at The Wheel Of Destiny but they still accepted that the underlying principles, if not necessarily the way they were presented, were sound.

It turns out that some markets were open to this new approach and others pulled up the drawbridge when they saw Schmitt and his insight knights approaching. "It influenced worldwide in a massive way because everybody was kind of forced to work with it," says one regional head of EMI in Europe. "Yes, there was very much resistance to it. Our market was very well resourced so we had great resources in terms of bringing this segmentation and the whole of consumer focus into life and everyday work. The whole company had that spirit so there was not big resistance to it here. That happened more in other countries like Italy and

Scandinavia. They did not like that new approach to the business, but it has been pushed through by Terra Firma."

Back in the UK, some, however, felt that Ernesto Schmitt was gilding the lily at best and recklessly bloviating at worst in terms of how transformative this all was. "It was a good tool," says one executive tasked with getting their team to use this thinking. "Although it might have been overdone because we had eleven different types of consumers, so it was perhaps taken too far. It was seen as the answer to all of our problems; it was going to save the world and it was going to save EMI. But it was just a tool."

For many at EMI, it often juddered and started to fall apart when going from the theoretical to the practical. The learning curve within EMI was too vertiginous for it to work across the board. "If you look at it today, you might say it was pretty primitive, but, for the time, it was very advanced," says a senior EMI executive. "The problem with that is that you had this analytics group that was being driven to produce all of this data and to try and get the marketing guys to both understand it and try to use it. But they were pushing it onto people who had no idea what they were talking about – because it was alien to the way that the music business ran. It was very hard for them to get acceptance of that. They pretended that they got acceptance of it but there was almost no real underlying acceptance of that as guiding the way in which you were going to market and present music into the marketplace."

Others believed that it was going the long way round to prove with science what staff knew instinctively from years of experience working in music. "We did quite a lot of consumer research and some of the work they did was valid," they say. "But they insisted on working from zero. So they were pretending there was no knowledge and spending millions of pounds getting to where we actually were already ... [It] produce quite elaborate and prescriptive ways of working that were often too inflexible to accommodate the differences in individual artist catalogue areas and market segments ... It was very detailed but not detailed enough to capture aspects of music purchasing."

Inevitably, there were some at EMI who felt this was all an enormous waste of time, money and resources. "They invested an insane amount of money into developing this audience research programme but without really speaking to the people who were going to use it," says one executive working on digital in the UK who was well used to data and analytics but felt things here were fundamentally flawed. "And without knowing how it was going to be used or why it was going to be used. They just wanted all this information and assumed that they would be able to apply it."

Another executive in the US claims that Roger Faxon, head of EMI Music Publishing, was categorically not a fan of this new thinking sweeping through the recorded music arm of the company. "Roger fucking hated Elio's focus on consumers at the expense of artists," they claim, suggesting a sectarian split was quickly evident between recorded music and publishing over this. "Under Elio, they had talked incessantly about consumers. It just wasn't something that people were able to get passionate about because consumers became second to artists. And artists would be, 'Fuck you!' Whereas Roger said we were going to put the artists first and whatever is the right decision for artists is ultimately the right decision for consumers and is the right decision for the business. It became a mission for people in the business."

On a less prosaic and more nuts-and-bolts level, Schmitt's shake up of catalogue was also key in lowering the overheads of an already profitable part of the company, making it run with even greater efficiency. As physical retail continued to crumble, the costs of manufacturing and, more importantly, storage had to be pruned back.

"Their ideas of stock control and keeping things tight and as one-off orders, rather than have stock around for a long time sitting on the shelves, was a good one," says one well-placed source. "They were quite aggressive on their discounting with the retailers. They stood their ground because they wanted to make a higher profit on product. Each product should have a profit margin of, say, 25 per cent. Whereas before we would have gone with something at 5 per cent if it made sense to us. They were a bit more rigid on that."

Another source backs this up, saying over-production of stock was a legacy problem from the 1990s when the company was seeing catalogue as a licence to print money. "There was a massive and bloated catalogue with EMI when nothing was ever deleted," they say. "There was a massive warehouse that stocked things forever. They brought in this very clever modelling which looked at the profit level of each album sat in the warehouse. There were tens of thousands of lines in the EMI catalogue that needed to be reduced. They came in and did it, getting it down to a few thousand lines. People might claim they can no longer buy a Val Doonican album because it's deleted – but we maybe only sold two of them a year."

Clearing the warehouses of waste was long overdue and a sign of a catalogue division now putting profits far above any sentimentality. But this Year Zero thinking accidentally bled into artist relations and the trickle that started in 2007 and early 2008 with Radiohead and The Rolling Stones defecting threatened to become a tsunami. If EMI saw catalogue as its biggest profit centre within recorded music, it was taking a cavalier approach to dealing with the acts that made up a considerable chunk of those catalogue sales.

A political minefield: fraught negotiations with EMI's biggest acts

In 2010, one of the most celebrated acts under the EMI umbrella took their entire catalogue with them and moved over to Universal Music Group. Having sold an estimated 170 million[5] albums for EMI since their debut album in 1973, in November 2010 Queen extricated themselves from the label that was so symbiotically associated with them.

"Between Ernesto and Elio, they managed to lose Queen," claims a senior source with knowledge of the negotiations that took place. "Jim Beach [Queen's manager] was probably the most loyal manager to EMI … The contract was up with Queen and Jim came to Elio and Ernesto with what he proposed should be the new deal. It was obviously much better for him and Queen than the old deal. There was a much smaller distribution fee and it was more like a distribution deal."

Beach was coming from a strong negotiating position, as a previous contract renewal would now return the band's masters to them (as Radiohead had wanted in their renegotiation). "There was a period earlier where a previous MD had renewed Queen's new albums on the basis that the old albums eventually reverted back to Queen a number of years later," they continue. "That period came up in 2010 when Jim came to EMI with his new proposal. So Elio and Ernesto played hardball and didn't take him seriously. Jim told them that this was his deal and he wasn't bluffing – so it was a 'take it or leave it' deal. Jim went around the corner and signed exactly the same deal with Universal. And they jumped at it … The Stones may have moved anyway, but Queen were completely and utterly fucked up by Guy's people – by Elio."

There were also fears that David Bowie was at risk of leaving during this time, effectively downing tools until it became clear what was happening with EMI and if Terra Firma's ownership of the company was going to deliver the goods. "They didn't understand artists and they didn't understand the mentality of artists," says a source on why Bowie had such reservations about the company at this time. "Bowie in particular in that period had no interest in dealing with them whatsoever. His catalogue was, to a point, signed up for a certain amount of time. He knew that and so he just shut down."

Bowie had apparently taken huge exception to suggestions that the vaults be cleaned out and that material that had gone unreleased for decades would now finally see the light of day. "Just because stuff exists is no reason, in my mind, to release it," he is reported to have said.

"Especially if I hate it. What is it supposed to prove? How fucking awful we were at times?"

Bowie may have been resistant to having outtakes and demos boxed up and sold at a premium, but the biggest archive act on EMI after The Beatles was less impervious. "Whereas David Bowie had gone, 'We'll do it our way and if we don't want to do it, we won't do it,' Pink Floyd kind of got wrapped up a little bit in some of the sales pitch," says a knowledgeable source of the reasons behind the elaborate release of a series of 'immersion' box set editions of classic albums such as *Dark Side Of The Moon* and *Wish You Were Here*. "To me, immersion is what warms the water in your house," they add.

A US executive at EMI was watching this unfold at a distance from the London office. They felt this was a direct result of using the logic of consumer segmentation, rather than the logic of a fan or a consumer, and taking it to the extreme. "They determined that certain people wanted to have a bunch of extras in those box sets – more physical things beyond the music that made the sets more valuable," they say. "I don't know who determined that the extras to include in the Pink Floyd box set were Pink Floyd marbles and scarves, but, to this day, there are few box sets that have been more mocked. As far as the Pink Floyd marbles and scarf being seen by Terra Firma as a 'triumph'? Ummm, you know, OK!"

There were also allegations of a serious crossing of professional boundaries in dealing with catalogue artists, making the 'going native' of some executives by dressing in jeans and leather jackets seem positively benign in comparison. "A typical Terra Firma thing was that if they got a communication with an artist, suddenly they thought they were close personal friends," says one source. "One guy felt that he and Nick Mason from Pink Floyd were like that [crosses fingers]. He didn't realise that Nick would go through executives, and has done, for years and years. They honestly did think that once they had dealt with an artist that they were best friends and they could go for tea around each other's houses."

This was not a one-off incident, according to the source. "They were trying to do something big with John Lennon," they add. "One of the Terra Firma people tried to engage himself with the Lennon camp – and it failed miserably."

Another executive reports that Schmitt's time in charge of catalogue was at risk of sacrificing long-standing and delicately maintained relationships with heritage artists or their estates because he was focusing too much on the mechanics rather than the products. "At the first catalogue meetings I went to run by Ernesto, all the agenda points were around the catalogue operating model and KPIs [key performance indicators]," they say. "There was no mention of The Beatles remasters campaign [for the box set reissues of their albums in mono and stereo in September 2009]. There was no mention of Queen, Pink Floyd or any of these issues. For them, in their consultants' world, it was much more important to create either 65 or 165 KPIs. It was a huge numbers of KPIs just for catalogue. Then there was their operating model where they would get obsessed with multiple regression analysis."

They add, "One of Ernesto's guys wanted to do analytical training for all the marketing people around the world to teach them multiple regression analysis and stata analysis – whatever that is. This was at a time when we were cutting all the travel costs for everybody and they were planning to fly everyone in to be taught multiple regression analysis. Even in small markets that spent nothing on marketing."

They continue, with mounting disbelief, "The Beatles remasters were due to be released a few months later and they hadn't even talked about it in the agenda. A couple of us, who were a bit more musically minded, asked them what was happening with The Beatles and Queen and we were hearing rumours that we might lose them. Then they started talking about them and it became a big issue. And then they took all the credit for The Beatles remasters campaign – which had actually been done before they joined."

As with everything related to The Beatles and EMI, things moved incredibly slowly and the four different parties – Paul McCartney, Ringo Starr, Yoko Ono for the John Lennon estate and Olivia and Dhani Harrison for the George Harrison estate – themselves moved at a glacial pace.

In April 2007, Neil Aspinall retired as Apple Corps CEO[6] and was succeeded by Jeff Jones who was responsible for pushing the reissues programme forward. Terra Firma inherited the project and took it to market, but it was very much controlled by Apple Corps.

So important were The Beatles to EMI that, early on in Terra Firma's ownership of EMI, Hands himself met with the surviving members as well as the widows of John Lennon and George Harrison. The meetings were, he feels, productive, but not every meeting with each of the four corners of The Beatles empire went as well as he wanted.

"I think the relationship by the end was good with Ringo [Starr], good with Yoko [Ono], good with Olivia [Harrison] but there was no real relationship with Paul [McCartney] at all," he says. "I met Paul once only. I met the others on a few occasions. Ringo actually left me a very nice note in my office once which was along the lines of, 'Don't let the fuckers get you down.' It was classic Ringo. It was very nice. I really appreciated it because I was having a particularly bad week when I found it. I found Yoko just extraordinary. She's an extraordinary, charismatic, sexy woman. I was quite shocked. I wasn't expecting that. I can see why she was both divisive within The Beatles and why Lennon just went for her. She is a force of nature."

With 75 per cent of the team around The Beatles on the same page as him, Hands explains why it did not run quite so smoothly with McCartney. "With Paul, the meetings were always with his representatives," he says of the day-to-day relationship, before outlining how his one direct summit with McCartney played out. "My meeting with Paul was totally commercial. It was very financial. My meetings with them [the others] were much more about art and the music. With Paul, it was very much, 'We are supporting EMI. If it wasn't for my money, EMI [would be in trouble].' But I wouldn't put The Beatles as a problem. I saw them as a total opportunity."

While EMI had perhaps been guilty of being too willing to acquiesce to the demands of Apple Corps, Ernesto Schmitt was not going to be quite so obsequious in his dealings with the company. One senior executive at EMI outlines how the relationship changed between EMI and The Beatles when Terra Firma came in. "It was a strange relationship [with Apple Corps]," they say. "From a creative standpoint, there was always a great deal of cooperation ... But there is a lot of history there. And the history was very fraught. But in that time, Guy made it vastly worse because he wanted The Beatles to allow EMI to do all sorts of things. He couldn't understand why they weren't letting him do what he wanted. Since Guy was never consistent in anything, he would say something, then a piece of paper would go out, but it wouldn't be what he said. That's the most important thing to avoid that you can possibly do as the talent only feels like you are trying to fuck them."

EMI and its biggest act were now at loggerheads in a way they had never been before despite their long and bumpy history of forced mutual dependence and occasional antipathy. "The relationship was poisoned because Guy and Julie [Williamson] felt that the guys at Apple Corps were nasty, greedy and untrustworthy," says the same source. "The guys at Apple Corps thought that's what Guy and Julie were! There was no bridging that gap."

That gap was about to become a ravine when EMI's catalogue head got involved. "The relationship with Apple Corps was unbearable," says Schmitt, who spent a year working to get a deal done with them. "That was because the remaining Beatles and their heirs had nothing but disdain for EMI. As far as they were concerned, their copyright had been stolen when they were young and they had signed up to contracts that they shouldn't have signed up to. It was felt that EMI had been riding on their successful coat-tails unfairly ever since. It was a constant feeling of hostility."

Rather than try and start from a positon of a clean slate with new owners at the helm of EMI, this deteriorated quickly. "Meetings with Jeff Jones [now head of Apple Corps] were always extremely unpleasant," continues Schmitt. "Whenever we were, very positively, trying to put forward an agenda to relaunch them digitally or remaster things, he kept on saying, 'No, you don't understand. I'm in The Beatles business. You're in the not-going-bankrupt business.' There was a lot that we wanted to do but they simply said no to everything. There was some belief that what we were trying to do was milk a sacred cow or we were desperate to make revenue. That is just not true. We saw opportunities but they just weren't willing to play that game."

Even though the mono and stereo box sets were a huge commercial success, Schmitt feels that this was not his department's best work, in large part due to the autonomy Apple Corps was granted. "This project was halfway up and running when I came in," he says. "In fairness, when it comes to the physical attributes, that was very much Apple Corps and Jeff Jones's remit. Nothing happened that Jeff Jones wasn't happy with … We executed on it but Jeff Jones really took responsibility for remastering it."

Schmitt was, however, able to add his own touch to the campaign, arguing that the box sets should come out on 9 September, the same day as game company Harmonix was releasing its *The Beatles: Rock Band* console game. "I knew that the games company behind it would be spending tens of millions on marketing going into Christmas," he says. "The prevailing logic at the time was that we should do the game first and then a few months later release the box sets. I said that we should make the two a big bang on 9th September 2009. Because then what you do is you have a big bang and you can effectively ride the coat-tails of the games marketing. That turned out to be spectacularly successful. You couldn't move without seeing marketing for The Beatles and that created huge interest."

Schmitt also struck a deal to sell The Beatles box sets via TV shopping channel QVC, an idea that came directly from results of their consumer insights research. "What we found was something crazy like 15 per cent of the US population self-declared themselves to be super-fans of The Beatles but owned no product at all," he explains. "That's a big gap. If you are a super fan but you don't own anything there is something wrong. What we found was that those people were simply not the kind of folks who would ever walk into a record store or even know what iTunes was … We realised we had to reach them through unconventional channels and so we did a deal with QVC. For the first time ever we sold very expensive products through QVC. We ended up shifting something like one million units through QVC alone. That consumer insight piece really helped connect the product with the right audience where they needed to be."

He is unconcerned that this might have been seen as crass or desperate – reducing the most deified band in popular music to having their music sold between promotions for 'slankets' and home-hairdressing products. "It's irrelevant if it's cool or not," he snorts. "The point here is that is where the consumers were going and it worked extremely well. The Beatles were the most successful catalogue relaunch in history."

The Beatles reissues might have been commercially satisfying for the catalogue department but they were not necessarily creatively satisfying. Instead, Schmitt believes the Pink Floyd reissues, despite the vociferous mocking in other parts of the company, were a better example of where his insights and segmentation strategy worked to its fullest effect. This, he argues, is his real legacy while at EMI.

"I think The Beatles are a poor example of the kind of work that we did other than through the way that we marketed and distributed them as the product development was done by Apple Corps," he says. "A better example is the Pink Floyd remasters that came out about a year later. We got all the members of Pink Floyd to agree to release not just one but five versions of every single one of their albums. There were the discovery and immersion versions and versions that ranged from £5.99 to £200 with completely different attributes and targeting different segments. That was a very complete set of remasters that we issued very much on the principles of the consumer insight that we had found. And it was hugely successful."

Published in July 2006, by the time Terra Firma bought EMI almost a year later the music industry was fixated on a book titled *The Long Tail*. Written by Chris Anderson, editor in chief of *Wired* magazine, the book's thesis was that online was inverting the retail model that previously focused on hits ('the head'), and now small sellers ('the tail') that were uneconomical to produce, distribute and rack in the physical world would now find a more viable commercial life digitally.

This was a Damascene moment for some digital utopians in the music business and chimed perfectly with Terra Firma's vision for EMI's catalogue. "They were obsessed with the long tail," says a member of the catalogue team. "They said that everything had to go up [on digital services] because if it's not up, it won't sell. Everything had to be digitised. Through the CD era, EMI was very good at exploiting its catalogue so there was a lot of stuff that had been digitised. I think they felt they could just ingest it all and it would be a self-fulfilling prophecy. That simply wasn't the case because the costs were enormous to do that in the first place. Much of this stuff had never even been mastered for CD. They had no idea, even if they had done that, where it would go from there."

Schmitt, however, argues that it provided an opportunity for EMI to do an audit and stock check of all its music on digital services like iTunes as well as physical retailers. "It is very easy to focus on the crown jewels and say what a great job we did on Pink Floyd and The Beatles," he says. "Actually what delivered the results for catalogue and EMI was not working on the big names; it was really carefully optimising on-shelf availability of product which was physical and repricing the catalogue that was digital. All of those things were what made the difference. It is the long tail – the millions of releases that we had – that either were or weren't available and which either were or weren't priced correctly."

He sent staff into major retailers like Walmart to check EMI's 100 biggest-selling albums against what was actually available on the shelves. "It had never been done [at EMI]," he says of the audit. "When we checked the availability of the top 100 albums, it came out as only about 20 per cent or so. Oops! Why is it 20 per cent? Then you do an exercise to try and understand why it's 20 per cent. And then you realise that no one had really been looking after this. So we made a big effort and we got on-shelf availability from 20 per cent to 75 per cent or 80 per cent. Then all of a sudden you find that things turn around. It was about frequency of supply and supply terms. There was a very big thing about not having stock sitting in retail and making it hard to be sent back."

This was all serving to improve an already buoyant part of the business and help futureproof it in a market that was transitioning from physical to digital. Some may have scoffed at the inclusion of scarves and marbles in a Pink Floyd box set, but that was to pale in comparison to some of the marketing ideas that were tabled during this time at EMI.

Several sources told this author the same story about the insights team being tasked with finding an exclusive retail partner for the Radiohead catalogue but having to think beyond the specialist music retailers. After profiling a typical Radiohead fan and mapping that across to high-street retailers, the results came back that the best place to sell Radiohead albums was in mid-level clothing shop Next. When asked about this, Guy Hands shook his head and said it was ridiculous. "I have never heard that!" he roars with laughter at the very idea. "It sounds complete bullshit! I can tell you Radiohead did not sell to Next customers. Next customers are not Radiohead fans. It's complete bullshit."

Other EMI sources swear it absolutely was an idea that was pursued before those behind it were talked out of it. "It might have been discussed in a marketing meeting but I can assure you that it never got anywhere close to me," says Hands. "And I would have regarded it as completely insane. Just complete nonsense. People don't go to Next to buy CDs! And Radiohead are not a Next band. It just makes no sense to me."

This was just the tip of a very ridiculous iceberg.

Exploiting the assets

Included in the EMI acquisition was the legendary Abbey Road Studios in Northwest London, made famous as the place where the majority of Beatles tracks were recorded. It remained a working studio. Terra Firma-appointed executives were tasked with finding ways to exploit the enormous brand recognition.

Some of this was led by Mark Hodgkinson. "It was about keeping the real studio heritage but thinking about how you could broaden that," he says. "Abbey Road was a fantastic asset. How could you make it bigger for it to be successful?"

One idea was simply using the name as a byword for exceptional audio quality, and creating branded musical instruments as well as recordings of concerts by EMI acts under the Abbey Road Live name that would be available to buy minutes after the act walked off stage. "That was seen by Elio as a game-changer at one stage," says one source. "There were some competitors [like DiscLive and Instant Live] but it was a tiny, niche business – and it still is. We were going to be the masters of that, including doing it for unsigned artists."

Just using the studio name was not, however, enough and a series of bewildering ideas were presented internally, all escalating in preposterousness. "One of the ideas was to have a visitor centre," says a senior EMI executive who recounted this in mounting disbelief. "You can't have Japanese tourists trooping in and out and expect to run it as a working studio at the same time. Then there was an idea about turning it into a hotel. They were wondering how they could make money out of Abbey Road. Almost as soon as they announced that they were looking at plans to turn it into a hotel, Westminster Council stuck a protection order on it. It got protected status and today it has listed status."[7]

Hands confirms this was the plan and says it almost came to pass. "We got very, very close," he says. "If it hadn't been for the issues around Citigroup, we were going to do a deal that would have put £40 million into redoing Abbey Road and making it a multi-dimensional visitor centre. You would be able to play with mixing machines. If holograms had existed then, it would have been wonderful. We were looking at getting planning permission. You could do a lot with that. The site is not small. It was going to cost a lot of money. We were going to keep what was there almost exactly as it was and then recreate something."

The biggest barrier, however, was raising the requisite financing and Hands suggests Terra Firma's strained relationship with Citigroup spooked potential financiers. "We had an investor who was willing to do it," he says. "What stopped it? Really Citigroup because no one was willing to do anything while Citigroup [was around]. People were worried that Citigroup was going to seize the business. What would happen if they seized the business halfway through something they were doing?"

Hodgkinson expands on the possibility of opening the studios to the public on a regular basis. "The idea of the visitors' centre came out of the fact that there were so many people coming to the studios and writing on the wall," he says. "We thought about how we could embrace that. Maybe have some of them come round, have a look and maybe charge an entrance fee. Some of those ideas were better than others."

He does, however, deny that turning the building into a hotel, or even apartments, went beyond being a vague idea that was quickly shot down. "I don't think that was ever a credible option," he says.

Other ideas apparently included installing two-way mirrors to allow visitors to eavesdrop on acts making records. That was until it was pointed out that being in the studio involves long periods of waiting around and short bursts of activity and would therefore make for a very dull visitor attraction. Plus, most artists themselves would object in the most strenuous terms to being treated like animals in a zoo. Not only that, the local residents, already having to deal with people in groups of four slowly walking over the zebra crossing for photos recreating the *Abbey Road* album cover throughout the whole day, would have resisted anything that brought more tourists to the area.

Hands claims it would not have been disruptive to the building's main function and it would have been business as usual for it. "The visitor centre wasn't going to change its use as a working studio," he claims. "It wasn't going to have any effect on that. It was just very expensive."

No matter. There were other – even more absurd – ideas.

"In terms of the segmentation, they looked to the airline model where people will pay for upper-class seats," says a senior EMI employee who was pitched some of these ideas. "So they were pursuing the whole VIP thing and they were going to have a Robbie Williams experience. They were going to have a golden ticket in the CD and somebody would win that. They would be helicoptered in and they would land the helicopter at Lord's [cricket ground, a ten-minute walk from the studio]. Then Robbie would escort the fan into Abbey Road and they would have a personal session. None of this had actually been cleared with Robbie's management."

They shake their head in disbelief at the memories they have just dredged up. "They came up with these crazy ideas! They just seemed to have these big, big, big ideas. I have no problem with people having ideas. You put it into the pot and you work around it – figuring out what works and what doesn't work. But these things were so fantastical and so missing the point – trying to get artists to do things that they clearly didn't want to do."

A well-placed source felt they went too heavily on brand-centric thinking, believing that everything in their line of vision could be turned into a brand and marketed as such. This might work in the world of FMCGs but it starts to unravel when applied to the creative arts. "You can't really brand artists because you can't tell them what to do, but what you can do is leverage brand partnerships," they say. "There was an odd and misguided sense of them thinking they could get artist to be more like brands. And more like their brands. So there was an element of trying to control artists and get them to do things that, in the real world, would only ever get done if it was the artist's idea. Or if the manager had been able to persuade them – but not a marketing executive. There was a belief that they could make that happen. That is why they hired Elio in the end – to make it a marketing-led portfolio of brands."

Other stories seem too ridiculous to have even been considered, let alone vocalised, but sources who say they were there in the meetings where they were discussed swear they are true. "There was a story that they wanted someone to curate the annual Meltdown festival in London," splutters one, "but they didn't realise that Bob Marley was dead!"

Another adds, "They were trying to do stuff with Lynx Africa – thinking it would be a great brand fit for Gorillaz. That kind of thing. You'd be like, 'WHAT? What's this? What *is* this?' Those people just had no clue. The worse it got, the more desperate it became."

A third offers this story. "One of their great things was to try and sell cheap Beatles albums in garden centres," they say. "I remember that was one thing that came up. Why? You think you're going to get a different market by doing that? You've kind of missed the point of it all."

The stories kept coming during interviews for this book. "There was an American football game at Wembley to try and promote the sport in the UK," recalls a UK source. "They wanted to get either Lily Allen or Kylie Minogue to sing at half time as it was being televised and had a satellite feed to the US and so if they did this it was going to break them in America. The fact was nobody gave a shit. There were just endless ideas that you got deflated by." Hands says he encouraged brainstorming and welcomed new ideas, wanting EMI to be more creative. He points out there is a long way from something starting as an idea to it being implemented and none of these so-called "ridiculous" ideas ever got put to him to be implemented.

There was also serious consideration of going through the EMI Archive in Hayes, which included equipment developed by the company over the years, contracts, photographs, rare recordings and more. It is claimed by one person with detailed knowledge of discussions that an auction house was appointed to provide a valuation of the artefacts held in Hayes and they came back with a figure of £5 million, which obviously piqued the interest of the new owners.

"I had conversations with people in the EMI Trust about the sort of content that they had and how we could bring it to life to create a much stronger identity around the assets that we had," says Hodgkinson of what he did here.

Another source suggests this was less about branding and more about plundering. Plus, there was the added complication of ascertaining who owned the rights in particular assets. "There was a whole idea about exploiting the archives and selling prints for all the pictures," they say. "Unless we could prove that we owned the copyright, they were trying to create a merchandise scenario for something we didn't actually have the merchandise rights for. They just thought that the archive was there to be exploited. Abbey Road was going to be some kind of museum, almost."

Those in the company involved in the EMI Trust took comfort in the fact that they knew the ideas being tactlessly tossed around and work-shopped could never come to fruition for one very simple reason: the assets they were grasping towards were all ring-fenced by the charity status of the EMI Archive Trust that was set up in 1996 specifically to ward off any commercial land grabs like this. "One of the reasons why the EMI Archive Trust was set up was to protect the EMI archive so that someone couldn't just buy the company and plunder the archive," says a source involved with the trust. "It was a separate entity as a trust which protected it from this kind of aggressive commercialism. A lot of it was down to the fact they didn't understand the rights they had bought. Their due diligence clearly wasn't as good as they thought it was."

One EMI executive argues that the fundamental problem with this new team digging through the archives was that they were driven purely by commercial interests and pursued that with scant regard for the cultural and historical significance of what they found.

"There was respect of the catalogue from the EMI side – from Tony Wadsworth particularly," they say of how things were run before the new owners arrived. "I would say that Terra Firma [just] understood the commercial importance of it all the time. It should always be important and it shouldn't just be utilised as a money-making exercise as and when required ... The problem was that they didn't respect the catalogue. That is where they went wrong. They didn't understand the worth of the physical catalogue or the artists themselves."

This all had a knock-on effect for the relationships with artists and their estates. A story circulated within EMI at the time about a senior Terra Firma appointee having a meeting with the widow of a major EMI recording artist that went so badly she sent a message back to the company that if she had to deal with this executive again she would "move Heaven and earth" to find a way to take her late husband's recordings to another label.

Cuts to the frontline A&R roster and serious slashing of the signing budget meant that EMI was effectively operating in the market with one hand – the hand holding its wallet – tied behind its back.

Leoni Sceti accepts this was holding the company back somewhat but felt the company did, despite this, manage to hold its own. "No question about that – it was a real concern," he says. "It was a concern that was magnified by the circumstances. But we did end up signing new acts that were being courted by Universal, Sony and Warner. Some we lost, of course, and some we gained. We had some good examples. Katy Perry was dropped by Sony[8] and look what we did with her."

He argues that during this time the insights team actually helped win acts over during signing wars with other labels – but they still had to convince acts that EMI was a viable label for them in the long term. "[When] we needed to sign somebody, I would send one of the guys from innovations or consumer insights to give them a view and a vision about Music Key and how we were the only ones who understood how to amplify whatever it was they were doing," he says. "It was unique to us and we did have our angle. But, yes, it was very tough. All the time there were two questions. One was: will my act be supported by enough people? The second was: will you go bankrupt? We had to talk through these two questions five times a day, every day!"

Those well versed in the A&R process, bidding wars and artist relations believed that the new systems and structures being put in place were undermining and negating a hugely important part of the company. The company was swinging from one extreme (the romance of the 'golden ears' of the A&R people) to another (where data defined all), meaning the spirit of the company was being stretched to breaking point.

"Terra Firma were very data-led and very marketing-led but they didn't understand the A&R process at all," says an EMI source. "They didn't understand … what that meant in terms of signing artists, recording music and making music … so they sort of pushed it to the side and told the A&Rs to get on with it. They were going to focus on how they marketed their artists and there were going to be different tiers and formats – a £60 album, a £30 album, a £10 album."

The same source recounts having a conversation with the insights team that had been put in place, about a key EMI act's imminent album. There was reference to their biggest global hit and a suggestion that they would sell more albums if all twelve tracks on that album were exactly like that hit. There was also, according to the same source, talk about halving signing budgets as that would make the deal more profitable, oblivious to the fact that other labels were chasing the same acts. "You'd have conversations like that all the time," they sigh. "The terms are contractual [if looking to retain an act] or the market actually determines them when we are trying to sign a new artist. The market dictates the value of an act."

There was a sense among some of the old hands at EMI that a war was being waged around marketing acronyms and that they were on the losing side. "They [Terra Firma] thought the people in the record industry didn't know what they were doing," says one executive with a long history at EMI. "It was all a bit amateur hour. They thought they could come in with best practice from the brand business – be that the matrix environment or more KPIs and pricing analysis – and find things that no one else has thought of."

There was also an isolationism at play that came from trying to make EMI different from the rest of the majors. The by-product of this was that, in coldly presuming the competition were flogging a dead horse, they took their eye off what the competition was doing better than they were.

"They also didn't understand that we needed to know when other releases were going out from our competitors," says one executive by way of example. "Douglas Merrill would ask in meetings why we were talking about our competitors' releases – and that we had to focus. I went to Elio and said, 'This guy can't run the new music board. He just doesn't understand the smallest thing. If you put out a Kylie record and a Rihanna record on the same day, you're probably not going to get your number one.' It was ridiculous. It was FMCG thinking."

A US executive drops in a hypothetical that is intended to illustrate just how detuned the new wave of leaders within EMI were to how the music business works – especially with regard to the convoluted world of promotion. "Pick two random artists," they say. "In week one, Lenny Kravitz performs on *Saturday Night Live* and his sales go up 6 per cent the following week. The next week, Coldplay perform on *Saturday Night Live* and their sales go up 17 per cent. Things like that were baffling to the experts at Terra Firma. They couldn't figure out that if acts go on *Saturday Night Live* why their sales are not going up the exact same percent. They were having a very, very hard time understanding exceptions-based causation correlation. They just could not wrap their heads around why sometimes this thing would happen and why sometimes that thing would happen."

Ultimately, they were trying to apply logic to something that was at the mercy of too many variables. "They were really, really struggling with getting their heads around a bunch of these things," suggests the same US source. "I think their insistence was that there must be a series of recognisable patterns and the industry simply hadn't been smart enough to uncover them. There was an implied narcissism in their approach that was off-putting. They thought there was going to be a way and they were the ones who were going to be able to do it."

Tim Clark of ie:music felt the underlying problem was that the new team could speak fluently when it came to marketing and branding but suffered from a form of aphasia when it came to talking to musicians about their art. "I felt that Elio, while he was clearly a clever guy, still didn't get the underlying fact of our industry – that it is based on artists," says Clark. "And that artists can't be pinned down. They simply can't. It is the nature of creativity. You cannot create to order. But it is very difficult when you are making art that is coming from the heart ... I think for them that it was always about products. I think it was always about confectionery! Ha ha!"

Another senior executive suggested that this stopped being just a case of the old guard of EMI facing off against the new guard of Terra Firma and was actually starting to break down into fiefdoms within the Terra Firma-appointed executives. Internecine fighting and jostling for position started to creep into the new management structures in 2009 and 2010 and this was because the structures themselves were fundamentally flawed and inherently encouraged pernicious politicking. It became like an executive version of 'sick building syndrome'.

"The structure didn't work as, at that point, there were an awful lot of powerful and influential people that were reporting into Elio whose objectives were not aligned and who were ultimately, I think, looking after themselves rather than EMI," says the executive. "Like David Kassler and Ernesto Schmitt. Ernesto was a friend of Elio's but he was undermining Elio every moment of the day. It was horrible to watch from my perspective. Was he jostling for the global CEO role? He would have been absolutely useless at it."

This new no-nonsense operational strategy did not go down well with EMI staff, who were used to a more affable working environment and command structure. "If somebody is telling you you're stupid and that you better fucking do what they tell you to do, people don't tend to do those things," suggests the same source. "Ernesto objected when anybody other than his team was dealing with marketing. Every time something came up and a local MD said that they couldn't really do that that way, he would say, 'It's none of your business! You have nothing to do with this!' He undercut any authority in the local territories. It was poisonous. Poisonous. Much of what he was trying to make happen was necessary, but he was just not capable of doing it. And Elio was incapable of managing him."

One senior source feels that the executives brought in were seduced by the glamour of the world they were now working in and this led to delusions of grandeur among a certain subset. "Guy Hands had brought in a lot of brand people who were in love with showbiz, the status and the glamour," the same source argues. "I wouldn't say these people were going native. I would say these people were star-struck. Going native could have been a positive thing. It could have been that they actually really put the artists first. They didn't."

Added into this was, for some senior observers, a corporate schizophrenia that resulted in Terra Firma trying to move 180 degrees away from the old way of doing things, and adding in the matrix system that ended up confounding when it should have been clarifying.

"You just didn't know who was in charge at that point or who was doing what," they say. "There were so many different work streams going on but no one had any real sense of who was in charge. They kept shuffling the deck the whole time. Elio came in but was dropped into this mixture of confusion and lack of direction, yet he was expected to run everything despite not knowing anything about the music business, not really knowing anything about EMI and not really knowing anything about Terra Firma. It was a pretty hard gig for him to get to grips with quickly."

It would have been fine if all this was happening behind closed doors, but stories and emails were being fed to the media and staff would gossip with friends and former colleagues at other labels. Everything that was happening in EMI very quickly entered the public domain and that brought whole new headaches for those trying to rebuild a company, knowing every move was being publicly scrutinised.

"There was a lot of leakage," laments Leoni Sceti. "It is a very leaky industry and people like to talk. It's very gossipy. Every time I wrote an internal email, it somehow leaked ... after the first time that I got caught, I was writing internally knowing that it was going to be read externally."

He does, however, feel this had some accidental benefits. "You adjust," he says. "I would say that the media shadow Terra Firma had, in that sense, for me was a plus. It took the attention away from what I was doing into the issues of ownership challenges and debt."

The end of 2009 saw some key executive changes with both Chris Rolling (EMI COO and CFO) and Ashley Unwin (COO for UK and North America) leaving Terra Firma. Both of them had been instrumental in the opening act of the company's ownership of EMI. Some saw this as symbolic as the company was moving into its next phase. Others just shrugged, now fully awake to the belief that everyone at the company, old or new, was ultimately dispensable.

At the same time, Terra Firma was reported to have injected £75 million into EMI to prevent it from defaulting on its loan from Citigroup.[9] The scramble to prop up the company and keep it out of the hands of Citigroup was to accelerate over the next two years.

During this period of asset mining and exploitation, as Terra Firma's team raced to find every way they could to maximise revenues, many things were safeguarded. Abbey Road was not turned into a visitor centre or a hotel. Gorillaz were not used to advertise a body spray. Radiohead were spared the indignity of having their catalogue racked beside chinos, ankle boots and pleather skirts in Next. Robbie Williams did not have to sit awkwardly in a helicopter on the way to Lord's with someone paying a fortune for the privilege. The EMI Archive was not turned into a glorified car boot sale.

But there was one significant casualty during this time. Built in 1906 originally as a theatre and then a TV studio in the 1950s, Byfeld Hall in Barnes, West London, was acquired in 1965 and turned into a recording studio. Olympic Sound Studios might not have had quite the same resonance for the public as Abbey Road, but it had an equally rich history. Acts who recorded there included Jimi Hendrix, The Rolling Stones, Dusty Springfield, Led Zeppelin, Queen, David Bowie, The Jam, Madonna, Prince, The Spice Girls, U2, Oasis and, yes, even The Beatles.[10]

The studio was acquired in 1987 by Virgin Music and eventually came under EMI's ownership. Terra Firma announced in December 2008 that Olympic would be closed and sold, with some suggesting it was sacrificed to protect Abbey Road. There was some public outcry at the cultural desecration happening here, but the deal went through in February 2010, with local businessman Stephen Burdge raising £3.5 million to buy it.[11] It reopened in 2013 as a two-screen cinema, restaurant and members' bar.[12]

It arguably kept its sense of history by being turned back into what it was before it became a recording studio. Some in EMI saw it as just Terra Firma, devoid of sentimentality and caring not one jot for cultural history, blankly selling off the company's history piecemeal. They thought, there but for the grace of God goes Abbey Road.

CHAPTER 10

Forming, Storming, Norming and Performing

EMI entered 2009 in mixed spirits. Apple's iTunes service revealed it was dropping DRM (digital rights management, limiting the number of devices music could be put onto or how many times it could be burned to CD) from all downloads – a movement that EMI had helped to kick-start in early 2007. That, however, was a legacy of the old management team, notably Eric Nicoli and Barney Wragg, and Terra Firma was keen to show that it had made its own profound impact on the company as well as the wider music market.

In terms of UK sales, the BPI's full numbers for 2008 reported that EMI was third, ahead of Warner, with a 13.7 per cent share of British album sales. There was also news that January that Robbie Williams was preparing to record his eighth studio album, with suggestions it could be out in time for Christmas 2009. (*Reality Killed The Video Star* was released that November.) It would be his last album in his current deal with EMI but it would be the first released under Terra Firma's ownership. Expectations were high that it would sell well, putting the curate's egg of 2006's *Rudebox* behind him and the company. A lot was riding on this album, especially if Terra Firma could retain him as an EMI act when his contractual obligations were fulfilled after the album arrived.

In the UK, Duffy and Take That (both Universal Music acts) were revealed as having the biggest selling albums of 2008. They were followed by Kings Of Leon at number three and Leona Lewis at number four (both Sony acts). Coldplay at number five and, then way down the chart of best sellers, Katy Perry at number forty-seven were EMI's only acts in the entire top fifty. In a falling market, where British album sales overall were down 3.2 per cent in 2008 from 2007, this was a lacklustre performance.

195

Better news was to follow in February when the IFPI announced that Coldplay's *Viva La Vida* was the biggest album globally in 2008, with sales of 6.8 million. EMI might have had a poor performance in its home market, but it could justifiably claim, for one album at least, to be a world-beater.

Buried in the 'news in brief' section of *Music Week* on 24 January was the news that Charles Allen, the former chief executive of ITV, had been named as a non-executive chairman of EMI Music, while Stephen Alexander (Terra Firma's operational MD) had become a senior non-executive chairman of EMI Music Publishing and Pat O'Driscoll (former chief executive of Northern Foods) was joining Terra Firma as operational MD. At the board level, Terra Firma was bulking EMI up for its most critical year to date.

This bullishness and optimism was dampened somewhat the following week when a report, *The Music Industry In 2009: Predicting The Unpredictable*, was published wherein senior executives and insiders outlined the key issues facing the business in the coming year. In it, Mark Collen – by then director at Mubito, a company running D2C (direct-to-consumer) sites for musicians, but former senior vice president of EMI Music – put the boot into his former employers. He predicted that EMI "will no longer be considered a major player by the end of the year" and that Guy Hands "will do his utmost to offload the recorded music side of the business". He also predicted more major acts and staff defecting, ending by saying that hopefully a consortium led by Roger Ames, or Warner, would buy it. "'EMI 2.0' will go down as a very high-profile mistake," he concluded.[1] This, by all accounts, was met with fury within Terra Firma.

Tim Parry of management company Big Life was less damning than Collen but still gripped by pessimism about Terra Firma's recovery plan. He was quoted in the same report as saying that EMI had "good execs" in Nick Gatfield and Rob Stevenson, but then outlined his reservations. "It is a question of how long will Terra Firma be prepared to keep funding a company that is doing so badly," he said. "I hope that it survives. But I worry that it won't."[2]

Not even eighteen months into its ownership of EMI, the outside diagnosis was one of grave concern. Charles Allen, coming into a company that was externally damned and internally fractious, knew he had quite a task in front of him.

"I was taking over from Guy as Guy had been chairman," says the former ITV executive of his appointment. "I had done some work for Guy before that and then he asked me to come in as non-executive chairman. The role really was to be the interface between him and the company." He was also to be a guiding figure for the chief executive, reacting to internal criticisms that Leoni Sceti lacked the requisite skills to be heading up a company trading in the creative arts.

"I was really [there] to be an industry mentor to Elio," adds Allen. "He hadn't been in the music industry as he had come from other industries. What Guy had wanted was someone who had worked in the media business. Because I had been at Granada and ITV for fifteen years, he wanted me to play that role. I joked with Elio about being both his mentor and his tormentor! This was at a time when there is so much change going on – both in the industry and within the company."

As with Lord Birt, his media background was not enough for some within EMI to welcome Allen as someone who would understand them and the nature of their work. "Charles Allen?" snorted one senior insider at EMI. "He was known at Granada as the man who went through the company killing everything. All of the budgets got cut. But they increased profitability just at the time when ITV started consolidating. So that enabled Granada to buy all these other TV companies. When he took over the entire company, they had no new programme successes whatsoever."

If Guy Hands was hoping that the double act of the former heads of a public service broadcaster and a commercial broadcaster was going to inspire the EMI troops, he was to be sadly mistaken. "Guy brought in Charles Allen and John Birt – the worst media executives in circulation who are actually unemployed," keens the same executive. "Oh, they've all come to EMI! That's who we've got!"

At least with his media experience, Allen knew that PR had not been Terra Firma's strength to date and so he had to undo a lot of the bad work that was done before his arrival, placating the upset and reassuring the anxious. He met with key contacts including the management teams behind both Robbie Williams and Coldplay as well as the surviving members of Pink Floyd. Also, no doubt hoping to repair the damage caused by Ernesto Schmitt, he met with Apple Corps.

"What they wanted was senior-level comfort," Allen says of many of these meetings. "They were reading all the things that were happening in the press and wanted us to tell them what was going on. Rather than shying away from it, it was about going to spend time with them. They knew that they could come to me at any point in time. Often they did."

He also had to reassure the wider artist community who had been spooked by media reports about deep cuts to the roster and budgets. "It was a key role that I played in terms of calming that down," he says. "It wasn't about dealing with boxes or products. Having spent fifteen years in the media, [I know] the talent can walk out the door or the talent talks back. It was about having the confidence to sit down, talk with them and listen to them."

Alongside this, one of the first things he did was to apply the brakes on the spiralling consultancy fees that dated back to the early weeks of Terra Firma's ownership of EMI. He estimates that consultancy bills before his arrival had topped a staggering £40 million. Hands denied the consultancy bill was this high and says the £40 million figure also covered things like redundancies. No matter. Allen felt the months of thinking and strategising by external consultants had to end and be replaced by enactment. "What had happened was that there wasn't really any operational implementation of it," he says of the consultancy work. "There was some good stuff in there, but what I did was I stopped all the consultants."

He felt that the ever-present consultants picking over parts of the business were a distraction to the staff who were trying to do their jobs in a period of intense scrutiny and uncertainty. He also felt that the outsourcing of work to a variety of consultancy firms meant that an integrated implementation of their ideas was nigh on impossible as they were not communicating with each other to share ideas.

"Because they had brought in four different consultants, there wasn't a joined-up plan because they had effectively all recommended different things," he says of the strategy documents. Allen was left to make sense of these and try to tie them together.

The old divisions between EMI's corporate office and its labels office were now at an end. In February, staff from Brook Green began to move into Wrights Lane, the thinking being that the company would work more cohesively as one, with Wrights Lane in effect becoming a physical manifestation of the matrix system. Staff at Brook Green had always had a healthy and tongue-in-cheek disregard for the 'suits' and 'bean counters' at head office but now they knew they were all ultimately pulling in the same direction. The relocation in 2009 was going to be slightly different as Brook Green staff were about to move into a space they knew was only available because of mass redundancies. And they were going to have to live cheek by jowl with their new taskmasters for the first time.

"When we were told we were going to move into Wrights Lane, that is when we thought people were going to start to be laid off because Wrights Lane isn't that big," says one long-serving Brook Green staff member. "It was a really awful time as you didn't know from one day to the next what was going to happen. Then you had a backdrop of blokes like Mormons – you know, Mormons on a Sunday morning, where they go around in shirts and ties? – walking around, measuring desks, lifting things up. You'd come in on a Monday morning and things had been taken down off the wall."

The same source feels that the move to Wrights Lane was more than just a cost-saving measure: it was a direct message to the staff at Brook Green that they were now under the full scrutiny of EMI's new owners. "We moved to Wrights Lane and they had won at that point," they say. "They had really won. By then it felt that there were more of them than there were of us. They wore their suits with no shame. At that point we were living in their world; they were not living in our world."

Initially Terra Firma staff had been accused of going native, dazzled by the world of music; now, the new system was so bedded in that the going native started to work the other way round for more opportunistic and self-interested staff members. "You knew who you were when Tony [Wadsworth] was running that company," says a source on how the old culture of Brook Green was eroded with the move to head office. "But you didn't know now. Some people could go into a meeting and come out being promoted because they said the right thing or power dressed. It was like the *Titanic*. You didn't know from one minute to the next who was going to survive and who wasn't. It was just elbows. That brings out the best and the worst in people, I find."

For some, the old 'them and us' divisions were harder to bleach away and behind the rictus grins, simmering resentments remained. "We had all of these people helicoptered into our division – all of these people who just looked like fucking weirdos," says one Brook Green evacuee. "And we wouldn't speak to them. We wouldn't say hello to them in the morning. That was because we didn't like them and also because we didn't trust them."

'They' became something to rail against and ideologically define themselves against for many who felt they were now in the belly of the beast. They also felt that the reason for working at a company like EMI – a romantic and overpowering love of music – was at risk of being gelded by a new working culture that had little emotional involvement in the 'products' that were being created and marketed by the company.

"Did they go to gigs?" a source asks rhetorically about the new line of Terra Firma-appointed executives they now had to work with and report to. "No! Never! They would never go to gigs. They were trying to run a business that they had no clue about how to run. That's because it wasn't like any business they had ever worked in. They couldn't work out how we did it. The arrogance of them was that they thought music people must be a bit stupid."

Invisible battle lines were being drawn on the floors of Wrights Lane, with paranoia starting to bite. Some long-serving EMI staff began to feel that talking to 'the other side' was an act of treason. "There was no way you could fraternise with them," one such person says. "The Terra Firma people weren't our friends. They absolutely weren't. There was a force field around them. You couldn't chat to them. You couldn't be seen to be talking to them. Some people crossed that divide and instantly there was a certain amount of distrust. 'Hang on a minute! How the fuck did that happen?' There was distrust like that."

A senior label source says they immediately took against the new executives coming in and imposing their rule on the company. They failed, the source says, to do anything to win the EMI staff over and change their gloomily negative view of what was going on. EMI old hands especially took against those on the marketing side.

"He was a fucking freak!" they say of a senior Terra Firma marketing executive that they would prefer not to name. "The stuff coming out of this guy's mouth! It was mad. He was a mild-mannered, suburban cheap suit-wearing guy talking absolute rubbish. He spoke in riddles! I have no idea to this day if that guy was an idiot or Stephen Hawking. I suspect the former. It was gobbledygook. It was madness. He kept talking about systems and drawing these nuts flow charts. He was talking about structures and systems. I was white as a sheet. He lectured all of us with a blackboard and was drawing on it."

The same source was equally cutting about another, nameless, Terra Firma recruit. "He'd go in marketing meetings [bored monotone], 'What's the brand essence of Laura Marling?' It was like marketing 101. This was a guy walking out of marketing school and trying to apply what he had learned about marketing petrol to records."

One source also claimed that some Terra Firma executives were not just struggling to get their heads around marketing musicians; they were unintentionally jeopardising the relationships EMI had with some of its biggest artists. "There was a meeting with one Terra Firma person and Terry Blamey, Kylie Minogue's manager," says someone who was in the room. "They were talking about the creative for the new album [2007's *X*]. He was quietly observant as we talked about choreography for the video and things like that as well as the bill for her stylist. He was wondering how we could make this a success based on what we already knew about Kylie. He alighted on the most identifiable thing about her which was her gold hot pants in the 'Spinning Around' video. 'Spinning Around' was seven years previously."

They continue, their hands clasping their face in horror, "I remember him saying to Terry, 'Just stick her in the gold hot pants again! Everyone will love it!' Even to the novice or someone who doesn't know anything about the music industry, that is not a good thing to say. If you work in the industry, you know that artist sensitivities and relationships are the top of the list. I have never seen a manager scowl at somebody so aggressively and just lose their shit. It was like, 'How dare you, as somebody who knows nothing about the music industry, come in here and tell me the way to sexually exploit my artist for your monetary gain? This is about my client delivering her art to her audience and not you demanding sexual exploitation.' The poor guy thought it was an innocent and jovial comment."

Such incidents were, fortunately, few and far between but they soon spread like wildfire around the industry, turning EMI at the time from something perhaps to be pitied by its rivals into something approaching a laughing stock.

Even though Mute Records was in a protected position within EMI, sitting more with the European arm rather than the UK arm, Daniel Miller was aware of the paranoia clinging like a miasma in the corridors of Wrights Lane. "It was all a bit Stasi-like," he says of this time when his label was brought into the main HQ. "Everybody was a bit cautious about what they could say. I would say things in passing that I'd find out later had got back into the system – in a very negative way. I just thought this was bullshit. Everybody knew that EMI was in a terrible state. Then after 2008, everybody knew that Terra Firma was in a terrible state!"

For the most part, however, Mute was allowed to continue operating as it always had done and was not under the same pressure as, say, Parlophone or Virgin. "For a long time I didn't really report to anyone," he says of where he fitted into (or, rather, didn't fit into) the matrix system. "I just got on with what I was doing. Once in a while somebody took interest. Or not. If there was a new Depeche Mode album or a new Nick Cave album, then people would pay attention."

Some senior managers having to relocate to Wrights Lane became very protective towards their staff members during this time – creating a bulwark between them and new tiers of executives brought in by Terra Firma.

"I told everyone here that they were going to be judged on what we delivered," is how one described their survival strategy. "I said, 'Fuck them [Terra Firma] and what they get judged on. But you, all of my team, this is what we will be judged on. So let's just get our heads down and get that right and we'll sail through this. We'll come out the other end – I don't know where it will be or who it will be with – but it will be all good. But we have to go through this pain to get there.'"

This executive felt they had found a common ally with one senior Terra Firma executive, however, and felt his treatment of staff was beyond reproach. "David Kassler was brilliant," they say. "He was the one person who came into the company and he asked questions. He asked how we did things and how he could help us. He was the first person who asked as opposed to everyone else who was telling us what to do. He was someone that the artists engaged with and liked."

Miller was also highly supportive of Kassler and felt he was the executive that he was closest to during this time. "All the other people from Terra Firma and their advisors whenever we met them – apart from Guy Hands, who was quite polite – were quite bluntly telling us what we need to do. They'd never worked in a record company before. The first meeting with David Kassler I remember really well. He said, 'I know nothing about this business and I need to learn from you guys.' That immediately set a much better tone! I had a good relationship with him." It was Kassler who Miller first approached in 2009 to start the process that would remove Mute from EMI the following year and he puts this down to the strong and close working relationship they developed from the off.

Leoni Sceti was burdened with pushing through the staff and roster cuts during this time, having to slim the company down to the level Guy Hands had talked about in his public statements on redundancies and A&R cuts. "He [Guy] made those objectives very open so the media wrote about it and everybody knew about it," Leoni Sceti says. "Then I was left to manage these 2,000 people that perhaps thought they weren't going to have a job tomorrow. And also to manage the managers of artists saying that if I took away their A&R guy or promotions person then their act wouldn't be as supported as they should be."

In his supporting role for Elio Leoni Sceti, Charles Allen explains that in his early months at EMI he was also tasked with, if not necessarily winning over the staff, then at least giving them the space to get on with their jobs. After so much upheaval, so much uncertainty and a rolling redundancy programme, he says he wanted the remaining staff to do what they were good at and what they were paid to do.

"We spent a lot of time just talking to people," he says of his meetings with staff. "They had got into this death-by-PowerPoint [culture]. Basically everything was a presentation; everything was a deck. That wasn't who they were. Talented people don't want to be creating presentations. We stopped all that. It was wasting time, frankly, on PowerPoint presentations which stopped them doing their day jobs … The death by PowerPoint got a bit silly. There was almost paralysis by analysis in terms of analysing things to death."

The management team put in place by Terra Firma were under intense pressure to hit certain targets and this did not let up during their time there. On top of trying to appease remaining staff members and help them to do their jobs better, David Kassler had tough financial objectives to push through. "For the first year, we had a budget of £60 million to hit and we hit that with a little bit to spare," he says. "There was a huge amount of cynicism from outside of the business and, to be honest, from inside the business as to whether or not that was achievable. We hit it. We hit it through top line growth, we made it through making our releases numbers and we hit it through cost reduction. That was a jump from £7 million to £60 million on recorded music. For me, that was proof that the model could work."

This also involved squeezing department heads and imposing tighter monetary controls on them, erasing the old ways of running projects where occasionally spending could run out of control. "People had got out of practice of having sensible budgets to cover sensible reporting, normal accounting practices and financial controls," he says on what he had to cauterise.

Right at the top of the recorded music arm of EMI, Leoni Sceti was having to pull the company out of a financial nose dive and return it to profitability – which was no small task as, by this stage, the recorded music market globally had been cratering for close on a decade. In 2000, the market had a trade value of $36.9 billion according to the IFPI; by 2009, this was down to just over $17 billion, but was actually closer to $16.3 billion when $785 million of performance rights, which were not included in 2000's tabulations, were stripped out.

Leoni Sceti suggests that "three fundamental changes" had to occur within the company to flip the decline into reverse. "The first was that, instead of being fully reliant on intuition, the company was going to understand consumer preference and use that consumer preference as an amplifier of that intuition; it was matching what I called the reason to the intuition. If you look at the revenue trend when I arrived, it was minus 9 per cent and the revenue trend when I left was plus 2 per cent in sales. That was the first pillar of change."

He continues, "The second pillar of change had to be about a systematically and a financially informed way to place investment. The music business on the catalogue side is a cash-generative, sustainable and constant business. It's an 'easy' business and it's a good business because it is easier to manage. On the new music side, it's a numbers game. It's like venture capital. You need to be as good as you can be at placing the right bets because those are the bets that pay for the whole system and pay for all the failures – which inevitably you will have. The capacity of screening what bets to act on had to be more data-based than they were."

He concludes his outlining of this recovery triptych by saying, "The third change was all about that digital black hole in which the industry

203

was. They were suing consumers and they were playing Whack-A-Mole [with piracy]. It was a whole fight against [them] as opposed to leveraging and embracing what in my mind was, absolutely no question, the future of music. As the future of music was going to be digital, the question was how we were going to deal with that."

He knew that what he was imposing internally at EMI was not necessarily going to be met with cheers of jubilation from the staff he inherited. This was something they were going to have to get over. EMI was going to have to take its medicine and the pill was not going to be a sugar-coated one.

"You need to be sure that what you're trying to do is correct and spend your time making sure that that's the case as opposed to making sure that what you were doing is liked," he says, bluntly. "Sometimes it is and sometimes it isn't, but that's not really the point of the game."

Leoni Sceti and his team were not naive enough to think that the staff at EMI were automatically going to fall cheerfully into line, but the hope was that by delivering results against the odds they could slowly win over the doubters.

Arguably much of the residual resentment of Terra Firma within EMI was a legacy of the first, highly schizophrenic, year where it seemed at the time that the new owners were struggling to keep a lid on things.

Mark Hodgkinson feels that this is not uncommon during takeovers and the trick is for everyone, as much as they can, to focus on getting through the pain barrier. "I think that was quite a new experience for EMI," he says of that first year under Terra Firma. "But I have seen it in other businesses where you go in and initially there are lots of things that you could do and it can sometimes be overwhelming because you are coming up with a lot of ideas and you need to think about which ones you're really going to focus on and make happen and which ones you are not. Some people will find that a really hard phase in the business because it's almost like challenging all the norms that you had before. It is always a hard time in a business. That classic 'storming-norming …' phrase [forming-storming-norming-performing] that is used in business. That was the storming phase. But you have to go through that to get to the other side, otherwise you'll just carry on as you are."

As a strategy, it was essentially playing the long game but, slowly, the obstinate and taciturn – helped by finally being afforded the wriggle room to get on with their jobs – were warming to at least some parts of the recovery plan. "I wouldn't want to say that Terra Firma were all bad because they had some genuinely good people – intellectually very clever and very rigorous," says one senior and long-serving Wrights Lane executive. "On the deal analysis side, they certainly brought a sense of rigour to the analysis of some of the new artist deals or acquisitions that had possibly being lacking in the old world. They would look at things slightly differently and bring perhaps more financial rigour to it than we had before."

At this stage, Terra Firma was dismantling a bonus system within EMI that it felt rewarded indolence and incompetence. Meanwhile the executives on the receiving end of the bonuses felt they had earned them, and they were a key reason why they had not upped sticks to go to another major label. News of this financial incentive now being terminated landed extremely badly.

"Terra Firma was introducing a new senior management contract for senior employees and it basically got rid of bonuses," says one highly ranked employee who was presented with new remuneration terms. "They had decided that the whole bonus system was a bad thing. That it was driving short-term behaviour rather than thinking about the long-term future."

There was, however, another scheme put in its place that Terra Firma would use to hold onto key executives and still reward them if – but only if – they proved their long-term loyalty to the new bosses by remaining at the company until the turnaround was achieved and the company was put back up for sale.

"Basically they came up with an equity plan," says the same top-level executive. "They said they would pay the base salary and there would be no bonuses – but they would give you shadow equity or an equity plan so that when they sold the business or re-floated the business, you would get a piece of the upside. They delivered this equity plan but it was so ridiculous. From memory, you didn't make anything unless Terra Firma sold the business for four times what they paid for it. We all thought they overpaid for it in the first place and were never going to get the money back. I was being asked to forgo my bonus in order to sign up for this plan that I didn't believe in. I said that it didn't make sense and no one was ever going to make any money out of it. Elio was putting pressure on people to sign the contract."

Rather than getting its most senior staff on side, the plan backfired somewhat and actually made them more suspicious of Terra Firma's motives and less hopeful about its chances of success. "It did feel that Big Brother was now in the room and it felt very uncomfortable for a while and that they were second-guessing every aspect of your job," the executive in question recounts. "Did I enjoy working here at that time? No. No, I didn't. I could sort of see what they were trying to do but they seemed to have very little sympathy or elegance about it."

One source has a unique perspective on it all, having gone on sabbatical early in Terra Firma's ownership of the company, returning a few years later. For them, the change inside the company during their absence was both profound and telling.

"By the time I got there the full weight of Terra Firma's mantra of, 'We're going to change the business,' had disappeared," they recall. "I think they had realised it wasn't working how they expected it to be. It felt that there was a lot less focus from the actual Terra Firma people. It was, 'How the fuck do we get out of this now?' rather than, 'How do we keep this going?' The impression I had was that there were two groups of people within it. There were the Terra Firma people and then there were the record company people that had been there for ages and were actually working their way around Terra Firma rather than working with them. There was definitely that split between the two sides. There were probably more Terra Firma people looking at sales and, luckily for the business, a lot less of them focusing on the other side of things. I think they had realised that that was too difficult to manage. That had changed, definitely."

EMI Music Publishing had a very different time from recorded music during the Terra Firma years and some on that side are less damning of the new owners. An executive in the publishing arm succinctly sums up the different experience the two sides of the business had during the Terra Firma reign. "I didn't take against Guy Hands in the same way some people did," they say. "But then I wasn't being fucked over by him every single week like a lot of people in recorded music were."

It has been claimed by some people at EMI during this entire time that a lot of the problems and complications stemmed from the fact that people brought in by Terra Firma were scared to make major decisions without first getting full approval from Guy Hands. This resulted in an impenetrable and damaging operational torpor. This was at its most pronounced during his time as CEO, but it is claimed the constant referral upwards did not change significantly when Elio took over.

"They were terrified of Guy and in awe of him," says a source who saw this play out multiple times. "They thought he had all the answers. You would have expected all of these people [former CEOs of other companies] to be a bit more confident. But they couldn't get to grips with the industry and the decisions that they needed to make. Things would get elevated up to Guy but then Guy didn't want to make all those decisions. He'd delegate them back down and they would gradually come back up. You could find yourself in a holding pattern. That's what I thought was going on."

Another, very senior, source claims that Hands himself was gripped by an inability to make hard decisions on things and this already aggravated the game of pass the parcel they saw repeated in front of their eyes. "I would say that Guy is not a decision maker," was their rather curt summation. "There were all sorts of investment issues. Say we wanted to make this deal for this artist and it was going to cost £5 million, it would go through circles in the team that was evaluating deals; it would just go round and round. You could never get a conclusion. The only conclusion was that the opportunity would go away. That happened a lot." They continue, "Julie [Williamson] was Guy's controller. She controlled the deals and she controlled everything on Guy's behalf. Every project that required capital had to go through the process that Julie was responsible for. Most Terra Firma people are very bright. There was nothing the matter with their intellect. But they were frightened to death of making decisions. They had analysis paralysis. That is the world that Elio had to manage."

Hands denies outright that such problems as 'holding patterns' and 'analysis paralysis' were in found within the company. He also denies claims made from several EMI sources that he is a dictator. "What I'm very strong about is process," he says. "That is about having everybody have a say. That means that somebody who wants to do stuff which is just them doing stuff, I tend to bristle. I say, 'Have you spoken to X?' It's a strange form of autocracy. With most autocrats, you go to them and say, 'I would like to do this.' If they say yes, you just get on and do it. Mine is exactly the opposite. You come to me and you say, 'I want to do that,' and I say, 'Have you spoken to Y?' To me, it's the exact opposite of being an autocrat. I am not quite sure what it is. A process junkie? I don't know what it is. It is not really autocratic. It really isn't."

He also says that he relishes people arguing with him, but what grates most for him is when a plan is agreed upon and one of his team does something off script. "That drives me crackers," he says.

Responding to accusations that he is a particularly bad boss to deliver bad news to, he raises his eyebrows quizzically. "No!" he laughs. "I take the delivery of bad news very, very well. I think I am probably one of the best people in the world to deliver bad news to. I am one of the worst people in the world to hide something from, though. There was a lot of hiding going on at EMI. There were a lot of people fiddling the numbers to get stuff through."

What internal decisions could or could not be made by Terra Firma recruits and executives may remain in dispute, but a very real – and growing – problem for the company was its crumbling A&R policy. EMI might have had the biggest album of 2008 with Coldplay's *Viva La Vida*, but this was a band that was signed to Parlophone back in 1999. EMI desperately needed to be finding the Coldplay or the Robbie Williams or the Norah Jones of tomorrow.

The budget for signing acts was significantly reduced but worse than that, EMI's standing in the market had been shredded. "The hardest thing was actually going out to sign artists," argues a senior A&R source. "First, Guy Hands was in the press every other fucking week and that was very bad publicity. For artists it was appalling. Was EMI seen as a toxic label? Absolutely. There was a period for two or three years where we couldn't actually sign anyone. No one would sign to us. Why would they? People thought it was all going to fall apart badly. No one wanted to sign to a company that was run by Terra Firma as they were reading all the things they were saying in the press about their own artists. They were very vocal in the press about the artists and the people who worked in the company."

This was going to starve EMI of the oxygen of new talent. Guy Hands might have balked at immediately turning EMI into a catalogue label, but it was now at a serious competitive disadvantage when trying to attract new talent. On top of this, the defection of acts like Radiohead, The Rolling Stones and Queen sent out a very stark message to artists and managers that EMI was having problems holding onto its biggest names. Then there was the ignominy of only having two albums in the fifty biggest sellers in the UK in 2008 – the market where it was supposed to be strongest. This became a vicious circle for the company. EMI, the industry was quickly concluding, could not get acts and even the ones it had were not so much slipping as racing through its fingers.

Into this maelstrom, with EMI struggling to regain its cultural relevance as well as its credibility within the incestuous and catty world of record label politics, came Andria Vidler, who was appointed as president of EMI Music UK & Ireland in April 2009. She was previously chief marketing officer at media company Bauer; her CV included being MD of Capital Radio, and she had risen through the BBC in the 1990s, becoming head of marketing for BBC News in 1996.[3]

Reporting to David Kassler, EMI Music's European president, she was effectively replacing Tony Wadsworth, who had left EMI some seventeen months earlier. Speaking to *Music Week* at the time of her appointment, she was full of praise for the new team for having "moved things on considerably", saying that "EMI is leading the way in the industry in changing how things work". She added, "EMI is already doing more than it is being given credit for." Major changes, she suggested, would not be coming from her immediately as she would be focused on "enhancing what is already working".[4]

Asked what EMI was like when she started there, she has a one-word summation. "Chaos." In a similar way to Kassler, she says she did not come into EMI proclaiming to have all the answers and instead spent her opening months working her way around the company to get a better feel for what worked and what needed to be fixed. Compared to the more combative approach of other executives through the doors before her, she was seen as a breath of fresh air by staff who felt they had been cast into a structural oubliette.

"What I didn't do was say I knew anything," is how she explains her opening gambit in the company. "I didn't go in saying that I had the solution for everything. That is what, I think, other people had done. What I did was listen."

She was, however, on the same page as Guy Hands in terms of where she felt the business needed to change and where it needed to make its money in the future. "What Guy Hands believed was that you could create a business that didn't rely entirely on singles and album sales – that there were multiple revenue streams within music," she said. "I believe in that 100 per cent. What I did when I came in was to say that I believed in this, but I thought the way we were trying to do it wasn't helping us."

To do this, she needed buy-in from the CEO of the company, saying she would use the marketing of the upcoming Robbie Williams album, *Reality Killed The Video Star*, that November as proof of concept. "I persuaded Elio to let me change the way it might work in the UK without upsetting some of the powerful men with big trousers," she says. "I asked them to let me see if this could work – and the Robbie album did work."

Robbie's co-manager Tim Clark has nothing but praise when talking about Vidler and the transformation of EMI in the UK, for which he saw her as being largely responsible. "We had a great time with Andria and her team," he says. "It really was back to the early days in the late 1990s and early 2000s. It really was back to that [time] when we had such a great team ethos. Everybody working together. It wasn't just the UK. It was Europe-wide and spread down to Australia. All the places where Rob was big, that album was a real success ... I felt that Andria was putting the company back on track and I felt that Roger Faxon was finally beginning to tackle some of the really core problems of running a rights company."

Vidler says she came into Wrights Lane knowing she had half a year, at most, to prove herself, get the company on side and drive through lasting changes. "I had about six months where I was pushing water uphill," she says. "Nobody in the old world of EMI was interested in somebody new coming in and saying they could do new things. I was also going against the grain of what Elio and Guy Hands had put in place. I didn't have very many friends in the first six months!"

She claims she was fully aware of just how badly the odds were stacked against her taking on this role. "I was walking into what could have been a six-month role," she says. "It could have failed. I could have failed like everybody else. What I was really impressed with was the spirit of the people and the commitment of the people who had just kept their heads down and who were loyal to the artists. I did believe in what Guy Hands thought – that you could create an all-rights management business and really support artists. So I was there to give it a go."

To her mind, the brand-centric logic being pushed by Elio Leoni Sceti was useful to a point, but it had to be translated for the music industry and she said her experience at the BBC was critical in this corporate exegesis. "The big difference between the FMCG world and broadcast and media is that, as a manager in the world of broadcast and media, you are not in control of the mic," she proposes. "You only can influence. You have to persuade a presenter. If I wanted Jeremy Paxman to trail something on the BBC at the end of *Newsnight*, I had to convince him that it was the right thing to do … You are not in the studio and it doesn't matter how many times you tell them to do something, unless they believe it they won't do it."

She explains how this was applied in the instance of the first major album to come out on EMI under her watch. "I came in and sat down with [his management] to talk about the Robbie Williams campaign, what they wanted to achieve, how the album fitted into the wider Robbie Williams plan and what it needed to achieve for Robbie's bigger and broader perspective. We talked about how everything needed to build together. The album was just one point and was not the whole of Robbie Williams."

This all landed well with the singer's team. "Once she [Andria] had been there for a while, we realised that actually she was making a difference and things were changing," says Tim Clark. "She did look at everything to do with the industry. She did have a grip on digital technology. She understood it. She knew it. She built a team that actually worked so much better together than in that whole unhappy period from David Munns and Alain Levy leaving to her taking up that position."

EMI in the UK might have been reinvigorated by the appointment of a new executive who better understood the music industry than some of her predecessors and peers, but the company was in no way clear of the jaws of debt. If anything, the repayment situation was getting worse.

"I worked hard in my twenty-eight years in business, but the amount of hours I put in during my two years at EMI were crazy; honestly I don't remember doing anything else other than working!" says Leoni Sceti of the workload he had to deal with during his time at EMI.

There were, he says, rigorous structures in place to keep expenditure in check. "[Having a dedicated] person in charge of the investment committee basically meant that everything that needed to be spent for artists, contract advancements and so on above a certain level had to go through very organised financial ROI [return on investment] sheets," he explains. "That's not too different from things in venture capital. The CIO [chief investment officer] was a very good brain and hand. That was basically helping me to make choices. The investment committee was me with my CFO and the two heads of A&R – Billy Mann and Nick Gatfield – for most of the time along with the CIO who was the guru of investment."

He feels this model delivered clear results. "That part worked because it avoided a lot of wastage in terms of spending too much money on artists that were really not being expected to return that money – or not in a meaningful way," he argues. "It was organised questions that the CIO and I designed for the people proposing investment. Why are we expecting to do this? Who else has done it? What is the maximum and what is the minimum?"

New – and different – signings were finally happening at this time and the hope was that, finally, EMI was back in the race. Shabs Jobanputra became president of A&R at Virgin at the start of 2009 and by May there was a restructuring of the frontline UK A&R team, placing Jobanputra alongside Daniel Miller of Mute and Miles Leonard of Parlophone in a new organisational framework. That same month, Jobanputra made his first signing, bring EDM (Electronic Dance Music) act deadmau5 to Virgin as part of a joint venture deal that saw EMI get a cut of his earnings from live music, recording, sponsorship, TV, film and merchandise. This was to act as an indicator of the types of deals EMI was pursuing and how it was going to both rebuild and reinvigorate itself.

"We tried to reinvent that model by developing shared risk and shared investment," says David Kassler of what was being accomplished here. "We did some very unique deals with acts like Swedish House Mafia and deadmau5 where we'd actually invest in the underlying business of the artist. We bought a 50 per cent share of the company and then we shared in pieces of all the revenue streams that came in for that artist."

A senior source says that good work was being done at this time but, due to the nature of the debt and the repayments, all of this still amounted to pushing against a locked door. "There were lots of quite exciting things beginning to happen," they say of this period of the company. "They had a much smaller release schedule and the financials were improving. After eighteen months or two years, you could genuinely see the progress being made in the financials of recorded music. But by that stage, that wasn't the game any more. The game was that Citigroup wanted its money back and the business was thundering towards a major breach of its covenants."

EMI Music Publishing was turned to on occasion to transfer cash to the recorded side of the business in order to help the company cover the debt covenants, but this was never going to be a long-term solution. It just delayed the amount of time Terra Firma was circling the plughole. "Guy had to come up with a lot of money every time a covenant came up," says a senior source with close proximity to what was happening here. "There was this huge effort to suck cash from wherever you could so you could actually make it all work." It was, in their eyes, doomed to unspool in a spectacularly damaging way. "You were driving this business in order to meet covenants as opposed to building an organisation that was going to be able to drive revenues going forward," they say.

In May 2009, EMI reported that David Kassler (EMI Music European president) and Ron Werre (president of EMI Music Services) were both becoming COOs, newly created roles in the company that made them the most powerful executives after Elio Leoni Sceti.

This came just after EMI announced its EBITDA had significantly increased in the year ending March 2009, its first full financial year under Terra Firma. EBITDA was up 219.6 per cent to £163 million, in part due to a £48 million year-on-year reduction in the cost of returns and other overhead savings. It also generated operating cash flow of £190 million (up from £142 million a year earlier), while turnover was up 4 per cent to £1.07 billion. Terra Firma announced it was on course to deliver the £200 million in cost savings it promised when it bought EMI.

"I am very pleased we have delivered this strong operating performance and would like to thank all the staff and artists whose talent, creativity and hard work made it possible," said Elio Leoni Sceti in a statement. "These results are an important first step in building EMI's future. We cannot afford to be complacent, however, since there is still a great deal of work to be done to restore EMI to its former greatness and we are doing it in the face of challenging economic conditions. Looking ahead we have some exciting new releases coming up, a much deeper understanding of the music consumer and a new engaged relationship with our artists to build on. Now it has established this platform, EMI can look to the future with confidence and optimism."[5]

This confidence and optimism was to be short-lived as two months later, Terra Firma was reported to be in talks with Citigroup to restructure its EMI debt. Guy Hands was said to be proposing that Terra Firma invest between £250 million and £300 million in EMI in exchange for the bank writing off around £500 million of the debt at EMI Music.[6]

As subsequent events were to prove, this was like taking a thimbleful of water to a forest fire.

CHAPTER 11

Dust and Soap

In 2007, digital sales made up 14.8 per cent of recorded music sales globally. Physical sales fell 13 per cent from 2006, while the IFPI reported that digital sales were up 34 per cent. Digital was still a small part of record labels' business but, crucially, it was the fastest-growing part.

In terms of how digital split by format and channel then, the distance of a decade makes it seem like a different world. Online sales (effectively downloads to computers) made up 48 per cent, mobile (effectively short-lived content like ringtones and wallpaper) made up 47 per cent and subscriptions accounted for a minuscule 5 per cent.

This was a bizarre but important transition period for the business. The arrival of Apple's iTunes Music Store in 2003 showed that, despite the enormous spike in illegal downloading and filesharing of MP3 files, consumers could still be persuaded to pay for music. Plus, the fact that they were prepared to pay several times more for a ringtone than they would for a full-track download was an indicator of how content was adapting to devices.

Apple was about to change the music (and wider content) business again in June 2007 when the first-generation iPhone was released. It was not the first smartphone, but it was the first one to really matter. In the coming years, the iPhone and the many Android-powered devices from rival manufacturers were going to burst the mobile content bubble as device owners could make their own ringtones and wallpaper, but they were also to offer the next evolutionary leap from the iPod. Digital music was no longer just portable; it was now also accessible on connected devices. The era of music ownership was going to give way to the era of music access.

Sitting in the wings was a Swedish start-up that was convinced people were going to pay a monthly subscription for music. It was not the first to do this. Rhapsody and the legal reincarnation of Napster were years before it, but Spotify's ploy was to use a limited free and ad-supported tier as a funnel to convert users into subscribers. The smartphone app ecosystem that the iPhone ushered in and that Android devices built on was going to make all that possible. Everything could happen on one connected device – from payments to playback. The future was already here; it was just going to take a few years for the public and the market to catch up. Even Apple had to accept this was the way things were going, eventually launching the Apple Music subscription service in 2015 as the death rattle of music downloads was starting to be heard.

This was all in the future, but the signposts were there in April 2008 when Douglas Merrill, who had a doctorate in machine learning, was poached from Google, where he was the company's chief information officer to become president of EMI's digital business. His appointment came mere months after EMI announced that Barney Wragg, its world-wide head of digital, was leaving and would be replaced, as it turned out on an interim basis, by Mark Hodgkinson.[1]

Symbolically, Merrill was going to be based in California, rather than London (although he would regularly shuttle between the UK and the US), sending a message that EMI was no longer hidebound by insularity. This was a company that was thinking and behaving globally, where it would drive its own digital future rather than slipstreaming the efforts of others.

Guy Hands, announcing the appointment, called Merrill a "proven agent of change who combines broad business intellect with a deep engineering background". His statement continued, "He has been a key member of the management team at Google which has created more value than any other consumer internet company by focusing relentlessly on tools that enable consumers to do things more effectively."[2]

EMI's two biggest digital developments before Merrill arrived were being the first major label to go DRM-free on iTunes in early 2007 and the problematic birth of EMI.com as a statement platform on Terra Firma's arrival. Merrill, as mentioned earlier in this book, was no fan of EMI.com and only took it across the finishing line because it was a project he inherited, but his priorities were much grander and definitely lay elsewhere.

He certainly had a wide-ranging remit, covering EMI's overall digital strategy and innovation efforts as well as working on business develop-ment and refining the company's supply chain. As part of Terra Firma's macro brief to bring external thinking to a music industry it viewed as having become intellectually lethargic, Merrill was a perfect candidate. He was a Silicon Valley veteran and Terra Firma was right in seeing the Californian tech sector as the new centre of gravity, not just for the music business but also for the content business as a whole. They now had executive feet on the ground where the future was being built – or, more specifically, coded – on a daily basis.

Speaking to *Music Week* on his appointment, Merrill said that top of his agenda was dismantling DRM in toto (not just on iTunes) as it was "probably not a good idea" because it "hurts users". He said his thinking and strategy would be informed by the fans and the musicians – trying to prioritise what they wanted and how they could be better connected. "We shouldn't do things that don't add value to fans and artists,"[3] he said.

He also came out swinging against received major label opinion that filesharing was devastatingly parasitic and could only be seen in negative terms, believing it could have benefits if the industry could just move away from demonising it. "Everyone thinks that filesharing is bad," he said. "However, there is some data that says that filesharing is good for some artists. If that is the case, then what does that suggest?" This dovetailed perfectly with Guy Hands's views and his desire to kick against conventional industry thinking.

At the time, a PR and legal war was raging across the industry. On the one side, record label trade bodies like IFPI (globally[4]), RIAA (in the US[5]) and the BPI (in the UK[6]) were presenting research, with academic support, that filesharing was costing it billions in lost sales and therefore they were justified in targeting not just operators of P2P (peer-to-peer) and torrent sites but also the "serial uploaders" (those making their digital music collections accessible via these decentralised services) upon which the services relied. On the other hand, open-internet lobby groups and bodies like the Future Of Music Coalition[7] were arguing that this could be beneficial to musicians and that the anti-piracy lobbying was the thin end of a disturbing wedge that was going to kill web freedom and modern democracy.[8]

The message was clear from Terra Firma: they were going to do things differently and they did not care if that angered the rest of the record industry. The industry, the subtext ran, had got themselves into this mess but Terra Firma was going to get them out of it – starting with EMI.

Merrill had been headhunted for the job and says the scheduling was serendipitous as he had been looking for a way out of Google for some time. "I thought I would do something fun," he says about why he accepted the job. "It was good timing."

With fresh eyes on an industry forced to play digital catch-up, he felt music companies were still philosophically fixated on the old ways of doing things back when they were the all-powerful gatekeepers with a stranglehold on distribution and marketing. This was, he believes, utterly unworkable and unviable in the digital age where labels had so much of their power taken away from them. The idea of trying to push music on consumers in 2008 was laughably anachronistic.

He did not, however, believe that 'free' had won and that consumers would never pay for music again. They would pay, he was certain, but the industry had to recalibrate its thinking about how, where and why they would pay. "One end of the problem was that the industry wasn't trying to understand what the customers wanted," he argues. "They were saying to the customer, 'Here is the one product we have. Buy this CD.' That was generally ineffective – to tell your customers exactly what they are allowed to buy as opposed to letting them tell you what they want to buy."

Hands, long of the belief that the music industry was built on false arrogance, having had things its own way for so long, was fully supportive of a new executive coming in and showing the record companies how to listen rather than dictate. "Part of what I felt was needed – and the discussions I had with Guy – was that EMI was going to be a leader in letting customers tell us how they wanted to pay us," Merrill says. "And we would find a way to make that work. We had great art, world-beating technology underpinning sales and marketing and we would be open to trying new things that were informed by what had worked in other digital domains. That was the sell."

Market size has always been a defining factor in commercial negotiations for the music business. This was key to the independent labels lobbying to prevent the Warner/EMI merger in 2000 and also their opposition to Sony and BMG merging a matter of years later. Consolidation in the market, they argued, handed the biggest companies an unfair advantage and was open to wilful abuse of power and position.

In a digital age where huge advances or equity stakes were offered by new music services keen to get into the market, the largest companies could effectively hold them to ransom, using their market share as their negotiating leverage. Services could, of course, launch without catalogue from the biggest labels in the world, but mainstream consumers would never flock to a service that offered only a portion of the world's music. Services were being held over a barrel and the biggest record companies were wolfing down everything they had in terms of money, leaving the crumbs for everyone else.

As the fourth biggest of the four majors, EMI was always going to struggle to be first in the queue as new services emerged and went out seeking licences. It was at the head of the queue in 2007 when iTunes did its DRM-free deal, but this was precisely because EMI was the smallest major and Apple was using it to force the hands of the other majors, getting the weakest major onside to convince the others to follow suit.

Merrill felt that EMI had become too caught up in an inferiority complex and this needed to change. "The other half of [my] strategy was embedded in the lawyers at EMI," he says. "That strategy was, 'We will do whatever Universal does, we'll do it after they finish it, we'll do it more slowly and we'll get worse economic terms.' It's not a bad strategy, to be clear. Universal is good. Following them is not a bad strategy. But it was not a situation where we were going to be winning."

Where Merrill felt that EMI could win was in pulling out of what he saw as the Pyrrhic victory of suing filesharers, and also using its audience insights division to better understand what its customers wanted: listening and not dictating.

Key to this was opening a dialogue with what the rest of the industry saw as its nemesis – filesharing services. And one in particular: LimeWire.

In the same month that Merrill joined EMI, the Digital Music Desktop Report was published that said LimeWire was the most popular P2P application in the world, installed on an estimated 17.8 per cent of computers. Given that computers could have several different P2P applications installed simultaneously, it was claimed that LimeWire actually had a 36.4 per cent share, far ahead of second-placed uTorrent with a 11.3 per cent share.[9]

The company had not yet been sued (that protracted process would begin in 2010) but it was commonly cited by the anti-piracy teams of industry trade bodies as a bad actor. To be seen talking to LimeWire in 2008 was akin, in the major label world at least, to making a pact with the devil.

Talking to filesharing services and trying to work out a settlement or partnership solution was not new. German media company Bertelsmann – before it merged its BMG music arm with Sony – had taken legal action against Napster soon after its launch but agreed on an armistice in October 2000 to work on a fully licensed relaunch of the service.[10] Napster ran out of financial road in May 2002, with Bertelsmann stepping in to buy the company's assets and invest $8 million to pay its creditors.[11] By February 2003, however, it was facing a $17 billion lawsuit from music copyright owners and creators for having invested $100 million in the service and therefore prolonging its life.[12] By September 2006, Bertelsmann had to pay Universal Music Group $60 million to settle the case Universal brought against the German media company for investing in Napster.[13] In March 2007, it reached an undisclosed settlement with EMI.[14] The next month, it paid $110 million to Warner Music Group in settlement.[15]

It was clearly a high-risk strategy to take straight out of the gates – and, if it went wrong, a ruinously expensive one; but Merrill was convinced this was the only way to move. Plus, Guy Hands was looking to cut EMI's contributions to record company trade bodies, partly because he saw their anti-piracy efforts as an enormous waste of money. "I wanted to come out of paying for anti-piracy because it was costing us a lot of money every year," he says. "And we frankly couldn't afford it. But the view was that we had to do that because it was really important that the industry made an attack on the consumer who was stealing. At the very least, we were going to get ourselves hated and at the worst, it was going to cost us more money than we would recover. But people just had very strong views on that."

Mark Hodgkinson says he had already opened up channels of communication with LimeWire early into Terra Firma's ownership of EMI. At the time, 'free' was seen as a dirty word in the record music, synonymous with theft. "When we came on board, [the industry's] attitude to digital and free content in digital was one of, 'We need to stop it,'" he says of the prevailing culture of the time. "As an organisation we had some pretty heavyweight legal efforts going into stopping free content being spread around the web. One of the early talks I had was with the CEO of LimeWire. I met with them with a view to saying, 'OK, if we wanted to legitimately share content with you, how could we come up with a business model?'"

He knew this was a risk, but the end goal was getting a licensed version of LimeWire off the ground rather than just dealing with it as it was. "Clearly what we weren't going to do was just embrace what was an illegal business model," he says. "My philosophy on consumer marketing is that you can never bite consumers."

Hodgkinson fully ascribed to Guy Hands's philosophy that the music industry was going about filesharing in completely the wrong way, seeing it as 100 per cent threat and 0 per cent opportunity.

A long-running legal case at the time was against Jammie Thomas, a single mother from Minnesota, who was hauled through the courts in the US after she declined to make a settlement with the RIAA. This was after being sent a cease-and-desist letter in 2005 when she was accused of making twenty-four songs available on KaZaA (later known as Kazaa). In October 2007, she was ordered to pay a $222,000 penalty to the RIAA after being found liable for copyright infringement.[16] The case was to drag on for years, but in 2008 it was frequently held up as an example of the music industry's sledgehammer approach to protecting its copyright. The longer the case went on, the more damaging the PR became for the major record labels pursuing her.

"I thought that was a brilliant story because it highlighted everything that was wrong about where the music industry was at that time," says Hodgkinson about why EMI under Terra Firma wanted to move in a different direction. "Trying to sue housewives is, for me, not the right approach. When consumers are wanting to access content, what you need to do as a business is work out how you can play in that space."

The thinking within EMI at the time was that P2P was a discovery mechanism and that the heaviest users were counter-intuitively the biggest spenders on music. For example, in 2005, consumer research company The Leading Question claimed that filesharers in the UK were spending four and a half times more on music than the average consumer.[17] This was also found by Demos[18] in its consumer research in 2009, for example, but claims of this sort were not uncommon in the early 2000s although they were often dismissed by the record industry as coming from flawed or selective data.

Merrill, the former Google executive, felt that viewing users of P2P and torrent sites as 'criminals' was the wrong way to go about addressing this, as it not only missed the nuances of what was happening on these services but was also pulling down the shutters on what could have been significant opportunities, if handled correctly.

While it only got to the most preliminary of stages, the LimeWire deal would have worked like a tasting menu, but one where rights owners like EMI, on both the recorded music and publishing sides, would have been remunerated. "They would have paid us a small fee for every stream played," explains Merrill of how he envisaged it working. "There was a bunch of math work that had to be done there as you had to make sure that you didn't undercut iTunes."

He accepts it was a daring plan – and one that would have certainly been met with enormous outcry among large parts of the music business – but he also feels there was a compelling logic to it, leading the consumer through discovery into purchase, with all stages being monetised in different, but connected, ways.

"People would use LimeWire to discover art, we would get paid a little bit for the discovery process, buying the asset would have been easy and the artist would also have got compensated; that was the tripartite pact," he proposes, saying it would have been a fairer model than other licensed ones in the market at the time. "It was about the artists getting paid fairly, but not all deals did that. So that was unreasonable. You have to get the music industry paid for what it does – and paid a reasonable rate for what it does. And to make sure that the person who is creating the customer experience is also getting compensated. So the customer has a good experience – and that good experience has sharing of value to pay all three of those people. And that is a hard solve. That is a very hard solve."

His remit – and the fundamental reason he believes he was employed by EMI – was that of being a disruptor; someone who would "kick up dust". Except the dust he was kicking up here was causing extremely watery eyes within powerful parts of EMI. "There were a lot of people still in the room who has been in the industry forever," he says of the internal opposition he faced. "A lot of old-time EMI-ers were still there. That was one of the things that became a little bit of a brake on innovation. These were people who had been doing this for twenty years or thirty years."

To his mind, those people still in the room were advising caution at the total expense of innovation, perhaps too caught up in (or too scared of) the past to do something genuinely pioneering. "These are people who remembered the Napster deal and then the Bertelsmann deal with Napster and how Bertelsmann got sued," he says of his adversaries on this. "I think they were all, understandably, going, 'Hang on! How are we different? Are we about to be Bertelsmann in this scenario? That was an expensive lawsuit!' The problem was that the world had changed a lot by that point."

Merrill also believes that he was not supported on this, where it mattered, at the highest level of the company. His plan might have chimed with what Mark Hodgkinson and Guy Hands had thought when they first came into EMI but he claims his negotiation of a "tentative deal" with LimeWire was immediately derailed by Elio Leoni Sceti.

"Elio knew about selling soap – he didn't know anything about music," scoffs Merrill of the executive who joined EMI a few months after him and strangled his most audacious plan at birth. "He didn't know anything about digital. That's not his background. So what this was [to him] was, 'Oh, you're doing a deal with criminals?' ... Elio didn't have the digital context, he didn't have the music context and he didn't have the art context to be able to go one level below. So he listened to people who talked like him, acted like him and dressed like him. It was an extremely undiverse [sic] crowd."

While this was a very visible pulling of rank on the LimeWire deal, Merrill says he already foresaw serious problems for his digital strategy when it was announced Leoni Sceti would be joining the company in the summer of 2008. "I always knew that there would be a CEO hired and I wasn't surprised by that happening as that was part of the deal," he said on coming into EMI when Guy Hands was the default CEO but was keen to bring in a full-time executive to run the company. "Guy's cool but [he's] not an operator. And you need an operator there. That's just rational. I did not expect the hire that Guy made. I think it reflected a different set of concerns. If you want to do a digital transformation, if you really want to be the leader in data and if you really want to be the person who changes the world, you should probably hire an innovator. We interviewed a lot of innovators. That was not the hire that Guy made, ultimately."

Even though he knew Guy Hands was on the same page as him with regard to P2P services as untapped opportunities, he was not willing to try and get Guy to overrule his new CEO. "I don't like organisational politics," he says of why he had to bite his lip on the LimeWire deal. "I don't like to try to whinge my way through things. I am a straightforward person – for good and for ill. It didn't really occur to me to wend my way behind Elio's back."

Meanwhile, Hands claims he was never told about this potential deal so it is unclear if he could have overruled Leoni Sceti's veto to get some sort of licensing arrangement through.

While believing he was lacking the backing he felt he needed from the top of the company, Merrill says that the sales team at EMI quickly bought into what he was trying to achieve. He says they had a clear understanding of where the market was going and why they needed to experiment more with downloads and move away from the deification of the CD, which was actually turning into a form of necrophilia.

"The sales guys were, to a person, some of our biggest supporters around," he proposes. "'Try this, try this, if we have to break the iTunes deal, let's break the iTunes deal.' It was obvious that the CD world was over … It was not going to be 80 per cent of the market much longer. And all of our revenue depended on selling CDs. The sales folk were really down with looking for the other answer. My major supporters in the LimeWire talks were the guys who ran worldwide sales. They said they would renegotiate with iTunes and we should try this."

He suggests there was a need to break a lot of conditioning within the company and this was to prove something of an uphill struggle for him. "EMI was, emotionally, a complicated place," he suggests. "A lot of the EMI folks had been there forever so had really been grown and groomed in the CD boom … The industry had been in this multi-year decline and there was a little bit of a hopeless feeling. And when you get a hopeless feeling, you do tend to get to thinking that you're in your bunker and you're going to stay in your bunker. I don't think that served EMI well."

At this time, in 2008, the CD was obviously a format in decline, but it remained the biggest revenue driver for record labels. On a global level, the record industry was worth $18.4 billion, of which $13.8 billion came from the sale of physical products – so effectively CDs still accounted for

75 per cent of the market. It drove the most income but it was atrophying, dropping 15.4 per cent between 2007 and 2008. Downloads were still growing at the time, but new entrant Spotify was betting heavily that the future was going to be about subscription streaming and access rather than purchasing and ownership.

Merrill says he was clearly not oblivious to this. He had come from Google which had paid $1.65 billion for YouTube in 2006[19] and had been developing the Android OS since 2005 to ride the coming wave in smartphone adoption. He was fully aware of where the big tech companies were trying to push the consumer and, therefore, the market.

Yet he says his plan was far from a radical slate-cleaning exercise within EMI and rather was more of a palimpsest, one idea overwriting the other. "I would like to say that I had some brilliant thought in 2008 about the future of streaming versus ownership – but I did not," he says. "At the time I just thought that streaming was interesting and [download] ownership was interesting. And they were both very different from CDs. We were thinking about CDs so we needed to start thinking about other stuff. My hope was that we would focus on how we would make streaming successful for artists – which was going to be very hard. We also had to think about how we could make ownership make sense in a marketing context. So how do you find the stuff?"

He adds, "I know at the time I didn't have a cohesive strategy for that because at the time my thinking was to try and support them both as hard as we could and have the market teach us if people wanted to stream versus buy and if they were the same people ... My idea at that time was just to try it, gather data and learn."

Merrill did, in his gathering of data and learning, have one senior key digital ally who joined the company a matter of months after he started there. Cory Ondrejka, co-founder of virtual world Second Life, was named EMI's senior vice president of digital strategy in June 2008. The two of them would be operating in accord.

"Cory shares my passion for driving technology and innovation in the digital music business," said Merrill in a statement on the appointment. "His unique experience building online environments, like Second Life, will be invaluable to EMI Music, as we create new digital communities for fans and artists. Adding Cory to the leadership team of the company continues to reinforce our commitment to the digital market."[20]

Looking back at the time he spent at EMI, Merrill feels Ondrejka was a fundamental addition to his team and brought considerable expertise and vision to the company as it was looking to define its digital path. "Cory is an extremely smart guy," he says. "And I think one of the best forward-looking people in the digital industry for years and years and years. I believed then, and I still believe now, that people want to engage with art. The challenge is to find the art to engage with and find people to talk to about the art. Cory has really thought deeply about how you make it simple for people to wander around these complicated spaces."

Music companies, Merrill believed, had focused a great deal of their efforts on products and pricing but had left notions of digital communities to third-party services like MySpace and the nascent Facebook. Ondrejka was able to bring ideas about digital communities right into the heart of EMI. "He built *Second Life*," Merrill says. "It is extremely complicated and has really high user rates. He had thought through the operations but, more than that, just mentally how you create worlds where folks can talk about things ... What is the best way to get fans to talk to other fans and to the artist? ... Cory is one of the best thinkers in the world on that topic and he did great work at EMI."

To achieve this, it was about taking the basic principles being forged by the insights division of EMI and parlaying them into the digital realm. "The first thing he did was push actual data analysis!" Merrill says of Ondrejka's initial goal. "Just data analysis and data visualisation. He did a really good job of just showing what the reality was. Then he helped design some of the things EMI tried to do a few years later. Things like the John Lennon Imagine community which happened a few years after I was gone. He was a big part of thinking through how to do that."

On paper, this should have all overlapped perfectly with what Ernesto Schmitt was doing in the catalogue and insights divisions of EMI. The reality, however, was very different. "I think maybe there was less delivery and more talk out of that effort," Merrill says of Schmitt.

He suspects that Schmitt was perhaps too territorial to work hand-in-glove with the new digital arrivals at EMI. "He never produced even a single spreadsheet when I was there," Merrill says of Schmitt, the subtext being that there was no love lost between the two. "He talked about it a lot, but I never saw anything. He probably went to work after I left and a lot of stuff got produced. One may wonder if that timing is not coincidental."

Others having to deal with Merrill and Ondrejka may not have clashed with them in the way it is suggested they did with Schmitt, but they felt the two digital heads quickly created a hermetically sealed world – a digital citadel in defiant isolation from the rest of the company – over which they had total control. Those they deemed to be outside were shunned. Or, more specifically, simply ignored.

There was initially a high degree of optimism about Merrill's appointment, but that quickly soured. "This guy Douglas Merrill was going to be the white knight who was coming in from Google and make EMI a digital business," says one senior source in the UK who was informed they would be working closely with him. It turned out that Merrill, despite regularly commuting between Los Angeles and London, was impossible to pin down.

This was backed up by several other senior sources at EMI during this time. "I didn't understand Douglas and Cory and what they were trying to achieve, quite honestly," says one source based in London. "I tried to have direct dealings with them, but they would not really engage." They say there was a degree of strategic obfuscation happening and they questioned if this was to cover up or distract from a dearth of ideas. "I never really saw anything come out of them," they claim. "I never really saw the digital strategy ... There was a lot of talk about how they were going to revolutionise the company, but I never saw what they were doing. It was quite concerning. It was really, really concerning. It wasn't that they weren't being transparent with their plans – I just wondered if there were any plans! ... I don't think he [Merrill] understood music and he didn't understand the content play. He didn't understand content. Period. He didn't understand how to work within a content company. That was my concern. It wasn't that we didn't get along. He just pushed me aside."

There was a similar standoffishness in the US as well, according to one high-level executive who recounts running into the same walls with Merrill and Ondrejka as their UK counterparts. "Douglas Merrill refused to meet with me," they claim. "Not only would he not meet with me, one time I found myself in the same place at the same time as him in the LA office. I went to his office to knock on the door and introduce myself. He was in his office apparently just having a sandwich. He wouldn't even come out to say hello."

Others questioned, once they did get to speak to them, if they were even up to the job of defining EMI's digital future and getting the staff behind them to achieve it. "I think Douglas Merrill was a terrible hire," is the blunt summation of one executive who had been working in digital at EMI for some time before Merrill's arrival. "He turned out to be clueless and annoyed everyone so he got fired. They lost a lot of ground in that time. His style was very car crash. He was very cheesy and Californian. It soon transpired he had no clue how to save the company. You know how every internal project has a code name? He was using *Lord of the Rings* references for his."

Another digital executive at EMI felt that Merrill was looking down on the digital team there as part of the past and, as such, they would have no involvement in his vision for company's digital future. They would work for him rather than with him. It was, for them, an echoing of how Terra Firma executives behaved when they first came into the company in 2007.

"There was that arrogant tone of thinking that we didn't know what we were doing," they say of their new digital bosses. "It was saying we had been working blindly for far too long and that they should take over. 'Now the big boys are here we'll start to make some money out of this. Don't you worry.' There might have been some good ideas, but there was no understanding of how to implement them based on rights or budgets. It felt like Douglas was only there for the short term to be able to put something on the table and walk away. Cory seemed a bit more invested in it. Cory was a good guy and a smart guy, but he had no understanding of artist sensitivities, copyright, the economics of the music industry and what you are able to achieve with budgets. He just didn't understand any of it and wasn't able to apply any of his knowledge here."

The same executive was spectacularly underwhelmed when Merrill's plans for the digital transformation of the company were shown to them. "I saw Douglas's digital strategy deck for EMI," they say. "It was seventy pages of hot air, basically. It had no meaning and no weight to it. There was no realism."

Mark Hodgkinson, being highly diplomatic, suggests that it could all have been down to a different working culture that just jarred with the way things were done at EMI. Rather than playing power games, it could have been caused by something as simple as cultural incongruity.

"I don't know why that didn't work," he says of Merrill's time at the company. "Douglas and the people he was working with had completely different backgrounds and therefore the language and the way he might express something as a digital person [maybe got lost in translation]. What was needed was someone who could interpret the Douglases and Corys of this world and interpret their very digital background into something that the guys in the music business could use."

Merrill, despite the disappointment with the aborted LimeWire deal and the indignity of having been handed the EMI.com project that he had no faith in, believes he did make a difference in EMI and helped set it up for the coming years of change. He is pleased with being key in ending the RIAA-driven lawsuits against filesharers and changing the conversation around that. "It's just throwing dirt on your customers," he says of what he regarded as foolhardy legal action here. "It's not a good structure. At the time, it was extremely controversial and the industry was generating a lot of enmity by suing everybody. And EMI was responsible for stopping that. It was very bloody and very controversial. I am super-proud of making that happen."

He also feels that he brought better efficiencies to the digital team that contributed to improved profitability at a time when, given Terra Firma's punishing debt covenant commitments, every penny counted. "A lot of material cost-cutting was required as was a lot of material realignment," he says. "A whole bunch of work was required and we did it. Ours was the only team that did it. That was partly by cost-cutting, partly by realignment and partly by getting a better relationship with Roger Faxon and using their [EMI Music Publishing's] resources. We did good things. Obviously that kind of stuff is emotionally painful and I don't mean to say that it was trivial – but it was good for the company." On top of this, he suggests that the preliminary work he did on big data eventually fed into the analytics arm of the company and helped it to work smarter.

In his additional role as COO of new music, he claims that "lots of contracts got renegotiated to make artist contracts better and less abusive" and that helped to tilt the power balance more towards creators than it had been in the past.

Merrill disagrees, however, with the claims from multiple sources within EMI that he created a digital fiefdom that closed out the rest of the company, isolated both him and Ondrejka and caused a misalignment of objectives. But he does accept there were things that fell through the cracks that, given a second chance, he would prioritise. "When I think of fiefdoms, I think you are off on your own, you never talk to anyone and no one ever sees you," he says. "We spent a lot of time talking about it and I was very open. But what I don't think I did was figure out a way for this maniacal focus on user experience, customers and artists to help A&R. How could I go and do that? Which now I would."

The ideological and strategic incompatibility between Merrill and Leoni Sceti was to contribute to the former's undoing at EMI. Tasked with being the architect of EMI's digital future, the fact that Leoni Sceti was denying Merrill the planning permission he needed – or simply rescinding his blueprints – was ultimately going to feed into Terra Firma's broader financial woes and lead to a denouement where either the digital head or the CEO had to step back or step down.

Merrill puts a lot of the issues down to two sets of wheels trying to pull EMI in different directions when they really should have been spinning concentrically. When asked about how he and his team were contributing to and reconfiguring EMI's digital marketing strategy, Merrill can barely conceal his exasperation. "We didn't have a digital marketing approach," he sighs. "We had a marketing approach ... What we have known for a long time is that digital marketing is marketing – and everything else is just part of it. It's not like you're rolling digital into everything else; you are rolling everything else into digital. The way

227

that we think about digital marketing is in terms of data strategy and implementation strategy and testing strategy and that kind of thing; which is possible in digital marketing and very hard in traditional marketing. That's the win. It's not digital marketing per se; it's data and testing. We were moving towards building some data-testing tools to get that done. A little bit of work got done in that space while I was there and after I left. But it was never a massive success."

Leoni Sceti and Merrill were coming at the same issues and the same problems but from completely different starting points and with different end goals in sight. With hindsight, it could never work. "Elio had a view of marketing that had to do with selling soap – where you do tests in stores and do things like change the colours," argues Merrill. "That's what he did and he was very good at it. But that is not what you do with art and that is not what you do with testing. So there was not a lot of support for thinking through digital marketing. Ultimately, that was unfortunate." In the end, Merrill lasted less than a year at EMI. By the end of March 2009, he was out.

If Hands was going to have to choose between his CEO and his head of digital, it was only ever going to go one way. "I think that was an Elio decision," says Hands of Merrill's sacking. "And I would have supported Elio. I think Douglas was very good technologically. I still believe one could have done something like that. And it would have transformed the music industry. When I look at the music industry today, and if I look at what we left in 2010, it hasn't moved on a huge amount since then. It has come back because the market has come back. But that is, to some extent, what we predicted in all our numbers."

Merrill is brutally honest and self-reflexive when discussing the reasons for his departure. "They fired me," he says bluntly. "[The reason was,] objectively I was not succeeding. I had done a very poor job of making the relationships that we needed within EMI and across the industry. I was the wrong guy for that job."

It is extremely rare that a senior executive at any organisation is so candid about why they left. They will often try and spin it that they wanted 'new challenges' or wheel out platitudinous lines about how they had achieved everything they wanted to in their time there. Or they will shift the blame and darkly allude to a conspiracy against them.

"It took me a while to get my head around the fact that my strategies were the wrong strategies," he says. "That's all on me. I want to be super clear. That's all on me … Objectively, I was failing. Why was I failing? There were a lot of reasons why I was failing. But ultimately, for me, I am a brutally blunt guy – for good or for ill – and I was failing. And I didn't have a strategy for fixing it. The external side of things is that it is not possible for one person to sit in an organisation kicking up dust and succeed. Because that person is not going to have enough ability to get anything done. It's just going to be annoying."

Perhaps finally accepting there was at least a grain of truth in the accusations that he built a digital isolation tank for both himself and his immediate team, Merrill says if he could go back to that time, he would be more inclusive rather than isolationist.

"I would have spent a lot less time trying to do things and a lot more time making relationships and understanding what this person needs and what that person needs," he proposes. "I didn't take any time to bring people along. If you want people to be with you on landing, they have to be with you on take-off. I didn't even ensure they were on the same plane on take-off!"

Merrill claims he knew his cards were marked as soon as Leoni Sceti took the top job. "The minute that Guy hired Elio, I was like, 'Hmmm – this isn't going to work,'" he says. "It was obviously hard for me. And sad for me. On the other hand, I feel like – certainly personally – it was the right thing for me. It was the right outcome for me."

One senior executive based in the US during this time suggests that an HR pattern was emerging. A new executive would arrive to trumpet blasts and exit to the sound of a sad trombone. "Most of them tended to be fired rather than leave of their own volition," the source says. "In the press it might have been said they wanted to spend more time with their families! There was a period when they had the golden child. Like Douglas Merrill. He was definitely the golden child for a while."

Indeed, Merrill's closest colleague and confidant Cory Ondrejka followed him out the door barely four months later. EMI was, once again, without digital figureheads at a time when it mattered most.

When asked if he felt like an outlier at EMI during this time, Merrill offers this response. "Oh yeah, I was off the charts. I was on some other spectrum! … You bring someone like me into an organisation because you want to kick up dust … You get dust, but you also get really good stuff. If you look back at my career, I have been kicking up dust in a lot of places and creating a lot of value. When Guy talked to me, and I was pretty clear on what I was good at and bad at, he was very clear that they were going to put a structure around me that would allow me to … make EMI the best place in the industry. And then they went and hired the guy who sold soap!"

Merrill trying to kick up dust and Leoni Sceti hawking soap was never going to be harmonious. If this was a struggle between Douglas and Elio, the former found to his cost that soap was always going to wash out dust.

CHAPTER 12

Revolving Doors

After the departure of Douglas Merrill and Cory Ondrejka, the rotating door at EMI did not slow down; if anything, its spinning was going to speed up as executives, artists and even labels extricated themselves from the company.

Looking at EMI from the outside at this point in its history, the signs were far from good. To slightly misquote Lady Bracknell in *The Importance of Being Earnest*, "To lose one executive, Mr Hands, may be regarded as a misfortune; to lose several looks like carelessness." But inside the corridors and offices of Wrights Lane, most staff were just trying to get on with things. They had no other option.

"There was a revolving door – in and out, in and out, in and out," says Andria Vidler, president of EMI UK & Ireland, about the executive turnover that was happening by this stage. "All they did was put their heads down. They didn't talk to each other. They put their heads down and they focused on what they were doing."

A source who was there when Terra Firma came into EMI suggests the company fell into a dangerously repetitive pattern in terms of appoint-ments from the beginning and this was to be a recurring theme throughout their time there. "After six months, it became apparent that Terra Firma did not have a plan for EMI," they say. "They would lose good executives and keep not-so-good ones. They hired some people who were not the best ones to hire."

Another long-serving EMI staff member was equally unflattering in their assessment of what they saw unfolding here as Terra Firma was entering its third year of ownership of the music company. "It was like a roll call of the opposite of saviours," they say. "'Here's your new saviour! Oh no, they're shit as well!' He [Guy Hands] was treating EMI like it was a start-up. It was a corporate company that didn't see the train of digital coming before it crashed into it. It was not a start-up."

They do claim, however, that the appointment of Vidler in summer 2009 was the best and most beneficial appointment that EMI's private equity owners had made in at least the previous eighteen months, suggesting a turning of the tide within the music company. Vidler was to prove a catalyst for unifying the often disparate and oppositional teams, especially those who felt they had been whipped into submission, or at least glum compliance, by wave after wave of Terra Firma appointments. "Andria Vidler was very good," they say. "She was good at employee engagement. She was a good leader. She was a people person. That's what you needed because Terra Firma were not that."

Arriving almost two years into Terra Firma's ownership of EMI, Vidler had not just a lot of work to do; she had a lot of work to undo. The company was listing badly at this time in terms of staff morale and Terra Firma were keen to see its investment come good; but the strategic flip-flopping that had happened in the opening act of its ownership had cost it valuable time. "They wasted the first year – and they wasted a lot of time and money," says a highly placed source during this time. "Guy would move executives around like they were on the chessboard – but it didn't really mean anything; it was just another reshuffle. There was just a lack of any real plan."

An additional problem, according to one very senior source at EMI, was that Guy Hands was vacillating dangerously in his decision-making and this affected the overall company by osmosis. He was also, according to the same source, autocratic and reacted badly to anyone disagreeing with him when he finally made his mind up. "Guy was not someone who necessarily listened to advice," they claim. "Or rather he would take advice and he would consult widely, but then in the end he would have his views and his views were usually the ones that won the day. He was very thin-skinned and that is what surprised me about someone who had been so successful. He didn't like criticism. He didn't like people telling him that they thought he was wrong."

When faced with opposition or criticism, it was alleged that Guy Hands proved explosive – the antithesis of the diplomacy some at the top felt he should be displaying in order to steer EMI into calmer waters. "He also had a very short fuse – and that was [from] people within EMI but also within Terra Firma," says one well-placed source, before citing an example of Hands clashing badly, and publicly, with one long-standing Terra Firma colleague. "I overheard a lot of bawling and shouting between them. Guy could get really irate really quickly. He had a very short temper. No one wanted to be the bringer of bad news to Guy. He did tend to kick the messenger. He had a very short fuse and was incredibly impatient when things weren't going fast enough."

Hands, when told this, denied it categorically, laughing that anyone would suggest even in the slightest that he was tyrannical or easily incensed, saying, if anything, he has mellowed with age. "I lose my temper sometimes," he admits. "A lot? Less than I used to when I was young. One guy once said, 'If you're not shouting then I get worried because it means you don't care.' Look, I get frustrated. My mind works slightly differently. I have a whole load of coping strategies because I am dyslexic. I don't follow things in a linear way, so I am bouncing around. People don't always understand and I don't always understand them and that produces frustration." Hands says there was a plan, and it was always clear that the existing management needed to be changed. However, the re-structuring had to go through a full legal consultation, taking into consideration each individual contract, the terms of agreements with artists, as well as the need to get Citibank's approval for any payments made; one executive was paid circa $20 million. He says the departures had to be understood in that context.

Terra Firma's perceived lack of focus and a combative approach to the staff it inherited was a toxic cocktail for those working under the new ownership. Rather than encourage the staff to move with it, the feeling was that Terra Firma was thinking more punitively.

"Had they gone in and been more action-oriented and made a few things happen, they might have got more buy-in from EMI staffers," says one senior source. "The staff were heavily demoralised. They felt it was death by a thousand cuts ... The more open-minded staff knew that it would be a bloodbath but they had to get through it and they could grow out of the ashes. But they were disappointed as there were holding-pattern decisions, nothing getting done but a lot of talk, plans, more plans, consultancy, more consultancy."

Some within EMI saw the problem with Terra Firma's strategy as being that it was based on total rejection of the past as there was a presumption that everything that had been implemented in the pre-Terra Firma years was flawed. Baby and bath water were both thrown out, meaning Terra Firma was left staring at an empty tub. It was not until it mellowed in its desecration of the past that it finally started to realise that the old guard were not necessarily obstacles to be knocked down; they could help lead it into the future.

During this period of great uncertainty at EMI, rival labels were circling, not like vultures but rather like hyenas collapsing in laughter. EMI's reputation was in tatters and its competitors made hits while the sun shone, never missing an opportunity to put the boot in, especially when it came to its on-off merger target since 2000.

"Warner happened to be on a bit of a hot streak at the time and I remember EMI being so defensive about it," says one Warner executive at the time. "They put out some crazy press release which said, 'What do you mean? We're still signing artists! Here's a list of fifty of the artists we have signed!' Big deal. It was a list of fifty names that no one had ever heard of. We were not saying that they couldn't sign artists. Anybody can sign artists. It's not that hard. The reality is about signing artists that have any prospects – and then having the ability to develop those artists on a global scale."

Someone who had served for decades in EMI believes a Damascene moment came when Terra Firma suddenly realised that, even though it was some distance off, success could be within its grasp if it was less frenetic in its attempts to get there. "To me, it never felt like it was going to work," they say of the first period. "It settled down a bit after the second or third year – when Nick Gatfield came in. Ironically, he was the old guard. One of the first times it started to settle down in the UK was when we brought some of the old guard back in!"

May 2009's restructuring of EMI's frontline A&R operations was arguably an attempt to have highly experienced label heads and talent scouts working in harmony. This was, it hoped, sending a message out to the artist and management community – as well as to rival labels – that the company might have dropped the pace in the last two years but it was now very much back in the race.

A creative triptych was presented to the industry where Shabs Jobanputra (Virgin), Miles Leonard (Parlophone) and Daniel Miller (Mute) would be leading the company from the front. All three had worked with and helped break some of the biggest acts in the world and Terra Firma was showing, at last, that it understood how important skilled A&Rs were to the company.

Except it was more of a strategic rebuilding in thought rather than deed. "It wasn't like we ever sat down together," says Miller of what this all meant in actuality. "There was Parlophone, Virgin and Mute and that was it. But we never had a joint strategy or anything like that. We [Mute] were very much standalone in the A&R sense. Maybe Shabs and Miles did but I certainly didn't."

There was, however, revised thinking about the importance of label heads and a more empathetic approach started to fall into place. "I just wanted to keep a real focus on the label, the business and what we did well," says Miles Leonard of how this trickled down to his role. "Daniel, Shabs and I were slightly protected because we were the only people who had the relationships with our artists, understood about making records and going into the studio. They didn't want to touch that or confuse that. It was a world they just didn't understand and they just didn't want to upset that."

It was under Vidler that things on the A&R front in the UK were starting to be turned around. This was not entirely down to her, but there was serendipitous timing. She came in as the culture inside the company was starting to change and she was able to marshal some of this positivity and optimism, which had previously felt like dwindling resources.

"I think the people who were left did an incredible job in keeping their heads above water under those situations," says one source who had left EMI by this stage but was in regular contact with colleagues who remained there. "And they did some interesting deals, like the one with Swedish House Mafia. That is like a template really for a modern deal."

Explaining how this all unfolded, Vidler says she had to deliver proof of concept to the entire music business, not just EMI, that the smallest major could not only sign acts and break them, it could also do so on new contractual terms. "When it came to signing artists, the thing that surprised me when I entered the world of music was that all the labels said they were going to sign ten artists and they would be lucky if two of them survived – and that was the way it worked," she says of the operational system that was in place when she joined. "But I don't work like that. I said, 'EMI does not have a great reputation at the moment. Neither does Parlophone and neither does Virgin … Nothing has a good reputation at the moment. So we really need to convince people that we're going to do everything we can for them.'"

The major label record business had traditionally run, if one is being complimentary, on a spread bet model. If one is not being so complimentary, it threw everything at the wall and hoped some of it would stick. As long as the handful of successes paid for the landfill of failures, it could stay in business. With EMI's reputation at an all-time low, and being at the biggest competitive disadvantage it had ever experienced, it did not have the resources or the market power to fall back into the old ways of working. Vidler believed EMI had to create new opportunities and show to itself, as much as to everybody else, that it could think, behave and – crucially – succeed differently.

"I said, 'We are going to sign five [new acts]. We are not going to sign ten. We are going to do five and do them brilliantly as opposed to doing ten but recognising we will only do two of them well.' That was my theory. We're going to do five brilliantly, we are going to plot and we're going to create deals that work for each artist."

Rather than taking a templated approach – as Warner Music was doing at time, insisting acts signed to a 360-degree deal that gave it a share of all revenue streams – EMI was going to build deals that were unique to each artist.

"We signed Swedish House Mafia and that was a completely different deal to the one that we signed with Tinie Tempah, which was a completely different deal to the deal that we signed with Emeli Sandé, which was a completely different deal to the deal that we signed with Professor Green and Eliza Doolittle," says Vidler of the key artists brought into EMI UK during her watch. "That was year one and there was one band we signed that didn't work. That was a good first year."

She says that all the deals done here were designed from the ground up and were malleable to the artist in question, where they were in their creative trajectory and what they were willing – or not willing – to do as part of the deal, outside of just their recording rights. EMI had done an all-rights deal with Robbie Williams in 2002 when his contract was renegotiated, so this was not uncharted territory; but there was a lot riding on the company proving that it could take unknown acts and break them on wholly new terms.

"For Tinie Tempah and Professor Green, they made more money from branding in year one than from music – because they worked with us," says Vidler. "And we got it right. We built that into the business model. I took the responsibility and the approach that we would stick with these artists and we would make them broad-revenue artists, not reliant just on albums or singles, and we would stick with them. If they fall at the first hurdle, we only have five so the business has to keep going with them; we have to be committed."

It wasn't all huge and credible successes, however. In November 2009 there was much bloviating in an issue of *Music Week* about the signing of Parlophone's first non-recording artist. Immodesty Blaize was a burlesque artist and the label had already invested in a film about her, *Burlesque Undressed*, planned for release in January 2010. There was no talk of her recording an album, but the "multi-faceted contract" she had signed with the label covered "a number of other revenue streams", including brand associations, live, merchandise and audio-visual. Miles Leonard added, "This is a move by Parlophone and EMI as a whole towards being a rounded entertainment company and to do that we need to broaden out into areas other than simply working with recording artists."[1]

It was to prove a one-off deal. It tanked and would not be repeated.

Running in the background of a lot of the other recording-led deals, however, was something much more interesting and innovative that was not talked about publicly at the time. Vidler says that all deals had to be approached from a conceptual starting point that they could, or would, run into problems and setbacks and, as such, alternative plans and contingency plans had to be ready and waiting in the wings if they were needed.

"In the meetings that I held I said, 'Well, what if that single doesn't work? What is Plan B? And have we already started it?'" she explains. "I ran a shadow budget throughout the year. The managers got used to thinking [what to do] if something didn't work ... What I was doing was re-educating the senior managers to think about only five artists rather than ten on the frontline and really think about Plan A, Plan B, Plan C and Plan D. We were also thinking about what we could do if these first initiatives didn't work."

This also, she feels, was able to bring more financial certainty to Terra Firma as it was increasingly desperate to boost revenues so it could meet its debt repayments to Citigroup and continue to hold onto EMI. "I was also able to satisfy the private equity business model which is, 'If you're going to deliver that at the end of the year, you're going to deliver that at the end of the year,'" she says. "The [music] industry tends to say, 'Well we don't know how it's going to work; an album might sell 100,000 or it might sell 80,000. We can't predict it so we can only run the business through the rear-view mirror.' I went, 'No. We can do better than that.' I introduced some basic business modelling which I knew could work because I had made it work at the BBC, Capital, Magic and Emap.[2] This was around how you manage creative businesses to deliver an end result. But at the same time I also focused them so that each artist [was the centre]."

There were also key marketing and retail changes introduced by Vidler in this time. Dissecting the dwell times of consumers on EMI-owned or EMI-affiliated websites (such as artist sites) meant that the longer they stayed browsing on the site, the more chance there was to tempt them with a purchase. "It was using the concept of hot and cold leads, which was very new to music marketing at the time but which was happening in different sectors," Vidler says. "You use analytics to really progress the conversation."

This also migrated into the bricks-and-mortar retailers who were key in pushing EMI's biggest-selling titles. Vidler felt EMI could grow its sales if it understood the product better, with consumer research conducted around the *Now That's What I Call Music* brand. The flagship releases under the *Now ...* umbrella were three double-CD compilations of recent chart hits every year, with a new title in the long-running series appearing every Easter, summer and Christmas. There were also *Now* ... compilations themed around things like decades and genres, but the three new titles each year were the blockbusters.

They found that in supermarkets it was mothers who were the main purchasers of the title. "It was safe music for the whole family to enjoy," says Vidler, but they found that it was racked alongside all the other hit albums and so it was overlooked as an impulse purchase. Vidler's plan was to pay for specific racking near the checkout, maximising the impulse potential among consumers.

"We doubled the size of *Now* ... in that first year when we changed the way we distributed the CD album," she says. "I knew that because that's what I did with magazines [at publishing company Bauer]. It was the same thought process. It's an impulse purchase. It's a bit of a treat and you're not going to seek it out ... I introduced that whole concept of what the consumer has in their lives and how you reach them."

Vidler's media experience – at the BBC as well as a magazine publisher and commercial radio stations – was regarded by some within EMI as part blessing (in that she understood how entertainment companies worked) and part curse (in that she was not always able to translate that across to music).

"Andria Vidler drove me to fucking despair because she didn't know what she was doing – but she did know radio and TV," is how one senior source who worked closely with her puts it. "She really fucking did. She was lost at sea as regards everything else, but ... she had worked at a radio station and had built it up successfully."

Multiple sources also report that she and Miles Leonard, head of Parlophone, would occasionally clash, with stories being offered up about them having screaming matches in the corridors of Wrights Lane in full view of staff. There were suspicions that Vidler did not rate Leonard as an A&R, pointing to the fact that many of the acts on Parlophone had been brought into the label by other executives and that Leonard himself had brought nothing of note. There were also suggestions that she found him frustratingly resistant to change and that his relationship with the managers of the biggest acts on his label was not as rich and productive as she felt it could have been.

There were other professional and personal reasons at play for their clashes, according to one source who worked closely with both of them. "While Andria was running that company and had everyone reporting in to her, people knew Miles was earning more money than her," they say. "So it must have been difficult from the off with the two of them."

Eventually an armistice of sorts was arrived at and the two found a way to work together. "Andria realised very quickly she should just let

Miles get on and do what he does – rather than try and interfere," says one source close to both of them. "The longer it went on, I felt she realised that was the best way to approach some of this. Just let people do what they do best ... maybe she had been told that this needed changing, that needed changing and those people were trouble, but actually they're not. They are only trouble if you poke them, but if you just let them get on with their jobs, they get on with it and they produce."

The curse of attracting new artists to EMI might have finally been broken – and it was hoped that the breakthrough success of acts like Emeli Sandé and Swedish House Mafia would see more managers come to their door – but the company still had a leak at the other end. Big-name acts out of contract and heritage artists whose catalogue deals were up for renewal were threatening to walk. Or were actually walking.

The Rolling Stones had already defected to Universal at the start of 2008 but salt was to be rubbed into the wounds when the reissue of their classic 1972 album *Exile On Main Street* went straight to number one in the UK in May 2010. This was the band's first number one album since 1994's *Voodoo Lounge*[3] but it was also the first album in British chart history to return to number one as a reissue. It might have been coming up on four decades old and trading on a growing sense of rock nostalgia, but it was a number one that EMI did not deliver for the band.

"I absolutely believe that the *Exile On Main Street* reissue would not have happened at EMI," says a PR who worked with several EMI catalogue acts over the years. "Mick Jagger and Keith Richards would not have let that happen under Guy Hands's watch as they thought he'd make an absolute mess of it. And rightly so, I believe."

Making a bad situation worse that month, Queen also announced in May that they would be moving their catalogue to Universal at the end of the year. It was reported that the band sold 664,000 albums in the UK in 2009,[4] suggesting a serious hit to the bottom line of EMI's catalogue business the following year. It is worth noting that their 1981 compilation, *Greatest Hits*, remains the biggest-selling album of all time in UK chart history, with over 6 million sales.

There was some comfort following on the heels of the Queen announcement when Chris Morrison, manager of Blur and Gorillaz, confirmed that Damon Albarn's various musical projects would remain on EMI – for the time being at least. "Damon was attracted to the company because of its heritage and prestige and for the moment this is still the case," he told *Music Week*. "We shall see what happens in the next year."[5]

The most painful and symbolic defection, however, happened the month before, when Paul McCartney signed a deal with Concord Music

Group – who had released his 2007 album *Memory Almost Full* – to move his entire post-Beatles catalogue out of EMI.[6] Few defections will have stung as much.

McCartney's most recent albums at that time may not have "set the world alight in the past few years" and "cost a lot to promote", according to one source, but the symbolism of him going could not be ignored. That said, the source feels Terra Firma was right not to overpay to keep him and it was in fact breaking a cycle of mollycoddling that the former Beatle had become well used to at his long-standing label. "They indulged him as he's Paul McCartney; they didn't indulge him because he sells records," they say. "He is the controlling element of The Beatles, and we were told in meetings that EMI indulged McCartney, and to let him do what he wanted because hopefully at some point he'd let them do what they want with The Beatles."

One long-standing EMI executive was watching equally long-standing EMI acts move to rival labels with mounting despair and laid the blame squarely at the door of Terra Firma and its inability to talk convincingly to artists. "They brought in people who had no experience or no understanding of the culture of music," they say. "The culture is everything when you are having a conversation with any artist. It is about understanding the vision of an artist and understanding the direction they are flowing in – and helping them to achieve the goals they want to achieve. It just ended up pushing against artists. We ended up losing artists. At that point we lost the Queen catalogue, we lost the McCartney catalogue, Radiohead famously left."

Another source backs this up and says the cultural mismatch between Terra Firma and acts on EMI was driving a wedge between them. "Terra Firma had no idea how to deal with artists," they say. "How do you speak to a Damon Albarn and a Robbie Williams in one go? You can't. It has to be individually. Tony Wadsworth did not deal with Robbie in the same way that he dealt with Damon. But Guy Hands saw them as the same. They were 'assets' that had to work harder and they were 'assets' to be stripped."

Even deeper into the catalogue, key acts and albums were slowly being chipped away. One British act with a solid run of hit singles beginning in the late 1970s and running well into the 1990s – on top of strong business in compilation album sales – was also looking to disentangle themselves from what they saw as a slowly collapsing EMI. "We had loads of meetings with them," says a source about the renegotiation talks. "But I got the feeling that their management didn't trust us to be around in six months' time. Us as employees but also EMI as a company."

As if artists and catalogues leaving EMI wasn't bad enough, an entire label departing was only going to put the other majors at risk of overdosing on schadenfreude by this stage.

In May 2002, EMI paid £23 million to buy trailblazing UK independent label Mute, home to Depeche Mode, Nick Cave, Erasure, Moby and Goldfrapp. The relationship worked out for a long time, but by 2008 founder Daniel Miller was looking for a way out of the deal.

Always regarding itself as European in outlook and ambition, Mute felt philosophically apart from the UK labels it was now sharing office space with in Wrights Lane. Plus, it felt that EMI's promotional and distribution network was letting it down. "We wanted to get all of our records released around Europe and that wasn't happening properly any more," says Miller. "They were mostly token releases with no marketing behind them. That was very frustrating for me because it was completely counterintuitive to the way that I had built the company. That was the beginning of us wanting to pull out, really."

The revolving executive door was making Miller anxious but the arrival of Andria Vidler did give him temporary hope that things could return to the way they were – where Mute ploughed its idiosyncratic furrow and could occasionally deliver artistically uncompromising acts that still sold large numbers of records to keep EMI happy. But this moment of respite was not to last. "Eventually I had a boss when Andria Vidler came in," says Miller. "But by that time what they wanted was for Mute to become just another EMI label, working in exactly the same way. I didn't really want that and thought it would be bad for our artists."

In 2009, he spoke to David Kassler about where he felt things were and were not working for Mute as part of EMI. Kassler, typical to form, was understanding and helpful, agreeing to help Miller develop a way to take Mute independent again. "It was all done in a friendly way; they weren't firing me and I wasn't walking out," says Miller. "It was like a soft Brexit. Mexit! Mute exit!"

Miller says the terms of Mute's severance were straightforward enough to work through but the process, where everything had to be ratified by several individuals, meant it dragged on for a year.

To rebuild the record label he started in 1978, Miller had to start again from scratch. "EMI owned Mute," he says. "Everything. The catalogue and the name. We just started figuring out what the best way to do it would be. It was quite a long process. And there were some acts contracted to EMI for longer than I was going to stay. And there were some acts who were out of contract. And there was some catalogue that we mutually felt that Mute could carry on working better than EMI – and to their benefit."

By September 2010, the deal was done and Mute was independent again. The staff relocated to new offices in Hammersmith and Miller was retained as an A&R consultant, working on acts like Richard Hawley and Goldfrapp who had to see out their own contracts with EMI. Another part of EMI's rich history had come to an end.

Earlier that year, however, the biggest executive departure since Tony Wadsworth in early 2008 happened when it was announced in March 2010 that Elio Leoni Sceti was leaving after just eighteen months in the job. As an interim measure, Charles Allen (non-executive chairman of the company) would become executive chairman.

Leoni Sceti claims that Terra Firma's debt situation with Citigroup, which began as a low rumble but had become a deafening roar by the start of 2010, provided his cue to leave. "For a couple of years, it was about turning the revenue around, trebling the margins of the profit and getting this discipline into the consumer understanding," he says of his primary responsibilities. "I turned it around from minus 9 per cent to plus 2 per cent, I got the margin from 5 per cent to 15 per cent and I put in this culture of the Music Key and consumer understanding. On the other side, the debt was not renegotiated and then there was this legal action with Citi[group], which decreased the chances that we would come out with a renegotiated debt. I needed to make a call about what the future of this was."

He continues, "Did it impact on me? It impacted on me in the sense that, at a point where I saw there was no renegotiation of the debt and there was no obvious good way out, I had to make a call. And I did make a call to leave because I didn't see that it was possible to come out without a renegotiation of the debt. In that sense it impacted on me. It forced me to make a decision."

Asked how his decision to leave was taken at Terra Firma, he had this to say. "At the end of the day it's not what they expected. But we managed through it. We [myself and Guy] are both very upfront individuals."

Hands has mixed feelings about Leoni Sceti's departure. He says his marketing and insights work was strong but he did not deliver the savings the company was expecting and, more importantly, needed. "Elio had a consumer background and so I think he was very, very, very good on making sure that the insights team established itself and sorted out the matrix reporting," he says. "Where I think Elio probably didn't do as much as we could have done was really on taking a harsher cut to the existing artists group and to our supply chain costs."

Hands suggests there was a strategic disconnect here and that, ultimately, worked against Leoni Sceti's viability as a CEO. He was given the benefit of the doubt in the opening act of his time as head of the company but was lapped by the work of another key department put in place by Terra Firma in terms of delivering results it was happiest with.

"Elio was of the camp thinking we could do it better [in terms of retaining artists and working them better]," Hands says. "There was an attempt in his first year to try and choose a number of artists and see if we could actually, through the traditional means, get them to be successful. I think that was moderately successful – but it didn't compare to what the insights teams were getting. The insights stuff really did work in terms of how we could take an artist, promote them and see if the artist was going to be popular out there."

There were, long before his September 2010 execution date, attempts to give the former Reckitt Benckiser executive the support system he needed to deliver on all his objectives, but this was to ultimately prove futile. And Leoni Sceti's mentor-turned-successor was also not long for the job.

"Charles Allen had been brought in midway through Elio's tenure to be the non-executive chairman of the record business," a senior executive says. "I think Guy's view was that this would give Elio a sounding board and someone to help him manage the business. I don't think Charles was all that interested in it and the issues were pretty tough. Charles liked being chairman of the record business and he certainly did the ceremonial things quite a lot. But he wasn't really that present in the business. But he did have thoughts about how it should be organised and run. As it was starting to fall apart under Elio, he had his own plan that he was putting forward. So Guy, in letting Elio go, put Charles in place [as executive chairman]. But it didn't take very long for Guy to realise that Charles was not the person to run that business."

One European label head was not exactly heartbroken when Leoni Sceti left and actually believed that things in continental Europe improved dramatically after his departure. "When Elio left, the degree of forcing people to act in a different way to how they did before kind of went away," they say. "You felt that in the UK people were relieved to not be under pressure all the time. Elio had a pretty harsh leadership style … There were no compromises. It was a very clear dictating style. David Kassler listened to people and he listened to artists. I would say this was a relief for a lot of people working at the higher level within the company around the world. Scandinavia was affected positively by David coming in because he had a great relationship with them. He understood this transitioning into the track-based business. He supported that and he gave those people a lot of freedom. He gave much more freedom to me as well. It was a good era."

Charles Allen was quick to deny rumours that he was being brought in as executive chairman to engineer a sale of EMI's recorded music arm to Warner. "[It] is absolutely not the case," he told *Music Week*. "I have come in to take this business to the next stage. I intend to put a plan together to encourage equity to come in and allow us to move forward. The team here has done a great job. We are seeing top-line growth."

He added, "My plan for EMI is very much a continuation of what we have been doing. The key was getting the right team in place. We have strengthened our senior team and put strong people in. We are in good shape there."[7]

Artist managers were generally supportive of the appointment. Tim Clark of ie:music said, "Charles Allen is a safe pair of hands and he's helped turn EMI around. They've made some much-needed changes and are very forward thinking, but what really needs to be done now is for the financing to be sorted so that the operational side can get on with the job."[8]

Bob Miller, manager of Corinne Bailey Rae, added, "Elio did a very good job in very difficult circumstances – he's done the job that every single record company around the world is going to have to do, but he has also connected to the artists."[9]

Allen was, however, not long for the role. He was swung into place in March to fill the hole left by Elio Leoni Sceti's swift removal from the company; but by June, he was moved sideways, becoming an advisor to both Terra Firma and EMI, as the head of the company's publishing arm, Roger Faxon, took over the running of the entire company.

Hands, reflecting on it all now, suggests the dismissal of Leoni Sceti was much more strategic than the music industry knew – or even guessed – at the time. It was, he says, all related to the worsening relationship with Citigroup and the bank's lack of faith in Leoni Sceti as CEO.

"We were going to try one last attempt to get an agreement with Citigroup and that was very much around the concept of having Roger [Faxon in place] and trying to cut the costs out of recorded," says Hands. "The question was whether we had Elio in charge of Roger or Roger in charge of Elio – and whether the other would stay."

The empire-building undertaken by the two was never going to be a joint effort. Just as Douglas Merrill was deemed disposable in order to retain Leoni Sceti, now Leoni Sceti was seen as collateral damage in the promotion of Faxon to run the entire company. Plus Faxon had an ace up his sleeve.

"It wasn't going to work to have one of them report to the other," says Hands. "[Roger] was close to Citibank and we had to make a decision in between Elio and Roger – and one of the reasons for us deciding on Roger was his closeness to Citibank. When you have one guy who is making a ton of money for the business and the other guy who is not making much, you are always going to choose the guy who is making a lot of money. It's just the way it goes."

Hands confirms that Leoni Sceti had voiced his growing concerns about the unsustainability of the debt repayments and how the company was struggling to stay afloat. Faxon, however, was considerably less despondent, which dramatically elevated him in Hands's opinion.

"Elio had made it clear that he didn't think the numbers could work out – that is true," says Hands. "He did not think we could sort it out. That is 100 per cent true. Faxon felt we could. Elio felt we couldn't and Faxon felt we could. We had simultaneously decided we were going to back Faxon."

It was felt that Roger Faxon could not only drive up company profits but would also be better placed to lower running costs. Being based in New York and having a good relationship with Citigroup, also headquartered in New York, was more than enough to move the needle most assuredly in Faxon's favour.

A long list of rapidly exiting executives, artists and labels might have looked bad coming into summer 2010, but things for Terra Firma and EMI were about to get worse. A lot worse.

CHAPTER 13

Rebuilding, Refocusing, Reimagining

"If you don't love music and if you don't love the people who make music, then get the fuck out!"

The elevation of Roger Faxon, formerly chairman and chief executive of EMI Music Publishing, to group CEO in June 2010 gave the company its fourth CEO in less than three years. To the wider industry, this executive schizophrenia may have seemed an outward sign of a company still struggling to define its strategy and its place in the market.

As Billy Mann put it, "The downside of all of the transition during that time, not just within EMI but all around, was that to have four CEOs in three years was like trying to plan a wedding with the girl of your dreams who changes fundamentalist religions every nine months."

But inside EMI – or certainly among the staff there who pre-dated the arrival of Terra Firma – Faxon's appointment was generally met with enthusiasm. He was very much one of them and they felt he innately understood the music business in a way that his two predecessors struggled with. After years of upheaval, they felt stability and corporate empathy was returning to the company.

Faxon had been with the company's publishing arm for the past sixteen years, having previously served as executive vice president and COO of Lucasfilm between 1980 and 1984 before embarking on a varied career that took in a stint as senior executive vice president at Columbia TriStar Motion Picture Group and a period as CEO of Sotheby's Europe. He arrived in Thorn-EMI in 1994 as executive vice president of business development and strategy, moving up to become executive vice president and CFO of EMI Music Publishing in 1998. In March 2007, he took over as chairman and CEO of EMI Music Publishing, replacing Marty

Bandier, with whom he shared the co-CEO role for a year as part of a succession plan.

Unlike Elio Leoni Sceti and Guy Hands, Faxon had come up through the company he now found himself running. Plus, this was the first time since 1998, after the departure of Jim Fifield, that the two sides of EMI were controlled by the same executive.[1]

"Roger came in and he really believed my philosophy and really exaggerated it," says Andria Vidler of her new boss. "[T]he philosophy was that we are only as good as we can make an artist and that we are a service for the artists. We are not bigger and better. Roger enabled me to do everything that we were doing."

The press coverage at the time underlined that – finally – a music person was heading up the company again. Except, according to those with a richer understanding of EMI's executive history, it was not quite that simple or straightforward.

"The criticism of Roger when he came into EMI Publishing was that he was a finance guy," says one long-serving executive. "He was always seen as the finance guy. The hilarious thing when he was appointed to the head of the whole group was it became, 'Hey! The music guy's back!'"

Others suggest this was not going to be the total reunification of EMI that some quixotically believed it would be, because the two parts of the company had become financially and ideologically distinct. Because publishing was such a profitable part of the company and the global leader in its sector, Faxon and his team had shielded itself from the massive and painful restructuring of EMI's recorded music division. Neither had it been guilt-tripped over Terra Firma's struggle to meet its debt repayments. Throughout all the Terra Firma years to date, EMI Music Publishing was, for the most part, untouched.

"I think the record company constantly felt that they were on the brink of failure," says Faxon of how the two sides of the company experienced the opening impact of Terra Firma coming in. "In publishing, we were extremely careful not to talk about our covenants to staff. My CFO, my COO and a couple of other people – we worried about that. But people in the organisation didn't worry about that. We went from strength to strength. We were able to keep the revenues rising. We were able to keep our market share improving. Our margins expanded quite meaningfully."

Publishing did have to make some cuts, but it was not put through the wringer like those in recorded music were. "We did do some reorganisations and we did let people go," continues Faxon. "But we explained to people what we were doing and why that was the right thing to do as it was building for the future. People in publishing never felt that there was any threat to their world. That was consistent with the way that Marty had run the business before. 'We are doing our thing. We don't worry about the record company. The record company isn't important to us. We are in our own world and just because the EMI name is on the door, that doesn't mean anything.'"

Hands says he was fully aligned with Faxon's vision for the company. "He and I had exactly the same view with regard to creating a digital rights company," he says, before adding that it was not going to be a simple marriage between the two parts of the business, in a large part because of the precarious relationship with Citigroup. "The issue was that we couldn't split out recorded music. If we had been able to split out recorded music, one of the things that we did look at was if Elio would want [to run] new recorded music and he felt that was too small for him. That was an alternative. Citigroup also didn't want it to split out, which we did."

Others within EMI felt that the notion of merging the two parts of EMI was great conceptually but the reality was going to be much bumpier. "Roger is funny because, and he would admit this, publishing always said they didn't want to be infected by recorded music's declining market and general uselessness," says a senior source. "Publishing even had a different logo. Then he's suddenly in charge and he's saying that recorded and publishing should be working together. Even though he was one of those people who maintained those silos big time. But Roger is someone who genuinely understands the business. Then it started to feel like the old days."

Faxon himself admits the structural divisions were there for years and became amplified in the 2000s. But he felt the digital upheaval that had pulled recorded music inside out and that was now starting to snap at the heels of publishing should be addressed collectively by the company, rather than having each side work in isolation.

"EMI had always been run, since the Jim Fifield days, as two completely separate businesses – publishing and recorded," he says. "There was very little, if any, coordination between them. There were fewer opportunities back in the 1990s, but as the [world] started to move away from physical goods into digital goods, what happens to a record company is that it becomes more and more a licensing organisation."

Faxon's vision for the newly symbiotic company was that recorded and publishing should think and move in unison, identifying and exploiting the creative and commercial synergies between them. He believed that the shift into digital had effectively forced the transformation of EMI from a manufacturing company to a licensing company. With this comes the rapid rise of data and whole new challenges in processing and interpreting that data.

247

"[There are now] third parties who you have to monitor and understand how their business is working in order to be effective at optimising your outcomes – so a lot of the internal disciplines of the business were converging," he says. "They still haven't fully converged today but they were converging [then]. We don't need to reinvent the wheel here. We know how to license and we understand what the licensing structure is, so let's take advantage of that. But you also had something else which was the fourth-largest record company in the world and you had, by far, the number one publishing company in the world whose rights extended over 50 per cent of the active repertoire in the world."

In the days of strong physical sales, EMI's recorded arm and publishing arm did have common interests but they tended to work in isolation. They had different executives leading them and different P&L [profit and loss] sheets – plus there was plenty of money being made in the CD market, which meant that coordinating activities was a rare luxury rather than a burning necessity.

"If EMI Music Publishing got a better deal at the expense of EMI Records, that was OK in the old world," says Faxon. "But in the new world, that was not OK. It was about bringing the elements together to have a mutual benefit for our songwriters and for our recording artists. What can we do that is going to build their careers and their income? As a consequence of us building their careers and their income, we prosper. Understanding that was really important to change the culture and also the operations. Without having the right culture, you can't actually succeed – particularly in a creative industry. The first thing was to get the culture right. But there was a very simple vision for the whole company."

Faxon was headquartered in New York but had been well used to commuting between there and London for years. He would have to be in London more frequently and working with whole new teams, so he held a town hall meeting in Wrights Lane soon after he took over as head of both publishing and recorded. "I asked the people why they were there," he recalls of this first big meeting in front of his newly expanded UK staff. "I asked these questions. 'Why are we here? Why are you here?' 'I need a pay cheque.' 'I don't think I could get another job.' I said, 'No, no, no. We're here because we love music. That's why we're here. And we love the people who make music. And if you don't love music and if you don't love the people who make music, then get the fuck out! That's who we are and that's what we do. It's time to make music and get it out there so that we are doing right by our artists and by our songwriters. Stop dwelling on your navel and talking about how the world is bad. We have huge assets and we can do all sorts of wonderful things.'"

On taking the job, Faxon had to end the old rivalries – sometimes healthy and sometimes poisonous – that had existed between the different sides of EMI. This was certainly achievable, but it was not going to be easy. "The politics between the two businesses [recorded and publishing] was legion in terms of the two management teams [prior to Terra Firma]," claims Charles Allen. "It was a very poor relationship. It was seen as one side would win and one side would lose. That is what needed to be managed and that is what Roger needed to do. He needed to come in and calm that team down. It felt like a takeover [by publishing], although they were sister companies."

Faxon was undoubtedly a popular executive at EMI and his promotion to the group CEO role ultimately meant that one of the most divisive executives at the company was overlooked for the same job and therefore knew their time at the company had come to an abrupt end.

Ernesto Schmitt, president of central marketing and global catalogue, lasted less than three months under the new structure before he exited. He claims he was being lined up to take over as CEO but his ascension plans were scuppered. "Elio Leoni Sceti fell out with Guy Hands," he claims. "Elio's recommendation was that I should take over as chief executive from him. Guy Hands and the Terra Firma team seriously considered that because they did see – their words not mine – the working agenda [I put in place] was the main value driver for EMI. In the end they hesitated. I was 37 or 38 at the time so I was a little bit on the younger end of the spectrum and they appointed the opposite of me … Roger Faxon and I are the exact opposite. Roger Faxon is very much an old-school music industry guy and had been at EMI for decades. His agenda was very much a traditional one of cost-cutting and streamlining. It was not at all a skills or insight transformational agenda."

He hints at a clashing and incompatible working relationship and vision for the company between himself and Faxon which meant that only one of them could stay. "Roger Faxon is the kind of guy who likes to have eight miles of clear water between him and the nearest guy," he says. "He presumed I had been a contender for the main role, [so] Roger basically said there was only [room for] one of us here. So I left."

Schmitt is also disparaging about Faxon's main strategic reshuffle of the entire company, feeling it looked fine on paper but was not the great transformation catalyst that some, including Faxon, claim it could have been. "Look, I see no reason why publishing and recorded music shouldn't have closer synergies. That's very true. But I don't think you can save the business on that basis. And Roger Faxon ultimately failed. It's not enough. Just saying you're going to bring them all together doesn't mean anything."

When asked what, had the top job gone to him rather than Faxon, he would have done and where he would have steered the company, Schmitt says it would have been a continuation of what he was already doing in the catalogue division and audience insights department, taking it to what he saw as its natural conclusion.

"I would have carried on with the exact agenda that we had, which was to take a consumer insight perspective, to have a very nuanced and de-averaged product offering and to build on the basis of technology much more advanced marketing platforms than the traditional marketing that the music industry did and still does today," he says. "All of the things that had earned the music industry its influence historically, in this current digital world no longer apply. The barrier to success is the discovery hurdle. The next generation of the music business in my view is a digital platform that connects consumers' preferences with content – and does that seamlessly at scale and effectively."

This switch-around at the most senior level of EMI came off the back of a failed deal with Universal that could have addressed the long-standing American issue and raised an estimated £200 million for Terra Firma. By this stage, the private equity company was thrashing around in the rising waters of debt to meet an investment target of £120 million by 14 June that had been set by Citigroup as part of its £2.6 billion loan to Terra Firma in 2007.

The Lex column in the *Financial Times* saw this as a sign that Terra Firma and EMI were a busted flush. It damned Terra Firma's position as "pretty bleak" and suggested the best thing for Guy Hands and his private equity company to do would be to "admit defeat and move on".[2]

This fell on deaf ears and Terra Firma chose not to move on but instead to press on. The plan, led by Charles Allen, was to sell EMI's North American catalogue to Universal. Analysts were calling it a 'do or die' deal and the very future of the company was hanging by a thread. "EMI is in a desperate situation," Claire Enders of Enders Analysis told *Music Week*. "The value of its equity has been written down by 90 per cent and, to his credit, Charles Allen is fighting hard on behalf of his shareholders, but the truth is this is an extremely stark scenario."[3]

It was suggested at the time that the deal could have been for a five-year licensing deal and that both Sony Music and Universal were interested. Neither, however, was prepared to go above £50 million, throwing Terra Firma into turmoil trying raise the money it needed to keep its head above water with Citigroup, having already breached the terms of its loan in March.

"At that stage, we were looking at whether we could shrink the business," says Allen of the deal that never came off, suggesting there was an alternative purchase strategy running in tandem with the sell strategy. "We weren't strong enough in North America. We needed to do something. Either we needed to buy something or we needed to sell something. We were looking at both options. Could we sell them that asset and then use that money to invest elsewhere?"

Given that catalogue was one of the key profit centres for EMI during this time, it seems counterproductive to think about selling it at all as its removal would blow a hole in the company's future profitability. "We didn't see that as a long-term business," is Allen's blunt assessment of why it was put on the auction block. "It was a business that would ultimately decline."

Terra Firma was, of course, in no position to be picky or take its time over a deal of this scale. "We as directors of the board had a fiduciary responsibility to make sure the company was solvent," explains Allen of the growing crisis they were having to confront. "That was a key thing. We were looking at the options and what we could do. We had the accountants in there and we had the lawyers in there saying that this was the information they had got and asking if we were still able to run the company."

Hands says a deal with the biggest record company had been sketched out but it was vetoed by Citibank. "We did look at a deal to split it [recorded music repertoire in the US] out on a licensed basis with a third party," he says. "That would have saved the company but Citigroup said no to that. And that was actually with Universal. That would have saved the company but we needed Citigroup's approval for it."

Even though it was presumed that Faxon was a safe pair of hands, Terra Firma's debts were spiralling perilously out of control. Faxon was tasked with bringing the two parts of EMI together at the precise moment that the entire edifice was threatening to collapse in on itself.

In May 2010, Guy Hands went to his investors to ask for an additional £360 million – three times what it needed to raise to appease Citigroup – which could fund EMI and, crucially, buy it breathing space into 2015, when Terra Firma could look to renegotiate the terms of its loan.[4] Within a matter of weeks, a number of investors confirmed they would collectively put in £105 million, but this was contingent on getting the backing of at least 150 of the fund's 220 investors before the money could be drawn down. Terra Firma would also have to present a 'compliance certificate' to Citigroup to prove it was in a fit state to meet the terms of its loan.[5]

"We went back to our existing investors to look at them investing more," says Allen of the panic to raise the funds to boost the business and ensure its long-term survival under Terra Firma. "This was about having sufficient funds to invest in the business going forward. It was around digital, the supply chain, having sufficient funds for talent. It was about having sufficient cash to invest in running the core business ... Insight was a big part of that. There was a lot of investment that went into that."

The £105 million raised here was reported to secure EMI's future into 2011, but some were seeing it as a Sisyphean folly. "All Guy [Hands] has managed to do is buy another year for the company," was Claire Enders' withering assessment at the time. "But this does not secure the company's future; nothing will unless it can develop a long-term funding plan."[6]

Charles Allen says Hands was leading this progression. "Guy was managing that process," he says. "He was the one going to see the investors. He was the one going to see everyone that he needed to get aligned with. He knew that we had to be compliant. Otherwise the implications of that were that they would pull the loan and he would lose the keys."

Allen adds that his role during this financially precarious time was to ensure the company remained active and focused on growth and to give it the protection it needed to carry this through.

"The team just carried on," he says, even though they were fully aware the sky above them was darkening. "It was really only myself and the legal counsel who were dealing with the board ... the company was getting on with [normal business]. My job was to protect them from anything that was going on above them and let them get on with things. If they didn't do their job, it took us backwards. If they didn't put out the releases and they didn't sign the talent, that would make the cash situation worse. The conversation we had with the senior team was for them to just do their day jobs. We told them not to worry about that and that we would get on and address it."

Hot on the heels of this freewheeling calamity came the news that the Pension Regulator was insisting EMI raise £250 million "to plug a gap in its pension scheme", with the Terra Firma board of trustees insisting Guy Hands make up the shortfall. EMI claimed at the time there were "issues" but that the deficit was £10 million, not £250 million.[7]

Speculation about the future viability of the company went into overdrive, with rumours now ricocheting around the music industry in June that Terra Firma was considering outside offers to acquire a 49 per cent stake in EMI Music Publishing. This was not helped by the concurrent news that the publisher was planning to cut at least six MD positions across Europe to improve its efficiency.[8] Later that month, Arjen Witte, the MD of EMI Music Publishing in the Netherlands, revealed that the Dutch office would be closing and fourteen employees would be out of work. To add insult to injury, the Belgian office also closed that month.[9]

Through the gloom, there were occasional shafts of light. At the end of August 2010, EMI announced it was buying e-commerce company Digitalstores to give it a competitive advantage in the growing D2C (direct-to-consumer) world where artists and their labels were selling music, merchandise and tickets online. EMI had already bought Loud-clothing.com in 2010 to extend its merchandising expertise, so this was a logical extension of the process.

Amplifying the positives, news of this acquisition was followed by Maltby Capital (the holding company for EMI) publishing its accounts for the financial year 2009/10. Revenues were up from £1.57 billion the year before to £1.65 billion, with the success of The Beatles mono and stereo remasters cited as a key driver alongside breakthrough acts such as Katy Perry and Lady Antebellum. They were still down, however, on the £1.8 billion reported three years earlier, crucially the financial period that just pre-dated the arrival of Terra Firma.

EBITDA (excluding restructuring) was up 14 per cent to £334 million and pre-tax operating profits jumped from £7 million to £121 million in the period, a swing into the black after losses of £258 million and £135 million in the preceding two years. Overall, EMI recorded a net loss of £512 million (after tax) for the twelve months but had an operating cash flow of £250 million compared to just £7 million three years earlier, with the company saying it was going to be able to meet its banking covenants with Citigroup.

Appearing in *Music Week*, an assertive Roger Faxon was quick to slap down suggestions that this was an outlier of a financial year propelled by a staggering 13 million sales of Beatles albums. He pointed to a Robbie Williams greatest hits album, a new KT Tunstall album and the break-through of Tinie Tempah and Eliza Doolittle, all of which would appear on the books for the next financial year.

He added, "We are not in a situation where the business is underper-forming – it is meeting all its bills … EMI is a strong business and getting stronger. There are two issues which are more important here – the underlying value of EMI's assets and the way the debt works within the covenant."[10]

Music Week editor Paul Williams used his editorial that week to say that EMI was "having something of a good run, growing its business in an industry that continues to shrink" but expressed concern about the creep in its net losses. Effectively, he said, "all that hard work and those successes" were being wiped out by the debt.[11]

Faxon – and Maltby Capital – may have talked a good talk with the performance of EMI in the most recent financial year, but the wider problems remained as Terra Firma scrambled to stay on top of its debts and try and make it through to 2015 when the grip Citigroup had around its throat could be loosened.

EMI said it had a "provisional commitment" from Terra Firma to stump up the £26.9 million it needed to meet the debt repayments, but that was just one payment and it still had to clear the other covenant repayments to the end of the year to stay in business. It also forecast a "further significant shortfall" when it would be tested again in March 2011, something that would necessitate Terra Firma going back to its investors to put more equity into the music company.

Faxon claimed this would not phase either him or the company. "The logic is pretty clear," he told *Music Week*. "They [the investors] would not have put £100 million into the business [in 2010] if they thought that this year or any year in the future they wouldn't have a business, so it's only logical that they put it in to make a return on the investment and they will continue to resolve the covenant issues."[12]

Despite all the gung-ho talk here, the debt tremors were becoming both more frequent and more pronounced. The question was no longer if but when the earthquake would hit.

* * *

Talking about EMI's performance in the past year was one thing, but Faxon had to be completely focused on its future. He roared into action, promising to break apart the conventional wisdom of A&R at record labels that accepted a 10–20 per cent success rate as normal and workable as long as the few successes paid off the losses of the others.

This chimed with Guy Hands's initial criticism of the business, that it had normalised failure, but he sought to solve it by different means. While Hands's strategy was to drop unprofitable acts and dramatically slash the frontline A&R budget to focus on just a handful of artists, Faxon's approach was to aim to have the bulk of acts on EMI's labels leap into profitability.

Key to this was dismantling the global business units that were put in place by the matrix system in which Terra Firma had invested so much time and effort. EMI Music Publishing had been spared the matrix model and so Faxon had no qualms about putting a new structure in place.

Faxon pointed out that EMI Music Publishing had a 95 per cent success rate in terms of seeing a return on its investment when signing writers and that, while recorded music would never be a 100 per cent successful endeavour, getting the majority of EMI recording acts into profitability was "very realistic" as far as he was concerned.[13]

Faxon told *Music Week*, "I know the world is very uncertain and there are all sorts of barriers to success but it's our business. We should be smart enough to help our artists find the way to succeed in the environment in which we exist and if we don't believe we can do it we shouldn't be in the business."[14]

Across a two-page interview in the UK trade magazine, Faxon explained in greater forensic detail what he was hoping to do in his new role, careful to avoid the word "vision" (as "it sounds so pretentious"), preferring to describe it as a "state of understanding". He said his goal for EMI was for it to be seen as a service company that worked with and for its acts in partnership, focusing on the connection between artist and fans "to extract the value".

He added that he understood why Terra Firma was so focused on the bottom line. "I think when a financially-focused owner comes in they are always concerned about, and rightly so, the financial risks that are being taken," he said. "A great deal of money, hundreds and hundreds of millions of pounds a year, is invested in artist development, releases, marketing, the creation of the recording, the music and so on and it's a creative business and therefore there is risk in it."

In order to mitigate the investment risk, EMI was going to have to expand into new business areas, work a lot smarter and make itself a company that, once more, people would aspire to work for. "This business will have a more diversified revenue base," he said. "It will be leaner and more agile than it has been. It will be a business that will absolutely put the artist first and itself second. It will be a place where people will love to work, people who don't fear for the future because they know they are making the future. It will be a business that loves music and yet sees it as something that is a mission. I don't know what [the other majors] are going to do. If they do the same thing as we do that will be great in my view for music and for the people who create music. We are just going to do our thing and are pretty convinced it will be successful."[15]

Faxon's decommissioning of Terra Firma's global business units meant the sacking of Ron Werre (COO of North America and Mexico), Billy Mann (president of global artist management) and Nick Gatfield (new music president for North America, the UK and Ireland). He said that on a conceptual level, these units were a good idea and brought additional value but, to his mind, they stood in the way of his plans to dismantle all barriers within the company as a whole to ensure everyone was pulling in the same direction.

Replacing the matrix was a set of hubs – North America, Latin America and 'Europe plus', which David Kassler would head and which included key European territories as well as Australia, Japan, Africa and the Middle East.

Looking back on this significant rebuilding and refocusing of EMI, where it was hoped that publishing and recorded would dovetail perfectly, Faxon explains in more detail his thinking and his strategy.

"The first thing that we did was dismantle the organisation [the matrix system] and move it back – not all the way, but part of the way as I wasn't about to delegate all this power back down into the territories as we wouldn't have the efficiencies and the coordinated effectiveness that we needed," he says. "We needed to understand that you needed local management to drive answers. We rebuilt the core management team and put most of the functions into two regions: there was the rest of the world, which was David Kassler's world; then there was North America. We simplified the organisation. We did rationalise it and we did actually move people around quite a lot. We did a complete review of the staff."

A senior source who saw all these plans being implemented argued that Faxon was lucky that the entire industry was in turmoil and so that did not make EMI stand out too much in comparison. That also ensured that the executive team stayed in place, in large part because no other majors had the budgets to lure them away, and they were paranoid about walking out in case they could not find a comparative post in a rival company.

"It was fortunate that the mayhem that Guy caused in the organisation was done in a period in which the rest of the record industry was not in great shape either," they argue. "What would normally happen if you had the purges that were going on and uncertainty in the Guy era, the best people would have left; they would have been stolen away. But they stayed and we actually had quite a talented group of people. But they weren't focused; they had lost their focus. On the A&R and label side, they were interested in the artists that were most important to them, but they really were struggling to build new artists and all of that. That hadn't changed. And [under Roger Faxon] that changed immediately."

One label source backs up this point about having nowhere else to defect to if they wanted to stay working at a major label. They also felt part of the reason they stayed was in the hope that the Terra Firma era – or at least the pain of the Terra Firma era – would end soon.

"Did I consider leaving at any point?" they say. "Yeah, but because I am so loyal to the company, I thought, and not in an egotistical way, that if I walk out I will be leaving some people and artists behind that we have a great relationship with and who have given so much to us. I just felt so loyal to them. Otherwise, God knows who they would have brought in. I loved our acts and I loved the team of people here. I thought, 'This will not last. There is not a chance in hell!' It was in such disarray. My plan was to keep my head down. I felt that in three years it would all be over. It was so obvious it wasn't going to last for ten years."

Guy Hands categorically denies that this flip into a hub model was a major vote of no confidence by Faxon in the matrix system in which he had placed so much hope back in 2007.

"The matrix system didn't apply to publishing," asserts Hands. "I think what he [Faxon] did was that he got people to start reporting directly to him. I think it was more that he felt he could basically cut costs by taking out the senior people alongside him and just have people report directly into him." He adds, "He had a huge number of reports in publishing and I think he simply just did the same thing in recorded."

As much as the matrix had been a mantra for Guy Hands and Terra Firma, the idea of a global rights management business became the hymn for Faxon and his team.

"Once Roger took over the whole company, we did a lot of work on how the company could be more proficient," says one senior source closely involved in all this. "We came up with this idea of a global rights management business, which we then repeated ad nauseam for two years. We also talked incessantly about successful outcomes for artists. Those two phrases – 'global rights management' and 'successful outcomes for artists' – were repeated again and again."

The most immediate impact of this executive restructuring was felt in the UK and the US, with executives in the major markets in continental Europe claiming they were actually under less pressure, rather than more, now.

"We did not really see a big change because Roger Faxon took over," says one European label source. "It just meant the direct pressure coming in from the UK was not that aggressive any more and was no longer ongoing. It was a more normal situation."

At the end of August, Iron Maiden's latest album, *The Final Frontier*, went straight to number one in twenty-two countries. This was a ringing endorsement for the label that had worked with the band for over thirty years, showing it could still help them deliver hits. And in October, EMI signed a joint venture with Guetta Events' *Fuck Me I'm Famous* to turn DJ David Guetta's club night into a global dance brand, proving the company could work with new acts and sign new types of deals in a rapidly changing market.

Then in October, Guy Hands scored a victory against HM Revenue & Customs in the UK over VAT payments on sample products (promo copies sent to press and radio). He pushed through the six-year battle, one that pre-dated his arrival at the company, and it ended with the European Court of Justice ruling that the UK was wrong to charge VAT on music sent for promotional purposes. The legal success would mean a "seven-figure sum" rebate going to EMI and it also set a precedent that would benefit the other labels.[16]

EMI was happy to take its triumphs where it could find them, but there was no avoiding the fact that they were somewhat bittersweet. "We were still struggling, though, because we didn't have any money," one senior source accepts. "Our marketing budgets were tiny. Universal would just outspend us on A&R and marketing. We were a shadow of our former selves. We were very shrunken. We were working well operationally, but our future was massively insecure because Terra Firma couldn't afford the mortgage. It just got harder and tighter each time. It was clear something had to give."

For one long-serving EMI staff member, the second half of 2010 was beginning to feel like a tentative renaissance of EMI. The company was also harking back to the good old days, by now hugely romanticised.

"We had finally started to turn the corner," they say. "We got through [the upheaval] and we were finally having some hits. From a PR point of view, we finally had a story to tell."

The closing weeks of 2010 brought a significant breakthrough for the company and gave it its biggest story of the year to proclaim to the naysayers – bringing to fruition something it had been working on for the best part of a decade. On 16 November, and after years of frustrating on-off negotiations, the entire Beatles back catalogue was finally made available for legal download. It was an iTunes exclusive and was something Apple co-founder Steve Jobs had made a personal mission. He had, after all, named his company in tribute to the band's Apple Records.[17]

"We love The Beatles and are honoured and thrilled to welcome them to iTunes," said Jobs in a statement. Paul McCartney added, "It's fantastic to see the songs we originally released on vinyl receive as much love in the digital world as they did the first time around." It was left to Ringo Starr to puncture any residual pomposity associated with the deal. "I'm particularly glad to no longer be asked when The Beatles are coming to iTunes," he deadpanned.[18]

It was a symbolic achievement but also an economic imperative, with Ben Rumley from Enders Analysis quoted in a piece by the BBC on the day of the deal saying that 10 per cent of EMI's sales in the US in 2009 were Beatles records.[19]

"It was a good deal for EMI and it was a very good deal for The Beatles," is Roger Faxon's summation of what happened in order to get the band's music on iTunes. "In my own view, it was well past the time it should have been done. There would have been more money on the table earlier. Jeff [Jones] and I went around the houses to make the digital deals and it was obvious that the place to go to was Apple. So we made the deal with Steve [Jobs]. We did it as a partnership between us to make the right deal."

Apple was quick to trumpet the scale of the deal's success when it announced that the band had sold 2 million tracks and 450,000 album downloads in their first week on iTunes. The timing could not have been better. EMI was going into Christmas with some positive news for a change.

But for Terra Firma and Guy Hands, the culmination of a long legal dispute with Citigroup and the thunderous roar of its debt problems were going to combine to deliver them the worst Christmas of their lives.

CHAPTER 14

Ob-La-Di EBITDA

A common summation of Terra Firma's time at EMI was that the company overpaid for it just before the debt markets collapsed; its recovery plan was always doomed as they did not know the industry; and they appointed all the wrong people to drive the change. This is partly true, but equally it is too reductionist. Terra Firma did as much good as it did damage to EMI, and the financial problems were partly of its own making but mostly utterly out of its control. There were too many moving parts here, some working at optimum speed and others snapped off or rusting over and becoming impotent, to allow for simple answers.

EMI was most assuredly on a path to recovery. How could it not be when staffing numbers had been so aggressively slashed and the running costs of the company squeezed so much they were almost choking? Was EMI going to be fully reborn by 2014, the date Terra Firma had in its mind when all the planets would align; when the recorded music market would finally start to pull itself out of the sharp decline that started in 2000; and when EMI was going to prove itself as the most match-fit major label and, therefore, the one that was going to reap the most rewards? Maybe. Possibly.

This, really, is a story of bad timing. The worst timing imaginable. Shockingly poor timing. Everything that happened was to happen at the wrong time – either too soon or too late. Like the inverse of that old maxim about great comedy being all about perfect timing, tragedy is all about abysmal timing.

The thing ticking asynchronously behind all of this, getting louder and knocking everything else off its natural rhythm, was the debt: that all hinged on the amount paid to buy EMI, the amount needed just to meet the debt covenants and the ambitious recovery plan that needed to work flawlessly to eventually pay off that debt.

Going right back to the start, between 2006 and 2007, Terra Firma had raised a €5.4 billion fund (known as TFCP III, short for Terra Firma

Capital Partners III) and had another €1.9 billion fund (around 40 per cent of what was termed TFCP II) left over to invest. Through its Limited Partner Agreements, it had approval to invest up to 30 per cent of each of these two funds, the plan being to sell down at least 10 per cent to co-investors, primarily Terra Firma's limited partners.[1]

Having missed out on buying high-street chemist chain Boots in April 2007 when Kohlberg Kravis Roberts submitted its winning bid of £11.1 billion, Terra Firma had to go shopping. Fast. This is why it was a last-minute bidder for EMI, which was planning to close the auction process before the end of May that same year, 2007.

To recap, Terra Firma, on the rebound from Boots, won the EMI bid, paying £4.2 billion for the company. Of that, £2.6 billion was borrowed from Citigroup to finance the deal. The remaining £1.6 billion came from Terra Firma and a consortium of around 220 investors. This was, by some distance, the biggest deal Terra Firma had ever pulled off. By its own admission, "it was over three times the size of the average deal we had done in the previous twelve years" but, because of where the company was in its fundraising and investment cycle, it "had made a strategic decision to consider larger deals" – hence EMI.

A confidential business plan that was presented to investors by Terra Firma was eventually leaked and was forecasting that EMI's projected pre-tax profits would go from £167 million in 2007 to £580 million by 2010. "This was despite almost every analyst predicting a fall in industry sales and earnings,"[2] wrote Brian Southall in his book.

Citigroup's aim was to syndicate the vast majority of its loan to Terra Firma, planning to hold onto no more than £223 million of it for itself, according to Hands based on information from Citi's investment papers. This was made up of £350 million of what was termed the securitisation bridge immediately following the acquisition of EMI, £48 million of the senior facilities (including rolling credit facility and interest rate hedging line) and £183 million of the high yield bridge. Of that total, however, Citi was seeking to reduce it to £223 million within 12 months once securitisation had been taken out.

In a buoyant debt market, this was a common presumption and a standard strategy. Terra Firma knew in this bubble it could raise the money it needed and Citigroup was confident it could sell on at least 90 per cent of the loan, mitigating its risk enormously and also giving it a cut of any potential upside.

Any economist, however, will tell you that bubbles, by their very definition, burst. From the 'Dutch tulip bubble' in the 1630s (where tulip prices increased by a factor of twenty before plummeting 99 per cent in 1637), through the 'South Sea bubble' (where shares in the South Sea

Company shot up by a factor of eight between January and June 1720 before collapsing) and the 'dot.com bubble' (that peaked in 2000 and popped in 2002), these were all warnings from history. Yet in a bubble, the same patterns are identifiable: a crass assumption that it can never end and, even if it will, a belief that normal rules no longer apply so investors can be as bold and reckless as they want, hoping to cash out before they become collateral damage.

As Terra Firma was looking to buy EMI, the subprime meltdown was about to happen, where high-risk mortgages and non-traditional loans that had been issued due to historically low interest rates (designed in part to re-stimulate the US economy in the wake of both the dot.com crash and the 9/11 terrorist attacks) went into default. This caused the biggest global economic contraction since the Great Depression triggered by the Wall Street Crash in 1929.

This was categorically no time to borrow £2.6 billion and yet that is what Terra Firma, oblivious to what was just about to happen, did.

"After the collapse of the sub-prime market in the US post-May 2007, the ability of banks to securitise any type of loan disappeared, along with their willingness to underwrite loans in the syndicated loan market,"[3] says Terra Firma in its EMI case study on its own website. It adds there were three major implications for the EMI transaction:

1) The cost of the debt was now exceeding what they had expected and planned for;
2) The financial covenants that Citigroup had put in place were now "more onerous than originally envisaged" and had been part of a debt package that both parties were originally going to refinance in 2008 via a securitisation programme;
3) "The loan made by Citigroup in advance of the expected securitisation was a lot smaller than the anticipated proceeds from that securitisation: Terra Firma therefore had to leave substantially more equity in the transaction to compensate."

As the securitisation market was effectively desiccated, Citigroup was unable to "syndicate its long-term senior bank bridge loan", according to Terra Firma. As such, the entire loan now rested with Citigroup, rather than (at most) 10 per cent, and they would have to carry the can. "Apparently the loans were considered not marketable [even by] April 2008 in light of investor anxiety about EMI's future, but by May it seemed that Hands was fighting to meet the financial targets set by the bank," wrote Brian Southall in his history of EMI.[4]

Equally, Terra Firma now found itself in a positon where 30 per cent of TFCP II and TFCP III was now tied into the EMI deal and not the 10 per cent it had hoped to have in there at most. "The problem was that the debt package that we had finally agreed with Citigroup, once the markets had changed, was a very different debt package from the debt package that we had envisaged when we did the deal," says Guy Hands. "The team who did the deal always presented it on the basis that we would always get our money back on publishing and with recorded music we could make a fortune on it or it could go wrong. We had a way of making a fortune on it, but the question was whether or not we could do it."

During this time, of course, Hands and his team – as well as their opposites at Citigroup – were desperately crossing their fingers that the EMI board would fail to get over the 90 per cent shareholder approval threshold, meaning they could all walk away from the deal with immunity and their reputations intact. They could shift all the blame onto the EMI board for the collapse of the deal, as they would have failed to convince their shareholders it was the right deal for the company. They could claim they had put in an offer in good faith and it simply was not their fault the EMI board could not convince the shareholders to go along with it.

Except, of course, the EMI board crossed the line at the last minute, meaning both Terra Firma and Citigroup had an enormous problem on their hands. The deal had to go through and both sides felt they were, in their own way, utterly screwed: Citigroup because it was not going to be able to syndicate the loan; and Terra Firma as it was going to hit targets that were now much higher than they had originally envisaged.

One senior source within EMI had an ominous feeling that now the shareholders were behind the EMI board, this would throw Terra Firma into an unenviable position, putting it at a punishing disadvantage that was going to be nigh on impossible to come back from. "The wheels had come off and both the debt markets and the securitisation markets had completely closed," they say. "There was nothing they could securitise so they were left with this enormous debt that was carrying huge interest rates. In terms of timing, they were very unlucky."

Hands and his team knew they had to do something to save their skins and try and find a compromise with Citigroup. "It didn't feel like a death sentence – it felt like we had to sort out the debt," says Hands when he learned that 90.3 per cent of EMI shareholders were backing the Terra Firma acquisition. "It was a debt sentence!"

In August 2007, a Terra Firma delegation flew to New York during an ominous and atypical summer downpour to meet with senior Citigroup executives, including Michael Klein and Chad Leat. Hands says they had rehearsed their pitch and their arguments over and over. "We had everything worked out," he says. "It was choreographed. This was the most important meeting we were likely to have – certainly in the next twelve months."

The Terra Firma ballet barely made it into the first grand jeté before Citigroup cut the music and told them that no deal was happening. They threatened to walk out and initiate legal action if Terra Firma continued with their pitch to recalibrate the loan terms in the wake of the global financial volcano that was beginning to erupt.

Hands says that he was asked to leave his colleagues and meet with the Citigroup representatives in a private room. "A huge mistake," he sighs. "In hindsight it was a stupid thing to do. I should not have gone into the room by myself. But Michael Klein was a friend and I felt comfortable, I suppose. Plus, to be honest, the emotional state that I was in and that we were all in was pretty extreme."

This meeting in New York was primarily to work out the issues around the interim loan, which matured in a matter of months, as the terms of the full loan had yet to be agreed. "We knew we couldn't pay off the interim loan, so if we didn't find an agreement with Citigroup on this interim loan then the company would go straight bankrupt," says Hands.

At the time, before the crash shook everyone into a more cautious and paranoid state, agreeing to a loan without hammering out every clause in advance was not uncommon. "It sounds ridiculous that you buy a company of this size on the basis of a bit of paper and you are then going to sort the loan out, but that is what people did," says Hands of these more innocent – or more reckless – times in the financial world. "If the market is good when you sort the loan out, you are going to get really great terms. It was ghastly. Citigroup weren't going to give us good terms."

Hands says the meeting with Klein and Leat went only one way – against Terra Firma. "We effectively walked out with a loan that was vastly worse than we had put in our expectations," he sighs.

What Terra Firma was hoping for was actually two loans from Citigroup – or, rather, a loan split in two and put against different parts of EMI. They wanted one loan for EMI Music Publishing which they knew was a solid business and did not need to change, so it was going to be an incredibly safe investment. Then they wanted another loan for the recorded music side of EMI which was the riskier investment and the part of the business that needed to be dramatically rebuilt.

"We understood the publishing business pretty well and we felt that was a steady stream of income which, in pretty much any circumstance, could pay our money back," says Hands. "Our view was that the publishing business could be securitised and we could add onto it by buying further catalogues. We were always going to hold onto publishing. That was what we were going to rely on to repay the debt and to give us our money back. We saw that as a safe business that we would be able to make two times our money on."

In the mind of Terra Firma, a loan against publishing was a form of security and could help mitigate against problems or challenges they ran up against with the recorded music part of the company. They would end up with a safe acquisition with its own loan and a difficult acquisition with its own loan.

Then the crash happened and all bets were off.

"Citigroup and Terra Firma could not agree on what the final debt package would look like," says Hands. This is where he feels everything started to unspool. The joint and several agreement was the opposite of what Hands desired.

Responding to widespread criticism that he could not be much of a financial expert if he categorically failed to spot this global economic crash coming, Hands concurs – to a point. "I would say they are 100 per cent right as banking is [an area I have a lot of experience in]," he says. "But I would also say that pretty much nobody else saw it … The British government didn't see it. The American government didn't see it."

He also subscribes to the thesis that it was impossible for the timing of the deal to have been any worse, before working through two parallel, if frustratingly hypothetical, outcomes. "My personal view is that if we had done the deal a year earlier at the same price we would have got it refinanced and been absolutely fine," he claims. "If we had done it six months later, we would have done it at a completely different price. Would we have done it six months later knowing the debt market was in free fall? We would have done it at a different price."

As it was, Citigroup would not compromise and refused to split the loans between recorded and publishing. There would be one loan covering the whole business. "You can't blame Citigroup for not giving us what we wanted – because the market had completely changed," accepts Hands. "From then on the relationship between us and Citigroup was a nightmare."

This was all going to fester over the next three years, from 2007 to 2010. Terra Firma stewed in the fact that it was forced to work with deal terms it did not want and Citigroup was left carrying a massive loan that it had planned to syndicate. No one was going to win here, but really it became a battle over who was going to lose the least. Within this, the terms were tilting more in Citigroup's favour than Terra Firma's.

"We got killed because we couldn't negotiate the terms after we had done the deal," is how Hands sees it. "And they got killed because they couldn't sell it down after they lent the money. You now had two incredibly unhappy parties with different timing objectives and different ways of getting out."

For Terra Firma, who had been roundly outmanoeuvred, the cliff edge loomed.

* * *

"It was probably the last big deal done for about three years," says Hands of the acrid legacy of the Citigroup loan. "Chuck [Charles] Prince, who was CEO of Citigroup, came over [to the UK] about a month after the deal was done and he was asked about the market. He said, 'While the music plays, one has to dance.'[5] I thought that was a great quote. When he said that, he was really referring to this deal. They had made the deal because the markets were very good. They wanted to win this deal. They wanted us to do the deal. We wanted to borrow the money and the market just collapsed on us. And it [the market] collapsed on Citigroup as well."

Effectively, Guy Hands had bought a company that he no longer wanted under financial terms that he had not envisaged and in a financial market that was, in his own words, "going to Hell in a handcart". To the public, and to the EMI staff he was now responsible for, he had to put on a brave face.

"I was scared shitless," he admits. "This was not a happy period. It was horrible. It was one of those awful things where you have a moral and a legal obligation to do something and you were just hoping that something would happen which meant you didn't have to. By contrast, you have [Eric] Nicoli and his team sitting there thinking that if this didn't happen then EMI was probably going to go bankrupt."

EMI was saved from bankruptcy and shielded from the cruel winds that had whipped it as a public company, now that Terra Firma owned it. But in taking EMI away from the brink of bankruptcy, Terra Firma was placing itself in a perilous position. At the time, the business press and music industry trade publications were speculating that the deal could have fallen apart due to the negative swing the financial market had taken. Meanwhile, EMI was sending out a message of confidence that it would all go according to plan – that the loan would happen and the shareholders would come onside.

It may have played out exactly as Eric Nicoli had hoped, but he became the first casualty of Terra Firma's plans for EMI in September.

With Hands now the reluctant CEO, Terra Firma had no other option but to rush through its restructuring plans for EMI. The debt package it now found itself holding was starting to feel like a parcel bomb. Terra Firma had to deploy everyone it had to try and hasten the speed of change and make it to the top of a debt hill whose slope seemed to get more vertiginous the more you looked at it. What the staff at EMI read as arrogance from Terra Firma's team coming in was, in a large part, merely panic dressed up in different clothes.

Hands deployed thirty-three Terra Firma people from the beginning at EMI – the thinking being that this would hasten the speed of change, quickly cut out the excess, massively reduce the overheads and drive up profits faster than planned – all to stay on top of the debt repayments it had to meet and not be overwhelmed by. He denies, however, that they came into EMI in a state of high anxiety. "It was all we could do to get it done really quickly," he says. "At the end of the day, we had to be in a position to cut the costs really quickly. We just didn't have the luxury of time."

He claims that in past deals, and without the added complication of a global economy in freefall around it, Terra Firma's standard approach was to put in one or two of its key executives at the start and move more cautiously and strategically in its restructuring from there.

If anything, Terra Firma, in throwing everything it had at EMI from the first day, did little to alleviate the fraught situation and in fact simply exacerbated it. With thirty-three Terra Firma executives charging pell-mell into Wrights Lane to enact change as quickly as possible, it is little wonder the EMI staff felt they were under attack and immediately put their defences up. Terra Firma needed EMI to bend, but with too many hands all scrabbling to bend it too quickly, it was at serious risk of snapping.

*   *   *

For those one step removed from the white heat of the Terra Firma debt, the financial situation had certainly progressed relatively calmly. But some EMI executives with a close understanding of just how the debt package was structured knew that the more time that passed, the harder it was going to be for the covenants to be met.

"Those covenants tightened in each period going forward," they explain. "The first year was a sort of 'give me', so that was OK. Then the next year it started to tighten. And by the third year it was like, 'My God!' The best thing that ever happened to him was Guy saying that he ought to go [as CEO]. I have to be careful here because I don't want you to take away that I think he was a bad manager and all that. He was just not in a circumstance that he had the tools to deal with."

They claim this was a unique debt situation and this is perhaps why, when it really unravelled, those outside of the company were shocked that anyone would tie themselves to the mast in this way. "Maybe nine months in, the covenants start to come in and now he [Hands] has to find money to fund it," they say. "It was the first time I had ever heard of a covenant that works like this. It's usually a ratio between EBITDA and debt. You need to get more EBITDA in order to make the covenants, but you can buy out the deficit. So effectively you can write a cheque and therefore you can just violate the thing. You just put enough money into the company and it is all counted as EBITDA – as opposed to capital. You can do that forever under these covenants, but it gets more and more expensive every time you do it because the covenants get harder and harder to meet."

They add that this only applied to recorded music, but not publishing within EMI. "Two things were underlying the way the structure of the deal was," they continue. "One was that Guy's projections of revenue and EBITDA were the basis upon which the covenants were set going out. That's one thing. The other thing is that they tighten because the lender – these are bank loans, after all – is trying to force the borrower to raise capital by issuing bonds and take it off the bank's books. Those two things made those covenants more and more difficult to meet; and therefore more capital had to be put into the business. Where did that money come from? It had to come from his funds. So he had to go back to get permission from his limited partners to be able to put more money in. They were not very happy about that! So he was under pressure there. Then he decided he was going to have to hire a full-time CEO. And that is where Elio came in."

The early signs and progress made by Terra Firma were, however, reasonably encouraging. Hands sent an email to staff saying that EBITDA in fiscal quarter 1 (April to June 2008) was £59.2 million compared to a loss of £45.1 million in the same quarter in 2007. Total revenues in the period were up 61 per cent to £228 million. He warned this was still "early days" and the market remained "extremely volatile". He did not, however, say if the £59.2 million in earnings would top the £180 million target that had been set by Citigroup as part of its loan extension.[6]

After that, it was a classic mixed bag of figures – occasionally surging forward and equally occasionally snapping back.

In October 2008, Maltby issued an annual review of its performance to the end of March 2008, reporting a loss of £757 million after tax compared to £287 million the previous year. Revenues were down 19 per cent to £1.45 billion. Restructuring costs for the year ran to £123 million, in large part due to 1,500 staff redundancies, with further restructuring costs expected to roll into the next financial year.

"Readers of this report may well be struck by the forthright presentation of problems and the absence of rosy assurances about the future," said Lord Birt in the report's introduction. "The main factor for the very large loss was continued poor operational performance, but more particularly accounting factors, in particular the revaluation of the balance sheet and the requirement to mark assets and liabilities to fair values. EMI now has a strong balance sheet and team with which to start a new era."[7]

Maltby added that its EBITDA of £164 million "had been wiped out by a variety of changes including £192 million arising from revaluation of its balance sheet; £123 million restructuring costs; £109 million depreciation and £520 million of net financing costs". It was calculated that this meant EMI had effectively lost £166,000 for every one of its employees. By the end of 2008, Terra Firma had reportedly injected £75 million into EMI to avoid defaulting on the Citigroup loan.

EMI half-year results (to September 2008 versus to September 2007)

	Half year to September 2007 (£ millions)	Half year to September 2008 (£ millions)
Net revenues	667	737
Losses	324	155
Frontline recorded music EBITDA	-12	+59

"It was also reported that out of a £250 million fund raised to cover the costs of restructuring EMI, £68 million had been injected into the company including a £16 million 'equity cure' to ensure it was able to meet its banking covenants," wrote Brian Southall in his book.

Covering all of 2008 and into March 2009, EMI's financial performance revealed an operating loss of £258 million on reduced revenues of £1.4 billion. In the middle of 2009, Maltby was given a £28 million cash injection to keep it inside the terms of its debt agreement with Citigroup and to stop it breaching its covenants. This £28 million equity cure came from a £250 million fund that Terra Firma had raised after buying EMI in 2007.

By July 2009, Terra Firma was reported to be in early talks with Citigroup to restructure the debt at EMI, with Hands suggesting that Terra Firma invest upwards of £300 million in EMI – but only on the condition the bank writes off around £500 million of the debt at EMI Music.

"Mr Hands has written to investors in Terra Firma's third fund, Firma Capital Partners III, a €5.4 billion buy-out fund he raised in 2007, for permission to invest the money in EMI but he requires 75 per cent approval," wrote the *Financial Times*. "Terra Firma has carried out a series of equity injections into EMI, including £28 million in March. This move signalled that EMI results for the six months to March 31 failed to live up to the conditions of the £2.6 billion in loans that Citigroup had extended to finance the £4 billion EMI takeover in 2007. Terra Firma was forced in May to inject more cash into EMI for the second time in six months, after it missed targets imposed in banking covenants. If this latest restructuring is successful it would mean that Mr Hands has invested almost £500 million [in total] in additional capital into EMI."[8]

By putting a fresh £300 million into EMI, the hope was Citigroup would write off £500 million of the debt, with the argument being that it would make EMI better financed and more solid so, therefore, Citigroup would have a better chance of syndicating the debt that Terra Firma had to pay back by 2015. In December, Hands came back with a significantly improved offer.

"City pension funds, insurance companies and foreign banks have been approached amid fears within Terra Firma that EMI could default on interest repayments to Citigroup, which bankrolled the £4 billion buyout of the music group on the eve of the credit crunch in 2007," reported *The Guardian*. "Hands's latest attempt to recapitalise EMI would involve Terra Firma and new investors injecting £1 billion of equity. But the plans could be contingent on him being able to persuade Citigroup to write off £1 billion of debt."[9]

Citigroup refused and this led to rumours that both Citigroup and EMI would split ownership of EMI.[10] Desperate times, it appeared, were calling for desperate measures.

By Christmas 2009, however, the two sides were about to enter into a protracted and messy legal battle over not just the terms of the loan to buy EMI but also the price that Terra Firma believed it had been hoodwinked into paying for the music company.

On the second weekend of December 2009, Terra Firma filed a £1.5 billion lawsuit in New York accusing Citigroup of misleading it over rival bids for EMI in 2007, thereby artificially inflating the sale price of the company. The minutiae of the lawsuit will be dealt with in the following chapter, but in the same legal action, Terra Firma claimed that Citigroup rebuffed proposals to restructure EMI "to soften the markets" and therefore push it into bankruptcy, planning – as the chief creditor – to seize control of the music company and sell it on for a profit.[11] This would play out for most of the next decade, with Terra Firma now, in its mind, stuck with a company it did not want based on loan terms it felt it was railroaded into accepting.

While Hands was absolutely convinced he had been tricked into overpaying for EMI, those within the company were split. "The definition of 'paid too much' is what you paid combined with what you did with it," is the blunt assessment of a senior source at EMI who had visibility on the deal. "Had it been successful, no one would have said they paid too much. They paid a lot – and the job of the EMI board was to get them to pay a lot. But not by conning them – because it was a public company. Everything that they saw was publicly published information. But the board's job was to ensure for its shareholders that it got a decent price."

They feel that a different owner, one who had taken a markedly different strategy when they got the keys, could have delivered a highly successful turnaround of EMI. "My view is that they paid a lot – I don't think it was much too much – but under different ownership it might have been successful," they say. "I think they fucked it up royally in the way that they managed it and the way that Guy changed the management several times … If you pay a lot and you fuck it up, then chances are someone will say that you paid too much."

Another well-placed source who saw every twist and turn of the deal between 2007 and 2011 believes many of their colleagues are quick to see it as the story of a hubristic private equity firm getting its comeuppance, but feels this is too selective with the truth.

"Lots of people are very down on Terra Firma and, look, there were plenty of idiots there, but I am not one of those people who really hates Guy or hates Terra Firma," they say. "The fundamental thing that people don't really understand is that they got fucked by the market. I don't think their ideas for EMI were particularly bad. I am sure, at the price they paid, Eric [Nicoli] absolutely ripped their arm off. They paid a lot of money at the top of the market."

They also feel the schadenfreude some at the company were to revel in with regard to Terra Firma's fate also absolves the prior management of any responsibility for the state EMI was in when Terra Firma took it over. "Terra Firma had inherited a broken business," they argue. "They absolutely had. There is absolutely no doubt about it … with way too many people and it just needed someone to take it by the hand and show them what to do with it."

Another EMI executive believes very simply that the timing was disastrous for Terra Firma. In their eyes, it could have worked, but just not at that time or at that price. "It was unfortunate timing," they say. "He [Guy Hands] overpaid and he didn't really know what he was buying. He didn't have any of the synergies that Warner had and yet he matched the Warner price – so from the beginning that made no sense. If he had held on until now, he would be looking like a star!"

Yet another feels that while Terra Firma was dealt a terrible hand by both Citigroup and the wider economy, they did not double down to try and flip a negative into a positive. Instead, they believe, Terra Firma went out of its way to make a bad situation considerably worse.

"Guy decided he was going to war with Citigroup but Citigroup was never going to sit around a table and negotiate a deal," they say. "I'm sure Guy would say they were never going to do a deal with him, but I don't think he ever gave them much of a chance. Plus, it was a horrendous first year. In the first year, the plan had been to securitise the music publishing business, to syndicate the debt and basically get the capital structure in place. In the middle of the financial crisis, the securitisation market was closed, Citigroup was left with all the debt along with a deep sense of fear and embarrassment. The stock markets fell a lot in that year which made the high price that he paid for EMI look very high indeed. Everything started to go wrong from the start!"

Having managed, for the most part, to just about keep on top of the debt repayments for the first two and a half years, by the start of 2010, the strain was starting to tell. In February that year, there were growing rumours that Terra Firma was at serious risk of losing control of EMI.

Maltby Capital, the EMI acquisition vehicle, had reported pre-tax losses of £1.75 billion at EMI for the year ending 31 March 2009. These included costs for impairment of intangible assets and goodwill (£1.04 billion), restructuring costs (£136 million), net finance charges (£722 million) and cash interest costs (£223 million). EMI had seen profits rise to £163 million in its recorded arm (a threefold increase on the previous year) and this was expected to rise to £200 million for the year ending 31 March 2010. The problem, however, was the "crippling interest payments" and "the need to meet the financial covenant tests from Citigroup".[12]

Music Week was ramping up the negative with a front-page headline posing the question: 'Time running out for Terra Firma?' It said that, despite the rising profits at EMI, the private equity company was now on "shaky ground" with regard to its most high-profile investment.[13]

In May 2010, the company figures for the financial year 2008/09 saw EMI's recorded arm report a jump in operating profit to £163 million.

Publishing, meanwhile, made a profit of £133 million. EMI Group overall reported a loss of £1.75 billion "including more than £1 billion in write-offs, restructuring costs and finance charges". This was despite revenues growing from £1.46 billion to £1.59 billion.[14] This sparked the race, as mentioned in the previous chapter, to raise the £120 million to hit the investment target due by the middle of June. In the end, by early May, Guy Hands had persuaded investors to put in £105 million to ward off Citigroup from taking control of EMI.[15] He had bought himself time. For now.

It was becoming clear that what had started as a mild quiver on the high wire for Hands was turning into an almighty wobble, his legs furiously flailing around to hold his footing. In June 2010, *Music Week* reported that Terra Firma was seriously up against it and was now considering selling a minority stake in EMI Music Publishing, "mulling several approaches" for a 49 per cent share in the publisher.[16]

While the financial and trade press was having a field day declaring the acquisition doomed and recommending that Terra Firma admit defeat – and thereby save at least some face and certainly more money – Guy Hands did not see it like that. He believed that, if they could just keep going through the turbulence, they would finally ascend to azure blue skies. "We put in money to save the business all the way through," he says of the constant battle to keep hold of the company, refusing to see the race to raise fresh capital as a case of throwing good money after bad. "We were making steps forward," he argues. "[As regards] the coverage ratios on the debt in terms of paying the interest, we were there. We could pay the interest. We didn't have any problem paying the interest. The issue we had was the valuation of the company."

He proposes that a number of factors need to be taken into consideration here. "If the loan has been securitised, the valuation of the company is irrelevant. As long as you pay the interest, people leave you alone. If we had got the deal that we had wanted when we were negotiating, we would have separated the business; or if we had said we could pay the interest then leave us alone. That's what's called covenant light. Because of the fact that the markets collapsed and everything was renegotiated and we couldn't do the securitisation, we ended up with a loan that was not a covenant-light loan; it had covenants and it had rules. One of the rules was an evaluation of how much the business was worth relative to the debt. That is something that varies over time depending on where the market is. It doesn't really reflect on whether or not the business can pay its interest."

A senior executive at EMI says Terra Firma ultimately had its hands tied here, especially given that the loan it was repaying was a single one and not split across the two parts of the business. "They were frustrated that they were being stymied every which way they went and they couldn't make progress on some of the big plans," they say. "One big plan they had was to securitise the music publishing business because the debt that they had used to buy EMI carried a very high interest rate. If they could securitise EMI Music Publishing and lend with effectively an asset-backed debt instrument they would be able to reduce their borrowing costs significantly. It would have been a viable option. EMI had looked at doing that long before Terra Firma came in. When EMI had high borrowing costs, it looked at doing securitisation as the interest rates that you pay on a securitisation are significantly less because it's backed by an asset that generates a solid income. They [Terra Firma] were going to do the same. The problem was that within about six weeks there was the global financial crash."

No matter which way Terra Firma was to spin it, however, the choir of analysts saying Terra Firma was doomed was growing bigger and louder by the day. One anonymous New York analyst pulled no punches when asked for their opinion on EMI's numbers: "All Terra Firma have done throughout this deal is demonstrate fully that they don't know what they are doing," they were quoted as saying in *Music Week*. "Sooner or later EMI is going to be pushed into bankruptcy at which point Warner will probably buy it."[17]

Elio Leoni Sceti took to the pages of *Music Week* the following week to argue the line that he was increasing both revenues and market share at EMI's recorded music arm. "Debt is a different story," he said, attempting to deflect the issue – or at least take some of the heat off himself. "It is a tale of two stories: the opportunities and the capital structure. That is not what I am concentrating on."[18]

Just over a week later, *Management Today* ran a lengthy feature on Leoni Sceti and his plans to defy the odds and turn around EMI. There was mention of his recent attendance at the Grammys, references to his "gleaming, perfect set of teeth" and lack of "anxious grey" in his hair. He revealed what he planned to say to staff in an upcoming address to those both in Wrights Lane and, via video link, around the world.

"I will tell them this business can beat the competition, it can grow market share, and that we will attract and retain the best talent," he said. The tone of the interview was relentlessly upbeat, despite a detailed breakdown in the feature about Terra Firma's mounting debt issue.

He talked about the power of brand marketing, the importance of listening to the customer and how EMI had diversified its revenue streams way beyond recorded music, categorically denying there was a black cloud hanging over the business. "I disagree," he said. "If you judge this business from the sustainability of the model, there is no black cloud hanging over it, because we're growing in a declining market, we're gaining share and we've worked out a way to bring creative momentum back. We've got four artists in the current US album Top Ten. There is no black cloud over this business."

He accepted there was still work to be done: "Every company has to look for efficiencies. Is there any fat left in EMI? No. Are there any efficiencies to be found? Yes" – and that it was only to be expected that investors would carefully scrutinise the business before putting money into it. "I would look at where the music industry is and look at the risk. I would assess how we propose to deal with that risk. In the end, it depends on how risk-prone [investors] are."

His concluding message was insistently upbeat. "I'm confident the business plan we present will be a good plan. I can only do my job. I'm staying focused on delivering a vision for this business – I'm very dedicated to EMI."[19]

He did not have to try and accentuate the positives to detract from the negatives for much longer – or try and hammer home just how dedicated he was to EMI. Mere days after the *Management Today* piece ran, Leoni Sceti was sacked.

* * *

There are plenty of EMI staff members and executives who claim to have been convinced at the time that debt was going to sink Terra Firma and risked pulling EMI under with it. Hindsight is, of course, 20/20 vision.

One senior executive claims they knew it was doomed from the moment they saw Terra Firma's recovery plan and overlaid that on its debt targets. "[Guy Hands] thought to pay the debts and pay dividends to his equity shareholders, he was going to multiply the EBITDA by five and six times," they say. "So what was your revenue in 2007 would be your profit in 2013. Here is an example. Your revenue is £150 and your profit is £25 and you say that your profit will be £150 in six years. You will have to add five layers of similar profit to get it to six times higher. We produced £25 of profit of EBITDA a year and we'd have to add on another £25 once, twice, three, four, five times. Every year we have to add £25 of EBITDA to reach that level."

This was, to their mind, utterly unachievable and he feels Terra Firma had all too easily presumed success when it should have been always questioning it. "To get to that level, you are the biggest company in the world by miles as you make more profit than the rest of the industry put together," they claim. "No one looked at these numbers! By the time anyone did look at those numbers, it was too late. The company was already bought. That was the issue for Guy. He could not have the appropriate attitude because his mindset had been distorted by the size of the money he had raised, the promises that he made and the size of the debt. It was a disaster from day one."

Under such a model, the debt gets completely out of control and it becomes impossible to pay back. The same source claims it was immediately obvious to them but it took Guy three years to find this out. "Thank you, go home, goodbye," is how they claim they predicted it would unfold. "This complete disaster was foreseen in September 2007 by us when we looked at it. 'My goodness. He can't be serious. What a debt!' You cannot just double the EBITDA in a year. Let's be wild and say that it's happening. You have to double it every year. How do you do that? The answer was that they were going to sign fewer acts, they were going to spend less and they were going to employ fewer people – and they would find a digital Holy Grail to save them. Then Guy embarked on hiring an army of digital guys on the west coast of America who were spending so much money on staff and nobody knew what they were doing."

Some EMI staff do not claim to be quite so prescient, however, and say they only realised how precarious it all was when everything started to fall apart.

"The problem they had was, pretty much from the start, they were under water on their loan," says one executive based in the US for the whole period of Terra Firma's ownership of EMI. "You could sell off recorded music for, say, £1 billion and you were left with publishing, which at the time would probably have cost £1.5 billion to buy. They were underwater from the start and you don't necessarily make the most rational decisions when you are in that situation. It's like being behind in your mortgage and you might be better cutting your losses but you think next month you can fix it."

Andria Vidler suggests that, taking the debt out of the equation for a moment, the turnaround that EMI so desperately needed on the recorded music side was most assuredly coming to fruition in the second half of 2010. "Guy's vision for what EMI could become was right, I believe," she says. "And I think we were proving it. As the UK gained momentum and success, we could lead artists globally. And the way that we worked globally without a big global internal team worked brilliantly. The way that we built campaigns with the American team was really successful."

The renaissance of EMI was happening; but that was not enough.

The noise of the debt may have seemed deafening by the summer but it was to feel as loud as a spider's footsteps compared to the court case that was about to open in New York.

CHAPTER 15

The Courtroom Showdown

Guy Hands had barely walked into EMI as its new owner in September 2007 when he started to have suspicions about the deal he had just committed to. He knew, after the stressful but futile meeting in New York in July, that Citigroup was playing hardball on the terms of the loan and Terra Firma was stuck holding a company it realised it did not want while being lashed to a debt package it desired even less. But there was something else niggling at him. He had no way of proving it – not yet – but he was starting to fear his long-standing friend, David Wormsley at Citigroup, had misled him about rival plays for EMI in the frantic weeks in April and May where Terra Firma appeared as a last-minute bidder and emerged the winner of the auction, paying 265p a share, an increase of 3p a share over what was apparently being offered by its closest rival.

Guy Hands was now hearing rumours that there had been no second bidder. Or, to be more precise, there was, but they had dropped out a few days before the auction closed – those crucial days when Wormsley was advising him to "not play games" with his bid, to go in at 265p and walk away triumphant as the new owner of EMI.

This was going to eat away at him for months but by the summer of 2008 he believed he had the evidence he needed to prove he had been wilfully misled to over-bid for EMI against a non-existent rival. This was compounded by the fact that Citigroup was a beneficiary of the EMI transaction on both the sell side, as a long-running advisor to EMI's board, and the buy side, as the bank providing the bulk of the loan Terra Firma need to complete the deal. (Terra Firma was to claim later that Citigroup had earned £6 million in advisory fees from EMI as part of the sales process and £80 million in fees from underwriting the loan to the private equity firm.[1])

A wash of conspiracy theories and a growing sense of betrayal were going through his head. Guy Hands had, he was sure of it, been stitched up – and stitched up by someone he believed was his friend. "I didn't know we had been misled until around April or May 2008," claims Hands. "I had suspicions that we could have been in October 2007 and I handed it over to the lawyers."

As his legal team began to dig into the issue, Hands was hoping that what he feared was, somehow, just not true. But if it was true, he was going to have to do something about it – namely take the issue to court, an end game he says he was desperate to avoid.

"From a business point of view, I did not want to take legal action against Citigroup in a million years," he says. "I just felt that would be professional suicide and was the last thing that I wanted to do ... Secondly, there were two of my best friends who were going to be involved in it – although at the time I only thought one of them would be ... One was David Wormsley and the other was Michael Klein. Although Michael Klein wasn't involved in the first suit, he was involved in the second suit [in London in 2016]. The last thing I wanted to do was to get involved in this."

He claims this is not quite the Shakespearean tragedy that some have framed it as being – that of dark betrayal among friends and a personal grudge that drives them to ruin. It was not, he argues, Guy Hands versus David Wormsley, with Terra Firma and Citigroup mere backdrops to a very personal rancour. Hands says he had an obligation to his general partners and if they and the legal team believed that legal action was the only course of action, then he would have to go along with them. "I knew I was going to be the key witness [but] it's not really my choice," he says. "I represented a lot of investors. I had over 200 investors here who had put up close to £2 billion so if the lawyers say that you've got a case, you don't really have much of a choice, to be blunt."

It took until December 2009 for the court documents, accusing Citigroup of fraud and of driving up EMI's sale price by misrepresentation,[2] to be filed in New York. It coincided with the leaking of a research note from Citigroup analyst Jason B. Bazinet in New York, originally circulated in October that year, claiming that if EMI did not merge with Warner Music then it could go bust.

"Without some financial flexibility on the part of the banks, Terra Firma may be forced to sell its recorded and publishing business to other players in the industry," Bazinet said. Should both music companies fail to pull off the merger – a merger that had been attempted or mooted multiple times in the preceding decade – then "the possibility of an EMI insolvency could increase".[3]

The leaked note was read by some as a strategy by Citigroup to undermine and destabilise the company, with some pointing to the fact that in the previous month Citigroup had rebuffed Terra Firma's offer to invest £1 billion in EMI in exchange for writing off $1 billion of the loan the private equity firm took out to buy the music company.

To outsiders, it might have seemed like a tit-for-tat response, but there had been a long lead-up to this very public moment of confrontation.

Those within EMI felt the legal action was in part because Terra Firma was convinced it had been misled, but they also believed that Terra Firma was waking up to the fact that EMI, in terms of the speed and scale of the turnaround needed, was starting to look like a very bad investment.

"Within the first six or nine months, the feeling was that they have been sold a pup," is how a senior EMI executive sees it. "I think his [Guy Hands's] wish came true that EMI was in worse shape than he had been led to believe. The numbers just weren't there. It was a lot worse than they thought it was and very rapidly they went into crisis management. They started off thinking that this was a jewel and that they could polish it hard and sell it off quickly for more money [but it didn't turn out that way]."

Chris Duffy, a lawyer at Boies, Schiller & Flexner in New York, was one of the legal team appointed by Terra Firma to gather evidence and build a case against Citigroup. "The original plan wasn't to bring a case or to not bring a case," he says of how the process began. "The original assignment was to take a look at the fact pattern and evaluate whether it supported a possible legal action in the US."

The next stage for him was to draft the complaint (the US equivalent of a writ in UK law). "This is your initiating paperwork that says you have this set of claims against this set of defendants," he says of how it works. "Then the defendants have to respond in the designated period of time. That is a very busy process, the lead-up to the case: the fact gathering for the complaint and then deciding what causes of actions to bring like fraud, like negligence, like breach of contract, whatever the case might be."

For this case, the primary approach was going to be a claim of fraud but there was a concurrent claim of negligence. The case was going to argue that Hands made a major business decision based on what they now believed to be untrue statements presented to him by Citigroup and, in particular, David Wormsley.

"The allegations that we made about these three conversations [at the heart of the case] were that David Wormsley told Guy Hands that there was another bidder still in play, that that bidder was Cerberus, the private equity firm, and that Cerberus was bidding at a certain price – at 262 a share and Terra Firma went in at 265," explains Duffy. "The allegation was that David Wormsley told Guy Hands several times that Cerberus were in, they were in at 262 and they'd either made the bid or were making it by the designated company deadline of 9 a.m. on Monday May 21st 2007 [the deadline for bids set by the EMI board] and that if Terra Firma was to win the auction, he shouldn't play games on price and should bid 265 to ensure they would get the company. Guy said that Wormsley told him he needed to bid at 265 in order to win the auction."

Key to the whole case, and something that became central to Terra Firma's claims when phone records were handed over as part of the deposition process, was what was said or not said during a number of phone calls between David Wormsley of Citigroup and Eric Nicoli on Sunday 20 May 2007, the day before final bids for the company had to be submitted.

Duffy says phone records show they spoke twice that day and there were other attempts to call that had not gone through – perhaps due to poor mobile connection or unavailability of the person being called – which suggested to Terra Firma's legal team that both conversations were deemed to be of the utmost urgency.

"The other part of it is that Wormsley had a long-standing relationship with Guy Hands. We argued that Wormsley knew that Guy would trust what Wormsley told him precisely because of that long-standing business relationship," says Duffy. "Part of our argument in presenting the case was that Wormsley likely viewed it as a positive for the acquisition to be made by Terra Firma instead of by anybody else; because not only would Citigroup make significant lending fees on the deal as the main lender to Terra Firma, it would also present a very significant opportunity for future business on down the line."

This potentially included a deal with Warner that would have run into billions and would have been, if successful, the first merger of two major music companies since Sony and BMG in 2004. "Within days of the successful bid by Terra Firma and before the acquisition actually closed, there was already talk within Citigroup about the possible next step as being either EMI buying Warner or being sold to Warner," claims Duffy. "That is the oxygen that investment banks run on – it's deals. Part of the presentation of our case was that the purchase by a long-standing client of Citigroup, and Wormsley in particular, would present more revenue opportunities down the line. That's separate and apart from the lending phase. There is also the possibility of additional investment banking fees by virtue of a possible deal with Warner."

The whole chain of events that would determine the fate of EMI under Terra Firma started with a process server showing up to Citigroup's New York offices at 399 Park Avenue – a 41-storey office building a few blocks from the south-east corner of Central Park that had been Citigroup's global HQ since 1961 – and delivering the complaint on behalf of Terra Firma. According to Duffy, Citigroup had a designated desk for the receiving of lawsuits. "They get sued a lot," he says. "This is part and parcel of high finance."

This was effectively a triptych lawsuit – against the parent company (Citigroup Inc.), the US banking institution (Citigroup Markets LLC) and the US investment banking part of the company. While Citigroup might have had a designated desk for this kind of thing, what was different about this case was that the complaint arrived at Citigroup without warning or prior notification.

"Often when you have a big corporate lawsuit like this, there are overt threats that are made in advance of the lawsuit. But it's not unheard of by any stretch of the imagination to have a lawsuit filed and served without there really being a clear advance warning. In this case, once the lawsuit was ready to file, Terra Firma chose to file it in a court of law rather than use it as a negotiation chip with Citigroup."

Citigroup was now on the back foot. Perhaps Terra Firma felt this gave it a psychological advantage – initiating legal action without warning against the bank that had lent it £2.6 billion and sending a clear message that it was not to be messed with. There was no going back from this.

Boies, Schiller & Flexner initially filed the litigation in New York State court, but Citigroup immediately, and successfully, moved to have it go through the federal court system. At this point the case was assigned a federal judge – Judge Jed S. Rakoff. A hugely experienced judge, Rakoff had served as a federal district judge for the Southern District of New York since 1996 and been an adjunct professor at Columbia Law School since 1988.[4] He was prone to being "sarcastic and kind of brutal" according to one witness who had seen him in court before. "That's OK in a judge trial, but when a jury is there it can be kind of harmful to make flippant comments," they say.

Rakoff was also no procrastinator. While some judges in the federal court system allowed the litigants to move at their own pace, Rakoff had a reputation for whipping his cases along at speed. "He gets the parties into his courtroom at the very beginning of the case and he sets a trial date – and that is a real date," explains Duffy. "A lot of judges will set a trial date early on, but it's tentative. It's not set in stone … We went in for that first appearance in January and we set a schedule for discovery – meaning exchanging documents and taking depositions – and the judge set the trial date for October, which was less than nine months away. There was a lot of work to do in a short period."

Citigroup had attempted to have Rakoff dismiss the lawsuit as its heads believed it should be heard in London, not New York. "They filed under the doctrine of what is known as *forum non conveniens*," says Duffy. "It is a motion that is very common in US courts when you have a lawsuit that has a connection to another country."

Citigroup's argument was that Terra Firma was based in London – although by this stage Guy Hands himself had relocated to Guernsey, one of the Channel Island tax havens – and most of the key meetings and dealings were with Citigroup's team in London. While it could have been a convincing argument, Terra Firma's team put forward, to Rakoff's ears anyway, a more convincing argument as to why it should be heard in New York.

With the clock ticking down, both sides had to work on their strategies and try to gather all the evidence they needed, the aim being to unearth as much detail as they could – including any smoking guns that may have been previously thought buried – in order to be covered for every eventuality.

Duffy feels Citigroup was intentionally dragging its heels with regard to document requests at the start of the process, suspecting they wanted to delay things so much that the case would be transferred to London. But when Rakoff ruled it would be heard in New York, they started to move at a speed more typical of such situations.

Documents running into millions of pages were eventually exchanged by the two sides, part of the protracted to-ing and fro-ing that happens in the US. "Typically, you make [document] requests that are more specific – and there will be dozens of them," is how Duffy explains the procedure. "[E]ach side makes a request and then the lawyers get on the phone with each other and say, 'Well, you've asked for all these things, but what do you really want?' Or, 'You've got to be kidding me? You can't mean that you need all this? It's too much. Let's get real.' Conversations happen from there and in the end something gets produced. Sometimes one party will say the other party didn't produce enough. There will be debates and discussions back and forward. It's a process."

The requests from Terra Firma's legal team included emails and phone records from Citigroup, but they could also access information held internally at EMI from before they bought the company. Additionally, they were able to request information from Cerberus – the other bidder in the final days of the auction. Even though Cerberus was not part of the litigation, it was deemed a connected party of interest and, as such, could be subpoenaed to hand over certain information.

"We got documents and internal emails from Cerberus and they confirmed that Cerberus had in fact dropped out of the bidding process," reveals Duffy. "That was significant. Before we got those documents, we had second-hand information that Cerberus had dropped out. That was a real validating moment when those documents were turned over. They confirmed that part of the story."

There was, naturally, an enormous amount of information that had to be sifted through and key to Terra Firma's case was the highly derogatory way that people within Citigroup had come to refer to EMI – a company they had been involved in trying to sell or merge for years before Terra Firma wrote its cheque.

A handwritten note from a Citigroup credit officer at the start of 2007 called EMI a "terminally ill cancer patient on chemotherapy", suggesting that Citigroup knew whoever bought the company was going to have a fight on their hands to keep it alive. The day after Terra Firma put in its bid for EMI, Jan Skarbek, a banker at Citigroup, sent his colleague Matthew Smith an email. "Well done!" he wrote. "I am amazed you got them to pay up for that old pup." Smith responded, "Thanks. Can't imagine why Guy bought it – he must have a Machiavellian plan."[5]

Terra Firma's case was building that EMI was seen internally by Citigroup at the time of the deal as, at best, damaged goods and, at worst, an utterly toxic investment. Even after Terra Firma bought EMI, the derogatory sobriquets for the music company were still pinging around Citigroup's internal email system. Two months after the deal was done, Smith received an email from Mark Simonian, a banker colleague, that simply said, "At long last you sold the pig ... "[6]

A pup. A terminally ill cancer patient. A pig. These were not, Terra Firma was arguing, ways to view a company that sold for £4.2 billion. This hardened the private equity firm's resolve that grand duplicity was at work in getting it to buy the company. Asked how he felt when, as part of the discovery process, it was revealed Citigroup was using such pejorative phraseology with regard to EMI, Hands very simply said, "I felt like complete shit."

In combing through Nicoli's emails to Wormsley, the team at Boies, Schiller & Flexner found the two men were discussing price issues related to the sale of EMI which the lawyers felt corroborated what Hands was arguing. There was no single 'Ah-ha!' moment in this process, rather it was about the steady accumulation of information to build up the picture and complete the argument.

"But there were many other documents along the lines of 'you've finally sold the pig' that did indicate that many people at Citigroup knew what a terrible position financially EMI was in," suggests Duffy. "There was another one about EMI being a cancer patient. There were others like that. And then we had the important email from Wormsley to Nicoli proving that Wormsley spoke with Guy the night before the bid was due, as we had alleged."

Before the trial, Hands turned to several friends and contacts for advice and help. Two of these worked as lawyers, one of them as a friendly support and the other to supplement the efforts of Boies, Schiller & Flexner. They both sat through the twelve days of the case. As such, they can offer an eyewitness account of what happened during the whole process.

The first was Terry Revere, a Hawaii-based property lawyer who had represented Hands in a property dispute there years earlier, their professional relationship turning into a close friendship. "Honestly, [it was] just being a friend for Guy – the chief morale officer rather than part of [the case]!" is how Revere describes his role. "We had the New York lawyers, the Los Angeles lawyers and the UK lawyers pitching in to get ready to fight [the case]. I said I could help where I could, so I came in on an ad hoc basis. But I was much more of an outside perspective than the people who were knee-deep in this thing for years."

The second was someone with litigation experience in the US that Hands had known for several years. Denelle Dixon-Thayer was senior legal director at Yahoo! from February 2007 before joining Terra Firma as its director of US legal strategy in February 2010[7] to help in the run-up to the court case in New York. "I was brought in to look at the strategy of what we should do and also to look at what had happened – how the EMI transaction actually took place, what was going on with respect to digital [in the industry as a whole] and to look holistically at what was happening and how we got to where we got," she says. "It was heavily focused on the potential litigation and then obviously the litigation once it actually took place."

Terra Firma had not been through a litigation procedure like this before in the US and so Dixon-Thayer was there to guide them through the process and work with Terra Firma's outside counsel. "A lot of what I was doing was trying to figure out how we were going to approach this from the standpoint of Guy's testimony or other individuals who were going to be called to testify," she says. "What was the best strategy for Terra Firma as an entity and Guy as an individual in terms of how to approach the litigation ... I was really a conduit for information and strategy for not just Guy but also Terra Firma generally ... There was a lot of work done to understand what had taken place."

As this was a jury trial, Dixon-Thayer was focused on coaching Hands and the other witnesses on how it worked, helping them refine and simplify their statements and responses. Jury trials can be won or lost on how clear the witnesses are in delivering their statements and during cross-examination. This was an incredibly complex case, but she had to get everyone on Terra Firma's side to ensure they were clear and, crucially, succinct in everything they said in the courtroom.

"Always in litigation, when you have a jury, you have to approach from the standpoint of making it simple for them," she proposes. "The hardest thing about this case that I found was that there was so much information and so much documentation – so much to bring to the table in terms of valuations, understanding the bidding process and what it takes to establish a fraud claim ... The most challenging thing about this litigation was trying to keep it simple. There were so many moving parts and so many players involved."

Key to all of this, from Terra Firma's side, was trying to prove that the Chinese walls[8] within Citigroup were compromisingly thin and David Wormsley was party to information that he should not have been party to, as far as Guy Hands's case was concerned.

"That was the most complicated part of the case – being able to show that," she claims. "In business generally, we know we have Chinese walls and inherent conflicts of interest that exist. But what we try to do, from a business standpoint, is we try to minimise that by operating with Chinese walls and making sure we protect the information and the access of each of the individuals by making sure that those walls exist and that they are strong. What we found here, and we believe there is sufficient documentation to support it, was that those walls were not strong and there was a flow of information that was likely improper; but most importantly, even if you forgot the impropriety of it, it was detrimental to Terra Firma in the bidding process and subsequent to that."

Terra Firma and its legal team might have been clear and fully convinced that this is what happened within the offices of Citigroup and, their logic ran, it had a deleterious effect on the company's position as the last remaining bidder for EMI in May 2007; yet all these things Terra Firma held as obvious and true were far from a given when evidence and arguments in a multi-day and multi-witness trial were laid out. "The challenging part of this is trying to get the jury to be able to piece together all these different pieces of the information flow and also the breakdown of these Chinese walls – that frankly most people understand exist in business – but which broke down here substantially," says Dixon-Thayer. "[There was also] the fact the debt side totally understood really where EMI was from the standpoint of the financial conditions, which were pretty horrific ... In the jury trial, my frame of mind at the time was very much that in the trial itself you need to figure out how to piece all of that together and to make it very simple – to put one brick at a time in the wall and let the jury build that wall with the bricks. That was the goal."

She says she spent a large chunk of her time working closely with Guy Hands, ensuring he understood the process and how it would play out when he was in the courtroom and on the stand. As a dyslexic, Hands found providing and refining his witness statement a painfully protracted process but understood this needed to be as clear and all-encompassing as possible as it would be doing a lot of the heavy lifting for him. But he also knew that, under cross-examination, all bets would be off.

"One of the most important things with a witness, and one of the things that I tried to do with Guy in New York during that time, was to calm him down," proposes Dixon-Thayer. "What happens with any plaintiff or any party in litigation is that oftentimes it becomes so emotional for them and they become so focused on the details that they lose sight of the larger picture. My job at the time was to try to bring it back to the larger picture."

There were suggestions that behind-the-scenes talks had been happening between Citigroup and Terra Firma to reach a last-minute settlement before the case opened. *Music Week* was implying at the time that one option was "Citigroup agreeing to write off a sizeable chunk of debt in return for a stake in Terra [Firma]".[9] This may simply have been pot-stirring or just wild speculation, the type the music industry press had long delighted in. Whatever the reality of the matter was, it did nothing to delay the inevitable. Both sides would have their day(s) in court.

A jury trial, by its very nature, is performative – for the lawyers as well as the witnesses. As such, getting the jury onside, or at least ensuring they have a positive emotional reaction to you, is something that can help swing cases. A related part of that performance is being able to communicate succinctly. Arrogance, uncertainty or verbosity from a witness are things that can quickly derail months of careful planning and scripting by their legal team.

"There is absolutely a performance element here," says Dixon-Thayer. "What the jury wants is to understand the story. They don't want to be entertained necessarily, but they don't want to be bombarded with information and details that aren't relevant to them. They want a clean way for them to be able to look at this and to join the dots together ... If you bore the jury and you make them feel that you don't believe that their time is valuable, you have lost already."

* * *

The case opened on 18 October 2010, just over three years after Terra Firma were given the keys to EMI. The company was seeking compensation for accumulated losses of £1.75 billion at EMI plus a punitive sum of £5.25 billion – bringing the damages sought to £7 billion, a little under twice what EMI was sold for. "The hearing … is being dubbed the trial of the century in City circles, as the reputation of two of the Square Mile's best-known moneymen hangs on the outcome,"[10] said *The Guardian* the week before the trial began.

Witnesses for Citigroup were revealed to be David Wormsley of Citigroup, in the court; Eric Nicoli, former chief executive of EMI, by video; Simon Borrows and Peter Bell of Greenhill & Co., who acted as advisors to EMI, both by video; and Guy Hayward-Cole of Citigroup, by video.

On the other side, witnesses for Terra Firma were to be Guy Hands in the court as a fact witness; Kirsten Randell, Tim Pryce, Riaz Punja and John Loveridge, all of Terra Firma, and all in the court as fact witnesses.

Before the case, Citigroup maintained that David Wormsley was unaware that Cerberus had pulled out of the sales talk before the deadline of 21 May 2007. "The evidence in this case is overwhelming that Citigroup has done nothing wrong and we firmly believe that Citigroup will prevail in this case,"[11] ran its statement.

The case opens

Day one of the case opened with David Boise, on behalf of Guy Hands, accusing David Wormsley and Citigroup of "playing both sides of the street at the same time" by acting as advisors to both EMI (on the sell side of the transaction) and Terra Firma (on the buy side). He also accused Wormsley of badly betraying his erstwhile friend, Guy Hands. Theodore Wells, acting for Citigroup, drove the line that Wormsley was unaware that Cerberus had dropped out at the last minute and, as such, was "an honest person and he never lied to Guy Hands".[12]

In the to-ing and fro-ing of the next eleven days, a lot of ground was covered and a lot of accusations were made, which were all strenuously refuted by each opposing side. In his 2012 book *The Rise & Fall of EMI Records*, Brian Southall offers a day-by-day synopsis of what played out in the courtroom. Choice quotes and developments include:

- Day one: Theodore Wells telling the jury in his summing-up of the opening day, "Mr Hands thought he had the golden touch, and he did for quite a while – until he bought EMI. And he can't get a do-over by saying he was cheated or tricked."
- Day two: Hands, on claims that Wormsley knew Cerberus had dropped out but misled Terra Firma into believing they were still in the running, saying, "If David hadn't made those statements we

wouldn't have been bidding on the Monday morning at all. It wouldn't have happened."

- Day three: responding to goading from Wells that this whole case was "because you wanted to blame someone else for your mistake in purchasing EMI", Hands simply responded, "That is not correct."
- Day five: Wells proffered an email from Hands's PR Andrew Dowler that mentioned claims in a *Financial Times* piece on the day the EMI bids closed that Cerberus was out of the bidding. "I don't even know if I read it," claimed Hands. "The *FT* gets things wrong on a completely consistent basis."
- Day seven: Wormsley claimed any bonuses he may have earned in 2007 were not dependent on any fees Citigroup would have made from lending Terra Firma the money to buy EMI. "I got no benefit in my bonus from the financing," he argued but did admit that Citigroup made money from the advice it was giving EMI on the sale as well as from the £2.6 billion loan it made available to Terra Firma.
- Day eight: Wormsley claimed he only played "a junior role in this transition" when accused of having hoodwinked Terra Firma into the purchase of EMI.
- Day ten: Judge Rakoff described the case as "a cat fight between two rich companies"; later that day he dismissed Donna Gianell from the jury after she was accused of contravening court rules by discussing the case in a lift in the court building with a fellow juror.
- Day eleven: Wells said that the notion Wormsley intentionally withheld the information from Hands that Cerberus had dropped out was nonsense and there was no written evidence to back it up. "This is corporate America," he said, even though Wormsley was based in the UK. "Someone would have written it down."[13]

Through the mill

"This lawsuit in many respects was quite a simple one," says Duffy on what the fundamentals of the case were and what their core arguments were going to be. "Even though there was a lot of money at stake, it was a much simpler lawsuit than many because it centred on those several phone calls, although Citigroup argued that it should prevail even if Wormsley did make the statements we alleged."

However, for Hands – despite his careful coaching from Dixon-Thayer about what to expect in a US jury trial – the process was to prove far from simple. It was to be a harsh awakening for him and the most gruelling three weeks of his life. "I think we were completely shocked by it," he says of his time in the courtroom. "We had no idea [of how a jury trial plays out in New York]; I had no idea; the witnesses from our side had no idea. They were all non-American witnesses. So, we flew everybody over there and we were all plonked into our hotels and then we were all called in front of a court. It was just a complete performance … It was mind-blowing. I think all of us were just gobsmacked. It wasn't anything we had expected or seen [before]. It made television seem very mild."

He describes Theodore Wells, the criminal lawyer from Paul, Weiss, Rifkind, Wharton & Garrison representing Citigroup, and commonly regarded as an exceptional white-collar defence attorney, as "an absolutely brilliant performer". Wells had defended Citigroup in a $2.2 billion lawsuit brought against it by the new management of Italian diary company Parmalat, stemming from the company's collapse in 2003, accusing the bank of aiding and abetting in massive fraud at the company.[14] The case ran for five months and the jury rejected the claims against Citigroup, instead awarding the bank $364.2 million in damages in its counterclaim, where it argued it was a victim of Parmalat's fraud.[15]

Wells had won – and won big – for Citigroup in the recent past and so was an obvious choice to take on this case. He was also known for his meticulous approach to jury trials, something Hands was to see in close-up after arriving at the court most days at 8 a.m. "He would come in every morning first thing before the trial would start and he would practise," says Hands of Wells. "He would have people sit in where the jury boxes were and he would ask them what he looked like, if he should go for this side or that side and how his expressions were. He was absolutely brilliant. We had a very, very brilliant lawyer as well – but he was a very technical lawyer [David Boise]. It became obvious, almost after the first day, that this was a case that was going to be won more on the performance than on the technical aspects."

He says, looking back on the case, that it was one driven and defined by the lawyers rather than by Guy Hands and David Wormsley as key witnesses. "It was the *Ted Wells & David Boise Show*," says Hands. "I think, at best, we were supporting characters."

He recalls he was on the stand for four days, usually from 9.30 a.m. until 4 p.m., an experience he found physically and emotionally draining. "It is very, very unpleasant," he says of his time in court. "It is very painful. I felt sorry for all the witnesses and the whole thing was just ghastly."

Talking about the jury's reaction to him as being on the stand for such a large chunk of the trial, he says, "I think they got very bored of me. I certainly got very bored of being on the stand. Wells would ask me questions but he wouldn't even really listen for my answer. He already knew what he was going to say. He called me 'Hans' all the way through and pronounced it without the 'd' as if I was German. He kept describing me as one of the wealthiest people in the world. I had a few court reporters who got quite interested in me! The whole thing was just very bizarre."

He describes his experience on the stand as "absolutely horrible", a situation that was compounded by his diabetes being worsened by the stress and pressure he was now under. "I found it really, really difficult," he sighs. "I had to keep going to the loo because, when your diabetes goes up, you end up having to urinate a lot. So, we had to ask the judge to give more frequent breaks. It was just horrible."

Wells may have been finicky in his planning and rehearsing, aiming for the perfect performance, but he, his team and Citigroup were not opposed to deploying mind games as well, according to those on Terra Firma's side watching from the gallery. "Citigroup actually – and I think this was more of a psychological thing [but] it was silly and I just thought it was amateurish – had a great wall between the Citigroup side and the Terra Firma side, stacking up at least fifty boxes of documents between their side and our side," recalls Revere. "It reminded me of the Wall in *Game of Thrones* or something."

Dixon-Thayer also believed that David Wormsley was using whatever he had at his disposal to try and win the jury over, not through what he said or how he stood when in the stand, but more covertly and subtly. "He had a book that he brought into the courtroom every day and he put it on the table so that the jury could see it," she says of what she took to be little more than a prop. "It was a book that was very popular at the time that lots of folks were reading. I can't remember the title of it but it was a very nice effect for the jury to have this personal connection with him … I'm not even sure that I ever saw him read it, but he had it in front of him."

In a jury trial, everything counts and so nothing should be left to chance. It seems that Citigroup understood this much better than Terra Firma did. Of course, using a book as a prop was not what this case was won and lost on, but a tiny thing such as that certainly contributed to the bricolage.

Citing both his dyslexia and his diabetes as major impediments for him in the trial, Hands knew this was always going to be tough, but he was dazed by just how tough it proved to be. Others saw him floundering early and knew this was going to seriously work against him and the whole Terra Firma case. "Guy is dyslexic and has dyspraxia," says Revere. "Guy picks things up and is normally better than the average person, but writing for him [is hard and] it's painful for him to read through stacks and stacks of material. It is incredibly time-inefficient compared to dictating things himself or having things read to him."

There was a feeling among some on his side that Hands's dyslexia was being used against him, with some reference to the lawyers playing on lengthy documents that he was not able to process as quickly as his opposites.

But for Revere, Citigroup's team ultimately outmanoeuvred Terra Firma's team in the eyes of the jury – the only eyes that really count in a trial of this sort. "It's sort of like a basketball game in terms of they are gonna score points," he says of the dynamics of a US jury trial. "The other side, when they start cross-examining, they're gonna score some points. That's the nature of the game. Citigroup's attorneys were the top guys in New York – and they got them. They could afford the top guys in London – and they got them. The other side did a very good job. It's like one of those situations of the fox has many tricks but the porcupine has one good one. Citigroup had a strong hand due to the passage of time."

He continues, "There is a ton of non-oral evidence that a big part of the case was boiling down to. Things like the phone calls and conversations and the nature of the relationship between Wormsley and Guy ... Their porcupine argument was that [certain claims] didn't happen."

For Dixon-Thayer, she believes it all proved too overwhelming for Hands. "The hardest part for Guy – as he was a representative of Terra Firma – was that there were so many facts to bring out," she says of the challenge he faced in trying to explain a complex story to the jury in easily comprehensible terms. "So, his time on the witness stand was pretty lengthy. That is hard for any jury; and it is hard for any witness in particular."

She believes Citigroup saw this as his Achilles heel and therefore kept him on the stand for as long as they could, slowly chipping away at him and his resolve. "A lot of details had to come from Guy and Guy was tired," she says. "It is a process that is incredibly tiring. Lots of preparation went into it. We had to look at it every day. I believe that Guy was on the stand for three [or four] different days. That's just a hard thing for anybody ... That's a lot of time for the jury to see somebody and to be able to start picking them apart. That is what actually happened I think with Guy. Did he do his part? He said all the things that he needed to say and I think he did quite well in terms of remembering different pieces and a lot of detail. It's just that he was on the stand for a long time."

She also says that if a jury trial is, in part, a beauty parade, then Wells had it down pat. "The lead trial counsel on the other side was quite good at playing to the jury and really having a relationship with the jury," is her summation. "This is one of the things you need to do as a trial lawyer; you need to have a relationship with the jury for your questioning of any witness. And he was quite good at that."

In court, Wormsley claimed he could not recollect the specifics of the phone calls for which Terra Firma had, in its discovery process, unearthed the records. "I don't remember any of the calls specifically," he told the court. "I remember speaking to him [Guy Hands] over the weekend on the subject of financing." When asked when he learned Cerberus had dropped out of the bidding, Wormsley said, "The first time I actively remember was when the complaint was filed. It is perfectly possible I was told before that."

He flat-out denied that he had told Hands before the bidding that he believed EMI's board would have accepted an offer of 240p a share. "I made no such comment," he said. "It was completely and utterly unacceptable for him [Hands] to suggest that 240 was acceptable or likely to be recommended by the board of EMI. I was furious. I demanded that he send written confirmation to EMI that I had never made that representation to him because I couldn't let that lie stand."

He did, however, accept that he may have told Hands "not to play games" with the price he was going to bid at, but claims this was in relation to a possible bid of 240p a share and not the 265p bid that won Terra Firma the auction. "I did not tell him to bid low, to the best of my recollection,"[16] Wormsley claimed.

There was a deposition for Eric Nicoli as a key witness as much of the Terra Firma case hinged on what he is alleged to have discussed with David Wormsley on the Sunday before the EMI bids were closed. He, and Wormsley, denied discussing Cerberus dropping out and that Wormsley kept the pressure on Hands to bid at 265p a share to ensure the sale went through. Nicoli's evidence was given in London and video recorded to be shown in the New York court.

Multiple senior sources have told this author that the EMI board would never have agreed to a bid of 240p a share in 2007. Even though the music company was teetering on the brink of collapse, anything this low would have been dismissed instantly and an alternative sale sought. That may have included quickly finding another private equity buyer or finding some way, even if it involved splitting the company in two, to merge with Warner.

Warner Music itself was tangentially involved in the case as part of the information-gathering process ahead of the actual trial. Forensic lawyers were sent to the Warner offices at 75 Rockefeller Plaza in New York to seize the computers of several key executives to comb through their emails for evidence of collusion.

"We got pulled into that lawsuit a bit," says one senior source based in Rockefeller Plaza at the time. "Part of the theory was that we were conspiring with Citigroup to undermine the value of EMI. It was a really interesting theory but it was completely false! Were we trying to lower the value of EMI? Yeah, but we certainly weren't conspiring with Citigroup to do it. We could do that on our own!"

Other details of note that emerged in the trial were that Hands had invested 70 per cent of his personal wealth (£100 million) in EMI before the buyout had started to wobble. Rakoff had also ruled from the off that Hands, were he to be victorious, would get no more than a quarter of the $7 billion in damages he was seeking. The stakes were still high – just not as high as originally thought.

Terry Revere, sitting in the courtroom watching the case play out, was increasingly convinced the evidence was crystal clear that his friend Guy Hands had been duped into buying EMI. He is unwavering in his assessment that this is still the case. "Guy is completely honest; he is honest to a fault, actually," he says. "With Wormsley, there is no doubt that the phone call definitely happened because we have the phone records. I believe Guy completely about what happened … When you break down the timeline over that weekend between what Eric Nicoli and Wormsley knew and then take into account that phone call, in my view there is 0.0 per cent chance that Wormsley didn't know the other bidder had dropped out. If you look at it, there is a 10:30 a.m. call on Sunday when EMI announced that Ceberus was withdrawing – this, to me, was the most ridiculous thing. Wormsley spoke with Nicoli about six hours later and the obvious question would be, 'OK. It's Sunday. It's a day before this auction closes. Are you guys just having a casual Sunday afternoon conversation about football or politics?' Of course, they would say, 'Holy shit! We're down to one bidder! What are we going to do?' Then of course the call happens … It is preposterous to me that Nicoli would not have said, 'By the way, I just found out a few hours ago that there is no other bidder. We are down to a single-bidder process' – which isn't an auction at all."

The end is nigh

As the trial reached its final phase, Hands claims to have had an overwhelming premonition that they were going to lose. The final straw for him was the dismissal of Donna Gianell from the jury. "She was heard to say in the lift, 'God, this is boring! How long are we going to have to keep sitting around hearing more and more evidence?'" he says. "The judge decided to treat that as discussing the case and kick her off.

By getting rid of her, you immediately get all the jurors spooked. It also spooked our counsel. Things started to unravel from there."

Gianell was also the focus on a hotly debated point by Citigroup's legal team due to her appearance in the credits for Michael Moore's *Capitalism: A Love Story*. Because the film was deemed to be anti-Citigroup, this was read as evidence that she was not impartial and thus could taint the jury's conclusions.

"The court was cleared of the jurors and then they played clips from a movie," recalls Hands. "It turns out that in this movie her husband was going to play an out-of-work Father Christmas who was picketing Citigroup. So they [Citigroup's legal team] asked for her to be taken off [the jury]. There really was no choice. She was going to have to be taken off."

Hands claims this was the tipping-point that flung them from cautious optimism to abject pessimism. "I think the heart went out of us when the juror was thrown off," he suggests. "She was the only juror who took notes. And she was the only juror who had a postgraduate degree. It was a very complicated case for a jury to decide. The fact that she sat there taking notes we felt was good for us because in a jury room she could say what had happened."

Everything, Hands feels, snowballed from there. Even his legal team abandoned him, knowing the jig was up. "The fight had gone out of our side – it was a disaster," he laments. "David Boise actually left before the verdict. He made his speech and just disappeared. He had another case on the west coast of the US, so he just left to catch his flight and that was it. It was very, very depressing."

On Wednesday 3 November 2010, after just four hours of deliberation, the jurors dismissed Terra Firma's fraudulent misrepresentation claims and exonerated Citigroup.

Dennis Posillico, a juror, said outside the court that "there really wasn't any proof" against Citigroup and that is why the jury sided against Terra Firma. He said it was Theodore Wells's summing-up that tipped the balance for him. "I felt [Hands] had a raw deal from Citigroup," he said of where he was originally wavering before Wells gave his closing statement. "Then I changed my mind."[17]

Hands claims that after the trial they spoke to one juror about why they sided with Citigroup. "[They] said they wanted to find in our favour but didn't think there was enough evidence," he says. "That fitted in with where we felt it was at that stage."

Evidence is one part of the issue here, but some who were in the courtroom claim Hands crumpled as a witness and his personality turned the jury against him. He knew going in that it would be a personality test

– and he failed in spectacular fashion. He was regarded as being verbose and imprecise, scatter-gunning too much information and peripheral detail that obfuscated things for the jury when he should have been charming them with clarity.

"Guy uses a lot of words – and one of the things that you need to do when you are testifying is that you should treat your words like you are paying for every one of them," says one courtroom source. "You just have to be very concise. That is a hard thing for somebody like Guy to do. In terms of the way his brain works, he thinks very, very differently ... Guy definitely had more to say; but the more you say, the more the jury feels like they are being thrown a bunch of information. And remember that the burden of proof is on the plaintiff. So, there was a burden that was on the Terra Firma side that the Citigroup side didn't have."

They also argue that Wormsley utterly outshone Hands on the stand and, as the trial went on, Hands found he was pushing against a closed door in trying to win them around. In a trial like this, you win by increments and Hands discovered that, from early on, he was having to ascend a slope that was getting steeper and more slippery all the time.

"David Wormsley did a pretty remarkable job as a witness," says the same courtroom source. "Once David Wormsley testified ... he made that connection that he was just an ordinary guy. That is definitely how he came off – very likeable ... And he didn't have to say a lot. The difference with Guy was that Guy had to carry the case. And Wormsley did not. Wormsley's best defence was to not remember. Or to not be very specific. Because he was playing defence versus offence. Whereas Guy had to be very specific and had to remember the details in order to prove the case. It was very different roles that they had to play. And Wormsley did a very good job playing his side."

Even Hands admits that Citigroup's legal team trumped his when it came to the closing comments, delivering the death blow to Terra Firma's case. "The summing-up they gave was very, very good," he says. "It was all about the fact that we hadn't proved the case. It was very strong."

For Dixon-Thayer, a plaintiff could have all the facts they wanted to back up their case, but if the narrative they present in a jury trial is too convoluted or meanders to the point of disorientation, then they will be undone. "From the litigation side, I think that the moral to this story is that you can be so right and you can have all the evidence to support it; but in a system where you really do have to keep it simple, it is very challenging when you are approaching a case of this magnitude," she says. "It is truly complicated. You have to really assess and maybe drop off some of the pieces that you can eliminate from the case to keep it simple for the jury."

Revere, however, feels Judge Rakoff was the determining factor in why the jury came down against Terra Firma – or rather how Rakoff conducted the trial was the determining factor. "The thing that screwed this all the most was, to be blunt, if the judge in New York gave the right instructions initially, then I don't think any of us would be here and the New York trial would have turned out differently," he says. "I am not calling Rakoff a dummy – as he is clearly not – but just like Michael Jordan might throw up an air ball once in a while, this was just the wrong instruction on the law. It's very difficult to get [the decision of] a judge of Rakoff's stature reversed. But to give credit to the lawyers in New York, they were able to convince the Second Circuit that Rakoff made a mistake."

The immediate speculation in the wake of the ruling was that Terra Firma could possibly now default on its debt and be forced into bankruptcy. If that were to happen then Citigroup would take control of EMI.

One EMI staffer, following the twists and turns in Manhattan closely from their desk in London, was not shocked when the jury ruled for Citigroup, but it made them, if only temporarily, view Terra Firma in a slightly more sympathetic light to how they had seen them in the preceding three years. "Guy Hands got a real spanking from Citigroup – almost to the point where you feel sorry for him," they say. "Citigroup are a Darth Vader-type force and, like the Death Star, they zapped them."

Music Week was harsh in its assessment of the way the case came to its conclusion. Its editorial suggested that its readers spare any sympathy they might have for Guy Hands and instead direct it towards the staff of EMI, whose future was now chillingly uncertain. Editor Paul Williams said Guy Hands "has lost the biggest game of poker in his life and, along with Terra Firma and EMI, he must suffer the consequences". He argued that it was a "spurious claim in damages" that Hands was seeking based on forecasts of EMI earnings. "The judge correctly saw right through that and Hands has had to head back to his Guernsey tax haven with his tail between his legs,"[18] he jeered.

Over a period of several months, this author repeatedly approached Citigroup and David Wormsley to speak about the case. They did not respond to initial approaches, and then eventually refused. In an email correspondence dated 20 December 2017, a Citigroup spokesperson said, "The EMI/Terra Firma transaction took place 10 years ago, in 2007. It was the subject of litigation in the English High Court in 2016, which concluded with Terra Firma unreservedly withdrawing in open court the allegations of fraud that it had previously made against Citigroup and certain employees, including Mr Wormsley. Terra Firma agreed to the dismissal of the proceedings and paid Citigroup's costs. As such, the matter is very much in the past and neither Citigroup nor its employees, including Mr Wormsley, will be making any further comment."

Planning the appeal

Rather than let the jury ruling stand, Terra Firma's legal team was preparing to swing back into action. Just over two months after the gut-punch jury ruling, on 12 January 2011, Terra Firma revealed it was going to appeal against the decision.

"Boies, Schiller & Flexner, on behalf of Terra Firma, filed a notice of appeal in the litigation against Citigroup," the private equity firm said in a press statement. "The appeal will challenge legal rulings made by the court in the litigation. Terra Firma remains committed to working on a resolution for EMI that will benefit all parties involved."

Citigroup was standing defiant. "As the jury unanimously found after a three-week trial presided over by a distinguished federal judge, Citigroup's conduct in the EMI transaction was entirely proper," it said in its own statement. "We are confident the appeals court will confirm that Terra Firma received a fair trial."[19]

It was understood at the time that Terra Firma was going to challenge technical details of the trial and that the appeal could take eighteen months to be processed. In the end, it took just shy of thirty months. At the start of June 2013, the Second Circuit Court of Appeals threw out the 2010 ruling. "[It] ruled that Judge Rakoff had incorrectly instructed the jury in the original trial on the English legal provisions relevant to the case, and that the matter should therefore be retried,"[20] according to the *Independent*.

Citigroup was unwavering in its position that it had been fully exonerated and the ruling was not in doubt. "The original verdict made clear that Terra Firma's baseless accusations of fraud were simply an attempt to gain leverage in debt restructuring negotiations," it said in a statement.

Terra Firma stood unbowed. "We continue to believe that we have a strong claim, and with the jury instructions now resolved in our favour, we expect to prevail in any subsequent trial," ran its statement.

Yet behind the scenes, just as he prayed in summer 2007 that the EMI board would fail to convince its shareholders to go ahead with the sale to Terra Firma, Guy Hands was hoping against hope that it would not drag on through an appeal and another debilitating court case. "To be blunt, I was not happy that we won the appeal," he claims. "It was just going to go on for the rest of my life ... It's terrible for us. It's probably terrible for Citigroup. It's certainly terrible for David Wormsley and me. And it just goes on. It's like the gift that just keeps on giving. Or rather the gift that keeps taking!"

In the interim period, Terra Firma, based on new information, reportedly filed additional claims with the High Court of Justice in the Manchester District Registry Mercantile Court in August 2013.[21] "Discussions happened between Citigroup and Terra Firma about whether it made sense to do the retrial in New York or London," says Duffy of how it all transpired. "In the intervening period, Terra Firma had initiated a new lawsuit against Citigroup based on some slightly different facts relating to the financing. They had initiated that in England. Ultimately both sides agreed that it would be appropriate to move everything over to England."

Hands, if he was going to go through this again, was keen to have it take place on home turf. "We felt we had lost to this judge once and we didn't have the heart to go back to New York again and go through the same process in New York again," says Hands on why they moved to have the second case heard at the High Court in London. "We just couldn't emotionally take it. Frankly, we didn't expect to win the appeal. It is very rare that you win an appeal."

However, by the time that the appeal came through and both sides agreed to have it heard in London, Guy Hands was no longer the owner of EMI. Mere weeks after its 2010 New York court victory, Citigroup landed a haymaker. It had snatched the music company away from right under Terra Firma's nose.

CHAPTER 16

Putting the Old Girl out of Her Misery

With the legal defeat in New York still ringing in his ears, Guy Hands returned to Guernsey to take stock of what had happened and, more importantly, figure out what could be done about it. The case for the appeal was being pulled together by his legal team but, as cowing as it was, there were bigger problems to deal with. The biggest, of course, was ensuring debt payments were made so that Terra Firma could hold onto EMI and not cede control to the company that knocked it for six in the US courts.

The music industry media started pointing towards a worst-case scenario for both Terra Firma and EMI. It suggested that the private equity firm would never recover from this and EMI would, once again, find itself on the auction block – either landing in the lap of another investment company or being put through the mortification of being carved up among the other majors. The prognosis for either side was not good.

"It would be a really great shame if it bites the dust – EMI is an institution and it would be extremely sad to see it split up," Blur and Gorillaz manager Chris Morrison told *Music Week*. Tim Clark, co-manager of Robbie Williams, added, "EMI is a great company and a great UK one at that. It has a great and iconic history … Were EMI to be split up it would be a great loss for the industry."[1]

The growing belief within the British music industry was that Terra Firma's debts were so insurmountable that the sale – and splitting up – of EMI was unavoidable. The narrative was already being sketched out: Citigroup would seize the company from EMI and put it on the market for a quick sale to the highest bidder.

The still unconsummated dalliance with Warner Music Group was marking its tenth anniversary and Warner chairman Edgar Bronfman Jr was not going to be drawn on if or when his company would make its move to buy at least a considerable chunk of EMI. There were rumours that it was considering a $750 million bid for just EMI's recorded music business and Bronfman was, inevitably, quizzed about it during Warner's earnings call in late November – an earnings call where Warner announced a net loss of $145 million for the previous year.

Bronfman said that EMI had seen an improved market performance recently but that it had "suffered since the Terra Firma acquisition". He said, "We have all been reading what happened with the court case," when asked if he was planning an EMI bid. "When we have something to announce – if we have something to announce – you guys will be the first to know."[2] So, he wasn't ruling it in, but he equally wasn't ruling it out. Same as ever.

Just as the year was closing, Hartwig Masuch, CEO of BMG Rights Management, expressed his company's interest – but only for parts of EMI. He said a total acquisition of EMI's recorded and publishing divisions would be a hard sell to the regulators, but its catalogue was tantalising. "It is no secret we are more interested in rights to masters than publishing,"[3] he told *Music Week*. BMG had just paid £107 million to buy Chrysalis Group so it was on a very confident – and very public – buying spree.

Like sharks sensing blood in the water, a feeding frenzy was about to begin.

Terra Firma loses its grip

To compound matters, a coup was brewing within EMI to defenestrate Terra Firma, while its guard was down, in the swiftest and most brutal manner imaginable.

"It wasn't lost on us that Terra Firma was under water on its loans and Citi was within its rights to call in the loan; we knew that, and we were waiting for that," says a high-level source at EMI on what happened next. "Roger Faxon, Leo Corbett [the recently appointed COO of EMI Group], Ruth Prior, who was the CFO, and Kyla Mullins, who was the general counsel, were the people who ultimately – under Roger's guidance – started to work on a plan to turf Terra Firma out of the business ... Once they were able to determine that Terra Firma was under water on the loans, they were able to essentially file for bankruptcy for the business, which would trigger the loans being called in by Citi. When you saw the stories around Terra Firma losing control of the business, that was something that Terra Firma didn't know about until after it happened."

One battle plan within EMI was to get the keys back to Citigroup and for Citigroup to round up viable buyers from the financial sector. "Citigroup puts the business up for sale and we are sold to private equity, so we have a five-year runway of trying to show that this was a successful business and delivering a successful outcome for artists and global rights management with a joined-up view of music and music publishing," was one senior executive's dream resolution to it all. It was to remain just that – a dream.

Faxon himself explains how this all played out in February 2011. "The directors of the borrowing company had to make a decision as to whether or not we would ever be able to repay the debt and, therefore, if we would be insolvent," he says. "Ruth Prior and I were the board! We determined that the company was insolvent and that it would need to go through receivership. But I was unwilling to take it through receivership in the normal way because then all the work that we had done – which was to make the business feel like it was winning, that it was absolutely on track and that the artists were trusting us to sign with us and do deals with us – would just bleed away. In order for us to do what we did, which was to go through what is called a 'pre-pack', we went through receivership in three and a half hours."

It was reported that Faxon – previously watching Terra Firma frantically scramble to get investors to pump in £105 million as an equity cure into EMI to keep it afloat – had been planning this move since the summer of 2010 and was just waiting for the optimum moment. He had been appointed to the assorted EMI/Terra Firma boards, notably at Maltby (the holding company Terra Firma set up for the EMI acquisition), in the summer of 2010 to coincide with his elevation to group CEO of EMI. Prior to that, he was added to the board of the corporate governance vehicle related to the company in January 2009. This all placed him in a position of great power and authority over the future of EMI.

Plans gathered speed in December 2010 when Prior, formerly finance director for portfolio business at Terra Firma, left to become CFO at EMI.

"In mid-January, Prior and Faxon approached PwC [Pricewaterhouse-Coopers] with a plan to appoint the accountant administrator to Maltby Investments," wrote Reuters at the time. "Under UK insolvency law, administrators can be appointed by either creditors or the directors of the company concerned if they believe it is technically insolvent. As the top company in the structure with exposure to the debt, Faxon and Prior could act without interference from Terra Firma … The administration enabled PwC to sell Maltby Investments' assets to principal creditor

Citigroup. The assets are immediate subsidiary Maltby Acquisitions Limited, which in turn owns EMI."[4]

Faxon's email to staff on 1 February 2011 explaining what had just happened – simply titled 'Message from Roger Faxon' – was quickly leaked to the media.[5] "In the last few minutes, we have announced that earlier today ownership of EMI passed from Terra Firma to Citigroup," he began, before explaining how the change of ownership took place.

"Well, when a company's value is less than its debts, one solution is to go through an administration process which allows the sale of the business in partial satisfaction of those debts. In our case it is not hard to see that our parent company Maltby Investments Limited (MIL) would never be able to repay the £3.4 billion it owed to Citi. With that being the case, it appointed an administrator who as an officer of the court was empowered to sell the EMI Group to Citi. This is sometimes called a 'pre-pack' because it can be done in a matter of hours – and that's exactly what happened here. EMI itself was never in administration. Where EMI came into the story was with its sale to Citi, which was followed by an immediate recapitalisation of the company which reduced our debt by 65 per cent."

He then put a positive spin on what it meant for the staff at EMI who had been through the mill in recent years. "Well first of all, it ends a struggle between our two principal stakeholders which has enveloped the business for most of the past two years. I'm sure that you'll agree that the distraction has at times felt unbearable. We will now be able to put behind us the controversy of the Terra Firma-Citi court case, the cliff-hanging drama of the 'will we or won't we meet our covenant tests' and of course the never-ending press speculation. I, for one, welcome a respite from all that, though of course we will never be fully free of press speculation – we are EMI after all!"

He added that the change of ownership effectively slashed EMI's debts from £3.4 billion to £1.2 billion, on top of which it had £300 million in cash, giving EMI "one of the most robust balance sheets in the industry". He then went on to say that Citigroup was prepared to "provide us with a stable and supportive environment to continue on our present course" but that, ultimately, the company would be up for sale again as "a music company – even one as great as EMI – doesn't exactly sit comfortably in a giant financial services company like Citi".

The narrative to staff was that Citigroup was going to give the EMI management time to stabilise the business and not force them through a quick sale. While he could not guarantee it, Faxon was adamant that the best future for EMI was to sell it as a unified company and not carve it up among multiple bidders.

"I have no doubt that the best possible way to yield the highest value for EMI is to keep our businesses together in pursuit of our strategy," he wrote. "As we move forward that will become evident even to the most sceptical observer. This is why I have every confidence that EMI will remain EMI for a very, very long time to come."

He ended by trying to assuage fears among the staff – who had been bloodied and bruised for most of the past decade – about what the end game would be. "[I]t is full speed ahead," he wrote as a means of rallying the troops, ending on what was perhaps an intentional pun. "No one should worry about the future – it is in our hands."

This was all an extreme and unexpected measure as far as Terra Firma was concerned, but there were numerous loopholes that had to be addressed after the trigger had been pulled. "It was the largest pre-pack to date in the UK – and probably still is," explains Faxon. "And it went faster through the process than any deal ever. In order to do that, Citibank was obviously the buyer for its own debt. We had to get antitrust approval from the Japanese, from the Brazilians and, most importantly, from the European Union. I had a pretty good relationship with the people at the Competition directorate and we went and explained our situation to them."

It did, however, move extraordinarily quickly. "While they [the team at the Competition directorate] would never say what their answer was going to be, they moved heaven and earth for us to get the approval, which had to go all the way from the commissioners and through the process at the centre and get the president to sign off for the clearance. That's what took the three hours. It would have been less except the person who was carrying it went to lunch in the middle! The whole point was that we wanted it to be seamless. You would wake up in the morning and the only thing that is different is that Guy and Terra Firma are out and Citibank is in. For the business, it was a non-event. Which is exactly what we wanted it to be."

It was, however, far from a 'non-event' for Terra Firma when it found out what had just happened. "In February 2011, Citigroup basically seized the company one afternoon on an hour's notice," says Guy Hands of the doodlebug that dropped on their heads. "They had basically gone to the directors and told the directors that they didn't believe the company was worth its debt."

One senior EMI executive explains just how the private equity firm was blindsided by it all. "Until that day [in February], Terra Firma had no idea there was anything going on," they say. "They knew they were in trouble, but they were bringing in new people to try and resolve things. They were still thinking the court case would give them some leverage to renegotiate the loans. They still felt that they had optionality there somewhere along the line. But from that day, they realised the jig was up."

Hands suggests that the reason why it was so easy for EMI to be taken away from Terra Firma was a legacy of adding Roger Faxon to the Maltby board after Elio Leoni Sceti was sacked and Faxon took over running all of EMI. "So, the Maltby board, which was there to represent the shareholders, also had representatives of the company on it," he explains. "That is an unusual situation and it was something that was debated within Terra Firma a lot. The normal structure is that you don't do that. And the reason you don't do that is that if the bank then wants to take over the company, it is quite difficult to persuade the shareholders that they should take over the company."

He suggests that with Faxon and Prior now both on the Maltby board, they were – as managers at EMI – representing EMI but they were also representing Terra Firma. "When Citigroup seized the company, instead of having to deal with Terra Firma representatives, they had to deal with EMI people," says Hands of what happened next. "They dealt with it in an hour. They literally turned up and our understanding is that they did it in about an hour. They said to Roger and Ruth that this is what they wanted to do, they had to do it, and they did it." He adds, "If it had been a Terra Firma representative, it is unlikely that they would have agreed so readily and so quickly."

Hands claims that, in this moment of crisis, Terra Firma took "the very open approach". Despite advice from some corners, Terra Firma did not move Maltby to France to avail itself of the country's bankruptcy laws in the wake of the New York court defeat. Such a move would have been a pre-emptive strike against it all going horribly wrong.

"One of the things after the trial that we were advised to do was to move the holding company – and the place we were told to move it to was France because the French bankruptcy laws are some of the toughest in the world for banks to deal with," he says. "In the UK, the court supports the bank – pretty well universally. In France, the court supports the stakeholders. So, you can't just grab a company in France. You have to go to the judge; you have to agree with the judge if it is appropriate; judges will often say no and say that what comes first is the employees or the artists."

He says that Terra Firma also declined to act on advice that suggested they change the Maltby board members so they could not be steamrollered by Citigroup. "In the end we decided to play a totally straight game and we didn't do anything to frustrate Citigroup," he claims. "When Citigroup wanted to take over, we just let it happen. Which was strange.

On the one hand, we fought as hard as we could for the company; on the other hand, we didn't really fight incredibly hard for ourselves. We did fight for our investors because we were advised that we had to; but the lawsuit was very much because we had legal advice that we had to bring it. The company [was something] we fought for as long as we could, but when Citigroup decided to seize it, we were a bit shocked because we didn't think that it was fair. We had done everything we could for the company and we thought the least they could have done was come and talk to us about it."

He remains conflicted and confused as to why Faxon and Prior would have so readily acquiesced to Citigroup's demands. "We were shocked that they just agreed to it," says Hands. "My view was that Roger trusted Citigroup completely and he thought it was the best thing for the company to let Citigroup take it over. He felt, as a director, that his duty was to do what was best for the company."

He said, however, that "cynics in my team" suggested that Faxon and Prior were bought off by Citigroup and that is why they agreed to the pre-pack that saw Terra Firma effectively evicted in a matter of hours. With no evidence to back this up, Hands felt powerless to do anything about it. He did try to get greater clarity on the suspicions of these cynics in his team, but he was blocked from doing so. "Citigroup would never give us key bits of information," he claims. "We brought a lawsuit to ask on what basis the company was taken away from us. One of the things we wanted was to find out what Roger and Ruth got paid. The reason we needed to know that is that it goes to motivation. We wanted to understand why they agreed to the transaction."

While some corners of the financial media reported that it all happened because Terra Firma had failed a solvency test, Hands says this was not quite correct. "It's not really a solvency test – it's really a net value test. It's basically asking which is worth more: the company or the debt? And they said the debt was and therefore they basically seized the company."

He remains frustrated that the company was taken from him so swiftly and feels that there was still a chance at that time for Terra Firma to snatch victory from the jaws of defeat. "In reality, the debt didn't have to be paid off until 2014," he proposes. "Who knows what the company would have been worth in 2014. In 2012, it would have met the tests quite easily. So we were a year short … Our view was that this business, at some point, would be worth more than the debt and we would get our money back. The market would recover. The company had recovered and we were making £250 million a year cash rather than losing £100 million. The EBITDA was 368 as opposed to 68. So, we were not concerned about the company getting there. Our concern was if Citigroup would seize it or not. We didn't think they would seize it. We were shocked when they did. Absolutely shocked."

His plan was effectively a waiting game – keeping EMI going through equity cures and additional investment, as they had done consistently throughout their ownership period – and just staying afloat until the financial markets recovered. Fine on paper, but Citigroup had stopped listening.

"Citigroup knew that we could make these debt cures because our investors had offered to give up £650 million to make debt cures and solve the problem," Hands claims. "We had an offer from the investors to solve it. The issue was that the investors wanted us to work on the basis that we separated the two businesses [recorded music and publishing], but they would still make cures as we went through. So we could get debt cures done."

He adds, "Citigroup knew that if they came to us and said that we needed to put X amount of money in we might well go back to our investors and get the money. They wanted to get rid of the debt and the only way they could get rid of the debt was to seize the company – so they just seized the company. And we didn't expect that. I don't think it was putting good money after bad. It was effectively buying an option. We paid £105 million for the opportunity to get to 2012. Unfortunately, Citigroup seized it before 2012. If we had got to 2012, we would have got at least 50 per cent of our money back. And Citigroup would have got all its money back. Now they sold it for as much as their debt was so we don't know how much they got back. Including interest and fees, they would have got all their money back. So Citigroup basically sold it as soon as they could get their money back."

* * *

Some senior EMI staff and executives argued that the whole thing collapsed like a clown car for Hands as he massively underestimated the size of the job in front of Terra Firma when they took the keys in the closing weeks of summer 2007.

His two favourite success stories to mention in meetings and presentations were Tank & Rast and the Odeon – both of which were effectively turnkey solutions (where immediate improvements can be put in place by the new owner). These were failing businesses but Terra Firma had gone in and identified the key problems. For Tank & Rast, it was clean toilets and better food; for the Odeon, it was popcorn and more comfortable seats. This is, of course, massively reductive as Terra Firma had many things to fix in both businesses, but these were the most visible and immediate changes that helped radically transform each of them.

The criticism of Hands from within EMI was that he believed a similar turnkey strategy was all that EMI needed. In essence: dump all the unprofitable acts and sack all the useless executives on massive salaries. The problem, of course, was that there were far more things wrong with EMI than there were at Tank & Rast or the Odeon. There was no turnkey solution. In fact, there were lots of locks, no one knew where they all were and the ones they found were rusted up.

Hands, however, denies that he applied turnkey logic to EMI. "The turnover in earnings we did at EMI was more than we have ever done at any business," he argues. "We transformed the earnings incredibly. The issue was the debt. There was nothing else which was wrong about the business. It was all about the debt; and the debt was all about the timing. The fact it was emotionally difficult and the fact it was painful was about trying to do it really quickly. You would normally do it more smoothly than that. Citigroup sold off a business which was very successful. The publishing business was very successful. The catalogue business was very successful. In new music, we had gained market share over those three years enormously."

He adds, "We had a number of really good acts at that point. We had our insights business that is now industry standard. I didn't think there were a lot of things we had to change in EMI when we bought it. We had to change the processes. We had to start re-spending the A&R budget on new acts rather than on old acts. We had to solve at some point, which we never got to, America. And we had to close down some of the corruption we had going on in the Far East and South America. We had to sort that out. Actually, when we looked at it, there were only four or five things we were trying to do with EMI ... Tank & Rast took us eleven years! ... EMI we did much quicker."

By the start of 2011, however, this was all academic. Terra Firma were now the former owners of EMI.

* * *

For the staff at EMI, uncertainty was becoming routine. Everything had been up in the air for so long that, like a disruptive rereading of Stockholm Syndrome, they were starting to get used to it. Abnormal was the new normal.

"The good bits of the company were just kicked for more," says one UK executive who feels that Terra Firma whipped the profitable areas too hard and just never got around to fixing the real problem areas. "It was a bit like Greece, where a few taxpayers just got asked to pay more and more. It was the same here. The good bits were screwed and the US was an ongoing problem."

Those who had survived to this point had, frankly, no other option but to do what they always did – keep their heads down, try and get on with their jobs and hope they would not be culled like so many of their colleagues.

"It made everyone work twenty times harder," says one long-serving department head of how they greeted the news that Terra Firma were out and Citigroup were in, albeit as custodians. "We were under pressure to break Emeli Sandé. We were under pressure to break Bastille. We were under this immense amount of pressure because, if we didn't do it, it would devalue the company. If we have hits, we will be worth more. And if we are worth more, we will get a serious buyer. And that meant we will have more chance of keeping our jobs."

The bitter irony of all this was that, at this stage in its highly colourful history, EMI was defying the odds and working incredibly well. It could have been the equivalent of a patient in a hospice suddenly rallying before slipping into a terminal decline; or it may just have been the effect of blessed relief at no longer being under the thumb of Terra Firma; but there were golden shafts of optimism – against the odds – cracking through the gloom.

"We were in good shape," says one executive of this most curious of times. "We had good people who knew exactly what they needed to do. They didn't need someone like an Ernesto [Schmitt] standing over them and telling them that this is the way it is going to be. They just knew their jobs and were creative enough to take things forward without being told they had to take things forward. Through it all, and all power to the staff who remained through all of that, they stayed true to themselves, they were incredibly professional, they were incredibly creative and they were still doing it, and still doing it very well, right to the end."

This carpe diem survival strategy was proof to one department head that, in the time of its greatest adversity, EMI could still come out swinging. "At that point we were having hits, but we were working out of our skins to keep our jobs," they say.

To salve the pain, EMI was going out of its way to ensure that staff felt valued. Everything might have been out of their control but there was a need to keep staff focused on the job in hand. Small but symbolic incentives were offered, like free breakfasts for all staff if the company got a number one record. This was EMI's 'blitz spirit'.

"I was telling my staff that if the thought of going to work on Monday morning was going to give them a nervous breakdown, that they could have duvet days," says the same department head. "The fact was we were under pressure and we had to make it work for ourselves and everyone else. Actually, it did really well."

For some, Citigroup's period of ownership was a mixed bag. Having been shunted in one direction under Terra Firma, it was jack-knifed back into the way things were before 2007 – yet there was something missing. "When Citigroup took over, it certainly didn't get any better and they went back to a regional structure," says one EMI department head who was by now starting to lose count of how many times EMI had been restructured during their time on the staff. "Under Citi, they were running it as if it was EMI in Tony Wadsworth and Eric Nicoli's day. David Kassler was Eric Nicoli and Andria Vidler was Tony Wadsworth. It was running on the old principles, but without as good talent. So you had a structure which was exactly like it was before Terra Firma – but with less able talent to run it."

For others, there was just elation that the Terra Firma era had come to an end. To them, things could not get any worse so, by default, things were only going to improve – no matter who took ownership of the company eventually. "It was, 'Thank God!' – as that was the best news we could have heard," one very senior EMI UK source said when the email from Roger Faxon landed in their inbox, announcing that Terra Firma was out and Citigroup, for now at least, was in. "And that [feeling of elation] was throughout the company. We still didn't know where we were going to end up, but we hoped we would end up as part of another music company because both Universal and Warner had shown interest. We thought there was no way we would end up with another private equity company."

To pour salt into Terra Firma's gaping wounds, they airily added, "When Citi had control of EMI, they probably did a better job than when Guy Hands was in charge."

There was a brief moment where EMI could have stayed as it was, under the ownership of Citigroup but with a leadership team headed up by Roger Faxon as he worked to bring his vision for the company – the recorded and publishing divisions working in lockstep – to fruition.

"It's hard to imagine that a major bank would want to own a music business – but I will say that not too long after they came in, Citigroup wanted to keep the business," reveals Faxon. "They really did. But obviously this was in the period after the crash and there were all sorts of banking regulations coming in and capital requirements [impacting on the business]. Those capital requirements were getting tighter and tighter and that meant they had to dedicate more and more capital to their reserves in order to hold onto the company. While they emotionally

310

wanted to hold onto the business – they loved the business – there was never in my mind any doubt that it was going to have to be sold."

While Citigroup might have expressed a polite – or passing – interest in maybe running EMI for a few years, some at EMI immediately got the sense it was seen as little more than a temporarily enthralling gewgaw for the bank in terms of its portfolio.

"If I'm honest, I spent more time giving guided tours of Abbey Road studios to the elderly statesmen of Citi," says Andria Vidler of the types of meetings she now found herself in. "But nothing changed. It was great until Citi said that they were selling … Citi don't hold businesses. They're a bank. I don't think they ever intended to hold us, even though they said they wanted to. Emotionally they might have wanted to, at least for a couple of years, which would have enabled us to get more done. I'm sure Roger hoped that he would have been given more time. But Citi said no."

Whatever fate was to befall EMI now, Faxon was adamant that he wanted it to be sold in its entirety, not crassly filleted by a variety of music companies keen to take as much as they could without spooking the regulators at the European Commission and the antitrust authorities in the US. "I was fairly vocal at the time that the business should stay together as there was long-term synergy and long-term value to be achieved by holding these businesses together," says Faxon.

That meant the initial wish-list of suitors, as far as EMI management was concerned, were from the private equity sector – primarily those based in the US. But, as the history of the music company over the past two decades had made abundantly clear again and again, what EMI wanted and what EMI got were very rarely the same thing.

The debt markets that sunk Terra Firma were still in such a poor state that they effectively mitigated against a clean sale of EMI. "As we got through the summer and into September 2011, what was happening was that the high-yield debt market was closing," says Faxon. "Before the crash, these guys wouldn't worry about that because it comes and goes, they could bridge it and it would be fine. But the truth is that they were uncertain about coming into a business and an industry that, even at that time, was very troubled. That's notwithstanding the fact that we were making a lot of money. Our operating margin was 22 per cent or 23 per cent of sales. The cash was there. It wasn't being consumed. We had a lot of cash flow. Obviously, all of that had to go to paying the debt service, but the value of the business that you would have to buy it at would still allow you to have a lot of free cash flow and to pay your debt service."

That meant only one real option: rival music companies keen to turn EMI's misfortune into their benefit. Or, at the very least, serve as a quick way to bulk up their market share in a dwindling recorded music business.

"In the end, the only bidders were music companies," says Faxon. "We had offered the business as either being sold as a whole or as separate pieces. Because we had done a huge amount of work for Terra Firma when they came in to assure them that we could separate the businesses and that we had all of the rights in the publishing business, we were able to stabilise all of the rights in the publishing entity for a securitisation that allowed us to be able to sell the business without much risk."

In the meantime, there was still a music company to run.

Business as usual ... in ususual times

In January, EMI signed a new five-year deal with Pink Floyd to mine their catalogue, in the hope that this would echo the success of The Beatles reissues in 2009 and their final migration to iTunes in 2010 – with hints of a possible move into a *Rock Band*-style game. "If you were to look at what we achieved with The Beatles it would be fair to speculate that we are looking to achieve similar results with Pink Floyd," Andria Vidler told *Music Week*. "The reaction to The Beatles shows that we can reach both existing and new fans through new products and new releases and we are confident that is part of what Pink Floyd want."[6]

As yet more speculation of a Warner/EMI deal whizzed around the business that February, European independent label body Impala made its opposition to such an outcome very clear. The same month, BMG hinted that it was changing tactic and, rather than seeking to buy EMI's recorded music archive, it was considering making a play to buy EMI Music Publishing, possibly turning to private equity firm KKR (which already owned 51 per cent of BMG) to raise the capital needed. Another name rumoured to be considering some form of bid was Apax, yet another private equity firm.

Gauging the industry's views on all of these potential outcomes, *Music Week* spoke to those with a long association with EMI about what they thought would happen and what they wished for the company.[7]

"This week it feels like EMI is starting to emerge from a three-year nightmare," said Tony Wadsworth, former chairman and CEO of EMI UK & Ireland, who had been out of the company for three years by this point. "It was clear more or less from day one that the outgoing owners neither understood [EMI's] values nor bought into them. Consequently, an acquisition that was made at a difficult time both in the economic cycle, and in the transition of the music market, was further hampered by Terra Firma's lack of empathy with both the company culture and the creative music industry." He argued that the team at EMI "will no longer have one hand tied behind their back" and praised "the strong leadership of Roger Faxon".

Dave Rowntree, the drummer in Blur, added, "For the first time in a long time the recording side of EMI is on top of its game." He cited the success of acts like Tinie Tempah and Bat For Lashes as proof of this. "So, it seems ironic that, while A&R and a lot of the company is working well, the business people right at the top can't get it right."

Meanwhile manager Tim Clark of ie:music said of Faxon's vision of a multiple-rights company, "I totally share that view". He added that a splitting of the company to sell it off in regulator-appeasing chunks "would be a ridiculous move". "This is because EMI right now are in a fantastic position," he said. "They have shed a lot of debt, have a good working catalogue and are making a profit." While his client Robbie Williams was technically out of his deal with EMI, they were "not discounting a new deal with EMI" or, he added as a careful caveat, "any other company".

Hopes of a Warner union were derailed slightly in March 2011. Rumours were growing about a potential sale of Warner Music Group, suggesting that Edgar Bronfman Jr's coy responses at the end of 2010 when asked if he would buy EMI were possibly a deflection technique.

Access Industries, operated by billionaire Len Blavatnik, was named as one of the potential suitors for Warner but other names being kicked around at the time included Sony Music Group, BMG Rights Management, Yucaipa Companies, Platinum Equity and Guggenheim Partners.[8]

The industry had to keep guessing for a few months as it was not until the beginning of May that it was finally confirmed that Warner Music Group had been acquired by Access Industries in a deal worth $3.3 billion. Inevitably this put a rocket up speculation that this was just phase one of Blavatnik's plan and that he would soon step forward with an offer for EMI.

Former EMI digital executive Ted Cohen – by this stage running Tag Strategic, his own US-based music consultancy – told the *LA Times* that a bid for his old company made enormous sense. "I would think that the next step for Warner is to buy EMI," he said, before echoing all the familiar arguments for a Warner/EMI tie-up from 2000. "[It] could be a very smart move. Where Warner is weak, EMI is strong. Where Warner is strong, EMI is weak. The two are very complementary."[9] Access

Industries was, for now at least, refusing to comment – something that did little to dampen the speculation that EMI was next on its shopping list.

During that time, of course, EMI had to go on the road to rustle up interest from potential bidders. "Citi clearly never wanted to own a music company and that wasn't their goal, but I would say they were responsible stewards for the company," says David Kassler of that interim period between the exit of Terra Firma and the next owner, or owners, coming in. "They made it very clear to the top team that there would be a sale at some point, but they wanted to stabilise the business first and figure out how they could best get their money back. They were responsible for about £4 billion of debts at the time and they wanted to get to know the management team and work with us on a sales process."

Kassler says that he was part of a team of six EMI managers who participated in the sales roadshow. "There was a bunch of private equity firms in the mix at that time," he says of the initial wave of interested bidders. "It was the usual West Coast private equity firms and New York private equity firms."

One well-placed observer says that the core EMI team on this sales roadshow was headed up by Roger Faxon and Ruth Prior and they were joined by Colin Finkelstein (EMI North America COO) and David Kassler (CEO for Europe and the rest of the world at EMI). It rumbled on for three months and, as it progressed, they perfected their pitch, which was initially made to private equity firms in the UK and the US. The continuing financial crisis, however, meant that music companies, partly by default, became the primary targets of the roadshow.

A senior source says they definitely presented to Len Blavatnik, the new owner of Warner Music Group. They also presented to Universal Music Group – but at this stage it was to the largest major's executive vice president and CFO, Boyd Muir, not Lucian Grainge, the company's global chairman and CEO, who did not attend the early pitches.

"They all had panels and they would ask the team questions," says this source. "We probably presented twelve or thirteen times." They add, however, that the New York court case between Citigroup and Terra Firma was expunged from the forward-into-a-glittering-future vision they were all trying to push to interested buyers. "The Citi court case was kind of irrelevant as it didn't play into the ownership story," they say. "The court case was just annoying. It wasn't the problem and wasn't related to the bankruptcy. It was just another example of EMI being fucked."

Various EMI executives were drafted into the presentations as and when they were needed, with one derisorily referring to the whole thing as "the dog and pony show".

As all three majors were circling and then booking seats for the roadshow presentations, others with a long history in the music industry stepped forward to kick the tyres of EMI. Among them, reportedly, were the founder of Island Records, Chris Blackwell, and 19 Entertainment's Simon Fuller (who also developed the *American Idol* format), who had pooled resources in June 2011 to form Blackwell Fuller to work on a next-generation music company.

"For me it was going through the release schedule for the next twelve months," says Parlophone head Miles Leonard on his role in these presentations. "I was talking about the culture of the company and the individual labels. [My presentation] was talking about our relationship with our artists and our vision for breaking new development artists. Then Andria [Vidler] would present a broader picture of the company, talking through our sales structure and the investments that we had made with other companies or businesses. But at no point did we divulge our artists' contracts."

On 20 June, the process was formalised as EMI issued a statement saying it had "initiated a process to explore and evaluate potential strategic alternatives, including a possible sale, recapitalisation or initial public offering of the company". To mitigate against any shame that might result from a failed play, it added that "there can be no assurance that this strategic review process will result in a transaction". This covered a variety of potential outcomes, but the smart money was on a quick sale.

By this stage, *The Guardian* was naming Len Blavatnik as the front runner – even though he was still awaiting full regulatory approval for his acquisition of Warner Music Group. BMG, with the help of KKR, were also said to be in the running. Outsider names included billionaires the Gores brothers, who were understood to have been in the steeplechase for Warner Music earlier in the year.[10]

Incredibly, during this time a totally unexpected bidder was trying to throw its hat in the ring: Terra Firma. Why on earth, many wondered, would Terra Firma want to try and buy back the company it had almost lost its shirt on and that had pretty much cost it its reputation for the next few years?

"The price would have been completely different," says Hands. "We paid £4.2 billion for it and Citigroup was selling it off for £2.5 billion, which was the price of the debt. They were selling it off 40 per cent cheaper. We had increased the cash flow ... so, we would have been buying a business that was in a far better state for 40 per cent cheaper."

It was suggested by Hands that Citigroup flatly refused to even entertain a bid from Terra Firma and it – as well as anyone it was bidding in conjunction with – was completely excluded, having to watch from the side-lines as a variety of companies fought over the pieces.

Carving up the spoils

Months of negotiations and refinement of bids went on behind closed doors. Then the latest bombshell – a double bombshell, in fact, in what had been over a decade of nothing but bombshells for EMI – landed.

Universal Music Group, owner of the biggest record company in the world, had won the bidding for EMI's recorded music arm, offering £1.2 billion for the company, reportedly outbidding Warner Music Group by £250 million.

Meanwhile, a consortium led by Sony – owners of the Sony/ATV Music Publishing division – had seen off BMG with a bid of £1.3 billion for EMI Music Publishing.

Roger Faxon's dream of EMI being sold as a whole now lay in the ditch.

The Universal bid shocked the industry. How could the biggest music major buy the smallest in a deal that would give UMG an estimated 38 per cent market share? How could the regulators ever clear that? It could never be allowed to happen. Could it?

Universal's parent company Vivendi said it would take on all the regulatory risk, which was its strategic play to get Citigroup to agree to sell to Universal, the bidder that came with the greatest amount of risk. Vivendi chief executive Jean-Bernard Lévy said the company would pay £1.1 billion of the sale price ten months from this date, settling up with the final £100 million on completion. The company talked a bold talk, saying it was confident the deal would go through.

This was the biggest high-wire M&A (mergers and acquisition) strategy the music business had ever seen and getting this all past the regulators would bring a painful and dramatic denouement to the whole saga in the coming years.

For now, the bifurcated deal – together making up just 60 per cent of what Terra Firma paid for the company four years earlier – meant that Citigroup could recoup £2.5 billion of its original loan to Terra Firma alongside £200 million in fees from the original loan to Guy Hands's company. All in all, Citigroup's loss in the deal came to just under £700 million, according to estimates.

"Bank insiders characterised that as 'a good result' given that EMI was bought at the height of the credit boom and is being sold in a downturn,"[11] reported *The Guardian*.

"Universal offered what can only be described as a ridiculous amount of money," says one EMI executive who had close involvement in the entire sales process. "Ridiculously high. Citi were thrilled and amazed by how much money they got for that business – and it had clearly been turned around over the course of a couple of years. I had a conversation with the lead banker on the deal afterwards and I said that we could have held onto the business for another six months and waited until the debt markets reopened and we'd have got more money. He said, 'Look, if we had been offered even £400 million less, we probably would have hung onto it; but the amount of money that was on offer was such that we were not sure that we would get it again.'"

Warner Music had put up a good fight and was at first shocked and then furious that Universal came in and blew it out of the water. Edgar Bronfman Jr had stepped down as chief executive of Warner in August to focus on the company's long-term strategies and future transactions, prompting speculation that this was a run-up to an EMI bid. One senior source at Warner in New York claims that Len Blavatnik then "asked Edgar to help with the EMI acquisition" as the company felt that Universal, in the closing weeks emerging as the strongest counter-bidder to Warner, was either bluffing or grandstanding with its EMI plans.

"We never thought that Universal was credible in it," they say. "We said, 'Jesus! This guy Lucian Grainge just moved to the US to take [former UMG head] Doug Morris's job. He is fresh in the job and now he's going to try and buy EMI? Is he crazy? Because if that doesn't happen then he's out of a job!' It was such a big risk and we never thought they'd get it through the regulators."

The same source reveals that, having just bought Warner, Blavatnik was perhaps too diffident in his strategy here. "Probably on the heels of a Warner acquisition, Len didn't want to stretch too far for an EMI one," they say. "He wasn't even sure that Warner was a good investment yet. Of course, it turned out for him to be a spectacular investment. If he could have done it all over again, he probably would have doubled his bid for EMI. He was not sure if he should stretch for EMI even though Edgar at the time was telling him he should go for it and to not let it fall into the hands of Universal."

Now that Universal had trumped Warner in confidence and deftly outmanoeuvred it, the Warner team was left feeling a strange mixture of awe and shame. "To Lucian Grainge's credit, it is one of the ballsiest moves I've ever seen in my career as he literally put his entire career at stake on this acquisition that we never thought would clear regulatory approval," they say, suggesting that the Universal head was treating it all like a chess grand master, thinking six moves ahead of his opponents and mitigating for every eventuality.

"What Lucian did, which was masterful, was to carve out assets for sale," they say. "He said he would package these assets – some are good and some are pieces of shit – and put a big price tag on it and invite people to pay $800 million for it. He ended up getting EMI and all the good stuff with it – maybe minus Coldplay – and then getting another great price on the secondary sale of the Parlophone assets. We [Warner] knew we had lost the big fight. Lucian had done what no one thought he could pull off. Then we had to pivot very quickly because we really wanted some of these assets."

For Roger Faxon, it was a defiant and daring play by Universal that, thankfully for them, worked out in roughly the way Lucian Grainge and his advisors hoped it would. "The single reason that the business was able to be sold at that time – and not only sold at that time but broken up – was that Universal took 100 per cent of the antitrust risk," says Faxon. "The world had not changed that much, by the way, on the antitrust front – certainly not in the European Union. In the United States, it was exactly the same. They never saw an issue of consolidation in the record business anyway – or in the publishing business. In Europe, they were absolutely opposed to the transaction. Certainly, the independents were extremely vocal, as they had been at the time of the proposed Warner/ EMI merger and in the Sony/BMG merger as well. That made for a very long and arduous process. It took a year. The publishing business was nine months in waiting and the record business was a full year – or a little bit more than a year."

An EMI executive in the UK felt, if not deflated by, then certainly resigned to, the whole process. After so many years of uncertainty and upheaval, they were just glad the end point was coming. They had lost the energy to keep willing the company they had worked at for so many years to keep defying the odds. It had to end and, they surmised, there was never going to be a pretty ending – so it might as well be now before it got any more embarrassing for the company than it already was.

"By that point, EMI was just a shadow of itself as it had been asset-stripped completely – it was just a shell, basically," they sigh. "Warner were trying to buy us – but there was the whole regulatory risk. Universal took it on; Warner didn't. We never saw that coming. We knew there would be massive job losses then. But for me it was a bit, 'At least we're putting the old girl out of her misery.' We had been through so many permutations. It is only a company at the end of the day."

As Universal signed its 'definitive agreement' to buy EMI from Citigroup, independent trade body Impala was quick to come out swinging, arguing this was a consolidation process out of control that would seriously damage indie labels in the market and, as such, would have a highly deleterious impact on culture.

It said it was confident that the deal would be "blocked outright". The independent sector had already lobbied to block Warner/EMI in 2000 and then negotiated huge compensation and divestment commitments from Warner in early 2007 when it tried again to buy EMI. It felt its arguments against consolidation were more valid now than they were then and, as such, the European Commission would listen carefully to it.

"Given that Brussels has taken a previous decision that Universal should not be any bigger, we would expect the sale to Universal to be blocked outright, even if it offers to increase the divestments it is prepared to make," said Helen Smith, Impala's executive chair, in a statement. "The same would apply to Sony if it buys EMI publishing."[12]

Universal felt impervious and was sure that the divestment commitments it offered up as part of the sale would be enough to see it approved by the regulators.

"To be honest, the roadshow was fine and the initial sale was fine," says Andria Vidler of what was to follow. "What was the most painful was Universal buying it and then having twelve months under scrutiny from the EC. That was horrendous … For about twelve months, David Joseph [chairman and CEO of Universal Music Group UK & Ireland] and I kept meeting but we weren't sure what was going to happen."

The EMI staff bore the brunt of this as no one was sure what was happening – what parts of EMI would go to Universal and what parts would be sold off as part of the divestment process.

"We were just like horses that were whipped – 'You've got to keep going. You've got to keep going. Keep going so you keep your job,'" recalls one department head. "So, you had people doing twelve-hour days. The way I saw it was that it was like I was on a liner and I was safe there. Every now and again a wave would come along and a dozen people would be swept over the edge. Of the dozen who got swept off, half of them would sink and the other half would get to a desert island where they would create their own community and would learn all the skills they never thought they would have to. The people left on the liner were always looking over their shoulder because they knew at some point they were going over the edge too."

EMI was frozen in this hinterland for almost a year, uncertain of what was going to happen to the company. It took until 21 September 2012 to finally reach some clarity. The deal had passed through the regulators in Japan, Australia and the US, and now the European Commission finally rubber-stamped it – but with a large number of conditions attached.

Universal would have to divest the company of labels and catalogue that brought in around a third of EMI's revenues as well as key catalogue titles. What this effectively meant was that Universal took Virgin Records (but not Virgin Classics), and it would have to sell Parlophone, although Universal had deftly carved out The Beatles' catalogue from Parlophone so they could take EMI's crown jewels. "Lucian got The Beatles," snorts one very senior former EMI executive. "But there is a limit to how many times you can regurgitate the catalogue."

Universal would also have to sell off EMI's 50 per cent stake in the *Now That's What I Call Music* compilation brand as well as its operations in ten European markets.[13]

On top of this, the Chrysalis label would have to be sold, as would EMI Classics and the Mute catalogue.

Daniel Miller had already begun negotiating his way out of the EMI deal in 2009, and by September 2010, he and his staff were independent again – just before the wave of debt capsized Terra Firma. His timing appears powerfully prescient but he says it was pure serendipity. "It was a combination of luck and necessity rather than deeply and brilliantly anticipating the market," he says. The catalogue, however, was sold as part of the divestment process, meaning Miller had to effectively start from scratch again.

Asked what would have happened had Mute still been housed within EMI at the time of the sale to Universal, he says, "I think it would have been very bad news. I think they would have taken the big catalogue titles and maybe offered me an A&R position and put me in with Polydor or whoever. It was a bullet dodged! We're still going."

While it was generally accepted that Universal was forced to divest more of EMI than it had hoped, the world's biggest music company was still spinning it as a victory. "We are delighted Universal Music will retain over two-thirds of EMI on a global basis, contributing to the accretive nature of the deal," it said in a statement. "With a broad array of EMI artists from Katy Perry, Emeli Sandé [and] Robbie Williams … to icons like The Beatles, The Beach Boys, Genesis and Bob Seger, we remain true to our vision: to invest in talent and grow the company to offer consumers more music and more choice."[14]

Joaquín Almunia, the European Commission vice president in charge of competition policy, effectively argued that Impala's many fears were utterly unfounded as Universal was going to be a good operator here. "Competition in the music business is crucial to preserve choice, cultural diversity and innovation," he said in his statement. "The very significant commitments proposed by Universal will ensure that competition in the music industry is preserved and that European consumers continue to enjoy all its benefits."[15]

Also buried in the approval terms was a fascinating clause that Universal would have to drop the 'most favoured nation' clause in its deals with companies like Apple for ten years. This had effectively allowed Universal to have its deal terms matched if another major managed to negotiate more favourable terms.

Impala, as expected, was not best pleased with the overall results but felt that the heavy divestment was proof the regulators had listened to their opposition, trying to take some positivity from something they had long opposed. "This decision has finally put a freeze on Universal's ability to expand further and sets a benchmark for constraining abusive behaviour across the whole market," said Helen Smith. "Following the approval of the Sony/EMI merger, however, this decision nonetheless reinforces what is already a powerful duopoly. Contrary to the basic principles of competition in cultural markets, artists and consumers will ultimately pay the price."[16]

Martin Mills, chairman of Beggars Group and a long-standing Impala lynchpin, added a dark warning about how this would affect the market. "It's good to see that the Commission has seen this deal as such a threat to the market that it has demanded and received truly swingeing commitments to divestments," he said, before delivering a stinging caveat. "However, that should not conceal that fact that Universal's arrogance has paid off for them, that they have destroyed a significant competitor, and that even with these divestments their ability to dominate and control the market has reached even more unacceptable levels. Anyone trying to start a new digital service will be realising that very soon, and we will continue to look to the regulators to monitor ongoing behaviour."[17]

A painful pulling-apart of EMI was to follow but, for now, Universal bathed in the warm glow of a (two-thirds) victory that few had believed could happen. Impala, meanwhile, had to take stock of what had just transpired and figure out what the upside could be for the independents in a market where four major labels had suddenly become three. Those larger independents with the resources could bid for some of the divested assets and take comfort in growing their catalogues, but the overall feeling was that the biggest player in the market had been handed even more power and, for independent operators, that could never be seen as good news.

Not even the furniture was safe

In Wrights Lane, the enormity of what had just happened was quickly felt. The dream of EMI remaining as a unified company was now dead and people were going to lose their jobs. Again.

Andria Vidler had to break the news to EMI staff about what had just happened at the European Commission and explain – as much as she could, given that everything was still up in the air – what would happen next. "I was shocked myself [that] I had to stand up in the atrium of Wrights Lane and tell everybody that the bit that was going to go to Universal was Virgin and that was all," she says. "We were really surprised. Universal wanted to break us into eight pieces and we fought that. I argued it was going to destroy it [EMI] and we managed to get it broken into four pieces."

A gallows humour gripped the building. After all, they were now well used to being bought, sold and squeezed almost to the point of asphyxiation. This was just another agonising chapter they had to steel themselves for. "That was a weird time," says an EMI employee who had been through several years of false starts even before Terra Firma arrived. "[At first] Parlophone were going, 'Yay! We're all right! We're going over to Universal! It's going to be amazing!' Then it flipped a week later and the Virgin guys were going, 'Ha ha – fuck you! We're going to Universal! We're all right! What are you guys going to do?'"

For the executives at EMI, they still had to steer the company and ensure that things were running as normally as they could under these exceptional circumstances, exceptional even for EMI in the light of its past decade of upheaval. There was something of a battle of wills going on between the executives at EMI and those barely half a mile down Kensington High Street at Universal Music UK.

"When Universal were told they could only have Virgin, I was 'owned' by Universal," says Andria Vidler. "I had to run EMI in a way that enabled EMI to be as strong as possible, which was slightly contradictory to what Universal wanted to happen. They wanted EMI to be as weak as possible [to be able to take more of it under regulatory approval]."

Beyond the conspiracy theories about Universal trying to enfeeble EMI during its sales purgatory, things started to collapse into childishness and pedantry between the two companies.

Universal now believed it owned two-thirds of EMI so it started to slowly take control of the assets it had bought. This was not, however, just the master rights to the bulk of the company's recordings, but also its fixtures and fittings.

"It was only then that Universal started playing silly buggers," is how Andria Vidler puts it, still visibly shocked that the biggest major behaved in the way it did. "We came in one morning and every desk lamp had gone from the building. The overhead lights were there, but every table lamp, every sofa, anything that wasn't labelled as being connected to an artist from Parlophone was gone." This included signed photos and posters of EMI acts she had on her office wall. This did not land well.

"I came in and I was horrified," she says of the drastically depleted office space she found. "The team was having a meeting with an artist that day and there were no sofas. Universal were called, but the truth is the items were theirs as they had bought the company and, until they knew where each item was going, they wanted to keep it all in storage. It was a difficult situation as they were preventing us running the business actively. It was very clever tactics."

Another senior EMI staff member backs this up. "Things [from the office in Wrights Lane] would disappear overnight – things that were deemed property of Universal," they said. "One weekend, they came in and took the kettles! It became really painful. You had people wandering around with tape measures, measuring everything up. You would ask what they were measuring up for and they wouldn't say. It was a very difficult period. There were very barren offices. There were just empty spaces all over the place."

Vidler was not going to roll over and let this happen. She fought for the return of their office fixtures and furniture to allow the EMI staff to get on with their jobs. "We got most of it back," she says. "But we didn't get the pictures back. Ever. I never got my Robbie Williams signed picture back."

Meet the new bosses

David Kassler was involved in helping to get the EMI deal through the Competition Commission examination, with Universal arguing that the market had changed enormously since the Sony/BMG merger and, because digital was a new challenge for everyone, it should be allowed to bulk up by buying most of EMI.

When it was decided that Virgin and other assets would go to Universal, EMI had to create a new division – called Parlophone Label Group (PLG), to hold all the remaining assets. It covered Parlophone in the UK as well as several European markets.[18] Kassler says he was running PLG for around a year as chief executive. That involved ensuring that it operated as normally as possible and was hitting its profit targets.

Warner Music was the lead bidder for PLG and, wary of the regulatory hurdles, suggested a series of divestments of PLG and Warner assets, offering them for auction to independent labels as a means of appeasing Impala. Kassler also had to oversee which staff members went where. "We had a very complex separation to do," he says of the lengthy process. "The separation went down to album level."

On 7 February 2013, Warner signed its definitive agreement, pending final regulatory approval, to buy PLG from Universal for £487 million in an all-cash deal. Both sides in the transaction trumpeted it as a victory for themselves and a victory for their commitment to new music.

"This is a very important milestone for Warner Music, reflecting our commitment to artist development by strengthening our worldwide roster, global footprint and executive talent,"[19] said Len Blavatnik, chairman and founder of Access Industries, the owners of Warner Music Group.

Lucian Grainge, chairman and CEO of Universal Music Group, added, "Following this transaction, we will continue with our global reinvestment program that is rebuilding EMI and ensuring that the company is able to reach its full potential. And we're satisfied that our agreement with Warner Music will provide a home for PLG artists."[20]

One senior source close to all these discussions felt that Warner was able to benefit from Universal's over-ambitious strategy here. Universal had bid for all of EMI knowing it would have to sell some parts of the company. In the end, the source claims, Universal had to sell off far more than it had ever anticipated – and sell it quickly lest it scupper the deal as a whole. In a way, they argue, Universal put itself over a barrel and Warner was only too happy to offer it a quick and (comparatively cheap) resolution.

"The price to Universal was that it had to basically sell [a huge chunk] of the business," they say. "The question is this: why would you do that? Because the destruction of value was so great but there was no way that it would have made economic sense to make that acquisition. They did get a very good price from Len [Blavatnik for Parlophone]. He went in on a pre-emptive basis to do it. He was looking to buy EMI at the time. He was making offers at the time. He did not believe the bankers when they said that, in order to play, he had to come up meaningfully from where he was. He didn't want to lose out again so he went and made a pre-emptive offer to Universal. That's really the end of the saga."

From there, Warner worked with Impala to sell off an estimated 25–33 per cent of the PLG assets to independent labels,[21] a process that was overseen by former IFPI head John Kennedy. It was so intricate that it started in March 2014 but took until the end of 2017 for everything that needed to be sold to get through the process. This ignoble syphoning-off of EMI's past was not how it should have ended. It was death by a thousand divestments.

And with that, EMI evaporated.

* * *

On the website of Universal Music Group, there is a section entitled 'Our Labels & Brands'.[22] It is covered with the many logos of the labels that now make up the world's biggest record company, most of which have been acquired as part of an aggressive industry consolidation programme. There's Island, Capitol Music Group, Mercury, Decca, Deutsche Grammophon, Interscope Geffen A&M, Verve, Republic Records, Def Jam, Motown, Blue Note, Polydor and more. Click on any of them and you will find a potted history explaining just how culturally and musically important they were, with a link to their official website.

And, if you look closely, there quietly sits a three-letter iconic logo of a slightly different stripe: EMI. However, it is the exception here as there is no link to its official site, simply because one does not exist – except, due to a post-acquisition quirk, in Australia where its branding remains.

But also on the main UMG website is a more telling placement of the brand.

EMI, the major British company, with origins dating back to 1897, that took on the world – and, for a period between the early 1960s and early 2000s, was winning – is additionally listed *after* the label it bought in 1992. "Virgin EMI Records UK," it reads, complete with a link to the official site.

After all that, after all those incredible highs and chilling lows, this is what EMI has been reduced to. A suffix.

Epilogue

"It's difficult to say that it wasn't the worst private equity deal in history"

The dissipation of EMI, when it became absorbed into the portfolios of two of its biggest rivals, was not the conclusion to the story. The company that bought it in 2007 had one final court face-off with the bank that shockingly snatched it back in early 2011.

Having lost in a jury trial in New York and then won the right to an appeal, part two of Terra Firma v. Citigroup finally moved to the High Court in London in June 2016 – just over nine years after EMI's board accepted Terra Firma's bid of 265p a share and half a decade on from its spectacular loss of ownership.

While Guy Hands may have argued that he "was not happy that we won [the right to] appeal" and that he "just couldn't emotionally take it", there was a staggering amount of money at stake and, arguably more importantly for those operating in the victory-hungry world of high finance, there were reputations to salvage.

"The private equity tycoon Guy Hands reopened old wounds from the financial crisis at the High Court today, beginning a new claim against Citigroup for more than £1.5 billion over his calamitous buyout of the record label EMI,"[1] wrote the *Daily Telegraph* on 7 June 2016 as the case opened. It was expected to run for six weeks – considerably longer than the case in New York – and would, crucially, be heard in front of a judge, but no jury.

Part of the trial was reasserting the original claims heard by the New York jury in October and November 2010 – notably Terra Firma's assertion that Citigroup and David Wormsley wilfully misled it over a rival bid from Cerberus for EMI, tricking it into paying a share price at the top of the market that was locked into an unpayable debt package. Citigroup and Wormsley, of course, maintained this was erroneous in the extreme and that they were wholly innocent of all charges. Terra Firma was seeking at least £1.5 billion in damages from Citigroup, a significant step down from the £7 billion it was originally pursuing in the New York case.

But there were new claims as well. Terra Firma was now accusing Michael Klein, Citigroup's global head of investment banking at the time of the deal, of having deceived Guy Hands about Citigroup's own (highly negative) view of EMI as a business and an investment opportunity. Klein, it was alleged, had told EMI head Eric Nicoli in 2007 that, if the Terra Firma deal collapsed, it would trigger a "clusterfuck of massive proportions".[2] On top of this, Klein and Chad Leat, a credit specialist at Citigroup, "misled about the bank's attitude to EMI's debts and pressured Terra Firma into increasing its equity investment in EMI by £205 million"[3] while cutting Citigroup's own risk in financing the deal.

James Oldnall was one of the lawyers representing Terra Firma, acting for Clyde & Co., initially before moving to Mishcon de Reya in November 2011. His background was in loan and acquisition dispute resolution, covering banking litigation and arbitration. He had a long and rich history of working with private equity firms in disputes and had numerous high-profile cases under his belt.

He offers additional details on the new accusations against Klein and Citigroup. "One of the primary differences between the American case and the English case was that additional allegations were made in England as to representations that were made by Michael Klein as to the quality of the business," he says. "The allegation was that Guy had asked Michael Klein, 'What do you make of this business? Is it good? Is there anything wrong with it? Is this a deal that I should do?' And Michael Klein made representations to the effect that, 'Yes, this is a good company and is something that you should do.' That was all around that 21st of May [2007] period when Terra Firma was evaluating whether or not to make the bid."

Hands was understood to be spooked by EMI's succession of profit warnings coming into 2007 and wanted assurance from Klein that the business was a solid one. In the week leading into the bidding deadline of 21 May, Klein and Hands reportedly spoke on the phone a number of times, with the former assuring the latter that he was about to walk into a good deal.

In the High Court, Mark Howard QC, acting for Citigroup, distilled his client's rebuttal of the claims down to a blame-shifting strategy by Terra Firma. "The claim is a manufactured claim because Terra Firma is trying to pin the blame for a disastrous investment onto someone else,"[4] he said on the first day of the trial.

It was a mammoth undertaking for all concerned. "There were about 1,000 court documents," recalls Hands of the run-up to this case. "I am dyslexic. I hadn't read them. There was no chance I could read them."

This was more than a rehash of the New York trial just transposed to the UK as, in the intervening half-decade, new evidence and new arguments were being added by Terra Firma's legal team.

"It was very difficult because we had already been through the trial once and were trying to work out what was going to happen on this one," explains Hands. "The decision was made to go through the whole of the previous trial and see what else could be done under UK law. The case was expanded. It was a similar case, but it was a little bit broader."

Oldnall outlines the core of the case as he sees it. "Citibank had an obligation under the funding documentation to keep all of the commercial information and financial information that was provided to it as a result of the lending arrangement," he says. "There were certain covenants that had to be complied with and so the company had to hand over financial records to Citigroup so that Citigroup could establish whether those covenants were being complied with. There was a duty of confidentiality in what the bank was allowed to do with that information."

He continues, "It was allowed to seek third-party advice in relation to it, but it had to give notice to EMI – or to Maltby, which was Terra Firma's holding company [for EMI]. It had to give notice of when it sent any of that information out. In late 2007, Citigroup notified Maltby that a senior banking lawyer has been provided with the information under the facility documentation; and certain letters were written from the bank to Maltby suggesting that there had perhaps been a breach of the financing documents. This was purely in relation to the financial covenants."

He says that the context for the New York trial was effectively unprecedented, with the subtext being that a retrial in London was hoped to right some of the perceived wrongs in that case. "It was a very odd case in that it was a claim being brought in New York by an English company against an American company," says Oldnall. "It was in front of a New York jury but subject to English law. That is very unusual [in the US]. It is very common here [in London] to have cases heard pursuant to foreign law. And it happened in America as well. But the thing that is unusual there is that it is in front of a jury on a civil case. Whereas here you have a judge only and they will receive expert evidence as to what the foreign law is."

Fundamental to the Terra Firma appeal after the New York ruling was that Judge Rakoff had got key parts of English law wrong and this had, in their eyes, an adverse effect on how the jury reached its final decision to vote in favour of Citigroup.

"A particularly curious aspect of the case was that there was English law expertise put forward at the preliminary stage, but the judge had

Epilogue

spent a summer in Oxford[5] chasing girls back when he was a kid and so he thought he was perfectly fine to understand English law!" claims Oldnall. "Immediately following the case, we launched an appeal on the basis that the judge had misdirected the jury as to how English law worked. That went to the Second Circuit Appeals Court in the United States – and the Appeals Court agreed with us – that Judge Rakoff had gotten the test wrong. Therefore, because it was a jury trial, rather than there being a reversal of the decision, you have to do it again! Which is quite strange to an English lawyer."

The shifting of the case to London was, in many ways, the whole thing coming full circle. When originally served with its papers from Terra Firma, Citigroup (despite being headquartered in New York) originally moved to challenge the jurisdiction, arguing it should not be heard in the US but rather in the English courts as the finance documents were English and, to their mind, the whole case had English law written all over it.

For the retrial, following the appeal, Citigroup again argued that it should not be heard in New York and should take place in London. Terra Firma acquiesced, partly because it did not want to go through a jury trial again as the complexities and nuances of what happened – and the basis of the claims – could fall through the cracks again.

While the terms of his appointment by Terra Firma to act on its behalf preclude him from answering directly when this author asked if Guy Hands had sought an out-of-court settlement before the case opened in the High Court, Oldnall makes allusion to what typically might happen in the final days before a case of this magnitude opened. "What I can say to you is that the civil procedure here [in the UK] expects parties to attempt to resolve their disputes without recourse to the courts," he says. "There is a court process. You follow it. In any litigation, there are always people exploring the concept of avoiding the need to go to court."

The move to the UK meant that Terra Firma's case against Citigroup could go into considerably more forensic detail than the slightly more simplistic version that had to be tailored for the jury in New York. "There are different styles," says Oldnall of the fundamental distinctions between the US strategy and the UK strategy. "You're presenting to jury in America which means you have to dumb everything down. Really, really dumb it down."

This was partly why Terra Firma felt it had lost in New York. Hands and other witnesses perhaps went into too much detail, confusing the jury and losing them at key points. Also, with the performative aspect

329

of US jury trials, there was an admission that Citigroup's team categorically outperformed Terra Firma's team. If it was a personality test dressed up in litigation garments, Citigroup had shone while Terra Firma had stumbled.

A detail-heavy approach in London, Terra Firma felt, would play better to the complexity of the arguments it was putting forward.

"Courtrooms here [in the UK] are unbelievably dull – very, very, very dull," says Oldnall. "The way that you win cases is by being dull, not by being exciting. It is forensic. It is death by a thousand cuts. So, we had to rework the claim so that it was no longer prepared in the Hollywood style and instead prepared in the forensic style. That is not to say that there isn't a huge amount of skill required in taking this complex thing and making it a performance."

He says there was a protracted build-up to the case finally getting to London. It began with the court papers (known as the pleadings) and both sides had to take the original American pleadings and conform them to the English court style. After that came the disclosure process where both sides exchanged documents. Because an estimated 10 million documents had been exchanged before the New York trial, it was felt this was sufficient to satisfy the English courts.

"The law firms have their own professional obligations to the court and to the other side, so they are not allowed to be tricksy," explains Oldnall. "It is not just based on trust; there are professional obligations. But that is only on the law firm. In England, when you provide disclosure, you have to sign a declaration that you have done this and that you have done that. There is a sanction if you haven't done it. There are kind of rules."

However, he adds a caveat. "But, as you know, rules are there to be broken! Lawyers have techniques that they use to test the veracity of the disclosure that has been provided. When you have a population that is as big as 10 million [documents], you can run all sorts of data analytics over it to see what is there and what isn't. You can see disparities. So, if one individual only seems to be sending emails but not receiving them, you can say that that seems a bit odd. As the law firm preparing the disclosure, you know yourself what these techniques are – so you don't necessarily want to fall foul of them. You will be saying to your client, 'Are you sure that this is everything? This doesn't seem right and we are going to get criticised.' It kind of comes out in the wash."

As the documents requested from Citigroup by Terra Firma had already been combed through by their legal counterparts in New York, the London-based team were satisfied they had done most of the heavy lifting here. But where the UK process differs significantly from the US one is that witness statements are critical parts of the trial.

Due to Hands's dyslexia, this was to prove an arduous and painful process, taking around a year to get it down in a form that everyone on the team was satisfied with. "It was a lot of work," says Oldnall. "His dyslexia did make it a slightly more challenging process than if you were working with someone who is in the business of writing things down. That took a long time. But also, it is a complex subject matter. A long period of time had passed and it was sometimes like being a hypnotist to try and get Guy back into the time and go through the emails to reconnect with that time."

There were mutterings from some in Terra Firma's team that, in both the New York case and the London case, Citigroup's lawyers pounced on Hands's dyslexia and used it as something to both beat him with and to trip him up. "I couldn't comment on that," says a diplomatic Oldnall. "What I am prepared to say is that cross-examination in the English civil court is not the friend of the dyslexic. That environment is incredibly tough for anyone. And even tougher [for someone with dyslexia]. He knew it was going to be tough. And it was."

Hands himself argues that – most assuredly – his dyslexia was used against him in the London trial and that this was both demeaning and anguishing for him. "The judge said he didn't know what dyslexia was – he made that quite clear," claims Hands. "They had said that because I couldn't read, they would read [the court papers] out to me. Having documents read to you and then being asked technical questions on them is very difficult to say the least. On a couple of occasions, I would ask what a certain word meant. [Mr Justice Burton] said, 'Mr Hands, surely you know what that word means?' I just felt completely humiliated. I thought I just wasn't going to be able to win and I just wanted it over. I didn't know what the judge felt. I couldn't get advice from my lawyers about what the judge might be thinking or what it meant."

On the second day of the trial, it was revealed that Hands had personally lost €200 million because of the collapse of the EMI deal. He added that his reputation in the City had been severely tarnished as a result, preventing him from steering Terra Firma to become a 'mega firm'.

Mark Howard, for Citigroup, argued that Terra Firma was trying to perform a 'shakedown' on his client to get the bank to settle the claims of fraudulent misrepresentation. He cited Terra Firma's filing of legal proceedings in a Manchester court in 2013 as proof of this 'shakedown' strategy as it had been done surreptitiously.[6]

Howard picked up on the fact that the Manchester filing had made allegations against Chuck Prince, the chief executive of Citigroup at the time, but they had been subsequently removed. Howard accused Hands of making these, in his eyes, false claims against Prince to embarrass Citigroup into settling. "That's not correct,"[7] responded Hands.

When asked by the judge if the fact that he and David Wormsley had discussed what Cerberus was bidding for EMI was a breach of confidentiality terms, Hands accepted it might be viewed as improper but was deemed standard market practice at the time. "I didn't think it was dishonest,"[8] was his reply when asked if being party to the details of a rival bid was honest.

By day three, Mark Howard was accusing Hands of having a "hazy memory" due to "gross discrepancies" between the evidence given in New York in 2010 and the evidence now being proffered in London. Hands's story, he said, was "all over the place".[9]

He accused Hands of reverse-blaming Wormsley for advising him to go in at 265p a share in order to defeat a rival bid from Cerberus. "You had a confusion in your mind about where the 265[p] came from and you have sought subsequently to attribute it to Mr Wormsley," said Howard. "The truth slips out. That is the truth." Hands denied it categorically, but Howard said it was "something you have made up subsequently".[10] He added later in proceedings, "The problem is, Mr Hands, your story is shifting and it is impossible to reconcile these different versions."[11]

On the accusation of having a "hazy memory", Hands, away from the white heat of the courtroom, now offers this defence. "That is what they tried to say – but that is not correct," he claims. "We never actually got on to the evidence I gave in New York. So that is not correct. What they asked me about was the confidentiality agreement [between us and Citigroup] which no one in New York had ever asked me for. And I couldn't remember that. So, they said, 'Mr Hands, your memory is fallible, isn't it?' And I said, 'Yes, my memory is fallible after nine years.' They took that and basically argued that my memory was now hazy. In that, they are taking stuff that isn't correct. They didn't actually ask me about stuff that I said back in 2007."

He feels Citigroup's team were trying to set booby traps for him by spotting inconsistencies in the various witness statements and testimonies he had provided over the past six years. "By then I had given two lots of testimony in court, one deposition and two witness statements," he says. "So, I had covered the same stuff five times. What they were trying to do was find some gaps in the five times which they could pick on. Actually, what they really picked on was stuff I hadn't even covered in any of the five times. It was really like a memory test."

Oldnall offers an expansion of this. "One of the reasons why Guy's witness statement is so complex is because the deal didn't close until the 31st of August [due to the shareholder approval process]," he says.

Epilogue

"There was a Mexican standoff, and this is all in Guy's [witness] statement, where both parties were in a difficult position. The acceptances hadn't been coming in, the market was starting to shift, the terms upon which Citi had offered the funding in May no longer seemed so commercially attractive. Guy couldn't understand why Citi wasn't prepared to sign up to the funding. Citi started dragging its heels on the funding and Guy sought comfort from Michael Klein and Chad Leat."

He continues, "[Guy] asked them, 'Is there something you're not telling me? Is there something about the business that is wrong and that you don't want to lend me the money any more?' They said, 'No, no – it's nothing to do with the company. It's all to do with the market.' The allegation that Terra Firma was making was, actually, it was about the company and Citigroup's own internal records show that they had quite a dim view of EMI and its ability to repay its existing financing. Its existing funding was £700 million and Guy was about to borrow £2.6 billion. If the company can't support £700 million, how's it supposed to support £2.6 billion?"

As with the New York case six years earlier, Hands got a growing sense that Citigroup was going to triumph again, and Terra Firma was going to be sprawled on the canvas, bloodied and broken. By day four, he had had enough and was not prepared to see if he could last the distance over six weeks. In a shock move, on Friday 10 June, the whole EMI/Terra Firma story came to a bitter conclusion when Hands withdrew the action. "I stopped it – nobody else did," says Hands. "The lawyers weren't allowed to advise me. Once you are on the stand, you can't be advised by anyone. So, you are not allowed to get any advice. You're not allowed to do that in New York either."

There were exceptional circumstances at play that he did not make public at the time but now says need to be factored in when trying to understand why he pulled the case. On the weekend before the case opened, his mother-in-law passed away and, as the trial progressed, the stress exacerbated his diabetes. This, on top of the bullying by stealth he felt he was receiving due to his dyslexia, forced his hand.

"My diabetes was out of control," he says as the trial went into its fourth day. "The judge kept asking me, if I wasn't feeling well, to tell him. My diabetes was seventeen and my sugar levels are meant to be below seven. When you get to seventeen, you find difficulty in focusing. I was having problems reading. On the first day, the judge said that I needed to go home and read the court papers that weekend. The problem was that I couldn't answer the questions. They were just asking me things that I couldn't answer. Part of that was that they were asking me things I never knew anything about. And part of it was that they were asking me

333

things that were pretty minor and which, after nine years, I hadn't really focused on."

Events had, he felt, become so insurmountable for him that he had no other option but to walk away in defeat. "I came to the conclusion that for us to prove that they [Citigroup] had committed fraud – and this was my conclusion, it wasn't anybody else's – was going to be very difficult. I was going to have another four days in the witness box because that is the minimum they said they wanted. Another four days in the witness box not being able to answer the questions because I couldn't think straight [was not desirable]. To get the diabetes back under control once you have lost control of it is quite difficult."

Asked why he did not move to ask for a hiatus in the trial due to medical reasons, he says, "I could have but I had been advised beforehand that that wouldn't look good to the judge."

He got a message to his legal team to speak to Citigroup's lawyers. Hands wanted them to give him permission to halt proceedings and confer with his lawyer. Citigroup responded that he could speak to his lawyer – but only with regard to settlement; they were not giving permission for Hands and his legal team to discuss any other aspect of the case.

"I asked him [my lawyer] on what grounds Citigroup would settle," says Hands. "Citigroup said they would settle if I withdrew the claim. So, we withdrew the claim. I said I just wanted to get out of this and we should withdraw the claim."

David Wolfson, himself standing in for lead QC Anthony Grabiner, issued a brief statement. "Terra Firma confirms it unreservedly withdraws its allegations of fraud,"[12] it said.

Terra Firma had agreed to pay Citigroup's legal fees – but only what the judge defined as "reasonable legal costs" – that ran to £8.5 million. They also had to agree that this was the full stop and that no legal action would be revived against Citigroup in the future.

And, with that, the last big private equity deal before the 2007 global crash, which had ended up in ignominy for Terra Firma and the desecration of EMI, finally rolled to a stop.

* * *

"We have always maintained that the allegations made by Terra Firma were entirely baseless and that Citigroup, specifically David Wormsley, Michael Klein and Chad Leat, acted at all times with absolute honesty and professional integrity throughout the EMI transaction," ran Citigroup's victorious statement outside the High Court. "We are very pleased that Terra Firma has unreservedly withdrawn the allegations, agreed to the dismissal of the proceedings and will pay Citigroup's costs in relation to this matter."[13]

Despite effectively losing twice to Citigroup, Hands was trying to draw a line under it all and focus on the future in his statement. "The matter is now closed," he said. "We have an exciting portfolio of companies, a talented and experienced team, supportive and loyal investors and €1 billion of capital to invest."[14]

* * *

Senior EMI executives who worked with Hands and under him during those years of Terra Firma ownership had plenty to say once the whole story was finally over. None were sympathetic to Hands or the very public and chastening drubbing he had received.

"His ability to rewrite history, you've seen," says one. "You've seen it in court cases. The trouble is that you will have no way of knowing if any of what he says to you is true. You will have no way of knowing … He is a piece of work. He is a very unusual character. Do not underestimate the size of his ego and his inclination to get very, very shirty if people have said unkind things about him."

Another adds, "Can he accept responsibility for his own mistakes? Or is he a bit Morrissey where it is always someone else's fault? I think he's a bit Morrissey. I think he thinks it was still the right thing to do and the plan was the right one. First the markets conspired against him because of the collapse and he could never have foreseen that. Then he was misled by EMI management as they were all trying to keep their jobs. Then he was deceived by the banks. I think he genuinely believes that Citibank deceived him in order to take his money and close the deal."

A third concludes, "[Chuck] Prince and Guy were fighting tooth and nail to try and get the deal to work. And Prince won, I guess, because he made the covenants that much tighter and all sorts of things. For somebody like Guy, this is – when you take this emotion out of it – where he is his most talented. And he was blinded to it. This is not a retrospective thing; it was obvious at the time that the markets weren't going to come back and he was going to get trapped. But ego gets in your way. He didn't want to back away and be seen as a failure. And Citibank didn't feel that it could back away as they would then forever be barred from doing high-yield transactions. But they both got caught up in their egos as opposed to the realities of the marketplace … I think Guy was in love with the idea of owning EMI. Like a lot of people in the financial world, they love music and he just wanted to own it. He built a confection of a story around what he would do. The business case that he was making to his investors didn't hold up."

As for Hands himself, he feels enough time has passed for him to be self-reflexive enough to accept the mistakes he made here and, in accepting them, try to come to some sort of peace with them.

Damian Reece of the *Daily Telegraph* had termed it "one of the worst private equity deals in history"[15] and Hands says he cannot disagree.

"It's difficult to say that it wasn't," he says. "From the point of view of private equity, yes. My job as a private equity person is to make money for my investors. I think we did a good turnaround of EMI, but it didn't help because EMI was still broken up by Citigroup."

Terra Firma itself has gone public on the bitter lessons it had to learn here and outlined the safeguards it has put in place to prevent it from being so spectacularly burned in the future. On its website is a document entitled 'The EMI Investment: An Analysis', in which the private equity company outlines how the deal came about, what its goals were and why the firm feels it all went so badly wrong.

"In light of our experience with EMI and the entire pre-credit crisis period, we have concluded that Terra Firma can mitigate the downside risks of these transactions by: prohibiting cross-fund investments; and reducing the targeted co-investment on any deal from 20% to 5%," it reads. "Going forward, Terra Firma will implement these structural limitations. Terra Firma will limit its concentration in any one investment to 15% with the intention of selling it down by 5%, leaving our funds with a net 10% exposure. We will also encourage LPs [limited partners] interested in committing to substantial co-investment to ensure that they are in a position where they are able to underwrite and commit to the deal at the same time that we do."[16]

It concludes, in part, by shifting blame towards Citigroup and the auction process back in May 2007, but also chastens itself for arguably walking into the deal with its eyes closed. "The risks associated with EMI were not fundamentally different from those that we assess with every transaction," it says. "Of course, we would never have purchased EMI on the day we did at the price we did had we known about the nature of the auction and the fact that without our bid it would have been busted. Regardless, what Terra Firma now intends to do, armed with these insights and lessons learnt, is to ensure that history is not repeated."[17]

Hands does, however, try and find some threads of glory amid the tattered fabric of defeat. "I think we changed the music industry," he says. "I really do believe we changed the music industry. For the better. Definitely for the better. I think it's a shame. I think there's things we would have done if we had had more time. And I think there are things we would have done better if we had had a better relationship with Citigroup and we didn't have the pressure of the debt."

EMI is the three-letter acronym that will haunt Guy Hands forever – both defining him and shaming him. No matter how big a deal he pulls off in the future, the disaster of EMI will always be thrown back at him. He told an audience at the LSE in London, a whole year and a half before the final face-off with Citigroup in the High Court, that EMI was "a name I try and forget".[18]

But try as he might to forget the name EMI, others will not, and so, against his will, Guy Hands is eternally fated to live in its shadow.

Appendix

Vox pops: assorted thoughts on why EMI ended the way it did

Having spoken to many sources for this book, this author heard a wide range of theories about why EMI ended the way it did. There is no simple reason – it was the snowballing of a thousand different factors over decades, some of EMI's own making, but many not. All that and, in the final two decades of its life, EMI had a run of phenomenally bad timing.

Staff would commonly joke that the acronym EMI stood not for "Electric & Musical Industries" but rather for "Every Mistake Imaginable". That was born out of typically British self-effacing humour; but in charting its final years, this epitaph now takes on a bleakly poetic resonance. In a darkly inappropriate way, one is left with the feeling that EMI wouldn't have had it any other way.

Here are just some of the closing thoughts and theories of those who, for part or most of their careers, were proud to have played a role, no matter how small, in the story of arguably the greatest record company that ever existed.

—

"There was this idea the EMI was just shit. But that was not the case. The people were great and the artists were great. It was the general circumstances around them that had nothing to do with the artists but had to do with the banking industry. That cast a cloud, in many respects unfairly, on things" – Billy Mann.

—

"I was really sad to see what happened to it. I was really sad to see a company that survived for over 100 years get ransacked and destroyed into less than its component parts in under eighteen months. That was shocking. I was also angry that people who had no understanding whatsoever didn't try to have any understanding of the world that they had bought into. I feel particularly sad at the outcome. It was just a catastrophe from start to finish, driven by egos who wouldn't listen but who had enough money to indulge in something that was fundamentally flawed" – senior EMI UK executive.

—

"We were not bringing in a lot of new art. We didn't really figure out how to monetise the art that we had very well and we didn't bring down costs. We had huge debt overlay. The Citigroup debt was weighing over everyone's heads. We had lots of conversations about it. Guy had got advised early on to do some relationship-building with those Citigroup folks and get some of that debt written off. Which probably they would have done. But that didn't happen for a variety of reasons … [The debt] was pricing for perfection. And we weren't perfect" – Douglas Merrill.

—

"It was a really tough time. This could have been an opportunity to really change the music industry and to both restructure contracts and restructure the economics. It was an opportunity to blaze a trail and set a path for the future – it was time to look at rights that had previously been ignored and then to reassess where we were with regard to changes in copyright and content distribution via the internet. At the start I was really excited when Terra Firma talked about wanting to do that. When it failed, not only was it a worry based on our jobs and job security, it was also a frightening projection into the future of what might lie ahead for all major labels. If EMI could have achieved all those changes, it would have set the tone for the entire industry and its future" – EMI UK digital executive.

—

"I think Terra Firma broke one of the best record companies there ever was. They are responsible for the fact that there is no EMI. And I think that's a terrible shame" – EMI UK executive.

—

"People took views. Was it a good time or was it a bad time? Frankly, it was neither good nor bad. It was some good and some not so good. What was good? What we achieved. What was not so good? The uncertainty for people. That is why people will remember some of the negative stuff. The stresses and strains. It was a very stressful time and there were a lot of moving parts. There isn't one truth here. Some people think that and some people think this. If you looked at the plan, it wasn't a bad plan. It was just that the timing wasn't good. It wasn't the business that failed; it was the debt" – Charles Allen.

—

"My view is that Terra Firma paid a lot – I don't think it was much too much – but under different ownership it might have been successful. I think they fucked it up royally in the way that they managed it and the way that Guy changed the management several times. He replaced them with people who didn't have a clue" – senior EMI Group executive.

—

"I think there were two phases to Terra Firma's reign. There was the first phase where Guy Hands was in charge personally. I wasn't there but from everything I read it was a disastrous year. I think a lot of damage was done then. There were a lot public statements that really didn't help. There was a lot of resentment and a lot of good people left. The second half was when Elio [Leoni Sceti] came in, Guy Hands stepped away, and Elio brought in a professional management team, including myself and a number of other very, very talented individuals and we did exceptional work. I would say the work I did at EMI is the crowning achievement of my career. At no point have I been able to come into an organisation – a sceptical organisation as well – and articulate a bold agenda around a consumer-led transformation that was then enthusiastically adopted by the existing team and that delivered very significant and tangible results. That was extraordinary. What we did was leading for the industry and, frankly, extraordinary in its own right. That was very much to the credit, ultimately, of Guy because he brought in a team to achieve that. We would have carried on and gone on to do, I think, really extraordinary things" – Ernesto Schmitt.

—

"When Terra Firma came in, I just looked at it all and thought, 'This is a mess. You're all cunts. I want to get out of here.' I was fascinated for a minute but then I was pretty comfortable with leaving. Well, they [Terra Firma] weren't trying to murder anyone, were they? But I don't think you can say that private equity necessarily has good intentions; the intention is to make as much money as possible. The legacy of Terra Firma? It's just the death of EMI, isn't it? It was the death of the label. The legacy? It's gone" – senior EMI UK executive.

—

"EMI is the story of the last gasp of the record industry. It's a flippant statement, but not only is Guy Hands the man who killed EMI, he is also the man who might have killed the record industry" – EMI consultant.

—

"I genuinely think that Guy and the team did want to change, positively, the music industry. They were prepared to say things that maybe if you wanted to smooth the waters, you just wouldn't have said. I do think that in some cases desire to say things in a straight, direct and sometimes very challenging way [meant] some would have taken that and misinterpreted what the objective was. The whole time I was there I very much felt that what we were trying to do was to make the music industry better – not to in any way destroy the music industry!" – Mark Hodgkinson.

—

"I think that the misunderstanding about Terra Firma is that it was only about cost. And that is not the case. The reality is that there is a true vision about repositioning companies in different ways that is better fitting the new environment and the new markets. There is a true market- and consumer-driven vision which is then enabled by some cost optimisation that gives you the cash to achieve that vision. I think that the market thinks that Terra Firma is just about slashing costs. I think that's a mistake. That's not the case … I would have wished for EMI to become independent financially and to be in a position therefore to buy Warner or others. It kills me the fact that EMI today has been broken into pieces and every other major owns a piece. It is not satisfactory" – Elio Leoni Sceti.

—

"I think Terra Firma came in very arrogantly. Do I think they came in with good intentions but executed them badly? Yes. I think they should have spent more time really understanding the business, getting to understand the people within the business and understanding the people within it that they needed to listen to and trust; but, bar a few people, they didn't trust any of them. They didn't respect our experience or our knowledge. They came in with an attitude of this is how they were going to do it and railroaded people – making some very big mistakes along the way. It was clunky and it was cumbersome. They were like a bull in a china shop. And they fucked it up" – senior EMI UK executive.

—

"EMI was top heavy with lots of executives paid an absolute fortune. It was ripe for a clear out; but it was drastic what happened" – EMI UK department head.

—

"The first thing is that it was a complete financial fiasco, disaster and insult to one of the biggest companies the UK has ever created. They [Terra Firma] destroyed the lives of thousands of people and artists. You know *The Bonfire of the Vanities*? It was at least that. There was such destruction. This company survived 110 years before Guy Hands took over. In three years, he managed to kill it. It's a pity. It's more than a pity. It's a corporate disaster. It's a creative and music disaster. It's a social disaster. And it's a human disaster. It's just terrible. Just because you were running some toilets on the German motorway, you think you're going to be running the toilets in a record company? Come on. This is beyond understanding. The second thing, I hope, is that this will become a business management case study at places like Harvard Business School of what not to do from day one to day 1,000" – senior EMI Group executive.

—

"I was really dismayed. I thought it was a real shame because a lot of what EMI did was right. Things like the relationships they were building with partners, what they were doing with digital marketing, what they were trying to do in terms of making the company lean and mean [were good]. I think a lot of what they were doing was so right and it was just a shame that they lost it" – Shamsa Rana, consultant to Terra Firma.

—

"Could Guy Hands have made it work? The conditions under which he bought it, it was impossible. No one would have done it. No one. It was a mistake from the start. I was with some of my senior management colleagues at the beginning, we looked at the deal he did and said it was never going to happen. If Guy Hands, instead of pushing to buy the company at the end of August [2007], had done his due diligence for six months [it would have been very different]. When you spend £4.2 billion on a company, don't listen to other people's advice. Listen to yourself. Because this is your fucking responsibility! Trying to be the biggest dealmaker in the UK? That's called an ego trip" – former EMI Group executive.

—

342

"One of the misconceptions is that the Terra Firma thesis was all about cost. Whereas actually what I think got Guy and Terra Firma excited about the industry in the first place were the digital changes that were happening. When you look particularly at China and India, the sheer number of people who are going to be coming into the middle classes there is just extraordinary. Did they get their models wrong with the timing of that? Absolutely. They forecast it happening much earlier. That was definitely an error in the model. I think Guy was right in terms of the opportunity but wrong in terms of the timing" – David Kassler.

—

"I think some of the intentions were good but I also think there were a number of not necessarily core Terra Firma executives – perhaps some of the people they brought in from the outside to help with this – who got a little star-fucked. The notion of hanging out with the Beastie Boys or Katy Perry was incredibly alluring, enticing and attractive. I get it. Those evenings can be memorable and a lot of fun. But the next morning, when the hangover wears off, those same people want to know what the plan is. You need good, solid, confident people that are going to write that plan and execute that plan. There was a lot of terrible politics and ugliness. I look back at it as a fairly unhappy and miserable time in my life. I am happy to have it in the rear-view mirror. It is unfortunate. There was a ton of really great, smart people who either lost their jobs entirely or were forced out of an industry that they really liked working in. It's a shame" – EMI US executive.

—

"It was like Alan Partridge taking over a record company. It was a miscalculation about how Terra Firma could turn around the company. It was something that had already hit an iceberg. It wasn't like it was about to hit it – it had already hit it. What's the difference between EMI and the *Titanic*? The *Titanic* had a good band!" – EMI UK staffer.

—

"I saw it as a tragedy. I cared about Terra Firma. I cared about EMI. I saw EMI as a great British institution and I wanted to see it thrive and flourish. I was absolutely confident that it was heading in the right direction and it would be a great company again. Terra Firma's steward-ship was very benign and indeed critical to its future success. With time, not only would EMI have grown strong again, but Terra Firma would have recovered its investment. I was operating elsewhere by the time that all of this happened, but it was a tragic outcome" – Lord Birt.

—

"It's kind of weird that EMI no longer exists. But life is life and sometimes these things happen" – Marco Alboni, former head of EMI Italy.

—

"EMI was an historically brilliant brand. It was inevitable that only the strong were going to survive through this revolutionary period [with digital]. It wasn't time for an evolution of the music business; it needed to be revolutionised. EMI had that opportunity to revolutionise, be bold and move forward aggressively. It just got hung up with itself and all the wasteful processes that went on there. Only the strong were going to survive – and in order to be strong, you really needed to be different. You needed to offer an alternative where artists and managers, as well as marketing opportunities, were coming to you rather than running away from you. I think they had a real fighting chance to re-engineer themselves into a 21st century record company before the others. Unfortunately that didn't happen" – senior advisor.

—

"Did I meet Guy Hands? Yeah, he used to be in the building and he used to walk around. If you were being very basic, you would say that he is everything that you hate. But that is too simplistic. He obviously is a really great businessman – but he fucked up" – Murray Chalmers, former head of press at Parlophone.

—

"In terms of comic timing, Terra Firma had the joke but they delivered the punchline at the wrong time. But actually, because of the way they began, they had the wrong punchline. The tumbleweed had already started before they even delivered it" – senior EMI UK executive.

—

"Well, Terra Firma were a bunch of fucking idiots. They just thought they were geniuses. The kings of the universe. And they weren't. They didn't understand the power of the artist manager. They just thought that we could tell the artist what to do. Managers are these massive power centres that you need to bring along with you. They didn't realise and that is one of the big reasons why they fucked up. In a way, if it wasn't Terra Firma, it would have been someone else. The company just wasn't strong enough in that market at that time. It just happened to be them. But they were all terrible in their own way" – EMI Group executive.

"It was terrible timing. Unfortunately, at the time that Guy invested in EMI and bought it, he realised it wasn't an EMI problem; it was an industry-wide problem. He came in as the whole bloody industry was imploding. It was going to take some really clever thinking to solve that … At the end, I felt that he destroyed EMI. And he destroyed a lot of careers with it. I absolutely accept that was unintentional but, at the end, he had done too rich a deal, he had spent too much money, he had loaded the company with debt – and that meant there was no way out. When you look back at it, there was absolutely no way that he was ever going to be able to turn this around having committed and taken on the debt. No matter how well intentioned [he was going in], he is a money man and he is an investor and this is what they do; they invest and they expect a return. He clearly invested with a view to making a return. I do think he was prepared to give it a longer period before making that return than he would normally. But unquestionably he overpaid and that was the killer mistake. That was the blow. It really was a sad, sad ending. It sort of dissolved. There's not really an EMI left" – Tim Clark, ie:music.

—

"Those six years were death by a thousand cuts. What's the difference between Tony Wadsworth and Guy Hands? Tony was someone who you believed in and Guy just wasn't" – EMI UK department head.

—

"Terra Firma was an example of bad market timing but also arrogance, a complete lack of understanding of the business, a complete lack of sensitivity to what artists go through and how difficult it is to be an artist. Those meetings with acts like Radiohead really showed their complete arrogance. Look at the people that they brought in! When you have no feel for the business, you come in with a sense of arrogance of, 'Hey – these guys must be stupid! They're music people – how smart can they be?' Their claim to fame was that they fixed the toilets at the rest stops for truck drivers in Germany. That's great. But I grew up in this business and the thing that I can tell you is that the good thing about the music business is that there is no barrier to entry for anybody, which is why I like it; but it can also be a bad thing because you got a lot of lunatics who probably should not be in any professional setting whatsoever" – former Warner Music US executive.

—

"They went in with good intentions but also with the arrogance of City people. City people have a God complex. They really do feel that they are omnipotent. Some of them anyway. Money does make the world go round in lots of ways. You can understand how it makes them absolutely power crazy. Yes, the intentions were to make a turn on the company and sell it for three times as much in five years' time. If that was their intention, then fine. At least the company would have been actually functioning. Instead, because of that arrogance and that feeling that they would succeed where everybody else has, in your mind, failed – but actually they haven't failed and they are just trying to reinvent a wheel that hasn't been invented yet – then it is going to fall apart. The end result of it is that in a four-year period, they managed to destroy a century-old British institution. I think that's some feat. I hope he [Guy Hands] feels bad about it. It was a failure and he can't blame on it external factors. He can't blame it on Citigroup. Even though he tried to. He can't blame it on the financial crisis. But he will blame it on everybody apart from himself. They managed to fuck up something which was, without being jingoistic about it, a great British brand that had, through the years, provided innovation, world-class brands, helped the soft power of the UK and been at the forefront of most new developments in music. They treated it like a German motorway service station" – senior EMI UK executive.

—

"People say Terra Firma killed EMI. Terra Firma did not kill EMI. EMI, one way or another, would have ended up in the hands of someone else – be that Warner or whoever. There was a degree of inevitability about that. Those were sad years for EMI. Those years were the downfall for EMI. The fact that Guy Hands and Terra Firma were at the helm [is almost irrelevant]. If it hadn't been them, it would have been somebody else. That's my view on it. They were just, in a way, the unlucky ones. They were the ones holding the parcel when the music stopped. But unfortunately there were no chocolates in the parcel at the end" – senior EMI Group executive.

—

"I was the guy who tried to save EMI – not knowing that it needed saving as badly as it did – and I failed. One doesn't like one's failure. I can blame timing. I can blame Citigroup. I can blame a lot of things out there but, at the end of the day, it was my responsibility. It's not great. Emotionally, I have to move on from it. It took up nine years of my life. I moved away from my family. I moved out of the UK. There were other issues, but this was a big part of those issues. By 2009, I couldn't go into a restaurant in London without people coming up to me. Literally not a restaurant. It didn't matter where I went, people came up to me and started talking to me about EMI … I want to learn from it. I can't say it wasn't an interesting experience. But at the end of the day, I need emotionally to try and forget it. More importantly, I can't let it define me" – Guy Hands, Terra Firma.

—

Notes

Prologue

1. https://www.rollingstone.com/music/news/hundreds-of-jobs-lost-in-universal-mega-merger-19990122

Chapter 1: Chicken Salad and Chicken Shit

1. Brian Southall, *The Rise & Fall of EMI Records*, 2012, p. 63.
2. Ibid.
3. Ibid.
4. http://variety.com/2013/biz/news/edgar-bronfman-sr-billionaire-head-of-former-mca-owner-seagram-co-dead-at-84-1200987175/
5. F. Goodman, *Fortune's Fool: Edgar Bronfman Jr, Warner Music and an Industry in Crisis*, 2010, p. 92.
6. Ibid., p. 93.
7. Ibid., p. 94.
8. https://www.theguardian.com/media/2011/jan/21/edgar-bronfman-jr-vivendi
9. http://news.bbc.co.uk/1/hi/business/797146.stm
10. Southall, *The Rise & Fall of EMI Records*, p. 81.
11. Ibid., p. 79.
12. http://www.ifpi.org/content/library/worldsales2000.pdf
13. In like-for-like terms, this figure should really be $14 billion as IFPI began adding synchronisation revenue to its numbers in 2010, partly to make the global decline seem less bitter.
14. http://www.washingtonpost.com/wp-srv/pmextra/jan00/10/aolmain.htm
15. http://fortune.com/2015/01/10/15-years-later-lessons-from-the-failed-aol-time-warner-merger/
16. Southall, *The Rise & Fall of EMI Records*, p. 100.
17. *Music Week*, 26.02.00, p. 11.
18. https://www.theguardian.com/media/2000/oct/05/citynews2
19. Southall, *The Rise & Fall of EMI Records*, p. 124.
20. https://www.theguardian.com/world/2001/oct/23/gender.uk1
21. http://www.independent.co.uk/news/people/profiles/nancy-berry-she-enjoys-the-rocknroll-lifestyle-the-trouble-is-she-works-in-rocknroll-9167174.html
22. Ibid.
23. Southall, *The Rise & Fall of EMI Records*, p. 75.
24. http://news.bbc.co.uk/1/hi/entertainment/1777172.stm
25. Southall, *The Rise & Fall of EMI Records*, p. 136.

26. Ibid.
27. http://www.telegraph.co.uk/finance/2737736/EMI-chucks-Berry-as-Levy-wins-record-pay.html
28. Southall, *The Rise & Fall of EMI Records*, p. 126.
29. Ibid., p. 127.
30. Ibid., p. 133.
31. https://www.telegraph.co.uk/finance/newsbysector/mediatechnologyandtelecoms/2792706/EMI-parts-company-with-Jean-Francois-Cecillon.html
32. Southall, *The Rise & Fall of EMI Records*, p. 157.
33. http://edition.cnn.com/2003/BUSINESS/11/06/sony.bmg.reut/
34. Southall, *The Rise & Fall of EMI Records*, p. 158.
35. Ibid.
36. https://www.theguardian.com/media/2003/nov/24/citynews.business
37. Southall, *The Rise & Fall of EMI Records*, p. 145.
38. Ibid., p. 68.
39. Ibid., p. 91.
40. Ibid., p. 96.
41. http://news.bbc.co.uk/1/hi/business/4242293.stm
42. Southall, *The Rise & Fall of EMI Records*, p. 68.
43. Southall, *The Rise & Fall of EMI Records*, p. 143.
44. https://www.theguardian.com/music/2015/sep/03/heavenly-records-at-25-saint-etienne-beth-orton
45. http://news.bbc.co.uk/1/hi/entertainment/1984966.stm
46. Ibid.
47. Ibid.
48. https://www.theguardian.com/business/2004/mar/31/money
49. http://news.bbc.co.uk/1/hi/entertainment/4225256.stm
50. Southall, *The Rise & Fall of EMI Records*, p. 179.
51. https://www.reuters.com/article/idUSL1781138320070718

Chapter 2

1. *Music Week*, 04.02.06, p. 19.
2. *Music Week*, 01.04.06, p. 2.
3. *Music Week*, 15.04.06, p. 4.
4. https://www.telegraph.co.uk/finance/2938217/Bronfman-could-profit-to-the-tune-of-500m-plus.html
5. https://www.forbes.com/2006/05/03/emi-warner-music-cx_po_0503autofacescan01.html#351937fae70e
6. Southall, *The Rise & Fall of EMI Records*, p. 181.
7. *Music Week*, 08.07.06, p. 3.
8. *Music Week*, 16.09.06, p. 6.
9. https://www.crunchbase.com/organization/permira/acquisitions/acquisitions_list#section-acquisitions
10. https://www.cnbc.com/id/20421309
11. https://www.telegraph.co.uk/finance/newsbysector/retailandconsumer/8379299/John-Gildersleeve-is-a-City-big-beast-still-driven-to-make-an-idea-succeed.html
12. https://nypost.com/2002/11/27/bmg-gets-fleeced-shells-out-2-74b-for-zomba-without-calder/

13. https://www.cnbc.com/id/16218216
14. https://www.theguardian.com/business/2006/dec/14/citynews.money
15. Southall, *The Rise & Fall of EMI Records*, p. 192.
16. https://www.theguardian.com/business/2007/jun/18/executivesalaries.executivepay
17. *Music Week*, 03.03.07, p. 1.
18. http://www.nytimes.com/2007/06/03/arts/music/03kozi.html
19. http://www.thisismoney.co.uk/money/comment/article-5160809/BIG-SHOT-WEEK-Terra-Firma-boss-Guy-Hands.html
20. https://www.telegraph.co.uk/finance/newsbysector/mediatechnologyandtelecoms/media/8067367/EMIs-Guy-Hands-Citigroups-David-Wormsley-and-the-fight-for-Dizzee-plc.html
21. https://www.theguardian.com/uk/2007/may/21/artnews.art

Chapter 3

1. *Music Week*, 02.06.07, p. 1.
2. https://www.terrafirma.com/communications/news/terra-firma/news-article/items/terra-firma-buys-tank-rast.html
3. https://www.terrafirma.com/communications/news/terra-firma/news-article/items/terra-firma-announces-acquisition-of-odeon.html
4. https://www.ft.com/content/9d353ae8-4820-11e6-8d68-72e9211e86ab
5. *Music Week*, 02.06.07, p. 2.
6. http://news.bbc.co.uk/1/hi/uk/8186922.stm
7. http://news.bbc.co.uk/1/hi/business/6926032.stm
8. *Music Week*, 11.08.07, p. 1.
9. Ibid.
10. https://www.theguardian.com/business/2007/aug/30/executivepay.musicnews
11. http://news.bbc.co.uk/1/hi/business/6968276.stm
12. Clasper, former BAA chief and ITV board member, was appointed to the EMI board at the start of November with a brief to fully exploit EMI's intellectual property. https://www.theguardian.com/business/2007/nov/05/media
13. http://www.independent.co.uk/news/uk/john-birt-the-devil-and-the-bbc-1336511.html
14. https://www.hollywoodreporter.com/news/terra-firma-holding-emi-150250

Chapter 4

1. EMI Music Publishing had just moved from its Charing Cross Road base in mid-September 2007 to take up residence in Wrights Lane, a relocation that EMI claimed had been confirmed before Terra Firma bought the company due to planned renovation to the building and major construction works in the area.
2. *Music Week*, 29.09.07, p. 1 and p. 3.
3. https://www.theguardian.com/business/2002/mar/21/2
4. If you are unfamiliar with this song from The Macc Lads' uncelebrated oeuvre, the fact they rhyme "binge" with "minge" and then crassly rattle though depressingly graphic "jokes" about the mechanics of bestiality should give you an indication of what it is like.
5. *Music Week*, 29.09.07, p. 3.

6. Ibid., p. 1.
7. https://www.theguardian.com/business/2008/jan/18/privateequity.musicnews

Chapter 5

1. http://content.time.com/time/arts/article/0,8599,1666973,00.html
2. https://www.theguardian.com/uk/2002/oct/03/arts.artsnews
3. Southall, *The Rise & Fall of EMI Records*, pp. 148–9.
4. https://www.theguardian.com/music/2016/feb/11/no-surprises-how-unexpected-album-drops-became-the-norm
5. Southall, *The Rise & Fall of EMI Records*, p. 84.
6. http://news.bbc.co.uk/1/hi/entertainment/8561963.stm
7. https://www.theguardian.com/music/2011/jan/04/pink-floyd-emi-single-digital-downloads
8. https://www.theguardian.com/business/2007/dec/02/businessandmedia5
9. https://uk.reuters.com/article/uk-radiohead/radiohead-frontman-takes-aim-at-emi-idUKN0160443520080101
10. https://uk.reuters.com/article/uk-radiohead/radiohead-frontman-takes-aim-at-emi-idUKN0160443520080101
11. *The Word*, issue 64 (June 2008), p. 98.
12. https://edition.cnn.com/2013/05/09/tech/mobile/ringtones-phones-decline/index.html

Chapter 6

1. *Music Week*, 10.11.07, p. 2.
2. Ibid.
3. https://www.independent.co.uk/arts-entertainment/music/news/hes-a-multi millionaire-himself-but-emis-new-boss-threatens-to-axe-stars-398771.html
4. https://www.theguardian.com/music/2015/sep/03/heavenly-records-at-25-saint-etienne-beth-orton
5. https://www.trendhunter.com/trends/kylie-minogue-facebook-app-kylie-robotics
6. https://www.theregister.co.uk/2008/10/27/emi_report/
7. https://www.telegraph.co.uk/finance/markets/2820466/Bringing-EMI-down-to-earth.html
8. https://www.independent.co.uk/arts-entertainment/music/news/money-to-burn-how-emis-profligate-bosses-filled-a-house-with-20000-worth-of-candles-761062.html
9. https://www.theguardian.com/media/2008/jan/09/digitalmedia.ventureproduction
10. https://www.theguardian.com/media/pda/2008/jan/16/emiconfirmsbarneywraggisl
11. The band's catalogue up to 1971 was controlled by Decca, part of Universal Music Group.
12. https://www.independent.co.uk/arts-entertainment/music/news/exile-on-main-street-becomes-stones-first-no-1-album-in-16-years-1981115.html

Chapter 7

1. https://www.theatlantic.com/technology/archive/2011/01/the-rise-and-fall-of-myspace/69444/
2. https://web.archive.org/web/20060819183610/http://internet.seekingalpha.com/article/15237
3. https://www.pcworld.com/article/166794/Facebook_Overtakes_MySpace_in_US.html
4. http://news.bbc.co.uk/2/hi/business/6034577.stm
5. http://www.futuristgerd.com/2005/01/08/music-like-wate-4/
6. http://www.nytimes.com/2007/05/31/business/media/31radios.html
7. http://news.bbc.co.uk/1/hi/england/tees/7057812.stm
8. http://www.independent.co.uk/news/business/news/emi-poaches-head-of-island-records-nick-gatfield-from-universal-music-810409.html
9. *Music Week*, 26.04.08, p. 2.
10. *Music Week*, 12.04.08, p. 15.

Chapter 8

1. Southall, *The Rise & Fall of EMI Records*, p. 241.
2. http://variety.com/2008/music/markets-festivals/emi-selling-china-business-to-co-1117990087/
3. http://www.independent.co.uk/news/business/news/emi-shares-dip-as-brazil-fraud-uncovered-421649.html
4. https://www.billboard.com/biz/articles/news/publishing/1319527/emi-music-publishing-moves-offices
5. https://www.billboard.com/articles/news/1045722/coldplay-prep-album-with-free-download-concerts
6. Southall, *The Rise & Fall of EMI Records*, p. 243.
7. http://archive.fortune.com/2008/07/07/technology/leonardemi.fortune/index.htm?section=money_latest
8. *Music Week*, 26.07.08, p. 4.

Chapter 9

1. https://www.telegraph.co.uk/finance/2792820/EMI-names-Reckitt-executive-Leoni-Sceti-as-head-of-recorded-music-division.html
2. *Music Week*, 15.11.08, p. 1.
3. Ibid., p. 15.
4. http://news.bbc.co.uk/1/hi/business/1378339.stm
5. http://variety.com/2010/biz/news/queen-leave-emi-for-universal-music-group-1118027132/
6. Aspinall passed away in March the following year.
7. Abbey Road was given listed status in March 2010 by culture minister Margaret Hodge, on the advice of English Heritage.
8. Perry, under her birth name Katy Hudson, began as a Christian singer and was dropped by both Island Def Jam Music Group (part of Universal Music

Group) and Columbia Records (part of Sony Music) before signing to Capitol Records (part of EMI) in April 2007.

9. Southall, *The Rise & Fall of EMI Records*, p. 252.
10. http://www.olympiccinema.co.uk/history
11. https://www.standard.co.uk/news/london/site-of-historic-olympic-studios-saved-for-the-community-8760516.html
12. http://www.theresident.co.uk/food-drink-london/restaurants-bars-london/barnes-olympic-studio-reopens-cinema/

Chapter 10

1. *Music Week*, 31.01.09, p. 2.
2. Ibid., p. 3.
3. https://www.campaignlive.co.uk/article/emi-music-appoints-bauer-media-marketer-andria-vidler-president/900517
4. *Music Week*, 02.05.09, p. 2.
5. https://www.billboard.com/biz/articles/news/global/1270895/emi-music-earnings-triple-to-246-million
6. *Music Week*, 25.07.09, p. 7.

Chapter 11

1. https://www.theguardian.com/media/pda/2008/jan/16/emiconfirmsbarneywraggisl
2. https://www.theguardian.com/media/2008/apr/02/digitalmedia.googlethemedia
3. *Music Week*, 12.04.08, p. 6.
4. http://www.ifpi.org/content/library/digital-music-report-2006.pdf
5. http://www.jstor.org/stable/10.1086/501082?seq=1#page_scan_tab_contents
6. https://www.billboard.com/biz/articles/news/1321840/bpi-investigates-honeywell-file-sharing-claims
7. https://futureofmusic.org/press/press-releases/report-finds-musicians-and-artists-use-internet-advance-their-work-connect-dire
8. An enormous amount has been written about these issues and arguments but this author would wholeheartedly recommend three books that collectively provide the full history of all the twists and turns here: *All the Rave: The Rise and Fall of Shawn Fanning's Napster* by Joseph Menn (2003); *Appetite for Self-Destruction: The Spectacular Crash of the Record Industry in the Digital Age* by Steve Knopper (2009) and *How Music Got Free: The End of an Industry, the Turn of the Century, and the Patient Zero of Privacy* by Stephen Witt (2015).
9. https://www.pcworld.com/article/144771/article.html
10. http://money.cnn.com/2000/10/31/bizbuzz/napster/
11. http://news.bbc.co.uk/1/hi/business/1994544.stm
12. http://news.bbc.co.uk/1/hi/business/2786573.stm
13. https://www.billboard.com/biz/articles/news/1350776/bertelsmann-pays-umg-60m-in-napster-settlement
14. https://www.reuters.com/article/industry-bertelsmann-emi-napster-dc/emi-and-bertelsmann-settle-napster-litigation-idUSN2639765320070326

15. https://www.reuters.com/article/industry-warnermusic-bertelsmann-dc/warner-music-settles-with-bertelsmann-on-napster-idUSWNAS7367720070424
16. https://www.eff.org/cases/capitol-v-thomas
17. http://news.bbc.co.uk/1/hi/technology/4718249.stm
18. http://news.bbc.co.uk/1/hi/technology/8337887.stm
19. http://news.bbc.co.uk/1/hi/business/6034577.stm
20. https://www.hollywoodreporter.com/news/emi-taps-second-life-founder-113440

Chapter 12

1. *Music Week*, 21.11.09, p. 6.
2. Emap became part of Bauer when the German media company acquired its magazine and radio divisions for £1.14 billion in 2007.
3. http://www.bbc.co.uk/news/10144577
4. *Music Week*, 22.05.10, p. 2.
5. Ibid., p. 3.
6. https://www.rollingstone.com/music/news/paul-mccartney-reissues-solo-catalog-with-indie-label-concord-20100421
7. *Music Week*, 20.03.10, p. 1.
8. Ibid.
9. Ibid

Chapter 13

1. Southall, *The Rise & Fall of EMI Records*, p. 276.
2. Ibid., p. 268.
3. *Music Week*, 10.04.10, p. 3.
4. *Music Week*, 01.05.10, p. 5.
5. *Music Week*, 15.05.10, p. 5.
6. *Music Week*, 22.05.10, p. 2.
7. *Music Week*, 29.05.10, p. 5.
8. *Music Week*, 12.06.10, p. 5.
9. *Music Week*, 19.06.10, p. 5.
10. *Music Week*, 28.08.10, p. 1.
11. Ibid., p. 4.
12. Ibid., p. 1.
13. It should be pointed out here that recorded and publishing are completely different business models and, at the time, labels paid for recordings, marketing, manufacturing and more, going hundreds of thousands of pounds into the red before anything could be released. Those at EMI's labels had long believed they were the risk takers at the company and their colleagues in publishing simply sat back and collected royalties. Of course this is a massive oversimplification, but it was true that labels were shouldering much of the upfront investment in new talent and the risk associated with breaking them.
14. *Music Week*, 18.09.10, p. 1.
15. *Music Week*, 25.09.10, pp. 16–17.
16. *Music Week*, 09.10.10, p. 4.
17. A long-running trademark dispute between Apple Corps and Apple Inc. dated back to 1978 and was only finally resolved in 2007 when Apple Inc. secured

all 'Apple'-related trademarks but agreed to license back certain uses of the name to Apple Corps.
18. http://www.bbc.co.uk/news/technology-11763650
19. Ibid.

Chapter 14

1. https://www.terrafirma.com/portfolio/current-investments/investment/emi-case-study.html
2. Southall, *The Rise & Fall of EMI Records*, p. 245.
3. Ibid.
4. Ibid., p. 239.
5. The quote was actually: "As long as the music is playing, you've got to get up and dance. We're still dancing." https://www.ft.com/content/5917b73c-28cc-11e6-8b18-91555f2f4fde
6. Southall, *The Rise & Fall of EMI Records*, p. 246.
7. https://www.telegraph.co.uk/finance/newsbysector/banksandfinance/private equity/3255399/EMI-report-reveals-757m-loss-when-Terra-Firma-took-over.html
8. https://www.ft.com/content/49193c44-6f0a-11de-9109-00144feabdc0
9. https://www.theguardian.com/business/2009/dec/13/terra-firma-emi-debt-crisis
10. Southall, *The Rise & Fall of EMI Records*, p. 265.
11. https://www.theguardian.com/business/2009/dec/13/terra-firma-sues-citigroup-over-emi
12. *Music Week*, 13.02.10, p. 1.
13. Ibid.
14. Southall, *The Rise & Fall of EMI Records*, p. 268.
15. https://www.theguardian.com/business/2010/may/12/emi-guy-hands-comment
16. *Music Week*, 05.06.10, p. 5.
17. *Music Week*, 13.02.10, p. 1.
18. *Music Week*, 20.02.10, p. 3.
19. https://www.managementtoday.co.uk/mt-interview-elio-leoni-sceti-emi-music/article/985298

Chapter 15

1. https://www.theguardian.com/business/2010/sep/07/citigroup-emi-deal-terra-firma
2. https://www.reuters.com/article/us-citigroup/citigroup-sued-by-terra-firma-over-emi-deal-idUSTRE5BA4J620091212
3. https://www.telegraph.co.uk/finance/newsbysector/banksandfinance/6805127/EMI-sues-Citigroup-for-2bn-over-fraud-and-lies.html
4. http://www.law.columbia.edu/faculty/jed-rakoff
5. https://www.ft.com/content/5917b73c-28cc-11e6-8b18-91555f2f4fde
6. Ibid.
7. https://www.linkedin.com/in/denelle-dixon-967a236/
8. A business term meaning boundaries that are set up within a business to prevent the leak of information that might lead to conflicts of interest.
9. *Music Week*, 23.10.10, p. 2.

10. https://www.theguardian.com/business/2010/oct/13/citigroup-emi
11. Ibid.
12. Southall, *The Rise & Fall of EMI Records*, p. 285.
13. Ibid., pp. 285–92.
14. https://www.paulweiss.com/professionals/partners-and-counsel/theodore-v-wells-jr
15. https://www.reuters.com/article/us-citigroup-parmalat/u-s-jury-awards-citi-364-2-million-in-parmalat-case-idUSTRE49J78Y20081020
16. https://www.reuters.com/article/uk-terrafirma-citigroup/citi-banker-cant-remember-key-calls-in-emi-case-idUKTRE69P4LX20101027
17. https://www.theguardian.com/business/2010/nov/04/guy-hands-loses-emi-fraud-case
18. *Music Week*, 13.11.10, p. 4.
19. https://www.theguardian.com/media/2011/jan/12/guy-hands-terra-firma-challenge-citigroup-emi
20. https://www.independent.co.uk/news/business/news/hands-lives-to-fight-another-day-in-court-after-terra-firma-wins-appeal-on-emi-deal-8640409.html
21. https://www.fnlondon.com/articles/citigroup-terra-firma-emi-group-legal-battle-moves-to-london-20140408

Chapter 16

1. *Music Week*, 25.12.10, p. 2.
2. *Music Week*, 27.11.10, p. 5.
3. *Music Week*, 25.12.10, p. 2.
4. https://uk.reuters.com/article/emi-prepack/ifr-emis-pre-pack-bombshell-makes-waves-idUKN0429587820110205
5. https://www.theguardian.com/media/2011/feb/07/emi-roger-faxon-email
6. *Music Week*, 15.01.11, p. 5.
7. *Music Week*, 12.02.11, p. 6.
8. *Music Week*, 19.03.11, p. 3.
9. http://articles.latimes.com/2011/may/07/business/la-fi-ct-warner-blavatnik-20110507
10. https://www.theguardian.com/business/2011/jun/20/citigroup-lines-up-emi-sale
11. https://www.theguardian.com/business/2011/nov/11/emi-sold-to-universal-and-sony
12. https://www.billboard.com/biz/articles/news/1160872/impala-says-it-expects-emi-universal-deal-to-be-blocked-outright
13. These were EMI France (including the David Guetta catalogue), Spain, Portugal, Belgium, Denmark, Sweden, Norway, Poland and Czech Republic. Meanwhile, Universal would have to sell its operation in Greece.
14. https://www.theguardian.com/media/2012/sep/21/universal-emi-takeover-approved
15. Ibid.
16. http://www.bbc.co.uk/news/business-19672277
17. Ibid.
18. Belgium, Czech Republic, Denmark, France, Norway, Portugal, Spain, Slovakia and Sweden.

19. https://www.billboard.com/biz/articles/news/global/1538515/warner-music-group-acquires-parlophone
20. Ibid.
21. https://www.billboard.com/biz/articles/news/global/1549326/warner-music-working-with-impala-merlin-to-sell-parlophone-assets
22. https://www.universalmusic.com/labels/

Epilogue

1. https://www.telegraph.co.uk/business/2016/06/07/citigroup-misled-guy-hands-terra-firma-into-buying-struggling-em/
2. Ibid.
3. Ibid.
4. Ibid.
5. Rakoff earned his M.Phil. from Oxford University in 1966. http://www.law.columbia.edu/faculty/jed-rakoff
6. https://www.theguardian.com/uk-news/2016/jun/08/emi-collapse-guy-hands-terra-firma-court
7. Ibid.
8. Ibid.
9. https://www.theguardian.com/media/2016/jun/09/guy-hands-denies-hazy-memory-over-emi-deal
10. Ibid.
11. Ibid.
12. https://www.theguardian.com/business/2016/jun/10/guy-hands-abandons-fraud-claim--citigroup-terra-firma-emi-takeover
13. Ibid.
14. Ibid.
15. Southall, *The Rise & Fall of EMI Records*, p. 311.
16. https://www.terrafirma.com/portfolio/current-investments/investment/emi-case-study.html
17. Ibid.
18. https://blogs.wsj.com/moneybeat/2015/01/19/guy-hands-admits-emi-deal-ended-terra-firmas-chance-to-be-a-mega-firm/

Note: all websites were accessed/re-checked in March 2018 and the information drawn on in the book was correct as of that date.

Index

About the Author

Dr Eamonn Forde is an award-winning music business journalist who has been writing about all areas of the music industry since 2000. His work has appeared in a variety of publications including *The Guardian*, *The Times*, *Q*, *Music Ally*, *Music Week*, *The Music Network* and *The Big Issue*.